A Culture of Confidence

A Culture of Confidence

POLITICS, PERFORMANCE AND THE IDEA OF AMERICA

Richard Nelson

University Press of Mississippi
Jackson

Copyright © 1996 by the University Press of Mississippi
All rights reserved
Manufactured in the United States of America

Paperback Edition 2010

The paper in this book meets the guidelines for permanence and durability of the Committee on Production Guidelines for Book Longevity of the Council on Library Resources.

Library of Congress Cataloging-in-Publication Data

Nelson, Richard, 1948–
   A culture of confidence : politics, performance and the idea of America / Richard Nelson.
     p. cm.
   Includes index.
   ISBN: 978-1-60473-575-8

    1. Political culture—United States. 2. United States—Civilization—1970–   3. United States—Politics and government—Philosophy. I. Title.
E839.5.N37 1996
306.2'0973—dc20   95-44457
                                                                CIP

British Library Cataloging-in-Publication data available

For Edwin M. Jessiman

Contents

Preface	ix
Introduction: Actor, Advertiser, Artist	3
1. Two Parables	9
2. A Culture of Confidence, A Culture of Doubt	24
3. The New Adam and the American Sublime	59
4. Edmund Burke and the Politics of Theater	80
5. The Neo-Burkean Renaissance	101
6. Max Weber and the Spirit of Confidence	128
7. Will Herberg's Crusade against Authenticity	167
8. Performance, Politics and Personality *Ronald Reagan, James Baldwin and Norman Mailer*	197
Afterword	233
Notes	237
Index	277

Preface

Ezra Pound, after reading *Tropic of Cancer*, asked Henry Miller if he had ever thought about money—what makes it and how it gets that way. The impertinent and impoverished Miller replied that he had never given it thought before, but now did so night and day. He then went on to write a satirical essay entitled "Money and How It Gets That Way," in which he pilloried the economists and intellectuals who grandly pontificate. If he could not settle the question, Miller said, at least he could *unsettle* it by pointing out that whatever money is and however it gets that way, "anything which can inflate today and collapse tomorrow has neither weight, substance nor value. It is not even gas, because gas, after all, answers to all three of these descriptions." Thinking about money, Miller concluded, may well lead to the collapse of thinking, but "when all the theories of economists are exploded, those who had the good sense to keep a 'mobile quantum of cash' on hand will be the least cruelly deceived."[1]

At the risk of falling into the very academic trap that Miller set out to mock in his essay, which was written in Paris during the depths of the Great Depression, I suggest that there is an answer to Pound's query. In fact, the answer is imbedded in Miller's satirical refusal to answer. Perhaps even more ironically, Miller's answer, I think, illustrates the common bond with the American national culture that the New Yorker and the Wisconsinite each affirmed in his attempted escape to Europe, the fabled center of Enlightenment civilization. That answer, and the central theme of this study of American national culture, is found in the word "confidence."

The word, as Miller implies, has a dual meaning. One usage contains the suggestion of deception, imitation, or illusion. A confidence game is always based upon a hidden transaction. The "mark" is offered a portion of the artist's own self-assurance. In exchange, the "mark" surrenders some object of material value. This aspect of confidence depends on a theatrical performance. Stereotypically, it is staged by the tawdry actor who pretends to have a European pedigree, the travelling evangelist who sounds pious, or the slick salesman who seems sincere. The classic confidence scam may be popularly associated with the American frontier or the big city, but it is usually an ironic morality tale. It warns against the wages of personal gullibility or vulnerability in a world where personal warmth and human dialogue seem to have disappeared.

The other definition of confidence involves emotional or physical reliance on some agent that serves as an instrument for achieving power or security. Such an agent may be the individual's own will, a method of organization, or some physical or psychological object suitable for an instrumental use. Thus, Miller appealed to "real" confidence as the alternative to a "confidence game" in matters of money, very much as he turned to the "genuine" culture of Europe as a refuge from America.

Despite Miller's antiacademic posturing, his argument concerning money is essentially the same one that Max Weber made famous in his essay *The Protestant Ethic and the Spirit of Capitalism*. For Weber's Hegelian conception of "the spirit of capitalism" was, at bottom, another way of identifying confidence. Weber said this "spirit of capitalism" could be challenged only through the Enlightenment ideal of science, which, he had to admit, was another expression of confidence. Indeed, Weber seems to say that the will to confidence is the foundation of the entire Enlightenment, whether expressed through science, aesthetics, religion, or nationalism.[2] The present study, therefore, may be simply described as a reconsideration of American national culture ninety years after Max Weber's visit to the United States and the publication of *The Protestant Ethic and the Spirit of Capitalism*.

The pervasive and inescapable power of confidence against which Weber rebelled and with which he identified in *The Protestant Ethic and the Spirit of Capitalism* was precisely the same scientific method that Francis Bacon had established in the seventeenth century and codified as the very essence of the Enlightenment. Fired with the spirit of discovering new worlds and reconstituting old institutions, Bacon, the patriarch of modern science, championed the possibility of a "great instauration," or reorganization of human knowledge, for purely instrumental ends.

In the *Novum Organum*, Bacon promised that he would "lay the foundation, not of any sect or doctrine, but of human utility and power," in order to "conquer nature in action." In the dawning twentieth century, Max Weber similarly recognized the power inherent in a utilitarian approach to nature and human institutions. He too saw the organization of power that was common to Calvinism and the scientific method. If Weber, chastened by the inhuman consequences of Bacon's utilitarian application of the principles of the inquisition to nature, echoed Bacon's own appeal to the higher standard of charity, Weber, also with Bacon, acknowledged the greater power of ambition. Once more, Weber went beyond Bacon's hidden political ideal of reconstructing a "New Atlantis." He identified Nature's first new nation, the United States, as a living "New Atlantis." For Weber, at the beginning of the twentieth century, the United States embodied both the political space and the cultural idea of utility. He recognized in America a manifestation of the organized Enlightenment will "to conquer nature in action."[3]

The America that Weber visited in 1904 was surprisingly close to the America of the agrarian frontier. Buffalo Bill Cody continued to stage his Wild West shows on both sides of the Atlantic. Jim Crow ruled in the South. Eastern cities were filling with a new laboring class, and Progressivism had not yet foundered on the shoals of World War I. Subsequently, two world wars and the Cold War would shape the cultural context of the United States, starkly separating the America Weber visited from the America of our own post–Cold War era.

I do not suggest that the Cold War created a new American national culture, but it did throw the existing tensions within American national culture into sharp relief. In a nuclear age, as well as one of mass entertainment and advertising, a far more intense glare is cast on the Enlightenment conventions of confidence and doubt. Paradoxically, therefore, the Cold War actually resulted in Weber's becoming immensely influential as an interpreter of American values. Existentialism, neoorthodox theology, and even the vogue of sociology itself found confirmation in Weber's ambiguous double vision of confidence and doubt in opposition to trust and personalism.

The Cold War crisis of American national culture, however, also resulted in an alternative answer to the problem of confidence and doubt through a renewed interest in the writings of the eighteenth-century politician and aesthetic philosopher Edmund Burke. His writings against the French Revolution fit well with those from disillusioned observers of and fellow travellers in the Russian Revolution. Burke recognized the utilitarian power of the very "idols" that Bacon wished to dispel, especially what Bacon called the "idol of the Stage." Burke drew a formal distinction between the sublime and the beautiful in terms that were similar to Bacon's in his division between science and charity and Weber's in his distinction between practical and utilitarian Calvinism and romantic and mystical Lutheranism, at the birth of a Protestant New World. That is, Burke, like Bacon and Weber, offered a theory of utilitarian power predicated upon the use of a working distinction between the instrumentalism of confidence and the relationalism of trust.

Burke, however, not only cogently recognized that emotion may be used for political purposes but also noted, as the German Idealist Weber did not, that the sublime is neither an expression of mystical religion nor necessarily moral in character. Essentially, Burke was a theorist of performativity, not of conservatism. From that perspective, Burke becomes a profoundly significant figure for understanding the twentieth-century American fascination with Hollywood, advertising, public relations and celebrity personality.

For similar reasons, the Burkean revival during the Cold War offers a window opening into the origins of the American national culture. When, for example, Herman Melville found himself engaged in a bitter and wrenching loss of religious and personal confidence, he expressed his doubt aesthetically through the conflict between Kantian and Burkean sublimes. His lonely dissent from transcendentalist hope in the American Adam gained a new relevance in the twentieth century. Melville's anguished confrontation with the problem of confidence, his eclipse, and finally his canonization, therefore, reveal a continuity in the American national culture from its Enlightenment sources, through nineteenth-century transcendentalism, to the Cold War and beyond.

The introduction of *A Culture of Confidence: Politics, Performance and the Idea of America* begins with a Weberian meditation on civil religion in the United States, and a Burkean conclusion about its role. I suggest that the Cold War transformed "the Protestant ethic" into the Judeo-Christian ethic, and that its inner dynamic, according to sociologists of religion such as Will Herberg (*Protestant, Catholic, Jew*) and Robert Bellah (*Habits of the Heart*), is consistently expressed in terms of personal and national confidence.

Chapter 1 offers two parables of the Cold War, one public and one private. Together, they illustrate the distinctions between confidence and trust and between the sublime and the religious. The pursuit of confidence within American national culture, in the context of the Cold War, is shown to have profound political, aesthetic, and scientific implications.

In the national election of 1992, the distinction between confidence and trust literally became a part of the campaign. In chapter 2, therefore, I begin with the Bush-Clinton campaign as a reflection of the crisis of confidence engendered by the Cold War. I locate its origins, as well as the subsequent national election of 1994, which brought Newt Gingrich to prominence as Speaker of the House of Representatives, in the Enlightenment convention of the frontier as a stage for performance. The same frontier conventions of performativity, I argue, have shaped the social sciences throughout the twentieth century. Performativity is not, therefore, synonymous with the recent vogues of postmodernism and deconstruction. Rather, it is a genre of rhetoric deeply entwined with Enlightenment values and institutions that are often misidentified with political and economic conservatism.

Herman Melville identified the problem of confidence and doubt with the American Adam. In chapter 3 of this book, his exploration of the sublime, as the province of the American Adam, is considered within the context of the twentieth-century Melville revival. Melville similarly provides the context for interpreting Bill Clinton's New Covenant and the virtual realism of Newt Gingrich. Both post–Cold War political figures are considered according to R. W. B. Lewis's categories from his classic Cold War text, *The American Adam*.

Edmund Burke, the single most significant Enlightenment theorist of performativity, is the subject of chapter 4. I suggest that Burke understood the political utility of the sublime as a rhetorical alternative to religion and as a practical instrument for modifying public emotion for organized ends. The Cold War, I argue in the following chapter, initiated a revival of Burkeanism in the United States, not just in political philosophy but in film and theater. In opposition to Louis Hartz, in his *Liberal Tradition in America*, I suggest that Burke was a significant influence upon American national culture from its inception to the present. However, unlike Russell Kirk and in agreement with Richard Weaver, I suggest that Burke's persuasiveness does not rest on conservatism but upon the performative rules of casuistry.

Max Weber's influence on Cold War America and the expropriation of his ideas by neo-Burkeans such as the theologian Reinhold Niebuhr are the subject of chapter 6. I suggest that perspectives similar to Niebuhr's may be found in the films of Frank Capra, and are echoed in counter-Progressive theories of science such as those of Stephen J. Gould and Thomas Kuhn. I also suggest that Burkeanism was challenged during the Cold War by such social critics and theologians as Paul Tillich and Martin Buber.

Chapter 7 considers Will Herberg, a prophet of Burkean politics who became a religion editor for William F. Buckley's *National Review* in the 1960s. In earlier years, Herberg had been a prolific editorialist for Communist papers such as *Revolutionary Age* and *Workers Age*. Through Niebuhr's influence, he embraced Judaism in the 1940s, and became an interpreter of existentialism. Though he aspired to be an American Martin Buber, Herberg repudiated Buber and existentialism in the late 1960s on Burkean grounds.

The rise of Ronald Reagan and the Political and Religious Right is explored in chapter 8, in relation to the New Evangelicalism of the Cold War and the new medium of television. Similarly, the cult of personality and performativity that Reagan perfected as an actor-politician is found in the rise of the celebrity-novelists James Baldwin and Norman Mailer.

An afterword contemplates the defeat of existentialist alternatives of personal responsibility to community through Burkean forms of performance. The consequence of replacing personalism with personality and identity with performance was a triumph of a culture of confidence at the expense of trust, and, therefore, of a culture of doubt, as well. With the transformation of existentialism, a conservative cultural movement of opposition to market values in the personal sphere, into a fashionable mode of performance, an important alternative to a national culture of confidence was lost. In practical terms, this meant that with the end of the Cold War, the ascendant American national culture itself became an indistinguishable part of a now-unchallenged worldwide market economy.

I especially wish to acknowledge the insights, criticisms and suggestions generously provided to me by Arthur Hill, Solveig Nelson, and David W. Noble. Certainly, I alone am responsible for any faults that have resulted from my failure to apply their insights properly. I also wish to express my deep appreciation to my wife, Jane Solveig Nelson, for sharing emotionally and intellectually in every aspect of the process that led to the completion of this project. Kirsten, Karl, Kristian and Britta were, as always, generous with their support and understanding, as were their grandparents, Solveig and Robert Bailey and William and Jane Nelson.

I wish to thank Laurie Anne Hopkins, Lisa Marin, Dr. Elizabeth Mancke, Ken Tudor, Elaine Hewes and Michael Hewes, George Schelling, and Jamie Nixon, among the many students, friends and colleagues who have helped me in innumerable ways. I deeply appreciate the thoughtfulness and patience of Dr. Richard Abel and the staff of the University Press of Mississippi. I owe Carol Cox a great debt for the high quality of her copyediting, both for her skill and for her sensitivity to my intentions. Her efforts improved the quality of the manuscript immeasurably. Thank you, as well, to Fletcher Cox, who went to great lengths in helping me to overcome the problems of translating from my nonstandard computer. I wish to thank Sheryl Davis for graciously permitting me to use the computer facilities of the Lamoine school. Thanks to the readers who offered their suggestions for improving the manuscript and to the staffs of the Bangor Public Library and Bangor Theological Seminary Library, who were always accommodating and helpful.

Finally, and especially, my thanks to Edwin M. Jessiman, whose personal integrity and humanity prevailed against imposing odds, and who understands the difference between trust and confidence.

Ellsworth, Maine
July 1995

A Culture of Confidence

Introduction

Actor, Advertiser, Artist

In 1955, sociologist of religion Will Herberg published a landmark study of American national culture entitled *Protestant, Catholic, Jew*. Herberg defined the elusive concept of an American national culture as a harmonious product of the interrelationship of two conflicting traditions. One of these traditions was pseudoreligious but actually political, a variation on the civil religions of classical Greece and Rome. It existed, he said, in an uneasy, but vital, tension with a countertradition that was truly religious. This second tradition, comprising Protestantism, Catholicism and Judaism, Herberg called Judeo-Christianity.[1]

Herberg grandly announced that it had become possible to discern this national culture and to differentiate its true from its fraudulent manifestations, despite the bewildering diversity and contradictory ideals of its elements. He believed that the methods of the social sciences had revealed an organic process of cultural evolution. America's fragmented cultural origins, he explained, had been transformed into a unified national culture through the process of social evolution. This harmonizing and blending of different traditions preserved distinctive ethnic and religious identities, he said, because Protestants, Catholics and Jews had in common a fundamental source. That source transcended religious sectarianism and political nationalism. Although he never named that organic foundational source with precision, Herberg suggested that American religiosity and secularism were both paradoxically derived from it, and that faith in faith itself was but a pale imitation of its creed.[2]

In 1985, in the midst of a profound realignment of American religious and political interests, sociologist of religion Robert Bellah and a group of his associates published *Habits of the Heart: Individualism and Commitment in American Life*. It was a best-selling effort to identify and revitalize that same foundational source of civil religion and its Judeo-Christian countertradition identified by Herberg thirty years earlier. Bellah, too, believed in the power of the social sciences to reveal the unity behind American diversity. For Bellah, however, the national character had become confused and disconnected. The two traditions, he and his research associates concluded, had lost their balance with one another. Bellah insisted that the recovery of a clear vision of American national culture was essential for both a moral and political revival in the United States at the end of the twentieth century. Only through understanding their true public values and ideals could Americans ask the basic questions of personal character and identity that desperately needed to be addressed. Public virtue and private virtue, political interest and religious commitment, needed to be considered together, Bellah explained, if Americans were to restore faith in the future and in themselves. Thus, once again in the 1980s, as in the 1950s, the balance between civic values and religious principles became central to debates about the health and the character of American national culture.[3]

The unity Bellah hoped to recover, he said, had been prophetically voiced by Tocqueville more than a century earlier, and it remained an undefined but living tradition among Americans in the "habits of their hearts." This natural source of virtue, Bellah and his associates wrote, was informed by the biblical and republican traditions, but it had been eclipsed by the artificiality of the expressive and utilitarian individualisms of the late Cold War consumer democracy. The original and pristine font of national culture, however, remained as elusive for Bellah as it had for Herberg, who three decades earlier had appealed to Edmund Burke to similarly establish a source of national unity through the organic values contained in the biblical and civic traditions.

Bellah and Herberg were convinced that a source of national unity must exist, even as its precise location and form eluded them. They offered similar trinitarian explanations suggesting that multiplicity merely hid a higher, transcendent unity. The lost source of national culture, therefore, seemed both real and legitimate, even if that source remained elusive and unnamed. For Herberg, the tripartite culture of Protestants, Catholics and Jews mediated multiplicity into an organic ecumenical model for explaining how national unity could transcend sectarianism.

For Bellah, however, writing in the Reagan years, a false trinity had eclipsed the national unity of post–World War II America. Relying on the tripartite schemes of sociologist David Riesman, who wrote *The Lonely Crowd* in 1950, and philosopher Alisdair MacIntyre, whose *After Virtue* appeared in 1981, Bellah decried the rise of the heretical trinity of the Entrepreneur, the Manager and the Therapist. These cultural personality-types, he said, represented the distortions of utilitarian egoism and subjective individualism in an acquisitive society. *Habits of the Heart*, Bellah said, was a call to restore the balance between expressive and utilitarian forms of individualism through the communally responsible influences of biblical and civic religious values. These, he said, would provide a language for recovering a genuine trinity of success, freedom, and justice, which would lead Americans back to the lost source of their organic national culture.[4]

This was a vision, Bellah insisted (as had Herberg before him) that was neither conservative nor liberal "in terms of the truncated spectrum of present American political discourse." It was neither a reactionary return to traditional society nor a radical rejection of all traditions. Rather, he said, it turned on "the criticism of criticism, that human life is lived in the balance between faith and doubt."[5]

Between the appearance of Herberg's *Protestant, Catholic, Jew* and Bellah's *Habits of the Heart*, momentous and cataclysmic changes in American society were transforming the nation, starkly confronting Americans with the fragile line between faith and doubt. In the midst of superpower brinkmanship, racial, class and gender confrontation, assassination and an eroding economic structure, the languages of civil religion and Judeo-Christianity continued to dominate expressions of anxiety and to offer the promises of a return to a lost source of national unity for Cold War Americans. Martin Luther King, Jr., Billy Graham, Daniel and Philip Berrigan, Jerry Falwell and Randall Terry are names that evoke the urgency and breadth of that appeal to the political Left and Right, as the issues of race, gender, militarism, and abortion have reverberated within the walls of legislatures, churches and synagogues, and homes across America.

One of the more passionate jeremiads to appear in the years between *Protestant, Catholic, Jew* and *Habits of the Heart*, and which delicately balanced the changing perspectives between them, was presented by historian John Patrick Diggins in *The Lost Soul of American Politics* (1984). Diggins called upon his fellow Americans to embrace a new integration of liberal individualism and Calvinist moralism, urging his readers to reclaim their national culture by choosing the balance between civil religion and Judeo-Christianity that had historically been advocated by Abraham Lincoln and Herman Melville. "Lincoln could agree with Melville," Diggins explained,

> that political meaning is bestowed not by victory but by sacrifice, and he too would offer an entirely new political vision of Christian atonement and redemption. In Lincoln the tension between classical politics and Christian values — between law and conscience, policy and magnanimity, an ethic of practical consequences and an ethic of ultimate convictions — would reach an apotheosis. Lincoln also bore "the failure of light" [*Billy Budd*], and from his anguished political thoughts and actions virtue, "true" Christian virtue, would rise to moral excellence.[6]

Paradoxically, Herberg, Bellah and Diggins shared a commitment to postmodernism, believing that by revitalizing American national culture America could escape from the false promises of modernism. Modernism, for each, had become identified with the expressive and utilitarian individualisms of emotional and material self-indulgence fostered by civic and religious tradition, as well as by the totalitarian reign of communist materialism. But postmodernism promised a return to the sacred, in which a sublime universality would replace the contradiction of opposing values and interests in the United States and in the world.

But is it possible to balance such contradictory and artificial traditions as civil religion and Judeo-Christianity, to preserve an organic national identity, as Herberg, Bellah, and Diggins assumed? Does Melville confirm that possibility with Lincoln, or were the fatal misprisions that brought death to Claggart and Billy Budd a diabolical contradiction to the legacy of Lincoln's murderous virtue for the Ship of State? Is postmodernism a break with the modern tradition, or is it a manifestation of modernism, feeding upon itself? If postmodernism is a break from the tradition, or the pseudotradition, of the modern, how can it serve as a basis for separating the false universals of modernism from the real universals of Judeo-Christianity and civic humanism, when, by definition, it must collapse all privileged distinction between the real and the imitative?

These are central questions for understanding the character of American national culture and its emphasis on celebrity personalities and performance. For, in the aftermath of the Cold War and in the shadow of the manifold failures of modernism and triumphs of postmodernism, it is now possible to recognize that there has been only one way in which the vision of Herberg, Bellah and Diggins has been and may continue to be sustained by twentieth-century Americans, and that is through a commitment to the mystical lost source of the American national culture they share.

That source may actually be located and named, as Herberg, Bellah and Diggins failed to do. But it may only be discovered and explored as the conceptualized balance of faith and doubt, as the frontier between the real and the imitative, the genuine and the fraudulent. A successful trinitarian explanation for American unity in multiplicity, therefore, may not be located in the notion of Protestant, Catholic and Jew, since we live in a society that now reflects global forms of self-definition. Nor, in an age that is resurgent with religious questions and political passions, may Americans be cynically reduced to the Entrepreneur, the Manager and the Therapist. Instead, the Actor, the Advertiser and the Artist represent the necessary core personalities for preserving the legitimacy of an American national culture in a postmodern age. For the Actor, the Advertiser and the Artist inform the sensibilities that shape postmodern politics as well as religion. They are able to bridge the abstract corporate interests of business with the most intimate senses of the self and to disseminate them through media images. The roles of the Actor, Advertiser and Artist have become vital in achieving the deceptions necessary for preserving established power, complementing the Therapist, who adjusts atomized individuals to the realities of power. The Actor, Advertiser and Artist, are in short, the smiths of American national culture. They balance simulation and dissimulation against each other to create a paradox: an original and genuine work of artifice.

The Actor, the Advertiser and the Artist are, of course, only ideal types, as the sociologist Max Weber has taught us to use them. They provide a symbolic function, rendering visible themes and contexts that might otherwise become lost in a web of social nuance and complexity. In its more recent postmodern context, therefore, American national culture continues to "exist," much as it did in the earlier modern contexts, but only as a manifestation of the sensibilities and qualities that Americans bring to it.

Alternatively, of course, the idea of a national culture may simply be abandoned as an unnecessary and unworkable abstraction, as a false association of ideas, and as a confusion of the aesthetics of the sublime with the sacred. Personalism, and the responsibility for preserving dialogue with others, may be privileged over individualism and the cultivation of the celebrity personality as a definition for achieving selfhood. Such an alternative was actually suggested in some forms of the existentialist movement that was briefly popular in the United States from the end of World War II until the early 1960s. More recently, some of these themes have been resurrected through the dialogical theories of Mikhail Bakhtin, a student of Dostoyevsky, who held Martin Buber's philosophy of dialogue in high regard. Bakhtin also has many affinities with the American social psychologist George Herbert Mead and has gained an increasingly wide following among postmodern literary and social theorists.[7]

But the history of the twentieth century in the United States, especially when seen through the lens of the Cold War, suggests that the Actor, the Advertiser and the Artist will continue to define America in the future as they have in the past, from Buffalo Bill Cody to Ronald Reagan, and from Henry James and Walt Whitman to James Baldwin and Norman Mailer. That past was focused through the transforming lens of the Cold War as a quintessential manifestation of American national culture. In considering the implications of the Cold War for defining American historiography and social theory, American philosophy and theology, and American theater and film, it becomes possible to recognize that the organic source of an American national culture is neither Jerusalem nor Rome, but simple confidence.

1

Two Parables

In the United States of 1959 the Cold War endured, as it had for decades and would continue to do for decades more. Communism had entered Cuba, the gateway to the Americas, that year. In *The Tragedy of American Diplomacy*, historian William Appleman Williams reflected upon the Cold War as a contemporary tragedy that had begun on that island at the turn of the century. Cuba, Williams suggested, was where American imperialism and idealism had married in the nationalistic fervor of the Spanish-American War. The happy couple had confidently crossed the threshold of an Open Door and given birth to an empire that led Americans to a political history of denial, self-serving exploitation, and unintended compromises. In the end, said Williams, Cold War America tragically subverted its own principles of revolutionary justice in the name of expediency and misdirected realism. According to Williams's analysis, once Woodrow Wilson, in the name of economic prosperity and moral virtue, had championed the Open Door against Lenin's vision of world revolution, the Cold War became the single universal reality shared by all Americans. For Williams and the revisionist historians who followed him, therefore, the tragic unfolding of the Cold War, through its persistence and the degree to which it was a catalyst for political, moral and aesthetic passions, shaped an entire American national culture.[1]

By placing the tragedy of American reform and economic ambition in the internal contradictions of the Open Door, Williams expressed the same moral doubts about the America of the Cold War that Norman Mailer was then presenting in his 1959 book, *Advertisements for Myself,* and which found popular expression in the leading film of the year, Douglas Sirk's *Imitation of Life*. "The shits are killing us," Mailer wrote provocatively, "even as they kill themselves—each day a few more lies eat into the seed with which we are born, little institutional lies from the print of newspapers, the shock waves of television, and the sentimental cheats of the movie screen." This was the moral dilemma of the ambitious actress, Lora, played by Lana Turner, and the tragic mulatto, Sarah Jane, played by Susan Kohner, in *Imitation of Life*, just as it was that of Williams's American political culture. All found themselves implicated in a society that subverted truth through propaganda and identity through imitation. The republic, Mailer concluded, was in real peril because the lies of American life "pipe us towards insanity as they starve our sense of the real."[2]

Yet, despite the disillusioned cry that the Cold War had subverted the real American values and substituted imitation ones, Williams urged a renewed confidence that tragedy could be transcended, very much as Wilsonian liberalism had promised, by reconciling contrasting truths. The homeless black mother Annie (Juanita Moore), of *Imitation of Life*, symbolized the same promise that disillusionment could be transcended, even after a life of false choices and fraudulent relationships. Annie, who launched Lora's climb to real achievement, imitated life by pretending to be her maid and acting as a surrogate mother for her neglected daughter, Susan (Sandra Dee). Early in the film, when Lora's future seemed most hopeless, Annie advised the down-and-out actress to act prosperous and trust the Lord. Later, Lora's pretense and drive for fame led to betrayal of those she loved and of her own principles. But it was finally the "real" pretense advocated by Annie and Lora's "true" instincts as an actor that allowed everyone in the film to find salvation.

Norman Mailer, in *Advertisements*, bemoaned the loss of creative nerve among twentieth-century American writers. According to Mailer, only John Dos Passos had achieved artistic greatness, with his 1937 novel *U.S.A.*, but he had been "beached on the dry sands of political integrity and had to live with the salt water of insufficient recognition." Too many American writers had betrayed their principles and talents in their ambition to gain fame and public acclaim. In Mailer's opinion Hemingway was the greatest talent and the most ambitious personality among his contemporary writers, but Hemingway's writing degenerated into mere pretense once he achieved the status of a celebrity. Only when one feels subliminally Ernest's head on the Cuban fisherman's shoulders in *The*

Old Man and the Sea, Mailer wrote, "does the fraud of the tale take on its surrealist's truth."

For, Mailer explained, becoming a public personality is essential to success in the writing game. The ambitious Mailer admitted to imitating Hemingway's self-promotion because he dreamed of achieving Hemingway's fame and Nobel Prize. "It is sometimes fatal to one's talent," said Mailer, "not to have a public with a clear public recognition of one's size." Mailer confessed that he, like Hemingway and Fitzgerald before him, had been guilty of dissipating his talent through compromise with mediocrity—a failure of nerve that constituted his own and America's imitation of life. But, Mailer wrote, echoing Lora's and Sarah Jane's redemption through the spiritually uplifting funeral service for Annie, "we are the cowards who must defend courage, sex consciousness, the beauty of the body, the search for love, and the capture of what may be, after all, a heroic destiny."[3]

Like Mailer, Williams decried the failure of nerve in America, and also like Mailer, he offered a radical analysis leading to a conservative conclusion. "The well being of the United States," Williams wrote, at least in the short run, depended upon "calm and confident and enlightened conservatives" who could see and bring themselves to act upon a radical analysis of America's history.[4] That history, in the wake of Williams's jeremiad, would reveal earlier cold war patterns in the national culture of the United States: the Federalist fear of revolutionary France, female emancipation and the consequences of slavery; Jeffersonian fears of the economic and territorial designs of Britain; the strained relations between the American North and South, leading to open hostility. However, it was the tensions of this last defining cold war, codified by Woodrow Wilson, which compromised the Progressive vision of industrial democracy in the 1920s and brought to an impasse attempts to revitalize national reform. The tensions of that cold war shaped American political values on the left as well as on the right during the 1930s, convincing the American media that the citizens of the post–World War II United States were living in an age of anxiety. That same cold war brought historians in the 1950s to the conclusion that the United States was a liberal society, trapped or liberated by its tradition of consensus, and it led many of their number to accept a republican ideology of conspiracy and redemptive violence in the 1960s, as an explanation for the tragic contradictions in American attitudes towards power in the light of Viet Nam.

The Cold War, therefore, not only shaped twentieth-century American historiography, but, above all else, it shaped popular attitudes towards community and individualism, power and morality, and pleasure and guilt in the public schools, at the movies, in churches, synagogues, mosques and temples. It made its presence felt on America's front porches through grave pronouncements by elders about armageddon and a coming apocalypse and in the whispered negotiations taking place among adolescents in the back seats of automobiles. It fueled the quest for a national culture among American social scientists, literary critics and the interpreters of the arts. The Cold War dominated the thinking of government policy makers and analysts, while, as the 1960s dawned, it turned the majority of young people in American schools and colleges into avid fans of *Mad Magazine*.[5]

Paradoxically, the United States in the Cold War was far from being monolithic and culturally rigid, despite the anticommunist propaganda permeating the whole society. Quite to the contrary, the Cold War, especially once it was named and brought to the public's consciousness following World War II, sensitized Americans to the ideological structure behind all political, scientific and religious orthodoxies, even as it justified enforcing conformity through them. Also paradoxically, it was the Cold War which rehabilitated regionalism in the South and West as the front lines of a national resistance to the totalitarian conformity of Soviet industrialism and to the decadence of American materialism. A southern literary renaissance challenged communist propaganda with a republic of letters, which itself served the purposes of propaganda, while New York intellectuals quoted Dostoyevsky and Tocqueville for the same contradictory purposes. And it was the Cold War which justified the cultural and political domination of the whole hemisphere by the United States, even as it undermined national ethnocentricity and isolationism in an international war against communist influence.

Such paradoxes, in which the perspectives created by the Cold War spawned the critiques of it, indicate a deeper significance than anticommunist hysteria and an unthinking acceptance of American foreign policy, on one side, and anticonformism and antimaterialism, on the other. They suggest that the Cold War reflected the existence of a national culture, which itself directed the influence the Cold War had on American lives and institutions, and which continues to live beyond the Cold War era. But, if such a national culture does exist, despite the discredit that the Cold War has itself brought to that convention, what could it be? Where would a universal national culture be located after Anglo-

America has lost its privileged status, when sectional identity has failed to preserve prophetic voices of national renewal, and when multiculturalism has revealed less a quilt of peoples than a fragmented field of conflict among ethnic, gender and class divisions?

Perhaps an American national culture could be located, however, if it were separated from the Cold War conventions that have embodied it while obscuring its presence and distorting its form. Perhaps the falsified manifestations of American national culture, which have made it such a doubtful quest for historians and social scientists at the end of the Cold War, could yield an insight into the national culture itself. If so, an American national culture might be located through an examination of the conventions of the Cold War, viewed as strategies among many previous ones, which Americans have used and discarded for preserving a collective sense of certainty in the presence of doubt.

One way to begin this process of reexamining the Cold War to reveal the national culture behind it is to look at two apparently unrelated events that occurred on opposite sides of the globe during the same year in which Williams considered the Cold War as an economic frontier, Mailer reflected on it as a sexual frontier, and Sirk contemplated racial passing as a boundary between true acting and false pretense in his remake of *Imitation of Life*.[6] Both these 1959 events occurred during the month of July. One was a very public display by political leaders of the international tensions that had brought the world to the brink of nuclear destruction; the other was an equally private meeting of anonymous men who were suffering from the psychological tensions of personal identities in crisis.

The public confrontation took place in Moscow, before television cameras projecting the images of Richard Nixon and Nikita Khrushchev all over the world. The American vice president and the Soviet premier each claimed to be the representative of a redeemer nation with the power to bring hope and prosperity to the masses of the world. Each offered the other certainty that the future had already been won, claiming that his nation had revealed the way to harness economic and technological energy that would save humanity from poverty and oppression. But the confident, and conflicting, promises these leaders made simultaneously implied a more ominous future, one that was threatened by the capacity to unleash that energy. The consequence of competing national ambitions, they themselves were forced to acknowledge, might be an apocalyptic nuclear conflagration.

The other confrontation, which took place behind the locked doors of Ward D 23 at Ypsilanti State Mental Hospital, was not between celebrity-politicians who represented themselves as the voices of their national cultures. It involved three mental patients and the psychologists who hoped to heal them and to liberate them from their delusions through a face-to-face meeting.[7]

Officially, the exhibition at Moscow, which Nixon had come to open, was a diplomatic gesture aimed at a mutual dispelling of dangerous illusions that Americans and Russians had about each other. It was presented as a practical and sincere effort to reduce the tensions that threatened to lead to a nuclear holocaust by celebrating the material promise of abundance also offered by technology as a vision of the world's future. But the American exhibition in Moscow was the perfect stage for political theater, as well as for diplomacy, and Richard Nixon had the irresistible opportunity to play a starring role. Even as he called for a new era of openness, Nixon was positioning himself for his coming presidential campaign. Speaking on Soviet television and generously advocating a new spirit of dialogue in which Americans would appear on Russian television and Russians would appear on American television, Nixon must have remembered his real audience — the forty-four million families in the United States who owned fifty million television sets.

The American trade exhibit that Nixon came to Moscow to open was constructed at Sokolniki Park. The exhibition, organized to showcase American products, was to advertise to the Soviet people — to the entire world — the superiority of the American free enterprise system over communism. It was also supposed to illustrate the idea, Nixon said, "that man does not live by bread alone." Lasting ten days and costing five million dollars, the exhibition promoted its contradictory agenda of spiritualizing material progress through a gallery of modern art, a Disney circarama movie, and Leonard Bernstein conducting the New York Philharmonic Orchestra. But its center was a ranch-style suburban home boasting a $250,000 model kitchen, complete with microwave oven, a futuristic dishwasher, and floor-cleaning robots, all directed from a master-control panel by a Russian-speaking homemaker from Peoria, Illinois.

In the midst of this technological fantasy of, and commercial for, the American way of life, the vice president of the United States "spontaneously" engaged his guest, Soviet Premier Nikita Khrushchev, in a spirited debate. Nixon insisted that only American free enterprise could provide diversity and the right of consumer choice; Khrushchev countered that communism had conquered space and, in contrast to American capitalism, offered workers real dignity. Khrushchev dismissed Nixon's claim that American technology liberated women from the drudgery of housework. Americans, he countered, mistook the worship of gadgetry for visions of freedom. If then-striking American steel workers could afford all this in their new homes, as Nixon claimed, so could contented Russian workers, said Khrushchev. When Nixon crowed that Americans had surpassed the Soviets in the technology of color television, if not in rocketry, Khrushchev was not to be outdone: "No," he said, "we are up with you on this, too."

This famous "kitchen debate" illustrates the obsessive preoccupation with power that shaped the technological and economic visions of American welfare capitalist and Soviet communist nationalisms at the zenith of the Cold War. Each of these leaders of what Ernest Lee Tuveson later called the Redeemer Nations tried to project an image of strength and authority, yet each found it necessary to offer the ideal of cooperation and mutual respect where claims of superiority could not be sustained. "You are strong and we are strong," Nixon intoned, and "in some ways you are stronger, but in other ways we might be stronger." Since both America and the Soviet Union were so strong, "not only in weapons but also in will and spirit," Nixon said, "neither should ever put the other in a position where he faces, in effect, an ultimatum."[8]

Nixon and Khrushchev struggled to negotiate between a messianic political ideology and the practical necessities of coexistence in a dangerous world. Nixon tried to appear natural and spontaneous for the benefit of television cameras. But he was as narrowly constrained by predesigned agendas as Khrushchev, and that made the contradictions in their Cold War debate transparently obvious as a staged media event, even at the time. Khrushchev was described in *Time* and *Life* as a showman, and in a *Look* feature article, Nixon was applauded by his college drama coach for the quality of his performance. Khrushchev, readers were told, "played the role of mimic and clown," but "the image that he seriously sought to project . . . was the image of a formidable man of power, frightening in his display of utter willingness to use that power." When Nixon put his arm around Khrushchev and apologized for failing to be a good host, it only served to underscore "the weird aspect of the whole performance."[9]

During the same month that Nixon and Khrushchev vied for international authority and argued about dishwashers, electric ranges, and other visible signs of economic grace, social psychologist Milton Rokeach brought together three patients at Ypsilanti State Mental Hospital for a different kind of summit meeting: one bringing together three men who all claimed to be Jesus Christ. Rokeach hoped that the resulting conflict might collapse their psychotic meaning systems and violently propel them back into sanity. The social psychologist recounted the story of this encounter, in what must be described as an unconscious parable of the Cold War, in his book *The Three Christs of Ypsilanti*. Rokeach said he was interested in studying the nature of belief systems and the ways in which they could be modified. He believed that delusional systems might provide an insight into this problem. What would happen, he asked himself, if three individuals who claimed the same delusional identity were forced to confront each other in a confined space?[10]

Rokeach was intrigued by the fact that the insane, despite such fantastic claims as, in this case, being the Son of God, do not deny the laws of physics. They do not think they can walk on ceilings; they accept the fact that no more than one person may possess a particular identity. Would multiple claimants to the same identity, therefore, experience a cataclysmic shock to their delusional belief systems? Would a chain reaction of violent emotion take them out of the rubble of their counterfeit realities and return them to their true selves?

Rokeach approached his experiment in social redemption with optimism about the power of science to explain and to heal through a violent act of refashioning the maladjusted self. Yet he also expressed a gnawing sense of disquiet at the recognition of the technical capacity to destroy the world behind his experimental metaphor. That capacity, Rokeach seemed to suggest, found an analogy in the potential for the individual to utterly destroy his or her own identity. He was deeply impressed and troubled by the fact that none of the insane men in his study had previously suffered organic damage. Each had once lived in the natural world as a functioning, normal human being, and had abandoned that world for an artificially constructed identity as Jesus Christ, the Son of God.

Significantly, Rokeach did not see this artificial transformation of identity as proof of an ambition to achieve grandeur. Rather, he described it as a desperate response to fragmentation, confusion and a loss of personal confidence. Indeed, Rokeach's Cold War social psychology appears similar to Rob Wilson's Cold War aesthetic definition of the postmodern nuclear sublime, which he says replaced the historically confident idea of the "American sublime" in the atom bomb's first light.[11]

The sublime is an aesthetic formula for psychologically balancing confidence and doubt as contradictory attributes of power, such as the polar experiences of terror and pleasure, vastness and littleness, or contempt and awe. The sublime enfolds the individual in a sense of power that is greater than any self, but necessarily also diminishes the individual as an irrelevant intrusion into the anonymous power of nature's law. Most important, the same sublime that expresses the psychological entrapment in the dual attributes of power also provides a practical strategy for using that power. It is a rhetorical strategy that lies at the very heart of the Enlightenment understanding of power, because it translates the natural into the artificial and renders it subject to instrumental use.[12]

Writing in the last days of the Cold War, Rob Wilson, in his book appropriately entitled *The American Sublime* (1991), offered a theory of sublime aesthetics to explain the deconstruction of cultural confidence. The American artist's celebration of force and technical mastery over nature, he said, has resulted in fragmentation of self and vision, due to a recognition of the overwhelming destructive power in nuclear weapons. The poetic participation in technocratic domination, he suggested, has led directly to the powerlessness of language among contemporary American poets. For, asked Wilson, how can the continuity of language be trusted, or the weight of words be preserved, against the technoscape of nuclear destruction? Yet Wilson's critique paradoxically reflects a far deeper commitment to his responsibility for preserving confidence than might be visible without the negative example of the three Christs. Indeed, Wilson's therapeutic approach to aesthetics parallels Rokeach's scientific faith that his patients' disillusionment might be overcome through a deconstructing of it. Rokeach and Wilson share the belief that the terror of nuclear annihilation may be used, instrumentally, to transform a shattered identity into a healthy one and to rebuild confidence through doubt.[13]

It is instructive, however, that Rokeach, in 1959, came to despair of his capacity to heal those determined "to trust nothing but mistrust," while Wilson, in 1991 at the twilight of the Cold War, still offered a promise of aesthetic hope in a post–Hiroshima and post–Auschwitz disillusionment with the technological domination of nature. These reversals in Rokeach and Wilson indicate that the "American sublime" did not deconstruct when, after 1972, Wilson found that it had become a conscious literary convention. Instead, it remained subject, even in a prescient critic such as Wilson, to the same oscillation between confidence and doubt that had always been characteristic of the sublime as an Enlightenment aesthetic of power. The pessimism of Rokeach and the optimism of Wilson, however, point to a subtle difference of great significance in their narratives. While the social scientist was experimenting with the phenomenon of competing identities among three subjects, he became personally committed to curing the three patients, to whom he had given the fictionalized names Clyde Benson, Joseph Cassel, and Leon Gabor, and to whom he dedicated his book. For Rokeach recognized that the three Christs were engaged in an elemental and direct struggle with their personal grounds of meaning. Wilson's poets, however, no matter what deep personal anguish might have inspired their writing, were considered artists who were in rebellion against a failed vision of the external world.

Once Rokeach personalized his experiment and attempted to look at the men behind the manufactured identity of Christ, he found his subjects to have identities that were already shattered. The Christs were, he said, losers in an entirely personal struggle against the evidence of the senses that had destroyed their trust in themselves, and with it their capacity for sustaining themselves through their anguish. Or, as Rokeach said that Leon, one of the three Christs, might have put it, "If your mother will betray you, who won't?"[14]

Rokeach quoted Helen Lynd's 1958 study *On Shame and the Search for Identity*:

> Sudden experience of a violation of expectation, of incongruity between expectation and outcome, results in a shattering of trust in oneself, even in one's own body and skill and identity, and in the trusted boundaries or framework of the society and the world one has known. As trust in oneself and in the outer world develop together, so doubt of oneself and of the outer world are also intermeshed . . .
>
> Shattering of trust in the dependability of one's immediate world means loss of trust in other persons who are transmitters and interpreters of that world.

Rokeach, however, qualified Lynd in a vaguely worded effort to make a distinction between confidence and trust, which Wilson did not make in his analysis of Cold War poetics: "[T]rust in the dependability of the physical world," he corrected her, "is rarely an issue in our daily lives." We do not find people becoming psychotic or neurotic because this physical trust is violated. Only in our complex group relationships, where we find trauma, punishment, shame and guilt imputed to individuals, is this trust called into question. Only in such contexts is the individual "likely to develop primitive beliefs that have no social support, whatever." These beliefs, "phobias for example, or obsessions, delusions, hallucinations— seem to be a second-best way of achieving constancy in the face of adverse experience," Rokeach surmised.[15]

Rokeach's distinction divided trust in the physical or instrumental sense of confidence in external reality from trust as a relational attitude towards others and one's self. He acknowledged that both are necessary requirements for healthy ego development. Ego identity, he wrote, confirming Erik Erikson's theory, "depends not only on trust in parents but also on trust in the dependability of the outside world." But, Rokeach insisted, against Lynd's Eriksonian blurring of the two, that it is trust as the capacity for relationship, rather than trust as confidence in the external world, which serves as the foundation of human meaning.[16] This distinction suggests that the three benighted souls who imagined they were the Son of God and the savior of the world were not really expressing a direct, phenomenological identification with the ineffable. Nor did they desire to die to themselves and to the world so that they could live eternally in goodness and power, as Rokeach supposed, confusing his own vague distinction between trust and confidence. Instead, as Wilson's explanation of the conventions of the nuclear sublime may help us see, the Christs were artful modifiers who instrumentally appropriated for themselves the associations of awe and reverence that they encountered in religious discourse. Though Rokeach's Christs were fragmented and suffering from a sense of personal inadequacy, these human wreckages nevertheless imagined themselves into a classically sublime state of ownership of the ineffable to preserve themselves from the reality of their own existences. In this way, they gained confidence that they could manipulate the power before which they felt unworthy, while they simultaneously created a legitimacy for their own failed lives of isolated hell.[17]

Rokeach called the core personal meanings of the men who identified themselves as Christ "primitive beliefs." He suggested that these psychological structures of personal meaning function much as do ideologies, as Erik Erikson used this term—that is, the "unconscious tendencies that underlie religious, political, and scientific thought." In another instance, Rokeach compared his psychological theory of primitive beliefs to the physics of the atomic bomb. He suggested that a primitive belief is the psychological equivalent to the nucleus of an atom. It contains great energy, and when it is released through fission or fusion, the structure of the nucleus and the atom itself is transformed. "Primitive beliefs are the nucleus of any system of beliefs; if they can be made to change, the entire system will be altered," he explained.[18]

If Rokeach used the imagery of nuclear power to explain how he, as a scientist, hoped to re-create harmonious lives out of shattered ones, the three inmates hoped to preserve their illusion of being Christs in order to appropriate the universal power of God for the same ends. He was forced to conclude by the end of his study, however, in an ironic moment of self-disclosure, which Wilson would surely not share, that psychologists "unlike the atomic physicists have not yet learned how to control reactions in order to achieve an enduring, socially desirable end."[19] Rokeach's confidence in science, however, could not conceal his shaken trust in human meaning, which resulted from his personal confrontation with the Christs' metaphysical despair. He and his science had failed to instil trust in men who asked a question he could not answer: "If your mother will betray you, who won't?"

The three Christs brought together in Rokeach's study were shaken, in turn, by their confrontation with living mirrors of their assumed identities. But instead of the expected explosion occurring, the initially intense feeling of dissonance each exhibited at meeting the other Christs soon eased. Faced with such a logic-shattering contradiction, each man merely sought to reduce the ensuing dissonance without renouncing his own claim. Instead of surrendering the false identity or of being inspired to live a life of holy dedication, each searched for opportunities to erode the legitimacy claims of his fellows. As time went on, Rokeach found, these men developed a kind of "peaceful co-existence," which was "based upon their silent bargain and a standardized repertoire of rituals designed to avoid the tension-producing subject of identity."[20]

Rokeach concluded his parable of the Cold War with an expression of his own need to preserve his capacity to trust in a mad world of superpower competition and nuclear brinkmanship and his confidence in science, which anticipated Wilson's confidence in art. When three paranoid men are deadlocked in the ultimate human contradiction, Rokeach wrote of his patients, referring also to the international political leaders, "they prefer to seek ways to live with one another in peace rather than destroy one another."[21]

In the epilogue, Rokeach underscored his need to preserve trust in the humanity of the Christs in order to preserve his own confidence in the science that had failed to cure them of their incapacity to trust themselves or others. Rokeach, therefore, attributed his failure to the ignorance of science rather than to the hopelessness of the patients. In doing so, he preserved his confidence in the enterprise that had brought them together. "This study closes with the *hope* that at least a small portion of ignorance has here been dispelled," wrote Rokeach, "and with the *faith* that as knowledge gradually advances the incurable conditions of yesterday and today become the curable conditions of tomorrow."[22]

By the time Rokeach was reflecting on and writing about his summit of paranoids, he must have been consciously comparing the event to Richard Nixon's self-initiated trip to Moscow through the U. S. Information Agency, the subsequent visit of Khrushchev with Eisenhower and Nixon in the United States, and their performances on stage before an expectant world of viewers, including himself. These three world leaders, like the three Christs of Ypsilanti, both disbelieved and believed in their own public roles as champions of destiny. The statesmen jousted before the cameras, just as the Christs had jousted in the privacy of their hospital ward. The protagonists of the international Cold War, first in Moscow and later in the United States, actually seemed to experience moments of mystical unity in their mutually exclusive beliefs that each redeemer nation, alone, was the hope of humanity's future peace through material progress. For, despite the warmth of the debate in Sokolniki Park, Nixon could say that "we welcome this kind of competition because when we engage in it, no one loses, every one wins."[23] Though Nixon invited Khrushchev to visit the United States in proof of his goodwill and international stature as a statesman, Eisnhower upstaged him by preempting the invitation before Nixon returned for debriefing. The Soviet premier accepted. He expressed a desire to visit Disneyland, and a spirit of harmony settled over Soviet-American relations.

The interlude in superpower animosity lasted only briefly. It was sandwiched between two sublimely elevated, yet deeply flawed, technical accomplishments: the January launching of Luna I, a Soviet moon probe that missed its mark to become the the first artificial planet, and the crash of the advanced U.S. reconnaissance aircraft, the U-2, in May 1960, when President Eisenhower was caught lying about high-altitude surveillance over Soviet airspace. An embarrassed editorialist in the *Wall Street Journal* wrote an epitaph to the July hope for reconciliation between East and West: "Up until now it has been possible to say to the world that what came out of the Kremlin was deceitful and untrustworthy but that people could depend on what they were told by the government of the United States." This confidence in the American government had been strained. "Now the world may not be so sure that this country is any different from any other."[24] Over the next two years, in the deteriorating game of high stakes competition that was being played by the superpowers, the world narrowly escaped a nuclear holocaust. Then the superpowers again stumbled toward détente and finally an unplanned and unexpected end of the Cold War.

Living now on the other side of the Cold War, we may recognize a significant moment of cultural self-disclosure in the events of July 1959 in Moscow and Michigan. That moment in international political space occurred in a time of transition that threw the conflicts within American national culture into sharp contrast with each other. The Eisenhower years were turning into the Kennedy years; a rhetoric of containment was being replaced by a rhetoric of new frontiers; a self-defined age of anxiety was giving way to an equally self-defined age of Aquarius. As such, these confrontations constitute one vantage point from which to consider the inner dynamic of an American national culture preoccupied with preserving confidence. In retrospect, we may view these moments at a trade exhibition and a mental hospital, as well as an artist's advertisement for himself and a film about an actress's imitation of life, as part of a larger cultural process. An American aesthetic approach to the sublime was visibly shifting from Walt Whitman's photographic realism towards Warhol's photocopied realism; or from Melville's masquerade in print, *The Confidence-Man*, to such masquerades in film as Jennie Livingston's tour guide to the voguing balls of New York City, *Paris Is Burning*, featuring Willie Ninja, who became Madonna's choreographer[25]; and from Woodrow Wilson's oratory of corporate progressivism to Ronald Wilson Reagan's rhetoric of populist corporatism, which cross-dressed twentieth-century American political categories.

Now that the Cold War has come to an end, the conventions upon which it was based and its continuity with earlier periods of crisis are clearer. As we may see in the first post–Cold War national election, the struggle against communism was less a struggle of ideology than a performance staged to win a rhetorical victory of national confidence. American national culture, therefore, does exist. But it does not exist in the fatally compromised terms of republican virtue, or Anglo-Protestant social conventions, or of abundance or liberalism. It exists not as a culture with confidence in some aspect of its tradition or in some symbol of its collective identity such as traditional family values or the political party system, the myth of the West or an American Adam; it exists as a culture, simply and purely, of confidence itself.

In a world of discredited universal claims, confidence is the one inescapably real and necessary universal that is beyond question in public and private life. It is so fundamental and inescapable that it has been all but invisible to philosophers and historians alike. No philosophers have devised confidence tests as they have devised truth tests. No history of confidence has been written. Nor would any responsible critic attempt to undermine confidence, even if attacking some false ground for confidence in his or her readers. However, should we once become aware of the insistent demand that we all have for confidence, of its singular necessity for personal survival, for practicing science and promoting religion, and for engaging in artistic production and business, we may begin to suspect its central role in defining the national character of the United States.

2

A Culture of Confidence, A Culture of Doubt

During the 1992 presidential campaign, when George Bush claimed victory in the Cold War, he found that it little influenced his standing in the polls. The economy had become the popular issue, replacing concerns about foreign policy and military experience. The incumbent found himself losing ground as the election approached. Bush sought to staunch the massive loss of voter approval for his administration by transforming the contest into a choice between change and trust and then into a referendum upon whom the voters could most trust to bring about change.[1] As an incumbent presiding over a depressed economy with no recovery in sight, candidate George Bush found it useful, as Ronald Reagan had before him, to exploit the disillusionment and lack of confidence voters were expressing towards the entire political establishment. "I'm very confident I'm going to win, not overconfident," Bush told a *Time* reporter in August, insisting those who predicted his defeat would be proven wrong. "And I think also," he explained, "I've demonstrated I can make tough decisions. And the people are going to say, Who do you trust to do those things? That's why I have this rather quiet confidence in the face of some of the darndest criticism I've ever seen." However, in running against criticism of his failure to sustain the Reagan Revolution, and, therefore, the record of his own administration, the president could hardly claim to offer a positive alternative to more government. In 1992, he was haunted by a crisis of confidence in government and the economy similar to the one that had led the voters to narrowly reject Richard Nixon for John Kennedy in 1960 when the Cold War was a live political concern. Nixon's emphasis on voter confidence worked against him when he failed to sustain the image of self-assured command during the television debates, as a tanned and confident-looking Kennedy emphasized the doubts and fears generated by the Cold War. Similarly, the fading of Bush's aura, after his high popularity during the Gulf War of the previous year, permitted Ross Perot, who modeled himself on Reagan, and Bill Clinton, who modeled himself on Kennedy, to successfully turn the president's own strategy against him in the polls.[2]

The explicit emphasis upon the rhetoric of trust and confidence in the 1992 election by all three of the presidential candidates highlights the pervasive, though largely unheralded, role of confidence in defining American political values at the end of the twentieth century. From the rhetoric of masculine confidence in Kennedy's Great Frontier to the frontier rhetoric of the New Political and Religious Right espoused by Reagan, the national mood had revolved around the promise to make America America again. The youthful death of the celebrity-politician Kennedy, followed by the debacle of Vietnam, had plunged the nation into a tragic sense that Camelot had ended, and that, as Daniel Patrick Moynihan grieved, America would never be young again. However, the actor-president Ronald Reagan did make America feel young again. He did so, Garry Wills suggests, because his own will to believe tapped the springs of the public hunger for belief—a belief soaring far beyond the small vote that elected him. For he had won election to the highest office of the land at a time of life when most people resign themselves to the end of their youthful dreams. In his mid-fifties and at the end of one career, Reagan entered politics, using his ability to sell confidence in conservatism as he had earlier sold Van Huessen shirts and General Electric's "products for better living." As a political spokesman and an advertiser, he projected himself as a confidence artist who was sincerely confident; it was a winning combination of qualities that Clinton and Bush tried to preserve in their own campaigns.[3]

Indeed, in October 1991, a year before the televised debates between Bush, Clinton, and Perot, *Time*'s Hugh Sidey wrote of a seemingly unbeatable Bush, "Not since Kennedy's time have discipline and determination been so pervasive in an administration." Bush, Sidey explained, had "carefully studied the leadership style of Ronald Reagan, which was to keep a public amiability while having a wrecking crew ready in the boiler room." Yet Bush's approval rating had been steadily falling, from a high of 86 percent in March to 60 percent in October. In hindsight, it can be seen that the comparisons to Kennedy and Reagan pointed not only to enduring personifications of political power, but indirectly gave witness to the doubt that had remained in the national political consciousness since Kennedy's assassination. In praising Bush's control, Sidey explained that neither Johnson nor Nixon had quite handled power right, and, therefore, had failed to command complete respect from their staffs. If Ronald Reagan had cheated Kennedy's fate, transforming doubt into confidence through two terms in office, it was also obvious that Reagan's magnetic hold on the public imagination diminished dramatically once he left a position of power.[4] Bush, and then Clinton, therefore, found themselves burdened with the same contradictory task: to use as models of confidence Kennedy and Reagan, former presidents whose appeal for voters was nostalgic and fatally identified with lost opportunity.

It is not surprising, therefore, that the supreme confidence enjoyed by the Bush presidency following the Gulf War—the second military triumph and personal victory over the "wimp" image since his coming to office in 1989—began to erode even before he faced Clinton and Perot on the campaign trail. In the last months of 1991, the media fed a stubborn public mood of political disillusionment by covering a series of performances that seemed only to confirm the duplicity of national leadership. Oliver North publicly linked former President Reagan to the Iran-contra scandal, with the publication of his autobiography, *Under Fire*, that fall. The marine lieutenant colonel had garnered national sympathy as a martyr to government duplicity in his testimony before the Iran-contra hearings of 1987. In his 1991 autobiography, North reemphasized his popular image as a loyal American who had been betrayed by his president, while standing by the marine code of *semper fidelis* at his assigned post as a mid-level staffer on the National Security Council.[5]

North had looked and sounded honest and somewhat naive during the hearings. His voice had cracked like Jimmy Stewart's when he spoke of his patriotic feelings and of his family and duty. But if North had looked and sounded like the hero of a Frank Capra film of the 1950s, keeping trust while the nation's leaders promoted their own interests, his autobiography revealed a deceptive cold warrior. North had operated clandestinely for many years with code names such as "Blue," "Mr. Goode," and "Steelhammer." The publication of his autobiography reminded his critics that many suspected him of inventing a far more central and daring role for himself in government-sponsored intrigue than he deserved.[6]

Between North's appearance in 1987 before the televised Iran-contra committee and the publication of his *Under Fire* in 1991, he had quietly amassed millions of dollars from donations and speeches to turn his own alleged exploitation by his superiors into a source of celebrity and political connection. President Bush, in contrast, appeared disingenuous in 1991 as he continued to swear that he had been "out of the loop" when decisions about swapping arms for hostages were discussed, and as former President Reagan exhibited real or feigned disorientation in his videotaped testimony during Special Prosecutor Lawrence Walsh's investigation into the Iran-contra scandal. Reagan's failure of loyalty to the men who served him, North scoffed, as he contemplated undertaking a political career of his own, "leaves as a legacy this videotape of a doddering old man. It's unbelievable!"[7]

Then, in October 1991, just as Sidey was praising Bush's political acumen and news magazines were highlighting North's allegations, millions of Americans turned on their televisions to watch Supreme Court nominee Clarence Thomas and law professor Anita Hill engage in a psychosexual drama, in which male sexual confidence was equated with the betrayal of female trust. Thomas embodied white male fantasies about black male sexuality and male nightmares of entrapment through female pretense. Hill embodied the aggrieved female victim of patriarchal power but also the debilitating moral authority of emotional indifference. She had turned the sublime—in this case, a former supervisor's masculine display of his vanity—into the ridiculous by exposing his alleged private behavior to public view.

Bush had ingeniously insisted that he had nominated Thomas because he was the best qualified applicant available, and also that he was an authentic black American, a phrase Cornel West argues discouraged moral reasoning because it presupposed elaborate political interrelations of interests, individuals, and communities that formed a "deceptive cloak of racial consensus" while seductively invoking "an undeniable history of racial abuse and racial struggle."[8] In the psychological space between the sexual demonizing of criminal Willy Horton in 1988 and the legitimizing of Judge Clarence Thomas's alleged pornographic approach to courting in 1991, it was not easy to discern whether the Thomas-Hill performance was scripted upon real intentions or a history of misperceived expectations that had passed between Thomas and Hill a decade before. "Even after listening to all the anguished testimony," wrote *Time* correspondent Nancy Gibbs, "who could ever feel confident that they knew what really happened?"[9] Nor was it clear whether the public fascination with the hearings was based upon the exploitation of Anita Hill's body or Clarence Thomas's, the first metaphorically raped and the second metaphorically hanged. Or, alternatively, was public hostility instead directed towards the uncomfortable white male senators of the Judiciary Committee? For it was the latter whose authority and legitimacy were assailed by Thomas and Hill together, once they were cast, by themselves, the media or a frustrated public, as victims of inept government and patriarchal insensitivity.

The Thomas/Hill melodrama implicated the embarrassed senators who were witnessing the performance before television cameras broadcasting the event all over the world. The vulgar self-disclosures and use of unprecedentedly ribald language in what were usually restrained and symbolically patriarchal hearings meant that Thomas and Hill were accidentally imitating singer Madonna's then-still-successful formula for turning explicit self-revelation into mystification about her real sexual identity and for turning her own exploited body and confession of psychological damage into an exploitation of public voyeurism. For, even though confessing psychological damage, Thomas won confirmation, and, while deeply humiliated, Hill identified herself with a revolution in attitudes toward sexual harassment in American public opinion. The Senate, however, was pilloried as an old boy's club, and members of the Judiciary Committee were portrayed as feckless old men. The subsequent 1992 election linked gender discrimination to the demand for political reform, as four women won new Senate seats.[10]

During that "election year of the woman," the media turned its light upon allegations concerning the private sexual indiscretions of the candidates. Bush preserved the Reagan image of male chastity despite rumors linking him to a longtime aide. Clinton, like Gary Hart before him, maintained the Kennedy image of sexual politics, but weathered the storm of public disgust for candidates captured in vulnerable situations, since no compromising photographs existed for Clinton as they had for Hart. Nor did Clinton exhibit Kennedy's or Hart's self-destructive need to test his nerve and to risk exposure through obsessive "womanizing" during the campaign. It was at this time, too, that the scandal broke in the national media over Woody Allen's affair with Mia Farrow's adopted daughter, Soon Yi, and charges of incest and sex abuse exposed his theatrical persona to public excoriation.[11] Allen had slowly evolved in his film persona from the comedic to the serious, and from casting himself as a shy and ineffectual Walter Mitty to the role of the confident male star of the

1950s. Just as he had reinvented himself through performance, the actor-director transformed his real-life humiliation and vilification into a performance of its own. He did so by making a series of public disclosures about his private life, while directing public interest to his new film, *Husbands and Wives*. The film starred the real-life combatants, Mia Farrow and himself, in similar, but fictionalized, roles.[12]

The Madonna-like power that North, Thomas, Hill, and Allen gained through their ability to turn ethically compromised events into performances and of Clinton's narrow preservation of his Kennedy-Reagan style as a political celebrity may be contrasted with the fall of televangelist Jimmy Swaggart after the revelation of compromising photographs and his tearful pleading for forgiveness in the fall of 1991 and with the earlier political death of Gary Hart for his ethical defense of his sexual behavior.[13] The public fascination with the private sexual obsessions of each of these celebrities reveals that sex and politics had both been consigned to the realm of theater in the waning days of American Cold War culture, and that when the public saw through theater, or, in Erving Goffman's terms, caught the actors backstage, they paradoxically demanded more theater. When celebrities stepped out of the role of performer to appeal directly to the public's trust, their self-disclosure only served to increase rather than decrease doubt about their veracity.

Simultaneously, in the relentlessly insistent world of news-entertainment, the videotaped beating of Rodney King had become a public performance through constantly repeated airing over television. It then became the center of a trial against his police assailants and, with their acquittal by a white jury, a source of conflict over the nature of visually reproduced evidence as simple fact or complex interpretation. The video, which graphically recorded more than fifty blows to King's head, did not convince jurors of police guilt, but did reveal the disappearing frontier line between crime and performance, trial and theater, and even cause and effect. For, upon the acquittal of the four white policemen on April 29, 1992, the largest riot in twentieth-century American history exploded in Los Angeles, with white truck driver Reginald Denney being videotaped by a news helicopter as he was dragged from his vehicle. The gleefully brutal assault on Denney by a few rioters who were responding to, or pretended to be responding to, the acquittal of King's videotaped assailants repeated and further confused the identification of news with entertainment and crime with performance.

In still another formally unrelated but parallel expression of the logic of performance, virtual reality was endlessly discussed in the popular press. Such films as *Cool World* and *Lawnmower Man*, both released in 1992, simulated the experience of virtual reality for film viewers, as the media also focused upon the disappearing distinction between fantasy and real violence in television and in evermore realistic video games and between celebrity and criminality in the matrix between ghetto streets and corporate entertainment in the world of rap performers. Perhaps the signature of the end of the Cold War national culture was in the then-current Disney film. The Disney studio's formula for coupling the terrors of modern experience with warm sentimentality literally made their films icons of America during the Cold War era. In this case, the film was the exotic, computer-animated *Aladdin*, which featured an ever-duplicitous blue genie, repeatedly and successfully asking the liberated but naive heroine, Princess Jasmine, to "trust me."[14]

Some of these national media events, which turned upon the postmodern confusion between the real and the simulated, were indicative of public disillusionment with government. Others revealed distrust of the nation's legal institutions. Still others revolved around the disappointment with national celebrities who failed to offer vicarious confidence through their stardom. But for the public and media critics alike, these contemporary post–Cold War events embodied the same cultural doubt that the philosopher Richard Rorty had recently maintained was eroding every claim of foundational authority that once supported the Enlightenment convention that knowledge is the reflection of the mirror of nature.

Rorty's philosophical challenge to the ocular metaphor of truth, *Philosophy and the Mirror of Nature* (1979), gave expression from the heart of the academy to the public doubt enveloping the late Cold War American political culture and anticipated the public fascination with simulation and self-invention that would capture the national imagination in the 1980s and 1990s. Rorty's exploitation of the intellectual doubt lurking behind the Enlightenment origins of philosophical confidence hinted that academic philosophy might be merely a sophisticated confidence game. That confidence game, he suggested, was grounded in an Enlightenment anthropology, which he described as "our glassy essence." The privileged status claimed by philosophers for themselves, Rorty argued, was a direct result of this self-serving anthropology. For it gave comfort and legitimacy to those who believed that the human mind could be so polished and perfected that it might reflect the light of Nature and mirror its truth. But, Rorty countered, a glassy essence might also be seen, according to the same Enlightenment conventions of reason, as a naturalistic fallacy, a confusion between essence and accident. Indeed, Rorty found the doubt about the glassy essence metaphor inherent in the scholasticism of Francis Bacon, who declared in the seventeenth century that the "mind of man" was "far from the nature of a clear and equal glass wherein the beams of things should reflect according to their true incidences . . . [it] is rather like an enchanted glass, full of superstition and imposture, if it not be delivered and reduced."[15] Such doubts about the very foundation of Enlightenment ways of knowing, Rorty recognized, were inseparable from doubts concerning scientific objectivity that was supposed to resolve them.

The Cold War origins of Rorty's challenge to philosophical essentialism may be discerned in his reliance upon T. S. Kuhn's 1959 essay on the social construction of reality, which was later published as *The Structure of Scientific Revolutions*. Rorty's influential argument in *Philosophy and the Mirror of Nature* was also formally similar to another Cold War touchstone, sociologist Daniel Bell's *The End of Ideology*, which, significantly, was published at about the same time as Kuhn's essay.[16] As Rorty announced the exhaustion of metaphysics and epistemology but not conversation, Bell had announced the exhaustion of the "old apocalyptic and chiliastic visions" but not the end of utopias. Rorty sought to undermine "the reader's confidence in 'the mind' as something about which one should have a 'philosophical' view, in 'knowledge' about which there ought to be a 'theory,' and which has 'foundations,' and in 'philosophy' as it has been conceived since Kant," as Bell sought to undermine the privileged status of traditional foundational ideas of politics that had, since Kant, defined politics and economics in the West. [17]

The corrosive atmosphere of doubt that Rorty shared with Kuhn and Bell, and through which they participated in extending the internal logic of the Enlightenment against itself, admitted a loss of standards for objective certainty, not just in science but in politics, and not just in theology and history but in the philosophical principles that have been claimed since the seventeenth century to underwrite them all. The loss of standards for objective certainty in the academic, political and popular cultures had reduced experience to seemingly limitless simulacra. The photograph and film were superseded by the photocopier and the videotape, raising doubts over what constitutes originality or even whether an original may be said to exist. Paradoxically, however, the elimination of originals, or philosophical essentialisms and political dogmatisms, have actually served to reinforce the need for preserving the true foundation upon which the entire Enlightenment project of progress was first established. That foundation is more basic than the scientific revolution, the rise of nationalism or the triumph of reason. For these manifestations of the Enlightenment that continue to define Western self-understanding at the end of the twentieth century are themselves constructed on the irreducible foundation of confidence.

Confidence, at this most basic level, may be defined as an active, utilitarian calculation of advantage. Though it seems an ephemeral emotion, even an insubstantial source of hope, confidence is actually the most basic of desires and pragmatic of tools. It may be won or lost; it may be searched for or preserved; it may be manipulated and supplied. It is the grease that moves commodities to market, the fuel that fires all economic activity. Confidence is an axis of abstract principle upon which conceptions of truth and wisdom turn. Indeed, it is the single recognized product that legitimatizes economic and political institutions, and it is the test of truth shared by the many philosophies, both materialist and idealist, that have competed as explanation systems in the modern West.

Confidence, in other words, is an instrumental approach to power. It may be contrasted with trust, which by its very definition eschews advantage and assumes social conditions of mutuality. Trust is woven into the fabric of primary social relationships, and, therefore, lacks the artifice characterizing confidence. Trust is innocent of ambition or ulterior interests, or it ceases to be trust. For this reason, trust becomes frayed when it is used for utilitarian purposes, and, once torn, is very difficult to restore. Confidence, however, is utilitarian, and grows through the achieving of instrumental successes. For this reason, when trust is torn apart, doubt replaces it, and an act of confidence is required in an attempt to re-create it. So long as memory revisits betrayed trust, confidence will be required to preserve the institutions and prevent the social forms of community from dissolving into chaos and despair. Confidence, therefore, is not necessarily instrumental in the merely vulgar sense; rather, it is a hidden aesthetic of power. It transforms doubt into belief through doubt, just as any original work of art is rendered authentic through its artificiality.

It is this quality that makes confidence an absolutely essential ingredient for the preservation of any modern political structure or social organization. As Edmund Burke wrote, "There is a confidence necessary to human intercourse, and without which men are often more injured by their own suspicions than they would be by the perfidy of others." When a particular individual or group loses confidence—as, for example, in the stock market or a political system, in a lover, or a product, or a scientific paradigm—confidence actually increases in value. The wearing out of old delusions, Burke observed, therefore only serves to encourage the invention of knaves. Neither health quacks nor political charlatans, he noted, actually deliver possession of the promised liberation from sickness or tyranny. Instead, they leave the people perpetually in hope.[18]

Similarly, the fashionably deconstructionist turn of recent cultural studies has essentially been an exploitation of the inevitable doubt proceeding from the most certain of Enlightenment truths. Indeed, confidence in a canon, or in the omnipotence of the authorial voice, or in scientific, religious, or philosophical orthodoxy, as every confidence artist knows, would be incomprehensible without a concomitant but suppressed doubt. Richard Rorty's neopragmatism has suggested that the crisis of confidence revealed in late twentieth-century postmodernism was not only anticipated in turn-of-the-century America, but was present at the creation of the United States, as a central theme of the Enlightenment in the eighteenth century. As such, it existed, as Burke's and Rousseau's social criticisms prove, well before an artificial world was fashioned through the culture-industry of television, film, public relations, government propaganda, and advertisement. Indeed, by locating the twentieth-century crisis of confidence in the failure of the Enlightenment metaphor of the mind as a mirror of nature, Rorty has implicitly acknowledged that confidence is itself artificially constructed, and that, therefore, no natural language for revealing reality is possible. Nor, for this same reason, may a mirror be constructed to artificially reflect natural truth, as positivists dreamed they might do for their less logically astute fellow beings.

Instead, Rorty argued, following T. S. Kuhn's theory of paradigm construction, reality is limited by what people are persuaded it shall be. Rorty claimed to find in John Dewey's pragmatism and in George Herbert Mead's social psychology of symbolic interactionism, upon which Dewey based his instrumentalist philosophy, a model for manufacturing confidence out of doubt by replacing rational objectivity with social solidarity.[19] Rorty shared with Josiah Royce, Mead's teacher and Peirce's student, faith in the possibility of preserving a frontier between social conformity and personal liberty. Rorty, the son of the independent Marxist journalist James Rorty, has identified that frontier metaphorically with a philosophy of "conversation." Royce, who had grown up a century earlier on the literal frontier of the California Gold Rush, located his conceptual frontier in a philosophy of "loyalty."[20]

Royce advocated his own version of the code of the West because he had observed with fascination the birth of new communities on the land. He explored the elements that gave these fledgling communities cohesion in his western novel, *Feud of Oakfield Creek* (1887), and through historical studies and philosophical inquiries. Royce advocated loyalty, much as Rorty promoted conversation, because he considered it to be the one quality that served as a meeting ground between individual initiative and social constraint. Conversation and loyalty, however, were not promoted by Rorty and Royce simply as philosophical grounds between self and society, but as processes for culture building. In each case, they offered a form of performance that had as its aim the creation and preservation of an organic community.[21]

To speak of an organic community as if it were a natural performance may seem oxymoronic. But Rorty and Royce agreed, from both ends of the twentieth century, that communities may be fashioned over time, and that individuals may collectively select and preserve those elements that will provide for an ever richer and more stimulating expression of shared meaning and problem resolution. This means that for the Cold War neopragmatist Rorty, as for Royce, Peirce, William James and Dewey before him, Enlightenment institutions and interests may safely surrender claim to privileged truth while paradoxically preserving confidence. This becomes philosophically possible, they all agreed, by accepting contingency, or radical doubt, as the starting point of all human interaction. Confidence may then be instrumentally defended by defining truth as rhetoric. It may be affirmed through "the will to believe," a phrase of Peirce's embraced by James, and it may be acted out through a dramatic performance, in terms of the "symbolic interactionism," that Mead developed out of Royce's psychological studies of learning social roles through imitation.[22]

Taken together, these strategies for preserving confidence through doubt share Edmund Burke's classic Enlightenment goal of creating a national community through historical selection. The idealist Royce and the neopragmatist Rorty, like Burke, could locate social discourse in some indeterminate and undecipherable past. That past, they agreed, is lost to memory, but it provides a formal source of social solidarity and common purpose, which may be evoked through rhetoric. For it is through the power of persuasion that a vision of an organic community must be artificially constructed, communicated, and then, if it is to be given legitimacy, preserved through masquerading as a form of naturalism.[23]

The idea of an organic community, however, is but an extension of the central Enlightenment metaphor of the frontier. The reason the metaphor of the frontier is central, and not peripheral within the Enlightenment, is that the frontier is not simply a conceptualized space between East and West. Nor is it only a geographical boundary between civilization and wilderness. More basically still, the frontier has served since the Enlightenment as a conceptualized space between confidence and doubt and as a stage upon which confidence may be acted out before the world. It is by virtue of this Enlightenment commitment to confidence that Richard Rorty's contemporary neopragmatic ideal of an organic community may be seen to parallel Herbert Blumer's and Erving Goffman's social theory of neosymbolic interactionism that defined social life as theater. For both Rorty's neopragmatic ideal of an organic community and Blumer's and Goffman's Hollywood-dominated vision of social role-playing from the 1950s were derived from Royce, who passed his views that social roles are learned through imitation along to George Herbert Mead and, through him, to John Dewey.[24]

This social psychology, based upon what Charles H. Cooley called the "looking glass self," had been embraced by a whole generation of Progressive social scientists. It expressed the profound doubt about the self and the meaning of history that Anglo-Americans experienced with the changing social conditions accompanying urbanization and industrialization after the Civil War. It was, however, a social psychology that interjected into that doubt a theory of confidence, a description of the mechanism by which the dominating and defining personality might effectively shape society according to a heroic vision. "Into the vagueness and confusion that most of us feel in the face of a strange situation, such a man injects a clear cut idea," Cooley explained.

> There is a definiteness about him, which makes us feel that he will not leave us drifting, but will set a course, will substitute action for doubt, and give our energies an outlet. Again, his aggressive confidence is transmitted by suggestion, and acts directly upon our minds as a sanction of his leadership. And if he adds to this the tact to awaken no opposition, to make us feel that he is of our sort, that his suggestions are quite in our line, in a word, that we are safe in his hands; he can hardly be resisted.[25]

Cooley, a long-time sociology professor at the University of Michigan, was intellectually drawn to German idealism, as were many of his academic contemporaries. He argued that heredity and environment must be viewed as a total organic process, not as separable parts of life, and that the individual and society were consequently parts of an organically whole community rather than divided entities. For Cooley, therefore, the self was produced by the society, but the society was, in turn, a product of the self, transmitted both from and to other selves through the imagination.

The convention of the looking glass self provided Cooley with a mechanism for reproducing an organic community through the power of communication, which could replace the failed agrarian community of his adolescence. However, as a classical Enlightenment formulation of knowledge, the looking glass self necessarily also suggested doubt. For the individual of "personal ascendency" was also required to sell that self to the public, making possible the ascendency of the confidence artist instead. Cooley acknowledged in *Human Nature and the Social Order* (1902) that "every one is something of an imposter." Unavoidably, Cooley explained, "[A]s social and imaginative beings we must set store by our appearance; and it is hardly possible to do so without in some degree adopting that appearance to the impression we wish to make."[26] Similarly, pioneer Progressive sociologist Edward A. Ross, of the University of Wisconsin, warned in *Sin and Society* (1907) that the new urban America had produced a new class of sinner, the criminaloid. This new social type, created by the forces of modern urban industrialism, existed at the frontier between respectability and criminality. The criminaloid, Ross said, practices his duplicitous war against society by "protective mimicry" of the good.[27]

Anglo-American writers, like the social scientists, found themselves trapped as well as liberated by the rhetoric of social constructionism in the new industrial era. Writers such as William Dean Howells, Mark Twain, Stephen Crane, Henry James, Walt Whitman, Frank Norris, George Washington Cable, and Kate Chopin were, as artists, dedicated to expressing their unique personal visions. Yet they found that they had to sell that vision to a consuming public. The conventions of realism and naturalism, demanded both by the artists' own sensibilities and by public taste, threatened to press them into the same service of nation-building and the same theatrical contradictions of industrial democracy as the social scientists experienced in their looking glass world. Henry James and Walt Whitman are two of the most significant examples of entrapment from this company of artists. They are particularly relevant illustrations, because they were transformed into symbols of aesthetic liberation in the American literary canon during the Cold War.

Henry James, novelist, playwright, and brother of the philosopher-psychologist William James, wrote to his brother on the publication of *Pragmatism* in 1907 that he, Henry, had always pragmatized without knowing it. He theorized in *The Art of the Novel* (1899) that art is an illusion cultivated by the artist through subterfuge to ensnare the reader's interest. Man, he wrote, combines the eternal desire for more experience with an infinite cunning for getting that experience as cheaply as possible. Like the confidence artist, the ordinary individual will steal others' experiences wherever possible. The more simply accessible the art is, James moralized, the more the consumer will try to avoid any uncomfortable part of the message.[28] James's artistic problem was how, as a professional artist, to write honest deceptions for a market-oriented public. The reading public, whom he was required to please if he was to earn a livelihood, James complained, instinctively knew how to turn the sublime desire for danger, which it is the artist's task to exploit, into a secure escape from discomfort, which the ordinary individual prefers.

James felt trapped between the sham worlds of aristocratic privilege and crass commercialism. He attempted to resist the market's tendency to turn him into a confidence artist by mastering an artistry of confidence so as to outmaneuver his wily audience and earn a living. He found a source for doing so, while escaping the aesthetically numbing trap of "fact," in the direct illusion made possible by the rhetorical immediacy of the theater. The play, in contrast to the novel, James explained, "lives exclusively on the spoken word—not on the report of the thing said but, directly and audibly, on the very thing; that it thrives by its law on the exercise under which the novel hopelessly collapses when the attempt is made disproportionately to impose it."[29]

The seamless communication between artist and public, however, eluded James. His plays were not successful. He had returned to the novel by 1895, using his untrustworthy narrators and duplicitous characters to create, as William James wrote, his "prismatic interferences of light, ingeniously focused by mirrors upon empty space." Henry James pervaded the lives of his forgettable characters so that, as Van Wyck Brooks noted, he everywhere replaced them through the powerful presences of his pretended absence. For Brooks, the satisfying illusion of

James's earlier novels was replaced by the insistently manipulative voice of the author's dualistic consciousness. A psychologist is not a novelist, Brooks complained, so that, for instance, the simple and emotionally direct character of Christopher Newman in the 1877 version of *The American* was spoiled in James's 1907 revision, when Newman "assumed the sophistications of the later James."[30] The author himself, however, who considered *Confidence* (1880), which explored both meanings of the word, to be among his favorites, saw it as simply returning from his sojourn in the theater with a humbled sense of the possibilities of creating a bridge between the "deceptive atmosphere of art," and the deceptive atmosphere of modern life.[31]

James's artistic doubts about the possibility of preserving cultural confidence and the doubts of contemporary social scientists were graphically combined in his reflections on the crisis in twentieth-century American national identity in *The American Scene* (1907). In the same year that Ross published *Sin and Society*, James wrote that an apparently secure sense of national identity is really the fragile creation of socially constructed reality, which may be easily shattered. It is formed on an individual level by viewing one's countrymen and countrywomen as one is used to seeing them, he explained, and it is instinctively preserved by "keeping the idea simple and strong and continuous." But a visit to Ellis Island, he said, places that confidence in peril. Observing the "inconceivable alien" and being forced to share the sanctity of American consciousness and the intimacy of American patriotism with the immigrant, James wrote, projects a lurid light on one's sense of national identity that shakes one to the depths of one's being. When James imagined this visitor to Ellis Island, he explained, "I positively *have* to think of him, as going about ever afterwards with a new look, for those who can see it, in his face, the outward sign of the new chill in his heart." In this new condition of doubt, James said, the alien threatens to take possession of the national culture by the sheer fact of his unsettling presence. The only way "to recover confidence and regain lost ground," he confided, dropping the mask of disinterested observer, is that "we, not they, must make the surrender and accept the orientation," despite being appalled by them. Under the threat of dispossession by a monstrous alien insistence, he concluded, "the art of beguiling or duping it becomes the art to be cultivated."[32]

Henry James had negatively reviewed Walt Whitman's *Drum-Taps* after the Civil War, but by the twentieth century he had come to recognize that the two had a similar mission—to negotiate the double meaning of confidence as the real and the artificial in industrial American national culture. Unlike James, who retreated to anonymous craftsmanship in England, Whitman cultivated his self-created role as America's authentic bard-prophet of industrial democracy. At the time of the Civil War, the middle-aged poet had failed to find self-fulfillment since wandering from his Hicksite Quaker roots. Nor had the author of *Leaves of Grass* achieved redemption by identifying with Dante or by surrendering his bohemian life style for purifying service as a nurse during the irrepressible conflict. Indeed, Whitman initially expressed profound disillusionment with the quality of postwar social values. "Genuine belief seems to have left us," he complained. "The underlying principles of the States are not honestly beliv'd in (for all the hectic glow, and these melo-dramatic screamings,) nor is humanity itself believ'd in." Instead, Whitman wrote dispiritedly in *Democratic Vistas*, "From deceit in the spirit, the mother of all false deeds, the offspring is already incalculable."[33]

The poet, however, soon found his voice in a mission to create confidence in a democratic national culture out of the rotting corpses of the many thousands dead on both sides of the war. Whitman's self-identification with national democracy as the "real thing," Miles Orvell points out, meant that he was at once a unique individual and a typical specimen. His poetic persona could claim to democratically encompass the whole, precisely as the photographer's singular vision may be reproduced again and again. Orvell suggests that Whitman quite consciously used the tension between the real and the imitative in photography for his own ends of self-proclamation. In doing so, the poet identified the photograph with celebrity status and with self-promotion, two dominating ideals in twentieth-century American popular culture that later made Hollywood synonymous with the American Dream.

By artificially blurring the perceptual distinction between the real and the imitation, the photograph also made it possible to multiply the number of original copies. Therefore, according to Whitman's use of the photographic metaphor, everyone could become an original democrat in the new machine age culture of urbanized America. Once more, if each ordinary and unexceptional individual would surrender himself or herself to Whitman's individual artistic vision, as he invited the masses to do, each anonymous soul could celebrate itself through Whitman's fame and personal apotheosis, to share in his cosmic self-confidence. It was, significantly, a view echoed by Charles Cooley, as well. We adopt the words of a Whitman and think of them as our words, Cooley said, "then being on the inside of it, as it were, it is our own self that is so expansive and happy."[34]

Whitman had learned from the Civil War photographers how to manipulate the art of the camera to organize fragmented experience into visual unity for national ends. The poet-as-camera translated himself into an instrument of aesthetic illusion to affirm the link between industrial progress and the organic evolution of American nationalism. In his appreciation for the rhetorical implications of the photograph, therefore, Whitman anticipated both Stieglitz's redemptive faith in modernism and Andy Warhol's voyeurism, on one side of twentieth-century consumerism, and the heroic engineer, celebrated by Buckminster Fuller and Norman Mailer, on the other. This mechanical aesthetic, produced through and in the camera, shattered the line between simulation and dissimulation, or as Whitman put it, "between being as against the human trait of mere seeming," or, in other words, between the real and the counterfeit.[35]

The process of transforming doubt into confidence, identified by Cooley and Ross as the duty of the social sciences and by Henry James and Walt Whitman as the central challenge to the artist in an industrial democracy, was part of a common sense of responsibility for building a national culture. Liah Greenfield has identified that Enlightenment process of building national culture as a "semantic transformation." That is, one form of community, which already exists, is transformed into a new configuration during a historical moment in time. Nationalism came to exist during the Enlightenment only after it had been made to seem natural through the evolution of language.

From the perspective of Greenfield's theory of nationalism as an association of ideas, the Progressive Era's social scientists, philosophers, and literary artists were primarily semanticists. Following the Civil War, and in the wake of the rapid social change the war helped unleash, they busily codified associations of personality, aesthetics, ethics, geography, population, and polity into a collective national identity. Then, the social scientists, in particular, used their various disciplines of history, sociology, anthropology, political science, and psychology to construct a network of linguistic defenses for new combinations of political and social power. Each of these defenses was, in turn, necessarily based on the same Enlightenment foundations of scientific instrumentalism and sublime aesthetics the social scientists shared with their contemporary literary artists and philosophers.

The Progressives collectively desired to discover the universal democratic principles behind earlier semantic transformations of "the people," which Greenfield suggests had been based upon abstracting the existing associations of family, church, or guild. But perhaps the idea of the frontier, a conceptualized space between confidence and doubt, was itself the pivotal center of semantic transformation. The lines between science, philosophy, and religion were still fluid at the turn of the century, inviting an identification with frontier associations. The United States was still dominated by Protestantism, and, indeed, many of the leading Progressive social scientists were either the children of ministers or had considered a vocation in the church. Therefore, given their frontier position between science and culture, religion and philosophy, and between the public and private, the Progressive social scientists were able to achieve what Stanford Lyman and Arthur Vidich have described as a sociodicy: a justification of society, in place of a theodicy, or a justification of the ways of God.[36]

Consequently, the contribution of the Progressive generation of social scientists to the invention of an American national culture lay in their use of the authority of science to substitute a sophisticated artifice of the sublime for the simple memory of the sacred, associated with the naivete and guilts of their rural youth. The sublime excitement of social reformation through science was compatible with the artificial naturalism of an organic community, which the Progressives associated with the dynamic evolutionism of urban growth. Associations of the sacred, on the other hand, were far more compatible with the tragic suffering among farmers "crucified on a cross of gold," a political slogan that became the death song for agrarian reform. Similarly, the Protestant theological convention of God's presence in His absence was poignantly experienced on the former agrarian frontier in foreclosed homesteads and apocalyptic visions of modern economic evils. Progressives instead offered the promise of new economic, political and cultural frontiers through national progress.

The Progressives testified to the compelling importance of the idea of the frontier as an Enlightenment convention for preserving American national confidence. The significance of that convention for defining Cold War America may be seen in the continuing and profound influence of three seminal Progressive social theories of the frontier: Frederick Jackson Turner's frontier thesis, John Dewey's formulation of an industrial frontier for postagrarian America, and Robert E. Park's urban frontier of marginal individualism. These three influential formulations of the Enlightenment frontier helped shape twentieth-century American values and institutions as the United States entered the Cold War following World War I. Subsequently, they continued to shape post–World War II American national culture through the work of the Cold War social scientists who followed the trails they blazed.[37]

In his now-classic revitalization of Turner's frontier thesis, *People of Plenty*, for example, David Potter appealed to post-World War II social science research to corroborate Turner's Progressive faith that American corporate nationalism was derived from physical abundance. That abundance, however, as Potter explained in 1954, was not based upon the primary frontier of nature that Turner had declared closed in 1893 but rather upon a secondary frontier of production. This second, artificial, frontier was the real one, Potter claimed. For unlike the agrarian frontier, the frontier of production was unlimited in its capacity to promote and sustain abundance, precisely because it was artificial and not natural.[38]

Potter knew that much of Turner's appeal was stylistic. Turner was perhaps the last of the major American historians to write out of Bancroft's nineteenth-century epic tradition and among the first to write in the professional prose of the historian as scientist. Therefore, the voices behind his narrative of the primary frontier were equal parts romantic poet and disinterested scientist. He had created an epic sweep of the imagination from that mixture of sensibilities to help the reader envision a succession of new frontiers, following upon old ones. In each cycle there was a completion but also a poignant sense of loss, as there was a return to primitive conditions when the cultivated soil became exhausted. Turner wrote of this ebb and flow of national vitality, as if he were viewing it from an all-seeing olympic height. His sublimely elevated elegy for free land was, however, not simply the sounding of a pessimistic note of doubt about progress. It simultaneously gave urgency and a sense of organic necessity to the growth of corporate national identity. Turner was calling upon Americans to find a way to imitate the vitality of the agrarian frontier in new forms by reminding them of their loss. However, he was not asking them to find a way to restore it.

This is why Turner rejected Populist insurgency against corporate economic interests. Indeed, Turner's eulogy for the agrarian frontier sounds more like Edmund Burke's eulogy for the natural virtue of the ancien régime than Tom Paine's celebration of democratic revolution.

This paradoxical attitude reflects Turner's Burkean ideal of corporate unity, which he shared with his instructor and friend Woodrow Wilson.[39] Though Turner identified with the West rather than the South, as did Wilson, he agreed with Wilson that sectionalism promised a way to restore national vitality and replace the exhausted geographical frontier. Sectionalism, the nationalist Turner warned, must not be distorted into a "sectional mirage" in which the part gives the illusion that it may encompass the identity of the national whole. Quite to the contrary, Turner said, the section must preserve the principle of cultural distinctiveness so that it may serve to check mob psychology on a national scale.[40]

Turner's faith in sectionalism was not, therefore, based upon nostalgia for a decentralized American past but upon a Burkean argument for maintaining order through tradition. After Woodrow Wilson assumed the presidency of the United States, Turner embraced the evolutionary faith that the elusive ideal of national unity might be achieved, despite an alien population and urban landscape, through national legislation. For, he reasoned, echoing Wilson's Burkean belief in the power of organic leadership to call forth latent national distinctiveness, the history of American democracy is not "a history of imitation, of simply borrowing." American history is a history of evolutionary adaption.[41] It was this theme of America, as an original imitation, that Potter emphasized in his Cold War revision of Turner.

For Turner, the closing of the primary geographical frontier of nature had presaged more than the passing of a virtuous agrarian way of life. It voided American uniqueness. It marked the triumph of imitation over originality and social rules of behavior over individualism. But Turner had attempted to answer those doubts about the new national culture by rhetorically transforming the idea of the frontier from an immediate natural experience into a reproducible process. He attempted to reproduce it through the agencies of sectionalism and national legislation. But, in 1922, the Turner who eight years earlier had warned against the illusion of the "sectional mirage" of mistaking the part for the whole, had become frightened by the consequences of the great nationalist war in Europe. Now, he warned the nation against the "sectional mirage" of failing to recognize the sectional basis of nationalism. "The American section may be likened to the shadowy image of the European nation, to the European state denatured of its toxic qualities," Turner explained to his postwar readers. Sections, as pale reflections of the European states, could provide a basis for national identity. Through the American solution of preserving sectional distinctiveness in national unity, Turner proclaimed, a *pax Americana* might descend upon "our sister continent of Europe."[42]

In the face of disillusionment, shock and apprehension, Turner had insisted there were new challenges and new frontiers to explore. "Let us dream as our fathers dreamt," Turner urged a class of graduating seniors on the eve of World War I, "and let us make our dreams come true."[43] By embracing the secondary frontier of production, Potter could later revise Turner to celebrate America as an original imitation. The dream could still come true in 1954. But, for Potter, the national ideal would be guaranteed, not through the uniqueness of America as a productive landscape, but through reproduction of abundance itself.

John Dewey's version of national corporate organicism offered an even more persuasive defense for confidence against doubt than Turner's in a postagrarian frontier America. Dewey's continuing imprint on American national culture may be found in Richard Rorty's Kuhnian argument that our world is invented through education and propaganda, in New Age indications that possible new worlds may be collectively imagined, and in environmentalist demands for a sustainable global economy. All these Deweyian implications for an instrumentalist approach to a fluid reality may be challenged, as fundamentalist and evangelical Protestants have done, as being an intellectual surrender to agnostic doubt. But Dewey preserved his Calvinist religious roots in his reliance upon confidence, which he affirmed in 1915, while still being conventionally religious and active in church activities. Confidence is "not *conscious* trust in the efficacy of one's powers," he wrote in *Democracy and Education*, "but unconscious faith in the possibilities of the situation."[44]

By 1928 Dewey had left behind his religious faith, but he remained dedicated to a credo of confidence, despite a world war and defeated hopes for reconstructing education and society. In a series of articles he sent from Russia for *The New Republic*, Dewey insisted that, despite evidence to the contrary, the Soviet Union really was a sublime new frontier. Dewey wrote that he found the Soviet Union to be exotic, at once Western and Eastern, on the very edge of the future while still immersed in the past. Moscow, he wrote, seemed "newer than any city in our own country, even than a frontier town," while Leningrad "speaks, even mournfully, of the past."[45]

Dewey was acutely aware of the failings of the revolution. He acknowledged that the Bolsheviks were not capable of shaping a society free from exploitation. Government capitalism, he charged, had replaced private capitalism, and the dictatorship of the proletariat was merely the mirror of bourgeois class conflict. But Dewey believed that a second revolution of human energy remained alive in 1928 that paralleled the failed revolution of 1917. The spirit of confidence was palpable in Soviet cities because, he said repeatedly, it was psychological. Popular energy was creating a new mentality, and Dewey sensed in it a compelling presence of the sublime. In Moscow, he declared, he felt the *"genius loci,* the lustrous sky, the illimitible horizon, the extravagant and tempestuous climate"; it reminded him of no Europe he had ever known.[46]

Dewey's confident view, as he used that term, of the course of the Russian Revolution accompanied his awareness of a growing estrangement between the revolutionary promise of a New World in the United States and a New World in the Soviet Union, in essence—the emergence of a Cold War. He feared that if this common promise of transition into a New World was shattered, the result would be despair and devastating civil war in every country of Europe. Dewey tried to preserve his faith against his growing doubts about the present by calling his readers to share in his confidence in the future. Savoring the sense of popular excitement around him, he refused to accept the pessimistic possibility that Columbus had merely extended the boundaries of the Old World. If a New World was possible in the United States, it must be possible in the Soviet Union; if the Soviet Union could manifest a new evolutionary beginning for Old World democracy, it would sustain confidence in the New World promise, which the power of democracy could still make come true in twentieth-century American national culture.[47]

The promise of the international frontier was at stake for Dewey in the failure of the Russian Revolution. The implications of that crisis for the preservation of his own confidence in the possibilities of the future may be seen in the publication of *The Quest for Certainty* the following year. *The Quest for Certainty* was Dewey's philosphical confrontation with the conflict between knowledge and action. The natural man, Dewey reasoned, fears doubt, and leaps at any opportunity to erase uncertainty. He explained further that the quest for certainty has been manifested in two cultural categories: the holy and the fortunate, and their ever-present opposites, the profane and the unlucky. "To secure the favor of the holy," Dewey wrote," is to be on the road to success, while any conspicuous success is proof of the favor of some overshadowing power—a fact which politicians of all ages have known how to utilize."

Dewey drew a Kantian distinction between two aspects of the noumenal sphere, the holy and the lucky, arguing that they both originated from the same desire to achieve confidence. The holy, he said, because of its surcharge of power and ambiguous relation to good and evil, evokes awe and must be approached circumspectly. The lucky object, however, is to be manipulated rather than to be approached with awe.

Moreover, the lucky thing tends to be a concrete and tangible object, while the holy one is not usually definitely localized; it is the more potent in the degree in which its habitation and form is vague. The lucky object is subject to pressure, at a pinch to coercion, to scolding and punishment. It might be discarded if it failed to bring luck. There developed a certain element of mastery in its use, in distinction from the dependence and subjection which remained the proper attitude toward the holy.[48]

Dewey, however, wished to escape the circularity of confidence and doubt that the appeal to the holy and fortunate held in common, and which pointed to their common origins in supernatural explanations for daily experience. The quest for certainty represents a false universal, Dewey argued. It is only a compensatory perversion for those unable to accept the uncertainty of life. Once more, Dewey concluded (perhaps in reaction to his own unfulfilled hopes of the previous year) that, just as supernatural solutions to the problem of doubt have failed to deliver mankind from the endless cycle of confidence and doubt, so too have psychological answers. Rather than simply surrendering to the inevitability of doubt, however, Dewey argued that subjective feelings of assurance and doubt may be transcended through promoting confidence in the ordinary facts of experience.

Though the cycle of confidence and doubt may be inescapable psychologically, it may be practically dispelled by action, Dewey explained. For action falls prey to neither the emotional indulgence of skepticism nor the false security of dogmatism. The search for certainty, he insisted, must become the quest for a method of control. Knowledge, therefore, is to be found not in capturing the real but in the correlation of differences among transient events. "Scientific statements as objects of these inter-relations," Dewey insisted, "are instrumentalities of control." This achievement of certainty through inquiry was not a philosophical abstraction for Dewey. He applied it to the problem of his own disillusionment with the Russian Revolution.[49] By 1937, Stalin's brutal collectivism, show trials, and purges would destroy the potential of the revolutionary change Dewey had hoped would transform the world. Still, Leon Trotsky, the revolutionary alternative to Stalin, claimed from exile to be the legitimate leader of a great social experiment that had been lost to fraud and deceit. A seventy-eight-year-old Dewey would brave death threats and insist on chairing an investigation at Coyoacán, Mexico, into Stalinist charges that Trotsky was himself a traitor who had sabotaged the Russian Revolution. The Dewey Commission would find in favor of Trotsky, before the revolutionary's assassination by a Stalinist agent in 1940.[50]

Dewey was one of the few public individuals in the United States who could successfully mediate such a performance, which permitted Marxists both to separate themselves from Stalinism and to preserve a defense of American idealism that even Trotsky was willing to embrace. Dewey's philosophical position, as Alan Wald points out, provided an alternative to Trotskyism because his pragmatic philosophy of the indeterminance of existence permitted those on both the Left and the Right to escape the logic of inevitable class warfare.[51] Students of Dewey such as Sidney Hook and Max Eastman found in his instrumentalism the same grounds for a Burkean program for creating an organic nationalism as did educators who continued to embrace Progressivism as an ideal after its political base had died with World War I. So did Edmund Wilson. He noted in *To the Finland Station*, published on the eve of Trotsky's assassination, that if Marx was not Euclid, neither was the Trotsky who loved to describe revolution as a parallelogram of social forces. "But to mold the living growth of a society," Wilson cautioned, "you must be aware of what people want."[52] From Wilson's perspective, Trotsky was ambiguously suspended between vision and blindness in this rationalist aspect of Marxism. Dewey, however, was pragmatically positioned as a commissioner in the inquiry, as in his philosophical arguments, to ambiguously support both Trotsky's revolutionary ideals and the values of liberal democracy.

Sociologist Robert E. Park's theory of racial transformation in the urban frontier was still another approach to national confidence through doubt. He integrated the fascination his teacher, Josiah Royce, had with the frontier phenomenon of the creation of new communities and the reform-oriented instrumentalism of another of his teachers, John Dewey, with the new urban commercial culture of twentieth-century America. Park not only applied Royce's idea of frontiers of race and urbanization to twentieth-century America, but also confronted in bold new ways the

Deweyan problem of instrumentalism in the dualities of simulation and deception inherent in the idea of confidence.[53]

Park's theory of racial and urban transformation may have been rooted in his reading of Hegel. Possibly, as his daughter intimated, Park was a hidden Marxist. Or, alternatively, these ideas may simply have been drawn from Royce's views of social and economic change. But whatever the source, Park's race cycle theory anticipated the postmodernist promise of vitality through deconstruction. His studies of cross-racialism and cross-culturalism among African-Americans and Asian-Americans anticipated the postmodernist assault on stable identity as a pattern for reproducing economic and social power among white Americans, and later, among heterosexuals. His background as a newspaper reporter gave him a practical view of scientific investigation and its relation to the publicity-driven forces of modern urban society. That combination shaped the Chicago style of sociology.

Park wrote that as a newspaper reporter he had learned that only the unexpected is news. Perhaps because of his instinct for news, Park the sociologist also argued that, psychologically, only the unfamiliar and incompletely controlled are interesting. This, Park concluded, equally explained the attraction of science, games, and sexuality. In principle, such forms of cultural gaming would include the more recent interest in the possibilities of cross-dressing and cross-gendering, though these were not actually addressed by Park himself. Park, however, did emphasize the importance of role-playing, and explored the meaning of popular associations of gender among racial identities, as, for example, in valorizing the convention that the Negro was the lady among the races. Indeed, through his theories of marginalization and self-invention, Park anticipated gay, lesbian and transsexual challenges to straight conventions about the boundaries of sexual identity.[54]

"It is probably no mere historical accident that the word person, in its first meaning, is a mask," Park wrote in an essay titled "Behind Our Masks" in 1926. "Our very faces are living masks, which reflect, to be sure, the changing emotions of our inner lives, but tend more and more to conform to the type we are seeking to impersonate," explained the onetime ghost writer for Booker T. Washington. What is true of personal psychology, Park insisted, was true of races and of nationality. "Indeed," he said, "every nationality, has its characteristic 'face,' its conventional mask."[55]

Park, who had studied briefly under Simmel in Germany, learned to identify the frontier with the marginal existence of culturally displaced persons. He contrasted such marginal persons to members of stable societies, who are "always consciously or unconsciously playing a role," and putting on a front, "as actors for the part are required to do." Lacking such stable markers, Park said, the person of mixed ancestry must creatively invent himself or herself. As products of the intersection of cultures, or organic revolutions, the individual of mixed race is the social product of a new civilization in the making; therefore, for Park, the mulatto, the mixed-blooded, is literally the new urban frontiersman. Such marginal figures, lacking models for imitation, are innocent of the duplicity of cultural role-playing. The marginal individual of mixed cultural background is a new Adam, more sensitive, more intelligent, and more spirited than either of his cultural antecedents.

It is by such urban pioneers, Park concluded, that new societies will be cyclically created out of the destruction of traditional cultures to restore confidence out of doubt. For, in Park's formulation of the race cycle as a form of organic community, contact brings doubt and conflict both in the personality of the product of mixed race and in the social relations between the races. This very conflict and doubt, Park explained, leads to a second stage, one of accommodation. At this middle stage, individuals are forced to accept each other and to live with one another by the very dynamics of the social process. Finally, doubts and conflicts are resolved in a new, more advanced, level of social harmony that emerges from the intermingled ashes of the separate races and the old social system. The race relations cycle, Park insisted, "is apparently progressive and irreversible." Though custom, immigration restrictions or racial barriers may slacken the tempo of the movement or even temporarily halt it, it can never be reversed. Most important, the race cycle theory represented for Park a model for the growth of an organic national culture. The race cycle would continue to build national identity through change, by at once expressing a commonly shared social language and preserving individualism. Despite a constant disintegration and reintegration of the society, national identity would grow ever stronger and more defined, shattering the conventions of race even while intensifying them.[56]

The frontier theses of Turner, Dewey and Park were more than artificial products of an industrially manufactured past. They were also strategies for renewing confidence through the doubts that inevitably followed from the failures of previous frontiers, which, they realistically prophesied, must occur perpetually in time and space. Dewey's humanistic evolutionism, like Turner's sectionalism and Park's race cycle theory, defended the promise that every conflict and doubt could serve as an instrumental proof for confidence. Indeed, the genius of these three formulations of social and political disillusionment and warnings against social chaos was that each successfully presented a blueprint for preserving confidence against the negative evidence of experience. Each did so by substituting sublime rhetoric for supernaturalism and social constructionism for metaphysics. Sublime rhetoric offered grand visions of power without the cosmic agencies of the holy or the lucky, and placed the ability to control human destiny and purpose in the methods of science and technology. Social constructionism confirmed the pragmatic conviction that the will to industrial and scientific progress made them attainable.

It is helpful to remember that the frontier conventions of Turner, Dewey, and Park grew out of their understandings of the actual historical frontier at the end of the nineteenth century. Their visions of the western frontier and its implications for American national culture were as much creations of the Enlightenment commitment to confidence as were the evolutionary theories of their contemporaries in the social sciences, or the vogue of realism among popular novelists and artists, or even the day-to-day experiences of working cowboys on the range. The post–World War II American West of Hollywood actors and cowboy presidents was, similarly, never simply a mythic place of the imagination, as many Cold War interpretations of the frontier since Henry Nash Smith's *Virgin Land* have assumed.

Since Smith and the "symbol-myth" school of American studies, which emerged after World War II, were simultaneously writing about both the historical frontier and the Cold War, their aim was to transcend myth, which they equated with ideology.[57] By virtue of their method for seeing through myth to an often tragic, but always ambiguous, human reality, the myth-symbolists could also bear witness to a democratic realism beyond illusion. But the Cold War perspective of the symbol-myth school resulted in a failure to recognize that myth is a subject for performance as well as of symbolism. They forgot, as Turner, Dewey and Park did not, that the frontier is real theater. As a place of genuine and false performances, the frontier offers both a conceptual and physical space where confidence and doubt, the essential and foundational problem of the Enlightenment, may be ritually confronted again and again.

This distinction between myth and performance may be clearly discerned, for example, in Theodore Roosevelt's pre–Cold War autobiographical narrative. In his election-conscious autobiography of 1913, Roosevelt described himself as a self-invented hero, who had made himself into a confident hunter of dangerous game and of other men. Yet he emphasized to his readers that he was "a foreordained and predestined victim," who had from an early age cultivated a great desire to be like the fearless men who could hold their own in the world. As a weak, asthmatic and fearful boy, he was impressed with adventure books. Roosevelt became convinced from his reading and daydreams "that at the outset almost every man is frightened when he goes into action, but that the course to follow is for the man to keep such a grip on himself that he can act just as if he was not frightened."[58]

After this is kept up long enough it changes from pretense to reality, and the man does in very fact become fearless by sheer dint of practicing fearlessness when he does not feel it . . . There were all kinds of things of which I was afraid at first, ranging from grizzly bears to "mean" horses and gun-fighters; but by acting as if I was not afraid I gradually ceased to be afraid. Most men can have that same experience if they choose . . .

It is of course much pleasanter if one is naturally fearless, and I envy and respect men who are naturally fearless. But it is a good thing to remember that the man who does not enjoy this advantage can nevertheless stand beside the man who does, and can do his duty with the like efficiency, *if he chooses to.*[59]

Roosevelt's autobiography shows again and again that the lesson he took to the Dakota frontier and from the other frontiers to which he continued to travel was the conviction that confidence can be achieved by will. His very admission that he never escaped a sense of self-doubt on the frontier or in politics defined his confidence in American democracy. If he had climbed from weakness to strength through practicing the stuff of his daydreams, so could others, providing they were born with the "right stuff" to begin with.[60]

Roosevelt's vision of the frontier as a place of performance where anyone could act a role or reinvent oneself was evident as well in the entertainment of his day: the Wild West shows and rodeos, the art of Frederic Remington, Charles Schreyvogel and Charles Russell, and the new film images of cowboys, such as those portrayed in Edwin Porter's *The Great Train Robbery*.[61] In these expressions of Roosevelt's world, as in his own rhetoric as a national political leader, the frontier pointed beyond myth to a more practical and fundamental experience of performance. It continued to do so after the world wars, in the images of John Wayne, Harrison Ford's *Indiana Jones*, and astronauts like Flash Gordon, James T. Kirk, and Neil Armstrong on the moon. It was present not just in Roosevelt's political rhetoric but in presidential rhetoric from Kennedy to Johnson and from Nixon to Reagan. Because the frontier is essentially a stage, it was and is both a literal space and imagined setting, in which individuals perform in new roles. By doing so, they may become new persons, reborn through the eyes of others.

For this reason, costume, self-invention, action, and promotion were always inseparable from frontier experience. The frontier was always a place where the authentic and the counterfeit vied with each other; it did not become so in imitation of the dime novels and industrial mythmaking of the nascent culture industry of the nineteenth century, as Henry Nash Smith and his followers suggested in their Cold War interpretations. Rather, these industrial forms for culture production mimicked the real performances of everyday experience in the West. A legendary hero such as William F. Cody, for example, who bears a central role in Smith's *Virgin Land* and in Richard Slotkin's *Gunfighter Nation*, was neither a man so deluded by his own legend that he began to believe it himself, nor an empty poseur, as he was depicted in Arthur Kopit's play *Indians*.[62] Rather than being a product of the entertainment industry or of literary and theatrical conventions from the East, Cody actually lived the life that he pretended to live. For, in order to claim his place of fame, William Cody had to contend with a number of other "Buffalo Bills," all of whom considered themselves the genuine and original one. The successful Buffalo Bill, who, like his competitors, was a genuine scout, Indian fighter, Pony Express rider, and buffalo hunter, did bring realism to theatrical performances about the Wild West by playing himself. But Cody was able to slip comfortably into the role of celebrity-actor, not because he blended "with his theatrical role to the point where no one—least of all the man himself—could say where the actual left off and where dime novel fiction began," as Smith wrote[63]; rather, he was so successful because he had really lived the role of a working scout in the West. Stage acting apparently occurred to Cody only when, on a visit to New York in 1872, he saw an actor playing him in *King of the Border Men*, a dramatization of Ned Buntline's 1869 dime novel of Cody's life.[64]

Cody was first boosted into the artificial world of New York society through his connections with the newspaper publishers and army brass he had met in his role as a scout and guide. They urged him to take a temporary leave from his army duties to visit the East and to undertake his own celebrity tour of 1872. Then, between 1873 and 1876, he divided his performance time between being a scout on the prairie and playing one on the Chicago stage. He and such friends as Texas Jack Omohundro and Wild Bill Hickok performed in several plays before Cody abandoned theater for the greater realism of the Wild West show, and Hickok, who also insisted on the right to portray himself, wandered back west and was killed by a man in search of a reputation.[65]

Cody's fame in the East had preceded him because of coverage by the *New York Herald* of his being a guide for celebrity hunting expeditions. However, he was able to secure the position of scout for such extravaganzas as Russian Grand Duke Alexi's hunting trip to the West in 1872 because he was a respected scout. Indeed, Cody had been named chief of scouts in 1868 by General Philip Sheridan, who later recommended him as Alexi's guide. Sheridan was impressed by Cody's courage and endurance in delivering dispatches through three hundred miles of hostile territory in less than sixty hours. On that basis, an unknown hunter garnering thirty dollars a month was rehired at a scout's top wage of seventy-five dollars. The next year, Cody was transferred from the Department of the Missouri to the Platte, a larger command, by General Carr. Cody was recognized for his scouting and fighting abilities in the campaign against the Cheyennes, cited for his contributions by the Secretary of War, and was paid, at least briefly, the then-extravagant sum of one hundred dollars per month.[66]

Cody was not unique as a working scout in developing a sense of the flamboyant in his horsemanship and shooting or in wearing dramatic clothing. The reputation of any scout depended upon his instilling confidence in the men he guided into hostile territory or through dispiriting conditions of cold, drought or rain. Scouts performed before soldiers and competed for fame against other scouts, as cowboys displayed their skills of roping and riding in competition with other cowboys before there were commercial rodeos. Cody differed from other scouts in donning a dashing costume to fight in the Indian wars in 1876 only in that he knew his colorful costume would be rendered authentic when the event was restaged during his Wild West performances. In dressing romantically, in choosing to ride forward to engage in single combat, and in scalping his defeated adversary, Yellow Hand, in one of his most famous exploits, he remained true to a vision of life in which recognition came for, and with, the quality of the performance. He was also an example of the power of performance, on the prairie or on the stage, in transforming the terror of the reality of personal death into an artificial source of confidence. Cody's own confrontations with death must have been unnervingly real; yet his dramatic re-creation of those personal moments could be repeated again and again on the public stage without leading to an emotional crisis.[67]

It was precisely this emphasis upon realism, as the currency of legitimate performance, that separated the greenhorn who looked the part from the frontiersmen who lived the part, in the eyes of westerners themselves. Even Buffalo Bill found that theatrical success in the East led some westerners to perceive him as an imposter when he was called upon to intervene in dangerous incidents in Indian country.[68] Cody similarly insisted on authenticity in every detail of his shows.

Cody's old friend and ranching partner, Frank North, was one contemporary westerner who may have recognized the origins of the idea of the Wild West show in P.T. Barnum's failed effort to stage a buffalo hunt as early as 1847. North advised Cody to "use some old hack horses and a hack driver," because "to make it go you want a show of illusion, not realism." But Cody refused even to call his performance a show. "It is the aim of the management of Buffalo Bill's Wild West," his program insisted, "to do more than present an exacting and realistic entertainment for the public amusement." The aim, the program notes explained, "is to PICTURE TO THE EYE, by the aid of historical characters and living animals, a series of animated scenes and episodes, which had their existence in fact, of the wonderful pioneer and frontier life of the Wild West of America." His West, Mark Twain wrote, was genuine "down to its smallest details," and old P. T. Barnum said enthusiastically that "they do not need spangles to make it a real show." It is significant that westerners such as Cody and Charles Russell, the cowboy artist who later worked on John Ford westerns to assure their authenticity, shared this perception of the frontier as a place for real performance with easterners such as Roosevelt, the novelist Owen Wister, and artists such as Frederic Remington and Thomas Eakins.[69]

Roosevelt, Wister and Remington, advocates of the strenuous life, were members of the Boone and Crockett club who sought to ritually promote the frontier virtues through fraternal initiations, hunting, and role-playing in authentic garb. They, like the genuine scouts they imitated, needed to bring their real performances from the West back to the East to preserve their own sense of confidence. Unlike them, the formally trained classicist Eakins never became identified with the West. But he was invigorated by his experience with the frontier when he briefly visited the Dakotas in 1887, after his dismissal as the director of the Pennsylvania Academy of Fine Arts.[70]

Many of Eakins's paintings and photographs, including the vast majority that had no western themes, such as *The Agnew Clinic* and *The Gross Clinic* and his various sports subjects in tension between movement and rest, explored the frontier between science and theater. His portrait of the famous ethnologist Frank Hamilton Cushing, however, provides one example of his aesthetics of realist performance as a commentary on the western frontier. Eakins painted the portrait in 1894, one year after Frederick Jackson Turner had delivered his address "The Significance of the Frontier in American History" at the Chicago Exhibition. The artist worked from a photograph in his studio, where he had painstakingly re-created an interior of a Zuni dwelling. Eakins portrayed Cushing in buckskin and earring, gazing down upon Zuni religious artifacts with an air of tragic insight. Cushing, who had lived with the Zuni for five years and had been initiated into the tribe's most sacred rituals, was painted as if he were a voyager from civilization into a primitive but disappearing culture. As an anthropologist who had immersed himself in native religion and myth, Cushing was painted at the edge of both worlds. He had, in Eakins's painting as in life, merged science with performance.[71] This would also be the driving ambition of a whole new generation of anthropologists, as trained by Franz Boas, who would follow Cushing into the field. Among them would be Alfred Kroeber, who placed the last Yahi Indian, Ishi, on display as a sort of living museum. Such Boas students as Kroeber, Alexander Goldenweiser and Edward Saphir would initiate the new science of anthropology into the evolutionary promise of pragmatism—that is, the idea that environment could transcend biology. Humans, the Boasnian anthropologists claimed, were defined by their performance rather than by genetics. In the very same terms, the frontier tradition of the other American social sciences after the 1890s turned upon the conventions of performance. In sociology and social psychology, American social scientists explored the practical possibilities of transforming doubt into confidence at the intersection of self and society, science and religion, and heredity and environment.[72]

This pragmatic frontier tradition, stretching through the twentieth century, is well illustrated by William James, who explored the borderland psychology of religious and scientific confidence and doubt. "We stand on the mountain pass in the midst of whirling snow and blinding mist," James wrote in his psychological study on belief, *The Will to Believe* (1897), "through which we get glimpses now and then of paths which may be deceptive." Since any choice may be right or wrong for safely descending the mountain, hope and doubt, James explained according to the same Enlightenment logic as contemporary deconstructionists, are sisters.[73]

It is, however, by the reason of this symbiotic relation between confidence and doubt, that every manifestation of confidence must also be an act of deception. Confidence succeeds against doubt only when, as a form of rhetoric, it suppresses doubt through the power of self-persuasion. In the terms of William James's pragmatism, as well as in Roosevelt's idea of the frontier and contemporary performance theories, the answer to the problem of doubt, therefore, may be found only in the will to believe. Indeed, when the will to believe is expressed through the dramaturgical forms of parody or pastiche, in an effort to explain a world of complete "simulacra," or depthless imitation, confidence as the source of dependence and autonomy has simply replaced confidence as the source of dependability and authority. In either case, the alternative connotations of confidence are actually implied by each other, and, therefore, add another dimension to the doubt that every act of confidence affirms.[74]

Confidence, therefore, is based upon a psychology of action, as is all performance. It is an instrumentalist strategy, a "quest for certainty," with "cash value," as John Dewey and William James respectively used those terms. Those seminal figures of the pragmatic tradition and their descendents who have extended their religious, scientific and social questions to those of the media and the body, intuitively recognized confidence as the central problem of any Enlightenment culture. Therefore, the conflict between modernists and postmodernists turns out to be a circular reproduction of the doubts implied in confidence and the confidence required to resist the personal and institutional paralysis of doubt.

The reciprocity between confidence and doubt guaranteed that Turner's agrarianism, Dewey's industrialism, and Park's multiculturalism would necessarily repeat manic cycles of hope and despair, without delivering resolution. Yet it is that same commitment to the logic and emotion of confidence and doubt that continues to define the contemporary American frontier of communications and information technologies. The negative consequences of this accelerating commitment to a frontier of performance, however, have exacerbated the problem of structural economic insecurity of workers, the alienation between generations and genders, the violence of the ghetto, the greed of Wall Street. The impact of those doubts sent shock waves through the national political establishment during the first post–Cold War election, which brought Clinton and a Democratic majority to Washington, D. C. However, as the O. J. Simpson murder trial subsequently confirmed, the massive public implication in the conflation of personality and politics and of entertainment and crime meant that those doubts led to a still greater need for confidence. For, even as the public avidly participated in the marketing of Simpson's personality, American voters simultaneously demanded harsher punishment for felons. Similarly, many Americans demanded an end to taxpayer support for unwed teenage mothers, while a nationwide threat to abortion clinic staffs intensified through murder and thousands of acts of vandalism and intimidation. Then the off-year elections of 1994 reconfirmed the paradox of greater voter doubt and, consequently, a greater need for voter confidence. It was a paradox that the recently dispirited Republican minority was able to ride to a political victory.[75]

The Republican landslide brought with it the triumph of the postmodernist politics of Newt Gingrich. The new Speaker of the House of Representatives promised to deconstruct the modern, centralized bureaucracy of welfare capitalism. The illegitimate son of a teenage mother, Gingrich promised to end welfare as an entitlement, and suggested that orphanages might offer a socially acceptable alternative to dysfunctional families. Gingrich also suggested that a program permitting poor people to purchase laptop computers might offer an escape from poverty. Though Gingrich's promotions of new approaches were applauded by some and pilloried by others, the former history professor understood the logic of postmodernism well enough to characterize himself as a conservative futurist who believed in a philosophy of "conservative opportunity." He urged his followers to read Alvin Toffler's *Future Shock* and *The Third Wave*, along with Tocqueville's *Democracy in America* and *The Federalist Papers*. Gingrich, perhaps more clearly than Clinton, understood that the public cry for deconstruction of the federal bureaucracy was less a cry for reform or a call to a renewed covenant of responsibility between public officials and their constituents than a demand for new styles of performance. For, as Garry Wills and Michael Kelly explained in 1995, Gingrich defined himself, even before he met the Tofflers, as a "modular person," someone who could construct and rearrange his elements at will. Gingrich simply translated his dream of national political power as a citizen-leader into the language of the Internet. He became an advocate of the practice of virtual politics.

Virtual politics is not an empty phrase but a phrase empty of stable content. Gingrich's use of that phrase expressed his practical insight that the "information highway" is, by definition, an electronic medium through which rhetoric may be directed at will. For Gingrich, the dawning information age makes possible a new sublimity and the ground for a conscious strategy for casuistically reformulating the elements of competing ideologies and interests into ever-new organizations of power. Information, Gingrich suggested, may now be practically used as blocks to build and dismantle modules of power alliances and common interests.

Gingrich's personal and political strategy of virtual realism did not depend upon substance but upon the ability to affect the basic processes through which public perceptions are organized. It did not seem to matter, as his critics and political enemies complained, that his agendas were often formally contradictory, or that frequently his information was wrong. For Gingrich aspired to be a director of a political countertheater. Virtual reality was neither a futuristic toy for the new Speaker of the House nor a troubling source of moral confusion, as it seemed to his critics. For Newt Gingrich, already falling precipitously in the polls a few months after the election, it was a practical new form of rhetoric for organizing power to achieve personal success and to bring a revolution to America.[76]

3

The New Adam and the American Sublime

Post–Cold War talk show hosts and information technologists, postmodern academics and postliberal Christians, new Democrats and Gingrich Republicans have one thing in common: the attempt to use the logic of performance to serve the political and social ends of reform. In doing so, they have found themselves implicated in the same contradictions of confidence and doubt as those identified by Edmund Burke, the venerable eighteenth-century parlimentarian, and William James, the reforming pragmatist of the late nineteenth and early twentieth centuries.

Both Burke and James were defenders of rationalism and champions of social virtue. But each was haunted by the irony that the confidence required to achieve the ends of Enlightenment virtue was equally useful as a tool of deception. So too was Alexis de Tocqueville, whose classic *Democracy in America* (1835, 1840) linked Anglo-American political institutions and the psychology of religion. Tocqueville, who appears to have been a seminal influence on the social visions of both Clinton and Gingrich, began his sociological effort to explain the national character of the United States out of his fear and fascination with the new nation's revolutionary movement towards social equality and to explore its implications for the future of belief. His perspectives on democratic nationalism, therefore, anticipated James and grew directly out of his high regard for Burke.[1]

The central theme that emerged from Tocqueville's travels to America, which was an extension of his own fears and hopes for Europe, was that equality of condition was the fundamental fact from which everything he observed stemmed, and to which all his observations led. The paradox at the heart of the fact of equality, he found, was that American democracy generates doubt precisely because it is predicated upon confidence and that Americans are a nation of imitators precisely because they place such a high value on individualism and authenticity. "At periods of equality," Tocqueville explained, "men have no faith in one another, by reason of their common resemblance; but this resemblance gives them almost unbounded confidence in the judgement of the public." As a result, Tocqueville warned, modern society threatens to turn everyone into an imitation of everyone else, and then to enslave them to the centralized government generated by their own drive towards equality. For, said Tocqueville, there are two contradictory revolutions at work in the principle of equality: one erodes confidence and trust in others because they are too like themselves; the other constructs confidence in a government to facilitate their pleasures, provide for their security, supply their necessities, divide their inheritances, and arbitrate their happiness.[2]

In the years immediately preceding the Civil War, Herman Melville, who, like Tocqueville, was a close reader of Burke, mapped the cultural contours of the Western will to confidence more fully than Burke, Tocqueville, or James.[3] Other writers such as Brockden Brown, James Fenimore Cooper and Nathaniel Hawthorne had considered the anguished implications of confidence and doubt and the problem of fraud and authenticity in the context of democratic society and religious belief. But Melville was the first American writer to explicitly acknowledge the existence of a culture of confidence behind American nationalism and religious faith. Once more, he implicated his confidence-hungry middle-class readers, with the authors who fed them, in a web of deceit. In his collection of short stories, *The Piazza Tales* (1856), Melville subverted his readers' expectations, often entrapping them through the use of an untrustworthy narrator whose comforting version of events fails to conceal an abyss of doubt below a thinly skimmed surface of assurances.[4]

In the short story "The Two Temples," for example, Melville's spiritually hungry protagonist finds himself excluded from a beautiful American cathedral. He has been turned away at the door by a "fat-paunched, beadle-faced man" because his threadbare coat marks him as a pauper. Though the protagonist has found it necessary to walk three long miles from the Battery to attend services in this "marble-buttressed, stain glassed, spic and span new temple," he informs the reader that he is not really poor. He is the unfortunate victim of a "false tailor" who had failed to deliver his promised new coat. Without the price of a bribe to get in, and sensitive to the fact that he looks like a poor man loitering outside, the protagonist-narrator starts to leave. But he sees a small door and slips in, wagering that it leads to the tower where he may join the worship unobserved.

Once inside, he feels as if he were in a magic lantern. Scratching a small opening in what turns out to be a false stained-glass window, the protagonist-narrator sees ragged boys being chased away by the beadle-faced man in the streets below. He ascends. The words of Christian comfort he had longed for, however, are too faint to hear from his great height. It is as if the noble-looking priest were on a distant stage, an actor in some weird performance. Soon the protagonist feels trapped in the tower, shaken by the earthquake vibrations of the organ and bells. The narrator's search for religious ecstasy has become an exercise in terror.[5]

The protagonist-narrator next appears as a stranger in London. It is a Saturday evening; thus the reader knows the sojourner has not yet entered the time of the Sabbath, though he has already left the place of promise, which is America. The forlorn narrator of the tale is drawn to a theater, mistaking it for a cathedral. Though impoverished, he gains admission through a workingman's charitable gift of a ticket. This kindness sets the narrator to thinking about the meaning of charity as an invitation to the sublime. Again, he finds himself climbing the stairs to a high place with ironic associations of prison; again, he watches the actor below. But this actor, who is portraying the satanic Richelieu instead of God's servant, seems to dispense a grace that the noble-looking priest failed to provide. A ragged boy who is selling refreshments in the crowd offers the lonely American traveler a communion cup of ale in rememberance of his "poor dad," who has gone to America seeking his fortune. The narrator-protagonist drinks to the lost man's immortal life, and is left to compare the charity of London—and artifice—to religion and to his earlier alienation in his native land.[6]

The Melville of "The Two Temples" superficially appears to have provided an aesthetic reclamation of the true sublime from a fraudulent sublime. However, Melville, who was also a student of Machiavelli, subtly suggests that the sublime may instead be negatively related to the experience of the holy. Melville reveals this suspicion only at the moment of the apparent resolution of the tale, when the curtain falls, bringing the performance to a close. "The enraptured thousands sound their responses, deafeningly; unmistakably sincere. Right from the heart," his narrator reports. But the protagonist uneasily intimates that sincerity in the second temple is merely a reflection of the insincerity of the first temple. The lack of charity and sincerity in the first temple literally makes possible the reader's recognition of those qualities in the second. However, for that very reason, the sincerity of the narrator's own experience is turned against himself. "And hath mere mimicry done this?" he asks. "What is it then to act a part?" If the sublime provides pleasure by imitating tragedy, what is an authentic sublime? What constitutes redemption?[7]

Beginning with *Moby-Dick* (1851) and *Pierre* (1852), Melville had made it clear that his aesthetic mission would require him to explore the terrifying implications of the sublime. The heart of that terror, his novels and short stories reveal, was an assault upon confidence. He identified the evils of class, racial and gender hierarchies with the sublime in *Pierre* and *Moby-Dick* and then more explicitly in shorter works. In "The Bell Tower," Melville repudiated both artificial industrial exploitation and the pastoral oppression of slavery. "The Paradise of Bachelors" scores those powerful men who "dine well up toward heaven" for their simultaneous industrial exploitation of the young virgins in "the Devil's dungeon," as the paper mill is called in "The Tartarus of Maids." The "Lightning Rod Man" similarly points diabolically towards the heavens to mock the public's obsessive preoccupation with confidence that "still dwells in the land; still travels in storm-time, and drives a brave trade with the fears of man." But it is his very loss of confidence that condemns poor Bartleby to his death in "Bartleby the Scrivener: A Story of Wall Street."[8]

Perhaps the most unsettling of these tales from the decade before the Civil War was "Benito Cereno," Melville's confrontation with the deceptions inherent in personal standards of morality and emotion and the masks of humanity and social order.[9] Melville was at once reporting the factual tale of a slave insurrection and fictionalizing it, locating horror within as well as around the innocent American captain, Amasa Delano. This was, on one level, a conventional use of the sublime, which made sea tales so appealing to a reading public in search of the exotic, the awesome and the unconventional, while rendering them safe through the narrator's all-seeing eye. Melville's earlier sea stories, such as *Typee* (1846) and *Omoo* (1847), had successfully navigated this commercialized public taste. But, increasingly in the 1850s, Melville went beyond the convention of fictionalizing the real to enhance the effect of the sublime by injecting the real into fictional tales of deception in order to subvert the pleasure of the sublime for his readers. He located this tale of exotic ocean terror inside as well as outside of the commerce of slavery, which Delano encountered on Benito Cereno's decaying Spanish ship. The scene of that ship, as a mixture of decay and ominous tranquility on one side and violent revolution on the other, presented a perfect setting for the sublime. Yet the unsettling death of Don Benito, after the order and tranquility had been restored, mocked Delano's desperate efforts to refashion his experience into a form of pleasurable sublime, as it does the reader's.[10]

At the conclusion of the story, Delano reflects confidently on the positive results of his accidently coming upon the Spanish slave ship, and of how beneficially his credulity had worked to bring chaos back into order, as it were, by reimposing slavery. Owing to Providence, Delano tells Don Benito, illusion had preserved his life. The temper of Delano's mind upon boarding the Spanish ship, undoubtedly like the reader's, was "more than commonly pleasant, while the sight of so much suffering, more apparent than real, added to my good nature, compassion, and charity, happily interweaving the three." This appreciation for the aesthetic of the sublime is the very quality that permitted the actual as well as the fictional Delano to "get the better of momentary distrust, at times when acuteness might have cost me my life, without saving another's."

The past is past, he tells Don Benito, concerning his terrible ordeal under the power of Babo, the leader of the slave insurrection, who had masqueraded as a loyal servant. "Why moralize upon it?" Delano asks the Spaniard. "Forget it." Nature, Delano points out, has already forgotten it. "See yon bright sun has forgotten it," as, he says, has also the blue sky. "Because they have no memory," Benito Cereno morosely responds, "because they are not human." Delano's bright confidence is clouded by the Old World shadows of gloom that envelop the Spanish captain. " 'You are saved,' cried Captain Delano, more and more astonished and pained: 'you are saved; what cast such a shadow upon you?' " "The Negro," is Benito Cereno's reply.[11]

In *The Confidence-Man*, which appeared in 1857, Melville went even further in questioning the American culture of confidence. Trust, or charity, Melville pointed out, is the vital relation that binds human beings to each other and saves them from metaphysical despair. Melville acknowledged that confidence is necessary in order to dare to trust, but he also reminded his readers that when trust is misplaced it leads to victimization and despair. The response to such disappointment is either the loss of confidence, which leads to an incapacity to dare trust, or to a loss of trust, which demands still more confidence in compensation. Consequently, confidence is a cosmic trap that had snared an expanding, restless and adventurous nation in its double meaning of bold assurance and insidious deceit. The double meaning of the confidence in which Americans had placed their own confidence, for Melville, shattered any possibility of separating the real from the artificial. Instead, the American culture of confidence was promoting the very confusion of the masquerade—the line between simulation, or imitating, and dissimulation, or pretending—that poisons all capacity to trust.[12]

Melville's own diabolical confidence game with the reader was based upon his identifying P. T. Barnum with American literary and political culture. Barnum had recently published a self-promotional biography in which he extolled his success as a confidence artist in winning public acclaim. This onetime blackface performer and purveyor of wild Indian extravaganzas, blackface minstrel shows and various scams that anticipated the Wild West shows of the 1890s also prided himself on his self-reliance and honesty as a businessman.[13] His favorite tales of his many adventures in show business were those that showed how cleverly he was able to outwit confidence artists. Such amateurish confidence games, Barnum suggested, failed because the perpetrators were mere imitations of the real thing: the incomparably original Barnum himself. As a result Barnum gloried in the denouement of his tale, in which he revealed himself as the real P. T. Barnum, while he equally savored the financial rewards that flowed amidst cries of "charlatan," and "humbug" from his more respectable critics.[14] For Melville, Barnum's good-humored honesty as a confidence artist reflected the same combination of values extolled by Ben Franklin in his autobiography, or by Emerson in his essays on self-reliance and the sublime experience of the over-soul found in contemplating nature.[15]

But Melville's identification of American culture with a great traveling confidence game was also a literary exercise in terror. Lurking beneath the tranquil surface of appearance was the evil consequence of a world in which trust and charity had disappeared. Melville's definition of the quintessential American culture of confidence as the devil's masquerade was portrayed through the cruelty and the gullibility of the passengers on the steamboat *Fidèle* towards a crippled Negro beggar. That persecuted black Guinea, who may or may not have been a blackface minstrel, was the first manifestation in the innocent West of what may or may not have been a legendary confidence artist from the East.[16]

The consequence of the American culture of confidence was also embodied in the character of the chilling backwoodsman of the West. This most primitive, and, therefore, most elemental, of Americans was a living metaphysics of confidence and doubt.[17] He was, for the same reason, a living contradiction to every idealist image of the sublime offered by American transcendentalists. Kant was a favorite influence on the transcendentalists. He had written in the *Critique of Judgment* that misanthropy could not be sublime since it was "partly odious, partly contemptible." But he also wrote that, paradoxically, pseudomisanthropy born of sad experience could be sublime because it could be the expression of a truly noble retirement from society. "Falsehood, ingratitude, injustice and puerility of the ends which we ourselves look upon as great and momentous, and to compass which man inflicts upon his brother man all imaginable evils—these all so contradict the idea of what men might be if they only would, and are at variance with our active wish to see them better, that, to avoid hating where we cannot love, it seems but a slight sacrifice to forego all the joys of fellowship with our kind."[18] For Kant, the sublime is an artificial standard we may choose at our best, for it "gives us courage to be able to measure ourselves against the seeming omnipotence of nature." Once more, Kant had insisted that the sublime is strenuous rather than languid, that it is simple rather than affected.[19]

All these attributes might be ascribed to the backwoodsman, but the result would be very much the opposite of the moral greatness that Kant predicted should follow from the moral character he associated with the sublime. Kant had also, however, warned that the similarities of the beautiful to the sublime, given the moral weakness characteristic of human society, could lead to counterfeit sublimes. Even simple relief from boredom at the conclusion of maudlin dramas, or allowing imaginary misfortunes to bring tears to our eyes, may fool us. When the weak and ineffectually beautiful masquerade as the noble and strong, he warned, the result is moral degradation and enervation, insensitivity, and an incapacity to respect the worth of our own humanity and that of others.[20]

Melville found that Kant and Burke, through their conflicting psychological theories of moralism and aestheticism, increased the very doubt and despair that each had tried to overcome by formally transforming emotion into an instrument for controlling nature. Burke thought the sublime could evoke terror, but Kant insisted that the sublime must transcend terror by the power of reason. Burke idealized the beautiful as unmediated virtue, but Kant questioned the possibility of such unmediated virtue in a sinful and often cruel world. Kant, ever the moralist, was dismayed to have to admit that "a cool observer, one that does not mistake the wish for the good, no matter how lively, for its reality, may sometimes doubt whether true virtue is actually found anywhere in the world." He was, therefore, almost certainly scandalized by the amoral and purely manipulative character of the sublime as Burke described it. Kant attempted to overcome the division between justice and power and to escape from the confusion between the authentic and the fraudulent, which Burke accepted. Kant, very much in contrast to Burke, found himself required to equate sublime power with moral virtue.[21]

Kant agreed with Burke that the sublime must be understood as an artificial creation of the human mind, and that religion, like the beautiful, must arise unmediated and direct from nature. The sublime, therefore, must be a product of the mind and not merely of natural emotion if it is to be considered by definition to be good, Kant reasoned, just because goodness is not natural to sinful human beings. Goodness could only be possible in this world, therefore, if it could be located outside of corrupted nature, in "the dominion which reason exercises over sensibility." Indeed, Kant argued, "feeling for the sublime in nature is hardly thinkable unless in association with an attitude of mind resembling the moral." For, said Kant, delight in the sublime in nature is negative, while delight in the beautiful is positive.[22]

The sublime, according to Kant, is suprasensational. It must be experienced as an act of imagination. When the mind sacrifices its own freedom to aesthetic law, the mind gains freedom by losing it and establishes the power of the artificial over nature. Thus, "the *astonishment* amounting almost to terror, the awe and thrill of devout feeling, that takes hold of one when gazing upon the prospect of mountains ascending to heaven, deep ravines and torrents raging there, deep-shadowed solitudes that invite to brooding melancholy, and the like—all this, when we are assured of our own safety, is not actual fear." It is rather, Kant explained, "an attempt to gain access to it through imagination," for the internal pleasure of feeling superior to nature. The association of ideas that makes the sublime possible and that links it to the beautiful, Kant concluded, depends upon physical conditions, but through the mind, as an instrument of reason, weak and ineffectual human products of nature become capable of leveling the power of nature and transcending it.[23]

Melville, with an artist's talent for making the abstract arguments of philosophers concrete, noted simply, under the heading "Containing the Metaphysics of Indian-Hating, According To the Views of One Evidently Not so Predisposed as Rousseau's in Favor of Savages,"[24] that it was impossible to know whether the backwoodsman's hatred of Indians was natural or the artificial creation of the social conditions created over generations. He also informed his readers that the portrait of this sublime or natural backwoodsman was fictional; yet it was derived from an actual document.[25] His backwoodsman was suspended between Burke and Kant, transforming him and them into messengers bringing a chilling word of doubt into the search for confidence.

Melville's metaphysical backwoodsman was revealed—or invented—as a man whose whole life had been shaped by his sundered humanity. The misanthropic backwoodsman had preserved his life by refusing to trust Indians, who, like the legendary chief Mocmohoc, might have simulated friendship to brutally murder him and his whole family. He was also, by virtue of his detachment, a metaphysical murderer. The backwoodsman, above all others on board the Mississippi steamship travelling through the heart of America, was, therefore, inoculated against the appeals for sympathy from the abused black Guinea and the confidence artist from the East, who may or may not have been one and the same. Nor would the backwoodsman, having surrendered his humanity, be capable of trusting the redemptive Christ of Easter, who was, perhaps, himself only an artist of confidence, or another version of the many religious prophets from the East who claim uniqueness.

The grim consequence for this disillusioned backwoodsman, who was sublimely or naturally dispossessed of confidence, was that he had become a human wreckage. The changing, restless bustle of progress and commerce had passed him by. He had become a living exhibit from P. T. Barnum's American Museum, like the "American Indians, who enacted their warlike and religious ceremonies on stage." The backwoodsman was a titillating exhortation to the audience watching the changing performances and "transient attractions of the Museum." His life was proof that if the public wished to escape disillusionment they must cling all the more tightly to their own confidences. Yet, in doing so, they were preparing themselves to become easy prey for the confidence artists lying in wait for them along life's way.[26]

A sense of confidence, the isolated and murderous visage of Melville's backwoodsman reminds us, is vitally necessary for cementing together those diverse, and often abstract, ethnic, economic and political interests that must somehow be joined if the legitimacy of any national culture is to be sustained. National cultures, which Benedict Anderson calls imagined political communities, are inherently forms of deception, or illusions, in the sense that they are artificial constructions masquerading as organic forms of society. They do not exist in nature, nor follow directly out of the social institutions of primitive community. They are, rather, simulations of actual kinship forms, raised to the level of universal abstractions. These pseudouniversals may be used to simultaneously dwarf and aggrandize anyone who identifies with them and the needs they serve for promoting confidence. This is precisely what Burke, in *Reflections on the Revolution in France* (1790), claimed the leaders of the French Revolution had done, and what Tocqueville found at work in the conditions of political equality in the United States and described in *Democracy in America*. It was the source of the magical powers of Melville's white-suited stranger on board the *Fidèle*, and the source of power for L. Frank Baum's Wizard of Oz in the Emerald City, patriarchal figures in two bitter, and barely fictionalized, critiques of nineteenth-century American nationalist rhetoric.[27]

The Melville revival, like the appreciation of Tocqueville and Baum and the denigration of Buffalo Bill Cody, was initiated by the Cold War. If there is a unique character to the national political culture of the United States, which embraces Burkean sentiments and is described in such classic Cold War texts as David Riesman's *The Lonely Crowd*, David Potter's *People of Plenty*, and Seymour Martin Lipset's *The First New Nation* (1963), it is that Americans have been free to invent an exceptional past for themselves as a nation that began in nature rather than in history.[28] This association with nature as pure spiritual and physical power has permitted Americans to identify themselves with natural abundance, or with an innate capacity for self-reliance, symbolized by the myth of the American Adam. Whether Americans have clothed their Adam in the plain style of New England Puritanism, wrapped him in republican independence, celebrated him in the democratic poetry of a Walt Whitman, or exploited him in the realistic style of modern advertising, American national culture has specialized in generating images of itself as an original source of direct, and apparently natural, confidence. But it is precisely that icon of the American Adam that became subject to a crisis of confidence during the Cold War.

The New World Adam, an icon of the American sublime, R. W. B. Lewis noted during the height of the Cold War, "was an image crowded with illusion, and the moral posture it seemed to endorse was vulnerable in the extreme." Yet Lewis, in his classic study *The American Adam* (1955), retained a faith in this "illusory" ideal that he sought to render useful again for sustaining confidence in the American national culture in a postliberal age. Lewis readily admitted that the narrative he wished to celebrate in Cold War America, by its very nature, had to be duplicitous in order to be inspiring. But he could not help but decry the then-fashionable, and perhaps more honest, European pessimism that had replaced it. Americans were presently embarrassed about sounding hopeful, he complained, and intellectuals, losing a sense of vitalism, had moved from correcting claims of innocence to promulgating "a cult of original sin."[29]

We had to get beyond "simple-minded adolescent confidence," he explained in praising the post–World War II reformulation of the American myth in the narratives of Bellow and Faulkner; "we may even have got beyond the agonizing disillusion that unexamined confidence begets." But he believed these novelists were telling us that substituting hopelessness for positive thinking would merely condemn America to the entropy of history. Americans, Lewis warned, must resist the temptation to distrust experience and nature if they were to relocate the vitality of literature and escape both the arrested development of innocence and premature resignation to the cynicism of original sin.[30]

The first post–Cold War presidential campaign, in 1992, echoed Lewis's call for a return to an Adamic myth in the name of chastened confidence. If building confidence out of disillusionment had become the transparent theme of American literature for Lewis in 1955, it had just as transparently become the theme of domestic politics among politicians in 1992. The nation's first post–Cold War national political contest, therefore, was waged in the traditional aesthetic terms of the myth of the New World garden and the dramatic conflict of the international cultural Cold War. The Bush campaign was essentially a psychological wager that the disillusioned voter might find it more difficult to rekindle faith in another heroic leader than to extract political promises from one who the public doubted had any principles beyond the desire to be reelected. Rather than making a vulgar appeal to cynicism, however, Bush's handlers were announcing the 1992 election theme of what Lewis called "the Fortunate Fall." [31]

As Adam's fall had erased his innocence, Lewis said, explaining the transcendentalist revitalizing of the Adamic myth, it delivered him and his race from ignorance and into the possibility of discovering a higher and more sublime wisdom. According to Lewis, the fallen Adam made possible a new hope of national renewal, based upon education and contrition rather than immediate grace. In the version adopted by the Republican campaign, a chastened President Bush repented his own loss of confidence in the nation's natural productivity and his yielding to the temptation of taxation by the seductive arguments of a Democratic Congress. Bush, alone among the candidates, was willing to admit that he had stumbled, and so, the contrite Republican president insisted, he alone could revitalize what Lewis had called the "party of hope," to restore citizen confidence in America's future.[32]

The practical public relations problem of selling the Fortunate Fall required a jubilee of rebirth. As the president opened the governmental storehouses to announce a renewal of abundance—and to win votes—he necessarily had to emphasize his image as a reconsecrated leader whom the citizens could personally trust. In promoting himself, he had to avoid projecting the negative image of a self-serving confidence artist, an image that plagued Bill Clinton, his Democratic challenger. Indeed, Clinton's youthfulness both compelled voters to view him as an agent of change and raised doubts that he could be entrusted with the awesome responsibilities of office. His draft record and rehearsed style helped to create an unshakable image as a "Slick Willy," who, his Republican opponents charged, had conned the American people into believing that a neophyte could run the country.[33]

Clinton anticipated the first of these appeals to doubt about his capacity to restore confidence in the American dream through his convention call for a "New Covenant." His was a call for generational renewal in which he identified himself as a New American Adam. In his acceptance speech, Clinton offered himself as a prophet of renewal who would help Americans transcend the Cold War ethos of containment and realize the promise of abundance. Benefitting from a sluggish economic recovery and skillful use of the media, William Jefferson Clinton moved from candidate to president. As he did so, he convinced the public that he might not be a callow confidence artist. Instead, like his idols Kennedy and Jefferson, he might yet offer a vision of political renewal to inspire confidence in the nation's future. Indeed, President-elect Clinton seemed to feel that his youthful meeting with President Kennedy in the Rose Garden had been a charismatic anointing of him as the man who would restore the broken covenant with the American people.

As a southern Democrat whose campaign may well have been saved by his having had the good fortune to have been born (though not raised) in Hope, Arkansas, Clinton began his symbolic journey to the White House on a bus, the common man's coach. He retraced the route of his namesake Jefferson to the scene of that president's inauguration two centuries earlier. President-elect Clinton affirmed his ability to absorb Reagan's corporate populism, selectively, into an organic corporate populism. Once more, he could do so by claiming direct descent from Jefferson's republican frontier, through John Kennedy's New Frontier, to take the reigns of leadership for a new political generation born after the Second World War.

Bill Clinton had positioned himself to win his lifelong quest for the presidency when, anticipating a future voter revolt against Washington, he moved to build a new base for national power in 1990 as chair of the Democratic Leadership Council. Newt Gingrich, with similar ambitions, had even earlier taken control of GOPAC. Beginning in 1986, he had transformed that political action committee from a lackluster organization into a $2.3 million recruitment and training program to build a new generation of Republican leaders. "Life is hard," he told these political hopefuls on promotional audiotapes, produced for the 1994 elections. "That is a major, major mistake we've made since World War II," said Gingrich on a tape called History and Leadership, "to suggest that life is easy and difficulties are the aberration." The opposite is true, Gingrich demurred; it is the good times that are the aberration. This, he continued, is the lesson of history taught by George Washington at Valley Forge and by Grant at Shiloh. It is through perseverance in the face of such hardships that victories are won.[34]

In 1994, Gingrich led his recruits on a counteroffensive against the Democrats by waging a contest of rhetoric through what he called "shield issues." That is, Republican challengers were urged to create negative associations with Democrats and to use key words to create positive associations with Republicans. He especially urged them to make the lack of voter confidence in Clinton a central issue. The cornerstone of that strategy was something he called a "Contract with America," which he persuaded a majority of the Republican congressional candidates to endorse. It was signed, with great fanfare, on the steps of the Capitol Building. These Republicans recognized, according to a campaign book that was published at the time, the need "to restore the fabric of trust between the American people and their office holders," since "public confidence in Congress and other institutions had reached its lowest point in twenty years."[35]

For his part, President Clinton expressed contrition for failure to sufficiently heed the angry voices of the electorate, and, in almost an echo of George Bush, for not communicating the reality of the good news about the nation's economic health. In his State of the Union Message of January 24, 1995, the president repeated his admission that he had made mistakes, "and learned again the importance of humility." Then, he renewed his convention invitation to establish a new covenant with the American people. It was a speech in which the president, portraying himself once again as a new Adam, called for a new beginning to the quest to restore the American Garden, and analysts agreed that he desperately needed to be reborn in the public eye if there was to be any hope for his political future. The Republican response was delivered by the governor of New Jersey, Christine Todd Whitman. She delivered her remarks from the statehouse in Trenton, New Jersey, on the site of Washington's famous victory in the Revolutionary War.[36]

Whitman had been a long-shot challenger to Governor Jim Florio in the 1993 election. She gained national attention less from her come-from-behind victory than from the fact that Ed Rollins, the leading Republican consultant, defeated Florio's consultant, Jim Carville, through her election. Both Rollins and Carville, who had engineered Clinton's victory over Bush and Perot, had entered into the Whitman-Florio campaign as full-fledged celebrity personalities. They drew such media attention to the race that Whitman became embroiled in a scandal before even taking office. Rollins bragged to reporters that Whitman's victory resulted from payoffs to suppress black voter turnout, a claim he later testified he made up to score points against Carville.[37]

Whitman had won the prize of the governorship in the proxy war between Carville and Rollins. She similarly won the opportunity, in answer to Clinton's address, to tout her success before a national audience as a stand-in for the patriarchs who led the splintered factions of the national Republican party—Senator Robert Dole, Congressman Phil Gramm, and Speaker of the House Gingrich. As a woman and as a voice of states' rights against federal domination, she could speak for the restive public mood against the "Washington beltway" crowd. Above all, she could promote herself as a Republican Eve by challenging Clinton's vision of a new convenant.

Was Clinton, indeed, a new Adam, she seemed to ask, or was he still the old Adam, continuing stubbornly in his sinful ways? "Well, there is nothing virtuous about raising taxes. There is nothing heroic about preserving a welfare system that entraps people, and there is nothing high-minded on wasting other people's money on big-government spending sprees," she intoned. Yet Whitman had necessarily staked her own credibility as the voice of virtue on the promise of national renewal. "It's clear that your votes in November sounded a warning to the president," she said. "If he has truly changed his big-government agenda, we say 'Great. Join us as we change America. Republicans welcome your ideas for making government not bigger, but smaller.' "[38]

For the post–Cold War American electorate and their political leaders, as for R. W. B. Lewis some forty years earlier, the American Adam had come to embody something other than a myth of innocence. The American Adam of the Cold War, and then of the post-Cold War, had become identified with the natural leader, crafty enough to preserve a balance between the illusions of innocence and the disillusionments of experience. This natural democratic leader had to be able to restore public confidence without gaining their private trust.

Lewis believed that the Adamic myth had been marked out in the past by prophets such as Horace Bushnell, who knew how to transform Puritan original sin into the hope of salvation. As a Cold War champion of the American Adam, Lewis, like his influential contemporary, the theologian Reinhold Niebuhr, quite willingly followed Bushnell in surrendering primitive innocence for sophisticated realism. As a practical political theorist, Niebuhr, who helped to codify and apply the lessons of realism for national leaders, did not wish to extend realism to the point of challenging confidence itself. Similarly, as a literary critic, Lewis acknowledged his ambivalence towards Melville for failing to preserve the illusions of realism while destroying those of innocence. Niebuhr and Lewis agreed, as would their political counterparts during the Cold War and after, that the illusions of realism, unlike those of innocence, were necessary. They were required for preserving political confidence in, as Lewis put it, "a still unfolding American scene."[39]

Lewis, therefore, celebrated *Billy Budd*, which, in his reading, marked Melville's triumph as an American writer. In that final work, Lewis said enthusiastically, the author achieved spiritual redemption over doubt, to affirm his confidence in the human condition. Melville achieved the apotheosis of Adamic democracy, according to Lewis, by aesthetically destroying innocence in order to restore it, just as Reinhold Niebuhr had destroyed the illusion of American exceptionalism in such books as *The Children of Light and the Children of Darkness* (1944) and *Irony of American History* (1952) in order to preserve the credibility of an American mission of leadership in the free world. The Melville of *Billy Budd* in the 1950s was a Cold War writer. He was interpreted, not only by Lewis but by the other leading American critics, as a conservative defender of necessary illusions. Captain Vere became the champion of confidence against both Billy's innocent sense of justice and Claggert's suspicious service to institutional order. Vere, in this reading of Melville, became the echo of Edmund Burke. He wisely recognized the primacy of traditional order, maintained through ritual, over the immediacy of revolutionary justice in a fallen world.[40]

Similarly, Lewis embraced the wisdom of ambiguity over moral clarity in his Cold War reading of Faulkner, as promoted by the Agrarian New Critics of Nashville and their New York intellectual allies at the *Partisan Review*. Like the Faulkner whose reputation Robert Penn Warren and Dwight Macdonald collaborated in restoring, Lewis's Faulkner represented authentic American creative genius.[41] He embodied the artist's ethical role of finding hope through despair. Faulkner, Lewis explained, was a witness to the "indestructible vitality of America," located in a redemptive space between "bouyant assurance and encircling doubt." This was the same conceptual space that the New Criticism identified as ambiguity and that Cold War political theorists, following Niebuhr, identified as irony. In each case, as in the post–Cold War era, the conceptualized American Adam inhabited the symbolic garden-space between nature and civilization, the real and the artificial, and natural law and the illusions constructed by the aesthetic imagination.[42]

The very existence and persistence of the myth of the American Adam, which is at the heart of American national culture, suggests the need to reconsider the conventional wisdom that historic Europe is the source of modern nationalism in general and of the United States's version in particular. America's writers and critics, from the earliest period of national consciousness, have routinely assumed that the young country was condemned to mere imitation of historically real national culture or cultures. But Benedict Anderson suggests that nationalism instead originated in the crisis of identity that occurred among the Creole-speaking populations of the exotic, but also exploited, Americas. The origins of the modern nation-state, he argues, may lie in the resulting doubt over identity and status, which, in turn, may have led to the question of who possesses title to the real national identity and who merely imitates it.[43] As such, the frontier, as Melville suggested in both *Moby-Dick* and *The Confidence-Man*, fatally defined the character of the conflict among races and genders that still permeates twentieth-century national cultures.

In the United States this contradictory pattern of envy mixed with contempt, or *ressentiment*, against perceived inferior doubles of the national ideal was already evident in the early nationalist period, when the cult of true womanhood was forged. Woman, as Eve, came out of Adam. Therefore, Eve, as wife, daughter, and mother, could be neither clearly separated from her husband, father, and sons, nor completely absorbed into their power through laws of coverture or the social conventions of masculine prerogative. Rather, though excluded from identification with public life, women retained a frontier presence, as deputy husbands, sellers of wares, midwives, or tavern keepers. It was at such frontier moments of public participation, however, in which the central Enlightenment metaphor of the frontier as a stage for performance made feminine identity most problematical. The birth of a new national identity out of colonialism made the laws of coverture, in which a wife's will was considered indivisible from her husband's, a divisive political issue. The identification of a wife with her husband's political choice to remain loyal or join the revolution became inseparable from the problem of individual accountability, personal rights and the legitimacy of the revolution itself.[44]

After the revolution, therefore, women's calls for rights in the areas of civic activities, education, and divorce were integral, yet deeply threatening, to the preservation of republican institutions. Mary Wollstonecraft's *A Vindication of the Rights of Woman* (1792) was perhaps the most direct and best-known confrontation with the gendered tensions of the early republic.[45] The British writer, who was revealed to have lived with a man out of wedlock some years before her death in childbirth in 1797, served as a lightning rod for fears of moral collapse as well as for hopes for ending hypocrisy in the former British colony. Consequently, Wollstonecraft was both embraced and vilified by American nationalists, who were confused by her double message of promoting the political virtue of independence while attacking the cult of true womanhood. This tension was inherent in Wollstonecraft's point of departure for her essay. For, beginning with her identification with Tom Paine's challenge to Edmund Burke in his pamphlet *The Rights of Man*, Wollstonecraft extended her attack on Burke's association of the sublime with masculinity and the beautiful with femininity to Rousseau's similar defense of the conventions of male and female spheres. Both, she suggested, were engaged in the same disguised celebration of power as a male prerogative.[46]

Wollstonecraft's challenge to that convention in the name of female confidence was recognized as an inherent implication of the revolution itself, and, not surprisingly, *A Vindication of the Rights of Woman* was greeted with the same mixture of sarcasm and burlesque as were the class-generated attacks against political deference by backcountry farmers. Similarly, pamphlets such as "The Humble Address of Ten Thousand Federal Maids"(1791) satirized the same fears of imitation that might threaten national identity, as did Hugh Henry Brackenridge's satiric Irishman, Teague O'Reagan, who humorously aped his urbane Anglo-American master in *Modern Chivalry* (1792).[47] A similar pattern may be discerned among nineteenth-century white audiences who gained pleasure from blackface minstrel shows, as Eric Lott has recently shown. Blacks were rigidly prohibited from participating in this apparent celebration of idyllic plantation life. Instead, minstrel shows featured white actors imitating stereotypical black imitations of white American manners. Blackface transvestism was especially popular, despite, and even because of, its outrageousness; it conventionalized the very core of Anglo-American national terrors of race, class, and gender into a single act of imitation for public consumption.[48]

These are examples of a ritualized performance used to evade the frightening implications of the real through a transformation of it into something artificial. It is a strategy for preserving confidence through the sublime, and therefore perversely mirrors confidence with doubt in the opposing fear that the imitation may replace the real. The result of this double bind of terror, *ressentiment*, has been expressed historically against women who enter previously male positions of authority or move into male preserves of activity, as much as against lower-class men or persons of color who do not recognize their places. Such women, social outcasts, and black "dandies" have routinely been derided for trying to mimic real men. Similarly, "real Americans," in the nineteenth and twentieth centuries, have been contrasted with "hyphenated Americans," or persons who are less than "100 percent Americans." This juncture of the imitative and the real and of simulation and dissimulation, as in any artistic production or any process of social engineering, manufactures confidence through simulating natural forms. It is at once an expression of organic community and a game of confidence.

This double implication, of the will to confidence as simulation and deception, may account for the ubiquitous presence of the confidence artist as actor on the American frontier, not only in Melville's and Baum's fiction, in Barnum's self-promotions, and in Buffalo Bill's Wild West shows, but in Kuhn's scientists, Rorty's philosophers, Warhol's Factory entourage, and even in the widely celebrated role of Madonna as an Andy Warhol in drag. It is the source of Gingrich's self-identification as a virtual Adam who would restore the promise of a fallen America. It was that same ability to challenge the conventions of established authority that Christine Todd Whitman brought to her response to President Clinton on national television, sounding the voice of individualist virtue and revolutionary conservatism.

Similarly, early Cold War writers such as Hemingway and Dos Passos—both of whom were indebted to Walt Whitman—were "semantically transformed" as frontier writers, or at least their messages that individual confidence must be fought for and won against an indifferent system of power was reconfigured in the post–World War II nationalist writings of Norman Mailer, as the Jamesian literature of national doubt was revisited in the writing of James Baldwin. Both Mailer and Baldwin would explicitly write on the frontiers of gender and race and between social theory and the traditional novel. Mailer and Baldwin would place performance at the center of their writings. They would conflate their art and lives as celebrities who felt compelled to live authentic theater by immersing themselves in the dangerous social issues of their day.

The concept of semantic transformation that Liah Greenfield applied to the problem of nationalism, and that may, therefore, be legitimately extended into the realms of national politics or to the nation-building aspects of the social sciences and the republic of letters, is another word for rhetoric. Transport is the experience of the sublime, and the sublime is a special form of rhetoric, evoking wonder or terror but not seeking to persuade, as do other forms of rhetoric. It is a language of performance rather than a language that is performed.

The classical writer Longinus characterized the sublime as a form of performativity, which illuminates, through artful uses of contrast, like lightning in a dark sky. The aesthetic contrast through which the sublime is encountered emotionally may be that of lightness and darkness, or vastness and littleness, or, more elementally, pleasure and fear. But the important point is that although the emotions of powerfulness, humility, grandeur and insignificance are themselves intangible, the sublime, as a form of rhetoric, makes them reproducible.[49]

The sublime alone provides the key to a culture of confidence, for only the sublime provides a formula for transforming doubt into confidence, terror into pleasure, the natural into the artificial, the fraudulent into the authentic, and the real into an imitation. Only the sublime provides a rhetoric of imitation that can mediate the line between simulation and dissimulation in industrial and postindustrial, as well as modern and postmodern, social eras. The sublime is the single Enlightenment aesthetic convention linking the post–Cold War covenant of Bill Clinton with the Cold War American Adam of R. W. B. Lewis and the performative perceptions of the Material Girl with David Potter's people of plenty. It is the substance of the frontier and the link between Melville's primitive backwoodsman and confidence artists, on one side of the twentieth-century literary divide, and John Crowe Ransom's *God of Thunder*, embracing a new fundamentalism, on the other. For the sublime extends from Locke to Kant, and from Dewey to Rorty, and it encompasses the children of Burke as well as those of Rousseau, from the revolution to the close of the Cold War—events that, finally, are mere episodes in the Enlightenment age of confidence.

But, as Melville and Tocqueville, Barnum and Buffalo Bill, and politicians from Wilson to Clinton and Gingrich have agreed, sublime rhetoric and social constructionism necessarily and simultaneously define society as theater and the individual as an actor. Together, they create doubt that truth may be separated from illusion, and as principles of social thought, they threaten to place social values in the hands of entertainers and demagogues. The American national culture from Jefferson to Clinton has, therefore, evolved through a context of pervasive doubt into ever-new forms of confidence. It has done so principally through the surprisingly broad influence of Edmund Burke. It has become possible to see, especially under the intense rhetorical combat characteristic of the Cold War, the Burkean conventions for using the sublime instrumentally to achieve political and aesthetic power. No other society has been able to apply Burke's insights so fundamentally as has America because no other national culture has been so able to claim an artificially natural national existence.

Burke's name, therefore, runs as a thread through the political and aesthetic history of the United States. But it is an obscure thread, made less visible by the skill of the Enlightenment parliamentarian's way with words, his sophisticated application of the rule of theater to politics, and his self-invented image of sincerity and of reasoned conservatism.

4

Edmund Burke and the Politics of Theater

Edmund Burke, with the odd exception of Russell Kirk to prove the rule, has never been included among the pantheon of fathers who are credited with establishing the national political culture in the United States. Though sympathetic to the American colonists, Burke always opposed their right to separate through revolution. Burke's reputation as a democrat was further tarnished by Tom Paine's famous pamphlet, *The Rights of Man* (1791, 1792), which personalized their disagreement about the French Revolution.[1] Yet Burke was not quite so lonely a prophet crying in the American wilderness as his admirers have pretended. In the eighteenth and nineteenth centuries, Americans and Europeans alike routinely read Burke's *A Philosophical Enquiry into the Origin of Our Ideas of the Sublime and Beautiful*, which appeared in new American editions every decade over the century after it was first published in 1757.[2] This popular reception assured that his rhetoric and his interpretation of the sublime would permeate American discourse about art, power and political virtue. The identification of Burke's variation on Longinus's discourse with the sublime, to the exclusion of the many other interpretations competing with Burke's, resulted from the fact that Burke alone went beyond philosophizing about the aesthetics of pleasure. As Mary Wollstonecraft recognized in her frustration with his patriarchal equation of the sublime with masculine power, the ever-practical Burke had developed a theory of the sublime that was as applicable to politics as to art.[3] Though the *Enquiry* was a pathbreaking psychological study of aesthetic pleasure, it was first and foremost a clever apology for the organized use of power in human affairs.

Edmund Burke's writings, as well as the writings of those who claimed to be influenced by Burke, from Tocqueville and Melville to Woodrow Wilson and Norman Mailer, appealed to a wide cross section of Americans in the twentieth-century context of the Cold War. This was true for the same reason that Burke's writing appealed to revolutionary nationalists of the eighteenth century such as Thomas Jefferson and Charles Wilson Peale, despite their disappointment with Burke's antirevolutionary message. That appeal was that his political aesthetic made it possible for postrevolutionary politicians and artists, as well as for Cold War artists and social scientists, to exploit the distinction between the sublime and the beautiful as a way of preserving confidence in the face of political and cultural doubt.

In the *Enquiry*, which Burke wrote as a young man and which defined the terms of all his subsequent writing, he contrasted the sublime with the beautiful. However, he did not do so only in the terms of masculine independence and feminine dependence, the notion at which Wollstonecraft so angrily chafed. Behind his metaphorical language, Burke more generally contrasted the sublime as an instrumental response to power, with the beautiful, as an immediate apprehension of power. He acknowledged the sublime to be artificial and manipulative. Because it is calculated and calculating, he wrote, "a true artist should always put a deceit upon an audience." The beautiful, in contrast, is immediate and untranslatable. Beauty induces emotions, such as love, as "the application of ice or fire produces the idea of heat and cold." The beautiful, in other words, is unmediated and authentic, while the sublime is contrived and imitative. Consequently, for Burke, the very disingenuousness of the sublime provides an aesthetic formula applicable to the resolving of the many psychological crises that may result from authentic experience.[4]

Pleasure, Burke's dichotomy assures, may be routinely constructed out of pain in a sort of emotional alchemy that parallels the ancient dream of turning base metals into precious ones. "In imitated distress," as opposed to real calamities, Burke wrote, "the only difference is the pleasure resulting from the effects of imitation; for it is never so perfect, but we can perceive it is an imitation, and on that principle are somewhat pleased with it." Indeed, Burke said, in some cases, it is the very fact of imitation that is the source of pleasure. Yet, he explained further, an audience does not experience pleasure in a dramatic tragedy by dismissing it as "a deceit, and its representations not realities." Instead, the "nearer it approaches the reality, the further it removes us from all idea of fiction, the more perfect is its power."[5]

In the year 1790, at the height of his political career, Burke used his earlier distinction between the sublime and the beautiful, which also implicitly presumed a distinction between the aesthetics of power and the spiritual immediacy of religion, to attack the French Revolution. It is this work, *Reflections on the Revolution in France* (1790), which most clearly exposes his dramaturgical strategy as a political theorist. It is also the *Reflections* that most impressed disillusioned Marxists and liberals with Burke's political wisdom during the Cold War. *Reflections on the Revolution in France*, therefore, bears close consideration as both an Enlightenment and a Cold War text.[6]

In the *Reflections*, Burke specifically applied his aesthetic theory of the sublime to the goal of discrediting the political claims of the supporters of the French Revolution. His strategy in doing so clearly appeared to former admirers such as Tom Paine to be a betrayal of Burke's own republican political principles. Indeed, Paine was so deeply stung by Burke's diatribe against the French Revolution because he perceived Burke's new position to be a duplicitous retreat from one that previously had been compatible with his own. "Such is the ingenuity of his hope, or the malignancy of his despair," Paine bitterly scoffed, that "it furnishes him with new pretences to go on."[7]

Burke's *Reflections on the Revolution in France*, however, was a mature statement of his dramaturgical perspective on politics. It was not in contradiction with his earlier principles, as Paine believed when he wrote his first pamphlet against Burke. Paine was, however, closer to the mark in his second pamphlet, in which he renewed his challenge to Burke's integrity and declared that Burke held a contemptible view of mankind. "He considers them as a herd of beings that must be governed by fraud, effigy, and show," Paine wrote.[8] These are strong words, but are not entirely inappropriate for characterizing Burke's rhetorical intentions in heaping abuse upon the French. For the occasion of his writing the essay that led Paine and Wollstonecraft to vilify him, and upon which his Cold War reputation for political wisdom rests, was not the revolution itself. Rather, Burke's essay, ostensibly presented as a frank reply to a letter from a young French gentlemen, was written to discredit the defense of the revolution in a published sermon titled "On Our Love of Country" by a nonconformist minister named Dr. Richard Price.

Burke argued, against Price, that politics and religion are formally incompatible because they address power in contrasting ways. Politicians, he said, play different parts in the theater of politics than do preachers, and confusing their roles is detrimental to the duties which each is required to perform in a fallen world. Politicians rhetorically manipulate power against each other, Burke suggested, while "no sound ought to be heard in the Church but the healing voice of Christian charity." These differing rhetorics, he insisted, were confused by nonconformists like Price, because they theologically rejected a national church while extolling a national politics. As a result of this muddle, the nonconformist Price was inviting a return to the chaos of the interregnum. His misplaced confidence in the French Revolution, Burke argued, was a threat to national tranquility because he failed to recognize that the French revolutionaries, like the English saints before them, had not achieved a rebirth of political religion but only the illusion of civic religion. The result of misreading civic religion as real rather than as a necessary illusion, Burke feared, was that the art of creating national confidence through political theater would degenerate into a confidence game. "We ought not, on either side of the water," Burke warned, "to suffer ourselves to be imposed upon by the counterfeit wares which some persons, by a double fraud, export to you [the French] in illicit bottoms, as raw commodities of British growth, wholly alien to our soil, in order afterwards to smuggle them back again into this country, manufactured after the newest Paris fashion of an improved liberty."[9]

Burke wrote that he had recognized, in the publication of Dr. Price's sermon and related documents, evidence of a "manifest design of connecting the affairs of France with those of England, by drawing us into an imitation of the conduct of the National Assembly." Though he expressed optimism that the British people "will not ape the fashions they have never tried," Burke clearly feared the triumph of similar nonconformist Protestant tendencies in England, adding, "nor go back to those which they have found mischievous on trial." While he professed to be unsure as to who had borrowed from whom in the development of their respective political cultures, Burke surmised that, in manners, the English had always been influenced by the French. Since "nothing is more certain, than that our manners, our civilization, and all the good things which are connected with manners and with civilization . . . have depended for ages upon two principles . . . combined; . . . the spirit of a gentleman and the spirit of religion," the fall of nobility and religion in France directly threatened England. "When your fountain is choked up and polluted, the stream will not run long, or not run clear, with us, or perhaps with any nation," he wrote to his young foil.[10]

In warning against imitation, deception, and counterfeit principles, as well as against atheism and sectarianism, however, Burke did not recoil from the illusions of political theater to embrace a higher truth of religion. Instead, assuming that all social roles were actually dramatic roles, Burke advocated that clergy should play a supporting role to politicians to preserve order. Institutionally, a religious establishment should stabilize political order, he argued against Dr. Price, not spread the principles of nonconformism by supporting revolutionary pretenders. The proper function of the church, in Burke's dramaturgy, as in every manifestation of the feminine, therefore, is to provide emotional relief, a psychological space "where one day's truce ought to be allowed to the dissensions and animosities of mankind."

Religion, Burke insisted, should inculcate, among the powerful and wealthy, or, as he describes them, "persons of exalted situations," "high and worthy notions of their functions." At the same time, he equally insisted, a "religious establishment, is necessary also to operate with a wholesome awe upon free citizens; because in order to secure their freedom, they must enjoy some determinate portion of power." The faith invested in the exalted, who "stand in the person of God, Himself," he explained, makes them accountable to their audience, while democracy is finally accountable only to itself. Therefore, "where popular authority is absolute and unrestrained, the people have an infinitely greater, because a far better founded, confidence in their own power." In an effort to combat the consequences of that advantage, Burke devoted the balance of his *Reflections* to an apology for the British tradition of political theater. He contrasted the British love of tradition with the innovative enthusiasms and violences promoted in the French National Assembly by contrasting the social consequences of the English Revolution of 1688 with those of the French Revolution of 1789.[11]

In Burke's view, the Glorious Revolution was preferable to the French Revolution because it was more orderly, provided security of property and individual rights, and permitted culture and religion to flourish. The Glorious Revolution had been able to preserve order, rights, and freedom because it did not confuse the artificiality of politics with the natural emotions of religious sentiment, as did the French Revolution. In other words, British political theater was better theater than French political theater because the former fulfilled the emotional requirements of preserving the illusion of natural sentiments, while the latter revealed their artificiality. In making this apology for the Glorious Revolution, Burke built directly upon the aesthetic distinction he had made more than forty years earlier, and which he had presented in the *Enquiry*.

As a political rhetorician, Burke found the sublime to be more useful than the beautiful because it takes the authentic, the real experience, and turns it instrumentally into an artificial one. "No work of art can be great, but as it deceives," he wrote. This was an assessment that necessarily included his own oratory, as well as the other performance and visual art he appreciated in others. The sublime, therefore, offered him a way to use aesthetic illusion as an Archimedean lever for moving the world and as a masculine expression of action that could dominate passive feminine awe before nature or nature's God. The French Revolution, however, extolled by Dr. Price as a radical democratic revival, was theater in the streets. It combined the cool art of political manipulation with the direct emotion of public excitement. As political theater, the French Revolution, therefore, threatened more than France. It threatened to set a precedent—that is, a standard of authority that might be imitated in new situations. It would, in essence, shatter the very distinction between the authentic and the imitative that constituted the foundation of good aesthetic taste and social order.

Burke had written in the *Enquiry* that theater might never fully envelop the reality that it represents. Choose a day to present the most sublime and emotionally compelling tragedy, he suggested, and hire the most popular actors, erect the most lavish scenery, add to it the greatest poetry, painting and music. The gathered audience, though erect with anticipation, will nevertheless empty the theater if they learn that a high-ranking criminal is about to be executed in the adjoining public square. For Burke, however, the French Revolution was both political theater, orchestrated and directed by the National Assembly, and a real political event taking place in the public square adjoining their chambers. It was a more exciting, exacting, and compelling production than any show he could have imagined ever being staged. Indeed, according to Paine, Burke never expected revolution in France at all, because he thought the French had neither the spirit to undertake it nor the fortitude to support it. Now, he looked with undisguised terror at the "most astonishing" revolution in history. Everything, he said, seemed unnaturally mixed into the frivolous and the furious, creating a "tragi-comic scene," with alternating contempt and indignation, laughter and tears, and scorn and horror.

In light of the events of 1789, therefore, Burke's former celebration of sublime pleasure evaporated before a direct experience of terror. Fear for the future of England gave a new immediacy to what had been a theoretical description of the artificially induced psychological pleasure of pain. Revolutionary France jolted him into a realization that such psychological pleasures could be wielded into a profoundly powerful social force. "We have seen an infancy . . . growing by moments into a strength to heap mountains upon mountains, and to wage war with heaven itself," he wrote. The compelling spectacle of sublime revolutionary theater and the tragedies it promised to engender would only intensify, he predicted, as it captured the public imagination throughout Europe.[12]

Therefore, in 1790, Burke did not applaud the art of deception, as he had done in 1747 and 1757. Instead he styled himself to be the guileless defender of the beautiful against the manipulative purveyors of sublime fantasy. In the year 1790, this was his one available directorial role as a nationalist and his one rhetorical avenue for preserving the status quo of political power in the British empire. He therefore evoked by turn emotions of sorrow and pity, humility and nobility, and tenderness and terror to excite an emotional defense of British national feeling in his readers. He marshalled his rhetorical skills to defend a spiritually elevated and materially civilized British nation of natural virtue, which he contrasted with an artificial and degenerate France brought to ruin by a small political cabal of amateurs intoxicated by power.

Burke artfully hid the fact that the British national culture he extolled to his readers was just as artificial as the new French regime or the older Cromwellean one, which equally terrified him. His object was to persuade his British audience of the sincerity of his delicate political apology for a natural nationalism and to marshal them emotionally against an artificial, imitative, and therefore fraudulent appeal to national feeling, as expressed in Dr. Price's sermon. To do so, Burke used the rhetorical strategy of appealing to a shared feeling of intimacy with his readers, while promoting a sense of distrust about the judgment and taste of his young and inexperienced French correspondent. By appealing to the notion of intimacy and to doubt, Burke established a literary, and therefore artificial, bond of trust between himself and his readers. By appealing to his readers' fears and doubts, Burke, himself an artist of confidence, fashioned a persuasive image of his own benign wisdom and the irresponsible naivete of the followers of Rousseau, who had managed to ruin France by placing her future into the hands of a government of confidence artists.

The whole of the *Reflections* is actually a clever literary orchestration of the tension between trust and confidence, the former expressed in the direct appreciation of that which is beautiful, and the latter with the artificial instrumentalism of the sublime. Throughout the essay, Burke contrasted the natural—whether of emotion, government, or religion— with the imitative, the fraudulent, and the artificial. He eloquently but disingenuously charged that the artificiality of the French Revolution resulted in an *imitation* of *real* art. In a subsequent work, *A Letter to a Member of the National Assembly*, Burke went still further and aesthetically challenged the sublimity of the revolution by promoting its appearance as the merely ridiculous. The French Revolution did not really offer theater, Burke insisted in 1791, but only a burlesque, not an economy of producers but of gamblers, not real confidence but a confidence game. The British national culture, on the other hand, was natural and traditional. Consequently, it possessed the solid virtues of sincerity, innocence and piety. It appeared, as Burke portrayed it, less sublime because it was more genuine.[13]

The source of Burke's fear of the French Revolution, which he raised well before its worst excesses, may be found in his definition of the sublime as a modification of power. Burke argued that the violent attempt of the French to re-create the patriotic religions of the Greeks and Romans was misguided, despite the fact that any revolution, by definition, is an expression of the sublime. Burke did not deny that this had been as true of the Glorious Revolution in England a century earlier as of the revolution in his contemporary France. However, he refused to embrace this recent sublime event as he had an earlier one, he explained, because the French revolutionaries had failed to restore the lost political innocence of aristocratic France, as had been done in England. They failed, he said, because they had confused sublime discourse, which is artificial, with religious confession, which is natural. Instead of reconnecting civic humanism with the divine by discovering natural law, the French revolutionaries, and the philosophes before them, had merely disconnected the sublime from the natural limits of tradition, especially religious tradition and manners.

The French Revolution, he charged, had perpetrated a fraud, not restored a natural form of civic religion, through the clever exploitation of a linguistic confusion. For Burke, the revolution was an attempt to create a new human constitution and a new social ethic by "everything which is spurious, fictitious and false; by everything which takes a man from his house and puts him on a stage; which makes him an artificial creature with painted, theatric sentiments, fit to be seen by the glare of candlelight, and formed to be contemplated at due distance."[14]

Paradoxically, however, Burke confirmed his own use of countertheater by attacking French theatricality. He attempted to legitimize British national culture by deriding French national culture as a mere theatrical illusion. Burke's rhetorical strategy was, of course, used to preserve the existing power structure of the state and its institutions, not to establish the theoretical grounds for a new polity. To the degree that he defended existing interests, therefore, Burke was conservative.

However, Richard Weaver argued in 1953, if Burke's form of rhetoric is examined, it is revealed to be one that is "fatal to conservatism," and Burke himself is revealed to be "very far from conservatism." This is because, for Weaver, method of argument is a better indicator of values than are principles. Conservatives argue from genus, or from the nature of the thing itself, Weaver explained, while Burke, on the contrary, argues from circumstance, which as a rhetorical strategy is essentially an argument from expediency.[15] The word "casuistry" never appears in Weaver's analysis of Burke's rhetoric. But it is casuistry, the venerable art and science of expediency, which may best characterize the blend of tradition and innovation in Burke's style of dramaturgical rhetoric, and it is as casuistry that Burkean rhetoric retained its continuing appeal for American political and aesthetic leaders in the twentieth-century context of the Cold War.

Casuistry has today gained the rightfully unpleasant, although unfortunately imprecise, connotation of disingenuous argument. However, casuistry has a more specific historical denotation as a science of ethics. Its function is to negotiate the contradictions that may arise between interest and conscience. More specifically, the practice of casuistry was an eristic strategy, in canon law or Calvinist ethics, for exploiting the ambiguous distinction between simulation and dissimulation. The practice of "holy pretense," as the Puritan William Perkins called it, was almost a growth industry from the late Middle Ages to the post-Reformation period. It spread through language as well as practice in the confused moral climate that resulted from Europe's expanding commerce, religious conflict, technological innovations and political centralization. A plethora of casuistic texts, manuals and commentaries appeared as the Middle Ages waned, feeding those hungry for guidance. At the same time, according to Perez Zagorin, the explosion of casuistic reasoning itself served to compound the moral perplexities of daily life. The line between truth and duplicity was increasingly experienced, not as a border that was only infrequently crossed by heretics and criminals, but as a frontier where many people lived and acted out their entire lives.[16]

Beyond its technical contributions to resolving the contradictions of behavior and morality, casuistry also demonstrated the increasing conflation of the theoretical and the practical in every aspect of life. In the century before Burke's birth, Catholic France's great innovator of deductive logic, René Descartes (1596–1650), intellectually defended the possibility of developing confident knowledge of this new territory of the mind and of experience through doubt. In Protestant England, the other great innovator who shaped the Enlightenment culture into which Burke was born, Francis Bacon (1561–1626), was the champion of new science. Bacon anticipated Burke's oppositions between the sublime and the beautiful in his earlier explorations of the frontier between sincerity and artifice and between representations of truth and its fraudulent misrepresentations. Bacon wrote essays with titles such as "Of Simulation and Dissimulation" and "Of Cunning," in which he noted the importance of confidence for taking advantage of the secret faults of others and for avoiding fearfulness and self-doubt. Bacon linked his celebration of the scientific method with a political suspicion of surface appearance that often masquerades as truth. It was, however, John Locke (1632–1704) who translated the political and religious conflicts embedded in the struggle with doubt and confidence and reality and illusion into psychological categories that were subject to social application. Locke provided Burke, like his near-contemporary, the American theologian Jonathan Edwards, with a scientific psychology of casuistic reasoning that served well the early Anglo-American fear of conspiracy, belief in regenerative violence, and enthusiasm for technological progress, all of which were as much implications of an instrumentalist definition of the will as the revivalisms that rocked and splintered colonial America in waves of emotional awakenings.

Locke was a medical doctor who embraced both the new science and his family's intense Calvinism. He was probably also an active conspirator against the Crown in the years before the Glorious Revolution. His life was enveloped in secrecy, and he often communicated his ideas through double-coded messages. He believed that the lessons of medicine might be applied to society, literally serving as a practical bridge of healing between diseased individuals and a diseased political body. Indeed, Locke pursued philosophical first principles in imitation of the way a medical doctor applies his skill in reading symptoms to isolate and treat some previously undiagnosed disease. Dr. Locke became convinced through his years of association with Dr. Thomas Sydenham, who was a brilliant epidemiologist and an equally staunch Puritan, that the best way to cure the body, or the body politic, was by curing the mind. He therefore developed his psychological theories, not as disinterested science, but as a practical therapeutic approach to minds diseased by the wrong kind of associations, such as Catholicism, dissenting Protestant emotionalism and what we today would call depression, which Sydenham pioneered in treating as a psychiatric condition. Where healing was not possible, Locke advocated purging such undesirables as Catholics, the poor, or the superstitious as a public health measure to protect other vulnerable minds from contagion.[17]

Locke theorized that illusion and ill associations with the environment literally make people mad, so his psychology of sensation was aimed at countering the negative effects of those associations. It was upon this Lockean psychology of a diseased will that the Puritan divine Jonathan Edwards constructed his hyperrealistic sermons to horrify sinners before an angry God. It was upon this same Lockean psychology that Burke later constructed his theory of sublime tragedy, in which pain may be transformed into a pleasurable experience.

Since Burke's practical description of the sublime is a conscious aesthetic strategy for turning terror into pleasure, it presents an insight into how Edwards could unconsciously, but just as artfully, use Lockean psychology to craft his jeremiad of terror, which he believed would lead his congregants to true conversion. Edwards was not unaware of the manipulative character of emotionalism, though he did not have the benefit of Burke's distinction between sublime and beautiful emotional responses to power. Edwards had joined with critics of the Great Awakening in questioning the legitimacy of emotion-laden revivals. However, he was theologically compelled to defend the possibility of the direct holy influence of God's presence upon the minds and emotions of believers.

Burke, however, in contrast to the New Light theologian Edwards, was a practical politician and a master illusionist who was interested in worldly rather than heavenly confidence. Unlike the Puritan Edwards, who inherited his Northampton pulpit from his venerated grandfather, Solomon Stoddard, Burke was born into Irish poverty. The product of a Catholic-Protestant union and without family connections to power, he was a man who lived between two worlds. He was an outsider all his life, but protected himself and advanced his ambitions by attaching himself to the fortunes of insiders. He might, for example, have personally identified with the oppressed Irish, the abused Indian people, and the exploited Americans during his political career, but he was too shrewd to confuse sentiment with sentimentality. Unlike his idealist near-contemporary, Burke developed and applied his Lockean psychological theory for manipulating public emotions in the service of an existing power structure. He carefully reinforced the prejudices already existing in the public to serve his own purposes.[18]

Actually, Burke's New Casuistry might well be described as a simple application of the lessons he learned from the Romantic painters to his political task of constructing rhetorical illusions in service to his political patrons. Like the artists, but using words instead of paint and brush, Burke appropriated the current fashion for the sublime into his theory and then into his speeches for the rest of his life. Like the artists, he applied aesthetic theory to the practical business of transforming real terror into an illusion, which could, in turn, be manipulated for public consumption.[19]

Burke distrusted popular emotion and eschewed unmediated religious truth, both because he feared the volatile power behind aesthetic pleasure and religious enthusiasm and because it did not suit his practical interests as a parliamentarian. He did not attempt to resolve the division between the beautiful and the sublime, or between the religious and the political, as, for example, medieval theologians had attempted to resolve the division between faith and reason, itself a conflict between versions of trust and confidence. Rather, the Reformation, which Burke defended as a necessary purge that guaranteed a stable civic community in England, had, for him, also witnessed a failure to resolve the contradiction between them. The Reformation had resulted from the inability to balance the conflict between instrumentalism in the scholasticism of Aquinas and Calvin, on one side of the nominalist-realist debate, and the mystical personalism of Nicholas of Cusa, Ockham, and Luther, on the other. From Burke's practical perspective, the resolution to this dialectical problem of reason and faith was through a pragmatic approach to managing power. He transformed the Augustinian division of the two kingdoms, one heavenly and the other worldly, into a metaphor of a single structure of order, which an established church must join with an established government in preserving.[20]

Edwards, in contrast, embraced both popular emotion and unmediated religious truth, because, though volatile, they were opportunities for demonstrating God's saving power in the life of his people. As a Calvinist theologian, Edwards assumed that the supernatural must act upon the natural emotions, for good or ill. He believed, as a child of the Enlightenment and of medieval scholasticism, that truth is rational. Therefore, he held that true believers could be discerned from deceivers, and that the holy terror mediated through the preacher's studied rhetoric could convey God's beauty and majesty to sinners, opening the way to God's forgiving grace.

Burke's contrasting distinction between unmediated emotion and institutionalized sentiment in religion was similar to his distinction between French and British political institutions in the *Reflections*. It was based, like his distinction between the sublime and the beautiful, upon his formal rhetorical separation of instrumental from relational speech. Burke's conviction that sublime power could not be merged with sincere faith meant not only that instrumental and relational speech were forever separate, but that, consequently, no religious revival could be sustained indefinitely to bring about the Kingdom of God on earth.

The Calvinist apologist Edwards, however, lacked an equivalent to a Burkean theory of the sublime. He was, therefore, vulnerable to his inability to discern under what circumstances the instrumental mimicked the metaphysical. That is, he could not be sure that what appeared to be a supernatural influence on ordinary emotions might not emanate from an aesthetic source rather than a holy or satanic influence. He paid for this conflation of the sublime and the demonic, however, with banishment from his pulpit in 1744 by a congregation that had grown surfeited with religious emotionalism.[21]

Burkeans in the twentieth-century context of the Cold War found casuistry both practically useful and frightening, a defense for traditional stability and an instrument for ignoring moral conventions that were inconvenient. For Weaver, writing in 1953, Burke appeared to be an opportunist and a liberal. At the same time, Russell Kirk, also writing about Burke in 1953, anointed him the crown prince of all Anglo-American conservative philosophers.[22] It was, precisely by virtue of this paradox made possible by Burke's grasp of the rhetoric of theater, that his writing could appear as conservative and liberal to anti-Progressives such as Kirk and Weaver, as both conservative and liberal to a Progressive politician such as Woodrow Wilson, and as the provider of a serviceable strategy of power to counter-Progressive intellectuals as different from each other as Reinhold Niebuhr and Norman Mailer.

Paradoxically too, though Burke is widely considered the leading historical champion against Rousseau, he curiously parallels Rousseau in his enthusiasm for the natural, his distrust of the artificiality of the modern, his anti-Enlightenment defense of Enlightenment values, and his faith in the practical possibility of a corporate polity that preserves individual freedom along with social order. He also parallels Rousseau, as Mary Wollstonecraft recognized, in his defense of masculine prerogative and his sentimentality concerning feminine virtue.

Despite their formal similarities, however, Burke's approach to politics as dramaturgy sharply contrasts with Rousseau's moralistic approach to politics through civic religion. In part, this is because Burke was present to witness the theatrical character of revolutionary nationalism in France and to address it through countertheater, while Rousseau was dead in 1787 and so could challenge nothing done in his name. In part, too, it was because Rousseau misread his own sublime ideals of utopian virtue as a direct apprehension of natural law.

Consequently, Rousseau's moralistic dream of a return to a natural order from the artificiality and decadence of the ancien régime, could easily be coopted by a younger generation in search of legitimacy for their rebellious attitudes towards a society that had lost confidence in its ability to resolve its internal problems. Rousseau's antitheatrical moralism provided justification for those who wished to use political terror to create a new social order. From their seats in the mountain and the plains of the National Assembly, and in the streets of Paris, competing factions of revolutionaries could claim they were acting in obedience to the self-sacrificing and lofty sentiments of political religion. But just because civic religion was actually only another disguised formula for appealing to sublime aesthetics, patriotism could be artificially created through fear, propaganda and, more positively, through national songs, poetry and plays. Soon citizen-soldiers were voluntarily flocking to defend the French nation from foreign armies. Nationalism, as George Mosse noted, began to define people's senses of virtue and their longing for respectability.[23] Yet even before the executions of the king and queen, the wars, and the terror, the belatedly honored Rousseau had posthumously gained the status of the prophetic voice of a new religion of humanity, and affirmed the pessimistic idea in his own writing that artifice both inevitably increases in society and inevitably corrupts all that it touches. Inescapably, therefore, the austere moralizing Rousseau was fatally implicated in the excesses and posturings of the revolution that followed his death, and Burke exploited those excesses of artifice as a propagandist for British nationalism.

Burke was uniquely situated to aesthetically codify the politics of performance at the very birth of modern nationalism, because nationalism is based upon sublime aesthetics rather than civic religious principles. Burke's formula for turning the terrors of the natural into the pleasure of the artificial would remain as central to Anglo-American national culture in the twentieth century as it did in the eighteenth. This remained true even when the problems of modernism, or political ideology, were not consciously recognized as Burkean, as they were for a Jefferson or a Wilson, so long as the strategy for resolving them was found in terms of performance rather than morality and in service to established institutions rather than in liberation from them. For Rousseau had acknowledged the contradictions of modernism as a moral dilemma that could not be resolved, while Burke had offered a strategy for escaping those contradictions through political theater.

The Cold War reminded the essayist and poet Peter Viereck that Rousseauvian moralism implicated the artist and the citizen in the contradictions of modernism, but that Burke presented both the citizen and the artist with an avenue of escape from those consequences through the rhetoric of performance. As early as the 1930s, Viereck argued that the evils of Soviet communism and Nazi fascism proved that Rousseau's civic moralism could never escape its own contradictions as an artificial religion. Rousseauvians could never return the West to political innocence by returning to the principles of political religion embodied in the Roman republic. Although the sociologists Will Herberg and Robert Bellah later claimed that a civic religion was fundamental to American national culture, Viereck's challenge to Rousseau in the name of Burkean values suggested that such civic religion was only an illusion. It was a rhetorical formula for promoting political theater, not a shared core identity as Herberg tried to argue decades later in *Protestant, Catholic, Jew* (1955) or as Bellah claimed in his classic essay "Civil Religion in America" (1967). Viereck assumed from his reading of Burke that such a civic religion could exist in the United States in the twentieth century only as a mechanism for manufacturing public consent. It could not serve as a source of organic consensus that could be mediated by political and cultural elites.[24]

Viereck embraced this conclusion through the same disillusionment as did Richard Weaver and Russell Kirk. During the 1950s, all three claimed to reject what passed for conservatism as well as for liberalism in the United States. These political categories had become entirely useless, Viereck explained in his 1953 book, *The Shame and Glory of Intellectuals*. As McCarthy raged, the Rosenbergs were executed, and Eisenhower attempted to steer a middle course between Taft Republicans and Stevenson Democrats, Viereck wrote that existing political categories no longer served to separate the artful dodger from the genuine dissenter. For this reason, Viereck explained, he was using the categories of liberalism and conservatism to describe psychological tendencies within American culture, not to denote political parties whose policies he supported or opposed.[25]

Contemporary American political values, Viereck said, together with literary and psychological sensibilities, were more accurately divided between the children of Burke and the children of Rousseau. The conservative descendents of Burke distrust human nature and believe in a political version of Original Sin, "which must be restrained by the traffic lights of traditionalism." The leftists and liberals are descendents of Rousseau, who "unconsciously assume the natural goodness of man—the less restrained in power the better." These conflicting temperaments, he wrote, are more fundamental than any political credo. They reveal the ethical and aesthetic "split between those who trust the 'natural goodness' of man and primarily want to release it from outer restraints, and those who fear his natural caveman propensities and primarily want to check them with *inner* restraints."[26]

Viereck's division of Americans into Burkean dissenters and Rousseauvian artful dodgers provided him with a valuable rhetorical distinction between real and artificial Americans. First, by substituting psychological restraint for political constraint, Viereck was able to defend cultural coercion while repudiating political coercion. Second, by rhetorically substituting political conservatism for traditionalism, he could conflate free verse, Romantic art, and anarchy with totalitarianism, while by circularly substituting cultural conservatism for political conservatism, he could attack both liberalism and conservatism as pseudoalternatives. Third, by extension of that argument he could claim that Nazis and communists were really only pseudoenemies of each other. Fourth, he could assert that he had made each of these rhetorical formulations not in the spirit of rancorous partisanship but in the name of a true conservatism, which was, by definition of his own will, indistinguishable from true liberalism. Such true conservatism and liberalism, Viereck cautioned in his fifth proposition for a restoration of a Burkean consensus in American national culture, could never be achieved politically through the failed Enlightenment ideologies that constitute party politics. It must be created, he wrote, through the coercion of an imposed traditionalism on the primitive violence characteristic of modern political passions.[27]

Therefore, Viereck, himself a literary artist, expected other artists and intellectuals of Cold War America to fulfil the vital role of culture-building as a means of nation-building. The responsible artist, he wrote, will reject the formless irrationalism of Romantic art and embrace the inner restraint of traditional classical art, to positively influence the national political values of Burkean conservatism. Meanwhile, because the true artist is always nonpolitical, as the true political conservative is indistinguishable from the true liberal, the artist will resist the outward demands of propaganda. By doing so, the true artist will serve his or her nation by preserving the vital inner vision of personal freedom, for a democracy must conserve the inner vision of freedom, as it presumably must enforce outward conformity through traditionalism, if it is to escape falling prey to totalitarianism.

Similarly, Viereck called for a new school of American historians whose institutionalized mission would be to research and inculcate in the popular imagination such Burkean defenders of the organic evolution of freedom as Gouverneur Morris, Rufus Choate, and John Randolph of Roanoke to replace "our revolutionary Tom Paine tradition." Since every human is a caveman by nature, capable of every insanity and atrocity, Viereck explained, "you must prefer art and artifice, classicism and formalized social convention to the cults of natural goodness, progressive education, and instinctive self-expression." For the same reason, Viereck continued, "you must prefer the 'conservatism' symbolized by the pruned and patterned gardens of Versailles to the 'anarchism' symbolized by the romantic barbarous jungle." The requirements of a democratic society to "prop up human dignity," Viereck insisted, justify the use of "powerful psychological safeguards." For Viereck, therefore, culture and politics finally shared a common dramaturgical responsibility for manipulating the sensibilities of the masses.[28]

It was by rediscovering Burke that Viereck located a theoretical foundation for restoring the cultural legitimacy of coercion through tradition in America. Burke provided an alternative approach to coercion through performativity when the terror and violence of the guillotine, the gas chamber, and the secret police had completely discredited the Enlightenment tradition of political coercion in Europe, and when it seemed it might yet succeed in the United States through the fanaticism of the communist Left or the radical Right. However, Viereck's neo-Burkean answer to the crisis of confidence in the Enlightenment itself might be said to have been based upon a confidence game, because his entire construction of freedom through coercion, his antirevolutionary defense of revolutionary values, and his antipolitical justification of political conservatism all depended, he acknowledged, upon "the clerks disillusioned even with disillusionment, revolting even against revolt."[29]

Viereck's political and cultural disillusionment, like that of his contemporary fellow poet and critic Paul Goodman, who made a similar plea for a true conservatism and liberalism in an age of artificiality in his book *Growing Up Absurd* (1960), was a sign of the crisis of confidence in the United States during the Cold War. In 1955 Viereck joined with Daniel Bell, David Riesman, Talcott Parsons and others as prophet to the self-consciously defined "age of anxiety," to warn against the radical Right. Viereck, Bell, and their whole coterie of anticommunist and antipopulist political and cultural elites, expressed the same essential message: "responsible" artists, intellectuals, and political and social critics must serve their nation by preserving confidence against doubt through illusion and manufactured consent.[30]

Viereck, however, complained that Americans were tragically hampered in their power to accomplish such necessary reforms because they had never embraced his political wisdom. Ironically, the irascible liberal Louis Hartz confirmed the conservative Viereck's lament in his classic jeremiad of consensus historiography, *The Liberal Tradition in America* (1955). Hartz claimed that true Burkean conservatism could not be found in the United States. Conservatism in the United States, declared Hartz, was merely a masquerade; behind the mask stood the grinning face of liberalism. The Harvard history professor reserved his most bitter sarcasm for the South because of its hypocritical facade of preserving Burkean tradition against the Lockean individualism of the North. Slavery, states' rights, and radical opposition to tariff in John C. Calhoun's politics and George Fitzhugh's sociology were as far from the organic corporate traditionalism of Burke, Hartz charged, as were the promotionalist schemes for industrializing the South promulgated by industrial entrepreneurs such as J. B. De Bow. He scoffed at the absurdity of a Comptean sociologist such as George Fitzhugh or a states' rights sectionalist such as John Calhoun posing as defenders of Burkean values. Instead of Burkeans, Hartz complained, "Southerners were false Burkes, halfway Burkes even in the time of their prime."[31]

Hartz wrote that the American national culture had been wholly formed out of transnational liberalism, which he called "Whiggery." It is a tradition that includes, he explained, English Presbyterians and Whigs, French Girondists and French liberals, and the American "petit-bourgeois" left and the "big-propertied liberalism" of the right. "Ultimately," wrote Hartz, "as with the Whigs, for all of the magical chemistry of American liberal society, we are dealing with social materials common to the Western world." Not only, therefore, did conservatism not exist in the fatal combination of Locke and New World abundance, but Turner's frontier of exceptionalism could not ever have existed because neither America nor its exploitable frontier was unique.

Hartz complained that Turnerian exceptionalism missed the point. American and European liberalism remained the same despite the abundance of land and resources that permitted Americans to live without European antagonisms. It was, he said, precisely those antagonisms that reveal the liberal mechanism in Europe, while it is their absence that indicates the same liberal mechanism at work in America.[32] Hartz, however, seemed unaware that his own jeremiad of the paucity of conservatism in the United States shared with Frederick Jackson Turner's elegiac frontier thesis a common historical argument for significance based upon the impact of an absence. Hartz's complaint, alongside Viereck's, that Burke was never imported into the American political consciousness, spoke eloquently of an opposite conclusion. Hartz and Viereck were their own best witnesses to Burke's importance for defining their own ideas of true conservatism and for establishing their interpretations of the failure of American liberalism as a form of Rousseauvian fellow traveling. Ironically for both Hartz and Viereck, therefore, Burke had become a central pillar of the Cold War through his very absence. Viereck and Hartz, along with other counterprogressives, had engaged in a kind of unconscious proto-Lacanian analysis to subtly transform Progressivism from a corporate conservative movement into a liberal one in the historical imagination. In empowering the idea of a patriarchal conservatism by its lack, they had subtly equated moral claims for individual responsibility with romanticism, while equating conformity to social convention with realism.

From this perspective, Hartz and Viereck simply affirmed Russell Kirk's positive argument, which he put forward in *The Conservative Mind* (1953), that a living remnant of an Anglo-American Burkean tradition still existed in Cold War America. Kirk had traced Burke's influence through the oppositional political philosophies of John Adams and John Taylor of Roanoke to the aesthetic visions of contemporary poets T. S. Eliot and Robert Frost. But, said Kirk, this Burkean tradition had been routed by the forces of radicalism. It lived on only as a small, critical voice of reason in a world of unchecked will and appetite.[33]

It was this common Burkean theme from the 1950s, of a noble lost cause of political virtue, which historian John Patrick Diggins used in the last decade of the Cold War to finally bridge Hartz's liberal jeremiad and Kirk's conservative jeremiad against acquisitive America and its critics on the left. Diggins appealed to Hartz and to Kirk in his jeremiad, *The Lost Soul of American Politics*, to defend a noble lost cause, not just of Burkean values, but of American national culture itself. Diggins called for a moral crusade of political renewal through the realism espoused by Reinhold Niebuhr, instead of the misplaced idealism that many historians of the United States had attributed to the republican tradition of civic virtue. Indeed, Diggins scoffed that the republican tradition of civic virtue was substanceless rhetoric. Mere words had fooled historians. They had confused the self-serving illusion of civic humanist posturings in pamphlets and broadsides for actual practice.[34]

But was the Burkean tradition in the United States routed, as Hartz, Kirk, Viereck and Diggins agreed? Or was the convention that Burkean conservatism was a noble lost cause, identified with the romantic South, a misleading conceit? Intellectuals such as Viereck, Hartz, and Kirk, politicians such as Woodrow Wilson, theologians such as Reinhold Niebuhr, sociologists such as Will Herberg, philosophers such as James Burnham, art critics such as Clement Greenberg and Dwight Macdonald, and playwrights and novelists such as John Dos Passos and Norman Mailer were all magnetically drawn by Burke's dramaturgical approach to power during the Cold War. They were drawn neither by the tragic nobility of a lost cause nor by the comedic possibilities of tilting at windmills. Rather, they were attracted to Burke's duplicitous rhetorical strategy, which they applied to their own versions of Cold War political theater. The neo-

Burkeans of the 1950s were consciously aware of the theatrical character of ideology, whether applauded as conservatism, denigrated as liberalism, or vilified as communism. They found Burke and his writings congenial because he was useful. They noticed his utility because they were attuned to the persuasive power of propaganda and the seductive influence of ideological rhetoric. This sensitivity to the dramaturgical implications of all forms of ideology was often, but not always, the result of disillusionment after an earlier attraction to Marxism with its conventions of masked interests and false consciousness. As sociologist Daniel Bell noted, the negative association of ideology with false consciousness, which Marx introduced, had become universally accepted by the Cold War era. It was an association shared by Marxists, liberals, and conservatives alike, despite the fact that it had the opposite meaning of pure rational thought when it was first coined in the eighteenth-century Enlightenment.[35]

Significantly, though the figure of Burke fell into disrepute following Wilson's tragic presidency, he gained even greater status after the Second World War, during the counter-Progressive era of consensus politics. Many of the disillusioned intellectuals who abandoned socialistic alternatives to capitalism, particularly Trotskyist ones, directly or indirectly appealed to Burke's writings to justify their retreat from utopian thinking. These anticommunist intellectuals drew convenient parallels between Burke's critique of the French Revolution and their own repudiations of the Russian Revolution. The Burkean view that politics is a form of theater provided a justification for a duplicitous rhetorical strategy for successfully promoting self-interested ends in a pervasive atmosphere of subversion and countersubversion. Burke provided an aesthetic and a political program for manufacturing confidence out of doubt and despair. He became the symbol of conservative integrity in an untrustworthy political world — the original historic voice of Anglo-American solidarity and a bulwark against modern totalitarianism.

5

The Neo-Burkean Renaissance

From the viewpoint of the twentieth century, the Edmund Burke of the eighteenth century had the historical advantage of remaining loyal to the British constitution and to tradition, yet supporting American grievances against the crown. Once more, he had repudiated the French assault on the monarchy, while he celebrated the Glorious Revolution, with which he associated America's grievances, contrasting its measured means and its restoration of order with the furious passions of the French Revolution. The "new conservative" neo-Burkeans of the Cold War could, therefore, claim membership in an unbroken Anglo-American political tradition. They could embrace the role of patriotic defenders of European values and American revolutionary liberty, and still repudiate the new Soviet communist order by associating it with the French revolutionary tradition.

Although, as we have seen, the neo-Burkean renaissance appealed to a wider circle of intellectuals than former Trotskyists, Burke's instrumentalist approach to the psychology of emotion especially resonated with the Enlightenment instrumentalism of Marxist praxis. Indeed, it was Marx, thinking of the French Revolution, who wrote that historical facts and personages are fated to appear twice—the first time as tragedy, the second time as farce—but his sentiments might easily have been inspired by Burke's *Reflections* and *Letter to a Member of the National Assembly*, which made exactly the same point.[1] For Burke, as for Marx, emotion was a raw material that could be instrumentally fashioned into organized social forms of power through the agencies of theater, art or propaganda.

Before and after World War I, as Wilson sought to shape public attitudes and institutions through Burkean oratory, the American cultural avant-garde discovered that, together, Marx and Freud extended the dramaturgical possibilities of social criticism. The new, anticommercial, theater movement, which emerged first in Chicago around 1910 and then matured in Greenwich Village, Washington Square, and Provincetown, insistently offered audiences emotional education into new levels of psychological realism. So too did the artists of the American secessionist movement, which began with Robert Henri's group, The Eight, around 1908, but later were eclipsed by their contemporary New Society of American Artists in Paris. Together, they turned American art away from what the New Society called the Decoration Trust. Such anticommercial art drew deeply upon the same Marxist and Freudian motifs that influenced secessionists in Vienna and Berlin, as well as, of course, in France.[2]

Then, during the 1930s, the Frankfurt school of sociologists brought their Marxian and Freudian critical theory to the United States. Exiled from Nazi Germany, this seminal group of social theorists, including Max Horkheimer, Theodor Adorno, Paul Lazersfeld, Erich Fromm and Herbert Marcuse, found a fertile ground of popular acceptance among American academics and theorists of popular culture. They warned against mass culture and the susceptibility of the modern mind to the domination of the authoritarian personality.[3] In theology, Paul Tillich, who had been a close associate of the Frankfurt scholars in Germany, brought a Marxist and Freudian message of alienation and dislocation to his American audiences when he emigrated from Germany in 1933. Before his exile, Tillich's theology of culture particularly emphasized the relation between the aesthetic and the religious in expressionist art. But Tillich did not return to writing about art again until the 1950s, when it was made politically safe to do so by the Frankfurt sociologists and art critics such as Clement Greenberg and Harold Rosenberg.

If Marxists and their new Freudian allies celebrated artifice as an industrial and cultural activity that promised to restore natural harmony to social relations and the private life before and after World War I, post–World War II Burkeans applied natural law to the process of fabricating aesthetic and political forms of "natural" authority. Conversely, however, if Burkean antimodernism scored the fraud and duplicity of revolutionary values and the triviality they spawned in mass culture, Marxian antimodernism decried the unreality of economic and cultural modernism, in which all that was solid melted into air. If the Burkean attack upon the fallen language of the French Revolution acknowledged the capacity of words to mask, rather than to reveal reality, Marxists attributed the same negative capacity to the fallen languages of ideology and utopia.

Not only, therefore, did the subversive power of rhetoric similarly shape Burkean and Marxist social criticism, but each used subversive rhetoric to promote necessary illusions as a strategy to counter false consciousness among the masses and the misguided elites who pandered to them. Marxists recognized the manipulative value of religion for preserving political interests, as did Burkeans, who found that quality useful. Finally, Marxists and Burkeans both fashioned a strategy for using natural law for utilitarian ends. Marxist Progressivism was based upon reversing the reactionary conclusions that flowed from the classical British economists. Burkeans reversed and stereotyped Rousseau's social criticisms to legitimize the existing interests of the educational, business and political elite.

Burkean "conservatism" met Marxian "radicalism" between the 1930s and 1950s, when former communists and sympathizers with the Russian Revolution discovered that they had misread the future. Trotskyism offered a halfway house for disappointed radicals, but neo-Burkeanism offered a mainstream avenue for rebuilding reputations. Many "new conservatives" imagined themselves as "new Adams of the fortunate fall," promoting themselves as Cold War realists. Most engaged in ritualized confessions at various stages of their careers, among them Richard Wright and Louis Fischer in the internationalist collection of essays *The God That Failed* (1949) and, much later, Norman Podhoretz's *Breaking Ranks* (1979) and William Barrett's *The Truants* (1982).[4] In each case, the prodigal son recounted his return to traditional values. Disillusioned idealists with tarnished reputations such as Sidney Hook, Daniel Boorstin, James Burnham, Granville Hicks, Midge Decter, Max Eastman, Gertrude Himmelfarb, and Irving Kristol were reborn as political sages who could claim succession in Burke's venerable revolutionary tradition of antirevolutionism. This was a strategy that mirrored the Marxist approach to power as counterideology.

Given the conditions of the Cold War, therefore, ideology as mask was transformed into mask as performance. Indeed, the rhetoric of theater pervades the culture of the Cold War from the era of Wilsonian propaganda to the House Un-American Activities Committee (HUAC) hearings, which Mary McCarthy noted were not aimed at gathering new information but were ritual performances.⁵ That rhetoric of performance constituted a victory for Burkeanism over Marxist analysis for such cultural leaders as Reinhold Niebuhr and Lionel Trilling and is a formula that may be seen in those influenced by Niebuhr and Trilling, such as Daniel Bell. His signature concept of disappointed Marxism and hopeful Burkeanism from the close of the 1950s was that of "the end of ideology."

The phrase "the end of ideology," which Bell popularized but did not invent, was a phrase that was endlessly repeated by social scientists and humanists alike throughout the 1950s. A slogan presented as an antislogan, it evoked a vague sense that a curtain had fallen on an episode in the Western struggle to achieve a virtuous civic community. Bell, who spent the rest of his academic career trying to explain exactly what he meant by "the end of ideology," always remained hopeful of a redemptive political, cultural, and religious future, despite a deep fear that memory was becoming too thin to preserve a living tradition capable of combating the degenerative forces of modernism into the next generation and beyond. For this reason, Bell said that he hoped that the end of ideology would not also mean the end of utopia, for the new generation needs passion and an outlet for those passions in "self-expression" and "self-definition" rooted in a stable memory, or tradition, of justice and order.

His argument, therefore, was that the future was both more hopeful and more dangerous because the old ideologies had become enervated and had degenerated into formalistic styles of rhetoric. They no longer were potent approaches for tapping emotional energy among the masses. Though these rhetorics had once been capable of igniting the sublime passions of self-sacrifice and visionary and apocalyptic fantasies, they had lost their aesthetic spark. Once vital as forms for organizing oppositional passions, they had become deadends to effective action among the twice disillusioned, whom Bell identified as his generation.⁶

Significantly, Bell used the same language to describe his own disillusionment with the ideological rhetoric of the Old Left, as did Old Left critics of commercial art such as Clement Greenberg and of commercial theater such as John Dos Passos and Elia Kazan. Even after his personal estrangement from radical politics in the 1930s, Bell continued to share a common view with the anti-Stalinist Left, that the meaning of life must be found through some "transforming moment" of personal experience. The creative energy of the artist, actor, or political activist, the twice-committed believed, could be released only if expressed in ways that were vitally connected to the emotional life of the masses. As early as the 1930s, however, Clement Greenberg echoed Frankfurt school warnings that kitsch could not permit the masses to escape manipulation because it too easily became propagandized. Later he suggested that the anti-Stalinism of the 1930s killed the aesthetic legitimacy of social realism in art and led from Trotskyism to art for art's sake, thereby heroically clearing the way for the abstract expressionist revolution that was to come.[7]

By 1959 Greenberg had replaced Marx with Burke, by way of Kant, Eliot and Irving Babbitt. They had become his new prophetic voices of artistic integrity. Abstract art, he claimed, was truly traditional art, since its form encouraged disinterested contemplation. Unlike the illusion of realism, he explained, the abstract form has a unity that may be taken in all at once. However, by eschewing the illusion of realism, abstract art could more naturally, more purely, and more disinterestedly approach the same goals motivating that realism in traditional Western painting styles.

The following year, in 1960, Greenberg traced the source of modernist art in the anti-Enlightenment values spawned by the Enlightenment. The Enlightenment threatened to turn art into pure entertainment. The falsely "[r]ealistic, natural art," Greenberg said, "had dissembled the medium, using art to conceal art." Modernism challenged this Enlightenment assault on the artistic experience by using art to call attention to art. That is, the real—the flat surface of the canvas, the shape of the support and properties of the paint's pigment—had traditionally been limitations to the artist in his or her effort to create the illusion of the real. Under modernism, said Greenberg, those limitations became the source of a new aesthetic experience of aesthetic confidence. The impressionists began this process, he explained, by leaving "the eye under no doubt as to the fact that the colors they used were made of paint that came from tubes or pots." Cezanne, in turn, sacrificed verisimilitude in his subjects in order to fit them into the rectangular shape of the canvas.

Such realism, however, while appearing to be a unitary expression of the natural, far superior to the illusion of mere representationalism, is not natural at all. Rather, it is a better artistic expression because it is a better confidence game upon the viewer. "The flatness toward which Modernist painting orients itself can never be an absolute flatness." The heightened sensitivity of the viewer to the canvas shatters the power of sculptural illusion, but in doing so succeeds in achieving optical illusion.

Such illusion, Greenberg insisted, was in turn based upon science, and, therefore, upon the cultural ground of visual experience alone, the basis of Western confidence since the Renaissance. In Greenberg's analysis, art, unlike religion, provides a link between the past and the present and between the personal and the social. Modernism is the very expression of tradition, not a break with the past. Abstraction preserves the authority of Western confidence through doubt by transforming the real into an illusion and by establishing the natural over the sublime, to achieve a Burkean solution to the problem of artistic truth rather than a Kantian one.[8]

John Dos Passos and Elia Kazan, though a generation apart, followed an odyssey similar to Greenberg's during the 1930s from their roots in the New Theater, moving from committed playwright and actor to reluctant defenders of American capitalism through the logic of their politics of performance. Dos Passos, the illegitimate son of a wealthy Wall Street lawyer of Portuguese descent and a southern gentlewoman named Lucy Madison, was trained in his privileged background to be an aesthete. Having studied art, music and poetry at Harvard, in 1916, after graduation and at his father's urging, he traveled to Spain to study architecture, and, apparently, theater, which also expressed the search for harmony and functional honesty within social space.[9]

Also, because of the circumstances of his birth, the hotel culture of his youth, and his Hispanic name, Dos Passos had come to feel like an outsider in America. Perhaps the distinctive combination of influences shaped his elite-democratic style of writing after World War I, in which his simple proletarian plays and novels exposed the ugliness of modern industrial life and contrasted it with the redemptive social potential in art. For Dos Passos in the 1920s and in the 1930s, the literary approach to social criticism blurred the lines between journalism and literature, and between real events and fictional events, reflecting the simultaneity shared in the art of modernist painters and in the cinema. The result was writing that was at once a scathing indictment of the fraudulent forces destroying American democracy and a celebration of America's cultural vitality.

His innovative 1937 trilogy, *U.S.A.*, for example, which Alfred Kazin said "breathes American confidence and is always so distinct in its effects as to seem simple," portrayed America as "complex, dark, and troubled." The work's very disenchantment gives it energy, Kazin concluded. Dos Passos mercilessly mocked the artificiality of Hollywood, public relations, interior decorators and the advertisement industry as the products of debased art, practiced by men and women who had surrendered their aesthetic vision to the forces of greed. *U.S.A* is a work, Miles Orvell noted, which is thoroughly rooted in the aesthetics of cubism and synthetic collages of the 1913 Armory Show.[10] But, like the earlier novel *Manhattan Transfer*, which Dos Passos published in 1925, *U.S.A.* also embraced the photographic realism and biographical narrative that was characteristic of Henri's New York secessionist artists. Dos Passos distorted space and time, embracing the whole world at once, but he also wrote journalistic prose that captured the newsreel and newspaper culture of industrial America and the echoes of ordinary speech. Dos Passos managed to write in both high and low style, capturing the two sides of the secessionist movement by writing with a balance between propaganda and artistic integrity that resembled the style of *The Masses*. That independent socialist magazine, which regularly carried the work of the New York secessionists, was edited by Max Eastman. Its radical style and antiwar stance made it a casualty of the censors during World War I, but it was reborn in 1927 with Dos Passos's support, and under party control, as the *New Masses*.[11]

It was a style, Dos Passos later acknowledged, that was also decisively influenced by his immersion in the new experimentalist theater after World War I. He had engaged in endless conversations with writer John Howard Lawson, of the New Playwrights Theater, whom he met in the Norton-Harjes ambulance unit during the war. Together they talked about how theater might be re-created on the models of the Moscow Art Theatre and the *Teatro Nacional* of Madrid, to bring emotional honesty and a greater sense of realism to the stage. Dos Passos felt that a national theater was the best possible organ for transforming predatory individualism and the greed for success that poisoned American values into group consciousness. His own first play, *The Garbage Man*, or *The Moon is a Gong*, as it was later renamed, was written in the midst of these discussions between 1916 and 1922. Dos Passos used jazz and vaudeville themes in part because he considered Yiddish theater, like the Madrid theater, to be true to emotional honesty and sociological reality. Genuine dialogue and true stage experience, which both versions of these people's theaters achieved, were missing from the commercial theater, Dos Passos charged, because they were missing in American society. A revitalized theater, he thought, would serve as a medium for promoting revolutionary social change.[12]

In 1924, a year before *Garbage Man* was produced by the Harvard Dramatic Club in Cambridge and Boston and *Manhattan Transfer* was published, Dos Passos wrote that American theater needed to move beyond the simple realism that film and photography had rendered obsolete. Theater, he argued, must instead cultivate emotional realism, unifying the fragmented bits and pieces of "our pigeonholed lives." Such modernist plays as Eugene O'Neill's *The Emperor Jones* and *The Hairy Ape* and his friend John Howard Lawson's *Processional* offered the potential for a new theater. The theater of emotional realism could exploit new rhythms of words and actions to "invade the audience's feelings by the most direct and simple means that come to hand." Dos Passos's interest in theater and his friendship with Lawson led him to become a director in the New Playwrights Theatre in 1926, and culminated in his visit to the Soviet Union in 1929. There, he attended theater nightly, and met a leading teacher of Stanislavsky's method, V. E. Meyerhold. He also met the great film innovator, Sergei Eisenstein, and embraced his use of film montage. Dos Passos was impressed by Eisenstein's use of that technique to direct, not just a dramatic performance, but space and time itself through rearranging it and synthesizing it in the cutting room.[13]

Dos Passos enthusiastically contrasted the vital Russian theater and film industry with the sick American theater. He attributed the health of Russian theater to its permanent staffs and regular companies of actors and to the freedom thus afforded them for engaging in experimental productions. American theater was hindered from achieving comparable artistic results, he complained, because companies struggling against budgets were unable to sustain permanent staffs and actors and because commercial values held by the public made it impossible to promote experimentalism.[14]

At the same time, however, he was alarmed by a smell of terror in the political climate of Stalinist Russia. That contradiction, between a flourishing aesthetic life and a decomposing political one, forced him to search for a new balance between political activism and artistic creativity in the 1930s. He did not find that balance in Trotskyism, as did many leftist American artists and writers, nor in Lovestonite communism, as did a smaller number of political activists searching for a viable alternative to the Stalinist Left. Rather, he began to look for it, as his father had, in an organic national consciousness that he believed resided in indigenous Anglo-American political institutions.[15]

That is why Dos Passos remained outside the party, despite his political agitation for leftist causes and arrest for syndicalism in 1931, while he was a member of the National Committee for the Defense of Political Prisoners. A vigorous defender of Sacco and Vanzetti in 1927, editor of *The New Masses*, and a proletarian novelist, he continued to regard communists with the same suspicion that his idol, Thorstein Veblen, had for capitalists. But his artist-heroes, like Veblen's engineer-heroes, were inseparably linked to the system of their own co-option. This was an irony that both Veblen, who died in obscure disillusionment in 1929, and the young Dos Passos, who wanted to save America, found intolerable.[16] Yet, despite his growing doubts about the Russian Revolution and his rapprochement with his father's politics in the 1930s, Dos Passos could remain aesthetically close to his Trotskyist friends. He did so, as a novelist and as a playwright, through the emotional realism of Stanislavsky's approach to acting—a systematic technique for breaking down a character's objectives and intentions and for turning the actor's emotions into an instrument for creating the illusion of reality—and through the psychological revolution in the modern perception of space and time in film montage and in modern art.

His return from the Soviet Union in 1928 preceded an indifferent production in early 1929 of his previously written play *Airways, Inc.* It was another of his less-than-successful efforts to use expressionist realism to attack the commercial values that permeated American society. After it closed, Dos Passos decided to resign from the New Playwrights Theatre. Complaining that the company could not decide whether they were interested in art or institution building, he then concentrated on writing novels. His disillusionment with communism continued to grow, as he extolled the Jeffersonian political tradition and voiced distrust of big government and big unions in the 1940s. Finally, he came full circle from his hatred of Woodrow Wilson and his war to his father's defense of Anglo-Saxon institutions and the Vietnam War. In the end, his desire for an organic national identity led from the search for a national theater to the search for a national politics, and, as it had for his father, to Burke. The dissident establishmentarian Burke had recognized that politics as theater was more effective than theater as politics, and so, finally, did Dos Passos. In the last decade of his life, on the pages of the *National Review*, Dos Passos would style himself a dissident conservative nationalist. He advocated Republican gradualism in civil rights, was virulently anticommunist, and attacked the misguided disruptions to social harmony fomented by the New Left.[17]

On the surface, Elia Kazan and John Roderigo Dos Passos were the most unlikely of cultural allies. They were the products of different generations and social circles. Kazan was the son of an unsuccessful Greek immigrant who was a rug merchant in New York, while Dos Passos's Wall Street attorney father had been born in pre-Civil War America. Yet both were drawn to experimental drama, film, and the novels of the 1920s. Both were entranced with the new techniques of emotional realism in the new theater movement, finding their creative attentions captured more by the practical details of stage construction and directing than acting. The two men shared a Cold War commitment to the use of theater to champion the cause of oppressed workers, which they later translated into a celebration of American nationalism. On a still more basic personal level, both were ambitious outsiders who used art to become insiders. Kazan had attended elite WASP educational institutions—Williams College and Yale Drama School—in the 1920s, while the older Dos Passos had attended Choate and Harvard before World War I. In each case the experience resulted in reinforced feelings of alienation from an elite world of wealth and privilege; yet at the same time, both men took advantage of the networks of opportunity provided by access to those institutions.[18]

In 1952, long after Kazan had repudiated communism, he testified at HUAC hearings against his old friends and old life. In that same year, Dos Passos, who also abandoned his old associations on the Left at the end of the 1930s, served as honorary head of the Writers and Artists for Taft Committee. By 1954 Dos Passos was no longer defending the New Playwrights Theatre of John Howard Lawson, but he continued to use the old techniques in the name of organic nationalism. So did Kazan, who was using the techniques he had learned from the new theater movement to feed the Hollywood and New York images of an American national culture in *On the Waterfront*. In 1954, too, Dos Passos published his anticommunist, anti-Hollywood, and anti-new theater movement novel, *Most Likely to Succeed*. The novel featured a thinly disguised parody of his old friend John Howard Lawson. It was also partly self-confessional about his own short stay in Hollywood.[19] Ironically, however, the protagonist of the novel also bore a striking resemblance to America's then-premiere director, Elia Kazan.

This fictional portrait of a brash young playwright and womanizer was a representation of everything Dos Passos disliked about communism and commercialism. The protagonist, Jed Morris, joined the left-wing

Craftsman's Theatre for the same self-advancing reasons and from the same misplaced idealism that had led Kazan to join the Group Theatre. Morris then rose to power in Hollywood, just as Kazan did. However, Dos Passos's morality tale parted company with Kazan's life in one significant way. Jed Morris's vanity and emotional weakness were so exploited by communist agents that he finally collapsed from the strain, while Kazan successfully made the transition from agitprop theatre to motion pictures and the Lincoln Center. Yet he too viewed his life in terms of betrayal and dissembling, which led from communism to commercial success and to both confidence and self-doubt.

In the end, the fictional Morris, like the real Kazan and Dos Passos himself, was transformed as the result of painful confrontations with suppressed doubts and false confidences. Each expressed fear of both the siren song of the communist Left and the lure of the fascist Right. Dos Passos looked nostalgically to a Jeffersonian past to escape this tension. Kazan embraced a corporate capitalist future. Their common rhetorical effort to discredit revolution as cultural fraud, however, helped channel cultural energy towards official power in the 1950s, and obfuscated the source of the artistic and moral constraints that shaped Cold War American national culture.

Kazan's significance for promoting a Burkean culture of confidence through self-confessed duplicity rested less in his eventual accomplishments as the leading stage and screen director of the Cold War (which he himself attributed to his powers of duplicity) than in his role in bridging the worlds of the anticommercial theater of the 1920s and 1930s and the corporate Hollywood of the 1940s and 1950s.[20] He did so as a direct result of his experience acting in the Group Theatre. There, Kazan learned the Stanislavsky method, or a version of "the method," as it came to be called, which was a system emphasizing the authority of the director and the necessity of a cohesive and stable group of actors. This combination made possible aesthetically greater realism and more dependably even dramatic performances. The Stanislavsky method provided a kind of system of quality control within the theater and film industries. Without the experience Kazan gained working with the Group Theatre, he could not so successfully have facilitated the absorption of the artistic innovations of the anticommercial theater into Hollywood film production during the 1950s, nor guided serious theater back from the little theater's insurgency on Broadway and into the corporate world of Lincoln Center.

The Group Theatre, which grew out of the experimental New Theater movement of the 1920s, was the inspiration of Howard Clurman, Stella Adler, Cheryl Crawford, and Lee Strasberg. Their dream of creating their own resident theater in America was realized during the summer of 1931 in Brookfield, Connecticut, with the financial backing of the Theater Guild and the private support of Maxwell Anderson, Edna Ferber, and Aaron Copland. Theirs was to be a theater company without stars, which would pay according to need rather than the dictates of the market. They would present serious drama, not Broadway spectacle, and would revolutionize American national culture. Like Dos Passos, the directors of the Group had taken the opportunity to watch the Stanislavsky approach in person, and incorporated his vision of total theater into their view, not just of the stage, but of political life as well.[21]

According to Clurman, the aim of the Stanislavsky system of acting is to enable the actor to attain an emotional truth on stage. If such truth were achieved in most productions, Clurman explained, there would have been little point in pursuing this system, which was not taught to novices but to experienced actors in each of their productions. "We were not satisfied with most of even the best previous productions, which seemed to us to show more competent stage craft than humanity or authenticity of feeling," said Clurman. "With few exceptions, what we saw in most shows was 'performance,' fabrication, artifice. Theatrical experience was, for the greater part, the antithesis of deportment rather than experience with direct roots in life. It seemed to us that without such true experience plays in the theatre were lacking all creative justification. In short, the system was not an end in itself, but a means employed for the true interpretation of plays."[22]

In 1924 Clurman had a bit part in a Provincetown Players production of Stark Young's *The Saint*. The play was not going well, and director Edmond Jones told the actors that theater should be like a light that the blind are made to see for the first time. It is a dream, he lectured them, that they come to view as a revelation. But Jones had complained to the troupe, "I do not see light, I do not perceive dream, I do not feel revelation." Clurman was touched by this speech, but, as a director, Jones had failed to make a connection with his actors. The Players were not enlightened by this criticism. They were merely embarrassed because "they did not speak his language, and he had been at no pains either to teach it to them or to translate himself into a language that might affect them." In other words, Clurman explained, effective acting rests not on the actor's rhetoric, but upon a rhetoric of theater that must be taught to the actors. "It was the leader's task," Clurman insisted, "to fashion a common language and common point of reference with those whom he hoped to lead." Clurman experienced that creation of a common language and purpose from the director brought in to save the production, Richard Boleslavsky, a student of Stanislavsky's who had come to America in 1920. It was from such inspiring examples, as well as from two exciting tours by the Moscow Art Theater itself in 1923 and 1924, that the idea of the Group Theatre was born.[23]

If the inspiration for the Group was centered in Howard Clurman, the driving force in defining and implementing it was Lee Strasberg. Strasberg stressed the absolute authority of the director in play production. His two cardinal principles for training actors in what he took to be the Stanislavsky approach were improvisation and affective memory. Both of these techniques were based upon intense emotional feeling, about which Strasberg was "fanatic," according to Clurman, and to which he made everything else secondary. Improvisation required the actor to confront problems that were emotionally analogous to those in the play. By acting impulsively, the actor would find solutions that could be brought to the play. In the second of these emotional techniques, the practicing of "affective memory," some very personal experience in the actor's past was used to bring intense emotional realism to a dramatic moment in the play.[24] The second of these approaches was no longer being used by Stanislavsky himself, because it was not stable enough to guarantee predictable results. Strasberg, however, continued to insist upon its use, even after Stella Adler returned from studying with Stanislavsky in Paris in 1934 and challenged Strasberg's version of Stanislavsky's method. That controversy eventually led to Strasberg's resignation and the breakup of the Group Theatre between 1937 and 1940.[25]

In 1932, the second year of the Group's existence, and with the country deep in the midst of economic depression, Kazan was hired by Clurman and Strasberg as a novice actor. He was fresh from Yale and without any other prospects at the time. He saw no future for himself in teaching or in directing community theater. Once more, he shared the Group's excitement at the possibility of transcending the artiness of the Broadway show and of achieving dramatic truth on stage. But Kazan lacked talent, at least in the ability to project emotion, which was Strasberg's major criterion for effective acting. Kazan managed to escape getting a pink slip, however, by making himself indispensable to the leaders of the company. He served in the kitchen and backstage, doing the detail work no one else wanted to do. He earned the nickname "Gadget," and proudly wore his worker's role in the Group, as he wore his worker's clothes in the street, sure that he was participating in the birth of a new order in society through his participation in a new artistic vision.[26]

Though "Gadget" Kazan resented the unacknowledged hierarchy in the Group, he subjected himself to it; he also joined the party, as the company achieved critical success. He did both because he needed emotional support, because he identified with their challenges to a hostile world, and because he was an opportunist. Kazan forthrightly admits in his autobiography that he played along to get along at the Group, just as he had done when serving his elitist fraternity brothers at Williams, when he had slaved away building sets and learning lighting at Yale, and as he would later do during the HUAC hearings after World War II. Through his self-abasement and his proud ambitions to become an actor and then a director, Kazan instinctively grasped the emotional power of performance. Already, in 1932, he understood that the secret behind the new approach of the Stanislavsky method was that it was more than a new technique of acting. It was a rhetoric of emotion, which he could use instrumentally to create realism on stage and to build confidence in life.[27] "Like many of you," Kazan later wrote to the readers of his autobiography, "I've worn the friendship mask; I often look friendlier than I feel."

But then, when I have what I sought, the mask would clatter to the ground, and what I truly am would be revealed. From time to time, I do what no one is prepared for, then someone is hurt or insulted or abandoned or simply puzzled. I let people come skin-close, until they trust me entirely and feel sure that I like them. But when the need is eased, the production opened, the seduction completed, I back away, suddenly become cool and remote, and those I've lured close don't know what happened. For years I declared myself an ardent liberal in politics, made all the popular declarations of faith, but the truth was—and is—that I am, like most of you, a bourgeois. I go along disarming people, but when it gets to a crunch, I am revealed to be a person interested only in what most artists are interested in, himself. I come on as a guy you can trust, but I'm just an ordinary, searching-surviving get alongnik, who doesn't like to be crossed, never forgets an insult, and, despite the ready smile, is angry a lot of the time—or at least looks angry, for reasons that are not quite clear. So I can't blame people for what they think of me.[28]

Kazan worked his way into being assistant stage manager for the first great success of the Group, their 1933 Broadway production of Sidney

Kingsley's *Men in White*. Then, building on that success, he was recruited by James Dombrowski and Myles Horton of the Highlander Folk School in Tennessee to direct his first film, *The People of the Cumberlands*. The film was given a private screening in the White House by Eleanor Roosevelt in 1938.[29] After *Men in White*, Kazan also became director of a collective of committed young players called the Action Theatre. Kazan reveled in the emotional power he wielded among them, as he imitated Strasberg's artistic authority. "They became my personal acting company," he remembered, "and I became, for a time, their hero." During improvisation exercises they would do anything he asked. Their emotion became so real, he said, that they had to be restrained from doing physical harm to themselves or others. Their dialogue was "absolutely true." Kazan's attachment to his players, however, was essentially one of power, and he eventually came to despise collective life among his actors, protesting that under the surface he was really an elitist. However, at the time, as an actor in such revolutionary plays as Clifford Odets's *Waiting for Lefty*, as a filmmaker, as a board member of a film cooperative called Frontier Films, and as an acting guru, he felt empowered by his collective identity as a communist and in his individual authority as a director. Like the other members of the Group, following the critical and financial success of *Men in White* on Broadway, he went out to take America by storm. They were like apostles of Jesus, he later remembered, "teaching, instead of brotherly love and the Ten Commandments, the art of Stanislavsky as filtered through Strasberg."[30]

Though Kazan repudiated many of his political commitments from the 1930s, testifying against his former friends and associates in the HUAC hearings of 1952, he did not repudiate the artistic values that he had developed at that time. Indeed, in 1988, he wrote that he still found that *Waiting for Lefty* thrilled him "to the verge of tears." [31] For the requirements of verisimilitude of dialogue and emotion that were absolutely central to the success of proletarian plays were also essential for the triumph of Hollywood cinema and advertisement, just as they had been for the great modernist plays of Strindberg, Ibsen, Chekhov and Shaw, near the turn of the century. Once more, such theater appealed directly to the desire for realism that the Wild West shows and naturalistic novels had prepared Americans to expect from the stage, without being able fully to deliver.

The decline of the Wild West shows and the new immediacy of radio and film intersected in the 1920s when Stanislavskian acting burst upon the American scene. Neither the modern theater, advertisement industry, film studio, nor political campaign could have delivered the new realism called for in the national interests of the Cold War and the corporate economy that burgeoned with it without a revolution in dramatic form. The Stanislavskian revolution in drama resulted in the complete disappearance of the theatrical style associated with the Old Vic. That stylistic change was not accomplished overnight. More "theatrical" styles of acting remained prevalent in American films until the Actors Studio began controlling access to the major acting opportunities after the early 1940s. Similarly, the anticommunist careers of post–World War II politicians such as Richard Nixon, Joseph McCarthy and Ronald Reagan were promoted because of voter-audience expectations. Many Americans found that theater was no longer so easily separated from the real, sociologist Erving Goffman suggested in his work at the time, and neither, by the 1950s, was there much distinction between entertainment and politics.

That same revolution in dramatic technique that Stanislavsky's method had codified had originally been useful to Stalin as he consolidated his power in the 1920s. Ironically, therefore, Stanislavsky survived the Stalinist era by achieving some of the same dramaturgical innovations for which he had been successful under the czar. Similarly, Elia Kazan, Lee Strasberg, and the acting establishment they created in the Group Theatre and, subsequently, in the Actors Studio, survived the American Right in the 1950s as a result of the same qualities of performativity that had made them useful to the Left in the 1920s and 1930s.

The translation of the anticommercial values of the Group in the 1930s to those of postwar corporate Hollywood and Broadway through the Actors Studio coincided with Kazan's own astute application of his artistic vision of serving workers to the serving of the national interest at the end of World War II. In 1946 Kazan and a group of Hollywood people had flown out to the Philippines and New Guinea to provide entertainment for soldiers who were wounded or preparing to return to combat. He considered the realism of war to have made the usual USO shows absurd, but he wanted to gain a sense of the reality of the war he had missed. Kazan found that he was energized by the desire for theater among the soldiers, and was surprised by their interest in his film *A Tree Grows in Brooklyn*, which they eagerly watched through many distractions. Then, during the tour, he contracted a jungle fever. He recovered with a resolve to re-create the Group Theatre experience and to build a truly national theater that would permit him to make the kinds of films and stage the kinds of plays of which he believed he was capable. This, he said, was the origin of the Actors Studio.[32]

Kazan had shed his communist ties during the war years, and, as a 4-F, he was free to make his way in Hollywood. He used the opportunity. In 1944 he signed a contract with Twentieth Century-Fox to direct five films over the next five years. Within a year after the birth of the Actors Studio, Kazan had three films in distribution—*Sea of Grass, Boomerang,* and *Gentleman's Agreement.* He was also directing two plays on Broadway, *All My Sons* and *A Streetcar Named Desire.* Kazan was working on two coasts, in two media, with access to the best talent available, and with almost unlimited funds to bankroll his efforts. Under those conditions, and given the new requirements for psychological realism that accompanied the end of the war, the stars were aligned for a director of Kazan's ambitions and training to establish a new version of the Moscow Art Theater for corporate America. The practical motivation for initiating his dream, however, seems to have occurred to Kazan later in 1946, after his return from the Pacific Theatre, with the critical failure of the play *Truckline Cafe.* It was written by Maxwell Anderson, an original backer of the Group, and coproduced by Harold Clurman and Kazan. That failure motivated Kazan to take the necessary steps to assure a supply of actors who were specifically trained for the kinds of productions he was promoting.[33]

It would be an exaggeration to suggest that Kazan created the Actors Studio by himself, or that it sprang only out of his personal vision. He was simply in a position to respond to a number of currents present in the political and economic climate of the country and the film and theater industries at the time. But, after voicing to Harold Clurman the need for a training system to avoid the problems that had marred the *Truckline Cafe,* he joined with Cheryl Crawford and Robert Lewis from the old Group Theatre, and such cast members from *Truckline Cafe* as Marlon Brando, Karl Malden, Kevin McCarthy, Peggy Merideth and Lou Gilbert, to create a studio for training actors in the Stanislavsky method.

The first meeting of the Actors Studio was held on October 5, 1947, at the Old Princess Theatre on Twenty-ninth Street. Among the guests were Arthur Miller and Tennessee Williams, the two leading playwrights of the post–World War II theater. Kazan warned the assembled actors on that first night of the seriousness of the commitment he demanded of them. Unexcused absences from classes would not be tolerated, he told them. "We want a common language," John Garfield remembered

Kazan saying, "so that I can direct actors instead of coach them . . . so that we have a common vocabulary." The studio is not a school, he insisted, but rather "a place to work and find this vocabulary."

Kazan's signature work occurred during this period: *A Streetcar Named Desire* and *Death of a Salesman* on stage and *A Streetcar Named Desire, Gentleman's Agreement, Viva Zapata!* and *On the Waterfront* on film. Those successes testified to the effective packaging of actors and the cult of the director. Time and cost were saved because directors could rely on a standardized formula rather than having to deal with many different styles and artistic interpretations. Significantly, Kazan did not originally include Strasberg in the Actors Studio because, despite his principles of absolute directorial control, his emphasis on emotional recall had proven too inefficient and created unpredictable results.[34] The Stanislavsky method, therefore, was not, as Richard Pells suggested, an unfocused and bohemian movement anticipating the fad of existentialism and the sixties youth culture. It was instead a Burkean formula for controlling the power of performance in the interests of efficiency in delivering a product that would bring corporate profits. It made possible maximum production together with a stranglehold upon artists' careers. By transforming acting into real behavior, the real world had become subject to control. The immediate experience of performance was harnessed as a sublime formula for producing packaged emotions that could be sold to the millions.[35]

Once more, the power of the Actors Studio, as one vehicle through which emotion could be rendered economically useful, coincided with the distribution of the new medium of television. Not only did the Actors Studio supply the actors and the stage managers for television drama, but as early as 1948 they supplied the shows for it on ABC and on CBS. Richard Boone, Martin Balsam, Mildred Dunnock, Tom Ewell, Julie Harris, Cloris Leachmen, E. G. Marshall, Nehemiah Persoff, Kim Hunter, and Eli Wallach are but a few of the names that became fixtures of the television world of the Cold War era, as other actors, directors and scenarists were blacklisted because of former communist associations, or lost legitimacy because they acted or staged from another tradition.[36]

Nevertheless, a Burkean formula should not suggest that crass commercialism reigned at the expense of artistic integrity. Commercial success had to be served, just as theater had to be useful as an ideological weapon for the Left, if art was to be grounded in realism to anchor the performance. Crass commercialism, like vulgar Marxism, was unacceptable, however, because it revealed only the surface character of an aesthetic experience. Consequently, a director such as Kazan was distressed when, by the close of his career, he perceived that the Stanislavsky system had become a racket. He really did, as a director, make artistic judgments that cost money in production. But, just as Kazan insisted that film was more real than theater because the camera is entirely limited to appearance, the confidence artist must appear sincere, even to him- or herself, if the performance is to be creditable. Once more, since the end of any Burkean performance is confidence, not a leftist commitment to social change or a rightist commitment to profits, the power of a Burkean position such as Kazan's was that it transcended either of these political limitations by rhetorically promoting realism as a pattern of performance. As Erving Goffman argued in *The Presentation of Self in Everyday Life* (1959), echoing Burke, Dos Passos and Kazan, "a character staged in a theater is not in some ways real, nor does it have the same kind of real consequences as does the thoroughly contrived character performed by a confidence man; but the *successful* staging of either of these types of false figures involves use of *real* techniques—the same techniques by which everyday persons sustain their real social situations."[37] For Goffman, living in society was literally an exercise in Stanislavskian theater.

In the post–World War II period, modernist visual artists were similarly expected to play the role of rebels against the establishment, looking into their individual souls to confront their alienation. Alcoholic despair and existential angst were proof of the authenticity of their artistic themes of anxiety and individual freedom, just as they were for artists in other media during the late 1950s. But rather than embracing the antitheatrical impulse of existentialism, which it mimicked, aesthetic rebellion in the 1950s was a highly stylized pose. Artists had become sufficiently conventionalized in the public imagination to press them into a special social role. That role most resembled Erving Goffman's description of stigmatization as a consciously assigned formula for social self-adjustment.

The stigmatized individual, explained Goffman in 1963, is asked to bear the burden of being for others what they decline to let him or her be for them. The social roles of stigmatization, consequently, are quite contrary to those of existentialism, as it was expressed in the writing of Dostoyevsky, Kierkegaard, or Nietzsche, though something close to this was suggested by the twentieth-century French existentialist-celebrity, Sartre. However, instead of an "authentic existence," based on the integrity of a chosen self, which even Sartre preserved from his nineteenth-century sources, Goffman presumed a performance in which a phantom acceptance of the stigmatized individual or group provides the base for a phantom sense of being normal. If a stigmatized person wishes to live as normally as possible in that assigned role of being "who he really is," said Goffman, then the best strategy may be "the one that has the false bottom; for in many cases the degree to which the normal accept the stigmatized individual can be maximized by his acting with full spontaneity and naturalness as if the conditional acceptance of him, which he is careful not to overreach, is full acceptance."[38]

Goffman suggested that the stigmatized individual may be an outsider for a variety of reasons: as the result of positive or negative qualities, for reasons of race or gender, or for crossing social boundaries or cultural norms. In this sense, therefore, such icons of the 1930s, 1940s, and 1950s as the lonely gangster or the hard-boiled detective, the misunderstood artist or the troubled adolescent, the dedicated crime fighter or the repentant communist and fellow traveler could all carry the conventions of the stigmata. In fact, Richard Wright wove all those conventions together in his celebrated 1940 novel, *Native Son*, a work that reflected Wright's immersion in the conventions of Robert Park's and Louis Wirth's Chicago sociology.

Bigger Thomas, the novel's social deviant, exhibited less self-awareness than Wright's later heroes, Cross Daimon of *The Outsider* (1953) and his underground man, who showed the influence of the vogue of existentialism in the France of the 1940s, where Wright had exiled himself. Young Bigger Thomas was, like the bulls Wright described in *Pagan Spain* (1957), a victim of socially projected guilts and aggressions unleashed by capitalist systems of exploitation. Indeed, throughout Wright's work, both before his private repudiation of communism in 1937 and after his public one in 1946, his male protagonists remain performers who attempt to escape suppression and repression from the blind forces of sub-conscious malice. His heroes, like the black bulls that were sacrificed in the ring, are unconscious victims who become conscious martyrs to the alienation they expose. Their existential choice is limited to embracing the stigmata revealed through the consciousness of their own isolation.

The success of *Native Son* made Wright a celebrity, and with that singular status for an African-American writer came a heightened conflict between the requirements of public performance and personal authenticity, as it did for other celebrity-writers of the 1950s such as

J. D. Salinger, Ernest Hemingway, Ralph Ellison, Thomas Pynchon, and Norman Mailer. The role taken on by these celebrity-writers, along with entertainers such as Lenny Bruce, Charlie Parker, and Liberace, comic book heroes such as Superman and Batman, and television's Lone Ranger, was to mediate the tension between actual and virtual social identities—that is, the condition of performance itself and the social role Goffman specifically attributed to the stigmatic hero.

Indeed, the cowboy heroes were the most conventionalized stigmatic figures of the Cold War period. They were ubiquitously present on television and in the films during the 1950s. They both idealized and abstracted the social deviant from the human community and were prime bearers of the stigmata of individualism. Therefore, like Franciscan saints, they remained outside of society and close to nature, living lives that were chaste and close to poverty. Television and film westerns were not, therefore, promoted as realistic re-creations of the West, as were the performances of Buffalo Bill and his imitators before the First World War. Nor were the westerns of the 1950s escapist romances of the carefree old West of the imagination. Instead, they were negative markers for social conformity, much as was a deviant "New American style" artist such as Jackson Pollock.[39]

Pollock's action painting merged the western regionalism of his teacher, Thomas Hart Benton, with the new international modernism, which was eventually named abstract expressionism. He was lionized as a larger-than-life individualist who splashed color across oversized canvases, reflecting the kind of commitment to action seen in silver-screen westerns. Action paintings and westerns alike visually symbolized America's heroic challenge to false materialist realism, whether embodied in slavish imitation of official Soviet art or in the mindless conformity of suburban American life, through a commitment to emotional realism. Both were art forms of sublime obliteration that eliminated contradictions through theatrical representations of violence. Other abstract expressionists, such as Franz Kline, Mark Rothko, and Clyfford Still, used the ominous colors and anxious tones of brooding European worldliness to add depth to the romantic individualism of the artist-hero that each embodied. "To express these times," a *Life* reporter explained in 1959, "they felt they needed a style that was tense, explosive, mysterious, and altogether new." They wished not to paint a picture of a suffering individual, the reporter explained, but "to evoke the actual sensation of suffering through the use of foreboding colors, clashing shapes or lines that hurtle restlessly across the canvas."[40] Their claim of affecting emotion directly, as an unmediated psychological performance, could be validated only through the artificial authority of the market. Art for art's sake, the manifesto of Cold War anticommunist aesthetics, therefore, insisted that each artist's authenticity depended upon the achieving of a unique individual style, which, once achieved, had to be maintained to assure dependable public recognition of the artist who created it. The work of art was a direct performance of the artist's personality, a piece of celebrity, which needed the unmediated recognition of its author to become genuine.

Paradoxically, too, the legitimate theater was becoming devalued and trivialized at the same time that theatricality was invading every aspect of life. The making and manipulation of images, therefore, increasingly dominated the relationships among all elements of Cold War politics and culture. This was not just because corporate economic interests bought performance talent to create a market for consumption through advertisement. The incorporation of the arts in post-World War II America was an acknowledgment, as well, that confidence could be preserved only through the same forms of entertainment media, public relations campaigns, and advertising as had raised doubts about the meaning and value of social experience in the first place. Because of the development of technical capabilities necessary for a comprehensive manipulation of emotional realism, theater and film became the vehicles for a revitalization of the sublime in an age of nuclear terror. They provided the cultural ground, as nuclear science provided the scientific ground, for achieving a virtual reality—of the self, in the former, and of the cosmos, in the latter. By definition, virtual reality is a purely artificial nature, and artificial nature is the very substance of the sublime.

Above all, that achievement preserved a common Marxist and Burkean front against existentialist personalism, which was a traditional and conservative alternative to ethical and political expediency. Indeed, the socially and theologically conservative Kierkegaard, who became known to Americans in the 1940s and 1950s, like the anti-Wagnerian, Nietzsche, challenged the legitimacy of a theatrical definition of personality as a substitution for personalism. Like Dostoyevsky, whose writing also gained prominence in post-World War II America, these social critics warned against the conflation of the sublime and the religious, a confusion that Jonathan Edwards had failed to recognize more than a century before. The image of existentialism as an innovative fad of modernist posturing, which led to revolutionary violence in the 1960s, was a characterization that gained credibility from sociologists such as Will Herberg and Daniel Bell and literary critics such as Lionel Trilling.[41] Earlier interpreters of existentialism, such as Martin Buber and Paul Tillich, argued during the 1950s that existentialism was drawn from medieval mysticism and classical Greek philosophical rationalism.[42] The 1970s image of existentialism as a false modern consciousness born of romantic posturing, or Trilling's wrong cultural road of following authenticity over sincerity, derived from Burkean rhetorical strategies for discrediting personalism. They were formulae for transforming personal responsibilities into theatrical performances to serve the advertising interests of a corporate economy.

One political expression of that Burkean strategy may be seen in the creation of the Congress for Cultural Freedom, a reprise of such Popular Front organizations as the First American Writer's Congress of 1936 or the International Association of Writers for the Defense of Culture. The CCF was founded under officially secret, but transparent, CIA sponsorship in 1950. Many "new conservatives" and chastened liberals, from ex-Marxists such as Sidney Hook, Clement Greenberg, James T. Farrell, John Dos Passos, and Richard Wright to non-Marxists such as Daniel Bell, Allen Tate, and Arthur Schlesinger, Jr., enthusiastically joined their voices together at international conferences and in CIA-sponsored journals of opinion. Together, they attempted to create a positive propaganda movement that would build a Euro-American solidarity and discredit communist propaganda. At the same time the CCF championed individual artistic and political freedom, its members worked to silence the ethical qualms of naive liberals and democratic socialists. Misplaced idealism, CCF participants and government sponsors agreed, played into the hands of totalitarian master planners. Although most CCF participants also distrusted the radical Right, they read the political Right as a benchmark of realism. They routinely attributed false consciousness to the Left, and cast aspersions on those who advocated a neutral or third way. The "end of ideology," which was a prophesy and battle cry for the CCF, therefore, was not a phrase of new beginnings and alternative utopias, as it was actually used. It was utilized as a rhetorical weapon for building a corporate, anticommunist security system through culture. It was an instrument for winning the Cold War, not an effort to extend dialogue.[43]

The institutionalized effort to shape American culture through secret government support of groups such as the Congress for Cultural Freedom, however, could not manufacture a common American stamp upon international art, literature and politics. That attempt, led by cultural moles and those involved in militarism abroad and by government bureaucrats, foundations, and former communists at home, would probably have been no more successful than was the Popular Front in winning the world to communism in the 1930s. At least in the United States, however, popular media cooperation with the government and semiofficial groups such as the CCF did reflect a national cultural unity. The unity was not that of a consensus, which counter-Progressive historians and social scientists thought they observed among Americans; rather, it grew out of a prior consent that had been won, or coerced, by the early 1950s from a wide cross-section of the public, including minorities, women and adolescents. While a power elite from government, academia, entertainment and business may be shown to have appealed to a nonexistent Cold War consensus for narrowly defined national ends in the post-World War II era, their success in persuading themselves and many other Americans that it existed still depended upon their ability to inspire a personal willingness to consent in that wide cross-section of Americans who shaped national public opinion. Modern art, both fine and commercial, and the Stanislavsky approach to acting in film, stage, on the political stump, and through images in advertising presented avenues of performance for manufacturing such consent and marginalizing dissent.

Successful smiths of public consent relied neither on propaganda nor coercion, though both existed and were pursued at the time. Instead, they followed a Burkean strategy for fighting the Cold War and for constructing an apparently organic national culture. One indication that such consent was preserved through a Burkean strategy, when Burke was rarely acknowledged directly by consensus intellectuals and social scientists, was the 1947 republication of Tocqueville's classic *Democracy in America*.

Russell Kirk noted that Tocqueville was "shot through with Burke," yet *Democracy in America* became almost a sacred text for counter-Progressive historians, sociologists, political scientists, and literary critics.[44] The privileged position accorded to Tocqueville by liberals and conservatives alike adds additional evidence that Burke's influence on American Cold War culture was far more pervasive than Hartz's myopic emphasis on Lockean individualism suggested at the time. It is one example of the way Burkean conventions of performance transcended liberal and conservative sensibilities during the Cold War.

Tocqueville's significance for the Cold War Burkean revival, which tended to reduce moral and religious aspects of personal responsibility to performance, may be usefully explored through the work of Marvin Meyers, a historian who had been a dissident Marxist in the 1930s. In 1957, two years before Erving Goffman published *The Presentation of Self in Everyday Life*, and in the midst of a dramaturgically oriented era of social analysis, Meyers published his influential monograph, *The Jacksonian Persuasion*.[45] Meyers's historical study, like Goffman's sociological one, was a study in manufacturing consent through theater. Goffman was influenced by the sociology of Edward Shils and David Riesman, and, therefore, assumed the social construction of reality, as did Meyers, who acknowledged his intellectual debt to the historian Richard Hofstadter and to Riesman. He also expressed reassurance in finding himself "in agreement with Hartz on many points, especially the value of Tocqueville for understanding American political thought and experience."[46]

The Jacksonian Persuasion was a book about political rhetoric and belief. Historians, Meyers explained, "dramatize politics because politics, especially in democratic communities, dramatizes life." Jacksonian politics, like Cold War politics, Meyers suggested, reflected the tensions and anxieties of democracy in crisis. It was a time of ideology and avarice, in which the innocence of the earlier republic had been lost, and a society that was "drawn fatally to the main chance and the long chance, to the revolutionizing ways of acquisition, emulative consumption, promotion, and speculation," was replacing it.[47] Meyers's mission as an American historian, he explained, was to search for "the major plot expressed in Jacksonian political appeals, with the hope that character, scene and episode" would be given order and meaning so that its lessons could be applied to the present. The central lesson that Meyers learned and communicated was that consensus could evolve from conflict. A balance of interests and a future of equalitarian promise could be restored in Cold War America, as in the nineteenth century, through the flawed process of a sometimes corrupt, and usually self-serving, party politics. History taught Meyers that if the persuasive appeal of Jacksonians had rested in their ability to tap the sense of fear and resentment the masses felt in their changing lives, then by happy contrast the Whig opposition affirmed the material promise that gave optimism to the American way of life.[48]

Meyers, however, found that the Whig conservatives who defended the corporations as engines of progress and resisted the view that economic depression anticipated the collapse of the social order were as blinded by their violent hatred of Jackson and as fearful of the masses as the Jacksonian democrats were consumed by paranoia and nostalgia for a half-imagined innocence. Once more, politicians, whether conservative or liberal, were all too prepared to compromise with the corruptions required for maintaining power and to surrender the "valuable interests of society to the pocket-pickings." The paradox of American national politics, Meyers concluded, certainly with an eye to contemporary politics, is that "out of the mouths of politicians have come the best public teaching of their times, but also, sadly, much mindless huckstering."[49]

Meyers found in Tocqueville not only the recognition of this democratic dilemma in the Jacksonian period but an ironic model of the intellectual of integrity prepared to transcend the "*trahison de clercs*" with the same commitment to ambiguity that the intellectuals in the Congress for Cultural Freedom were attempting to institutionalize. This was, above all, a style of dispassionate, but knowing, appreciation for ambiguity in moral matters that reserved conviction for matters of strategy. "The community shares many values," said Meyers, and "at a given social moment some of these acquire a compelling importance." The political expression that is given to these values Meyers called "a persuasion." It was this rhetorical massaging of the acquisitive instincts of the lawless individual that had saved Jacksonian Americans from themselves. Tocqueville, he said, had observed the living principle of democracy in the archetypical American. Meyers characterized this American Adam as the paradox of the "venturesome conservative." Status anxiety, insatiability, and greed were embedded in American national character, he learned from Tocqueville, along with the love of freedom, fear of change and equalitarianism. Meyers praised Tocqueville for his paradoxical vision, which contrasted these antithetic forces of liberation and servitude to reveal both the source of social conflict and the "tameness in the marrow of the tiger's bones."[50]

Above all, Tocqueville had created for Meyers, and for a whole generation of consensus historians, a vision of a democratic sublime, terrible in its conformity, empty of conscience, and terrorized by change, yet grand in its expansive drive to realize itself, in its power to erode divisions within itself, and in its ability to embody the ideals of sacrifice for the future. Tocqueville and his incessantly quoted *Democracy in America* offered students of the American national character a frightening sense of irrelevance before a natural process of revolutionary change and a personal sense of significance through the law of equality. He provided a Burkean witness who approved of the American Revolution, distrusted the French Revolution, and legitimized the national obsession with preserving the supposed uniqueness of American national character through the social sciences.

By confusing the distinction between consent and consensus at the heart of Cold War America, the historians and social scientists who, like Meyers, embraced Tocqueville, blurred the distinction between politics and culture and between coercion and conversation. Therefore, Burke seemed on the surface to be irrelevant to what passed for both liberal and conservative realities in the United States. Few could find reason to believe that the Burkean virtues of aristocratic traditionalism, civility, piety, and classicism could ever define the American way of life. But those who longed for a Burkean revival of humanism or of political conservatism, as well as those who dismissed those possibilities, missed the substance for the style of Burkean ideas. They did so because, in Burke, the style is meant to hide the substance. As a politician and as an aesthetic theorist, he was interested in manufacturing consent where consensus did not exist, not in nostalgically promoting a noble lost cause of social harmony. Consensus suggests a common purpose and perspective, which may be achieved in a family or community through dialogue. But consent requires neither; it depends upon the power to manipulate doubt and confidence. That was the power offered by Burkean conventions to successful Cold War intellectuals, politicians, and artists, because that was the power used by Burke against the supporters of political dissent in England, France and the United States to preserve British nationalism in the eighteenth-century Enlightenment age of revolutions.

6

Max Weber and the Spirit of Confidence

Warren Susman (1927–85), among the most perspicacious of American Cold War historians, wrote that every critical perspective on American consumer culture, whether Marxist radical or middle-class liberal, is finally derived from Max Weber and his analysis of the iron cage of modern materialism.[1] Susman was deeply ambivalent about this Weberian perspective on the character of American national culture. Though critical of many aspects of what he chose to call the "culture of abundance," Susman also wished to offer an affirmation against the pervasive pessimism he felt was Weber's negative legacy for Americans. Like Susman, most American critics have found Weber's analysis compelling but have simultaneously sought to escape the implications of his ideas. Ironically, therefore, Weber's ideas, which challenged American confidence even as they affirmed its necessity, have spawned an equally divided response from his readers. Like Susman, most American readers of Weber have sought at once to affirm and to deny the implications of his analysis for the nation's future.

In *The Protestant Ethic and the Spirit of Capitalism*, Weber presented a complex morality tale about the triumph of "the iron cage" of the modern world over the religious world of the Middle Ages. That work was also a masquerade behind which he sought to preserve his own balance of freedom and discipline against the contrasting implications of America. In *The Protestant Ethic*, Weber contrasted the natural spontaneity of Lutheran reciprocity towards the world, Gemütlichkeit, with "the narrowness, unfreeness and inner constraint" of Calvinism, which was literally destructive of spontaneity. In making this dichotomy, Weber was particularly interested in the psychological sanctions that originate in religious beliefs but are then transformed into cultural directions, persisting long after the distinctive features of the earlier beliefs have been eroded by time. He recognized that, historically speaking, Calvinism and Lutheranism could not really be divided. For not only had Calvinism "spiritually" grown out of Luther's influence, but Lutheranism could not have achieved "permanent concrete" success without Calvinism. In saying so he announced the double bind at the heart of his thesis: Calvinism was both necessary and destructive to the Lutheran Reformation, as Calvinist asceticism was necessary to the capitalism that destroyed it.[2] Weber could not offer a dialectic in order to resolve this history. For, although the natural spontaneity of trust required the artificial instrumentality of confidence to sustain it, spontaneity could not survive its own routinization. Weber could not surrender his need for trust or romantic spontaneity, but he needed confidence to believe in the possibility of trust and to fulfil his responsibility of vocation. How had such a tragic double bind come to pass?

Weber's method for answering this question was to return to a moment of origin of the "disenchantment of the world," by artificially separating the Lutheran and Calvinist understandings of vocation. This, he believed, would unlock the secret of the continuing cultural implications inherited from the transformation of the West since the sixteenth century.

The Lutheran idea of vocation, which affirms the individual in the place and within the limits God has provided, Weber explained, meant that "ethical principles for the reform of the world could not be found in Luther's realm of ideas." Luther, therefore, could not be identified with the rise of capitalism because "Lutheranism, on account of its doctrine of grace, lacked a psychological sanction of a systematic conduct to compel the methodical rationalization of life." In the Calvinist conception of the calling, in contrast, "the emphasis is always placed on the methodical character of worldly asceticism, not, as with Luther, on the acceptance of the lot which God had irretrievably assigned to man." The Calvinist steward must be willing to become wealthy for God's glory, "hence the faithful Christian must follow the call by taking the opportunity." The subtle difference between making the best of what God gives and getting the best one can get for God's glory "had far reaching psychological consequences," according to Weber, "and became connected to a further development of the providential interpretation of the economic order which had begun in scholasticism."³

Essentially, then, Weber's problem was the same one identified by Burke and echoed by Melville in *The Confidence-Man*, and which Perry Miller and Reinhold Niebuhr made central to their readings of Weber in relation to American Puritanism: openhearted trust may be the vital spirit of human relations, faith in God, and indeed, of all redemptive hope, but trust is impossible to sustain without confidence. However, Weber's own divided attitude toward ineffectual but natural Lutheran romanticism and dynamic but utilitarian Calvinist realism has tended to obscure his careful reservation that Calvinism did not create capitalism. Rather, for Weber, Calvinism and capitalism shared a common utilitarian ethic, which capitalism needed in order to overcome religion. That ethic, for Weber, could be identified only by locating a common religious moment of value that did not participate in the formula of power shared by Calvinist asceticism and capitalism. Since, Weber insisted, "Luther can not be claimed for the spirit of capitalism in . . . any sense whatever," he provided Weber with a myth of the origin of the capitalist spirit, in the isolation of dynamic confidence from passive trust, and the subsequent victory of pure confidence over trust.⁴

Weber identified this pure confidence, as a dynamic force of self-creation, with the United States. Like Luther's Reformation, America was a new country, a point of origin at which the passage from spontaneity to routinization and democracy to bureaucratization could be observed. Weber traveled to the United States in 1904, visiting New York, St. Louis, the Tuskegee Institute in Alabama, and distant relatives in North Carolina and Virginia. He was interested in observing, in a firsthand way, the problems the new society faced: racism, immigration, labor unrest, city management. But Weber's trip to the United States came just after his completion of the first half of *The Protestant Ethic*, and it was particularly the relation between American Calvinist sects and the spirit of capitalism that absorbed his attention. Thus, *The Protestant Ethic*, which was completed upon his return to Germany, drew personally on his own family history in Germany and America. In his great sociological study, he embedded himself within his analysis of the common cultural dilemmas of Heidelberg, Germany, and the Blue Ridge Mountains of North Carolina.⁵

Weber reflected on his experiences during this trip to the United States in an essay, "The Protestant Sects and the Spirit of Capitalism."

Noting the historical linkage between confidence and religion, he explained that " 'the sinful children of the world' distrust one another in business but they have confidence in the religiously determined righteousness of the pious." Weber found contemporary evidence of the continuing reality of this association of religion and capitalism in the America of 1904, despite his belief that asceticist sects were in a state of decay, rotting into "the mundane passions" that reduced them to a pure essence, without internal definition.[6]

While riding on a train through "Indian territory," Weber interviewed a travelling salesman, who explained to Weber why doctrine was unimportant in America, while church membership was very important. "Sir, for my part everybody may believe or not believe as he pleases," said the salesman. "But if I saw a farmer or businessman not belonging to any church at all, I wouldn't trust him fifty cents. Why pay me if you don't believe in anything?" Similarly, at a baptism in North Carolina, Weber's relative explained to him that acceptance into the fellowship of the sect through adult baptism was essential for a successful business career in the area. Being accepted into a voluntary sect, like the Baptists, he learned, stood as a guarantee of respectability. "This stands in contrast to membership in a 'church' into which one is 'born' and which lets grace shine over the righteous and the unrighteous alike," Weber concluded. Clearly, the confidence placed in the member of a voluntary sect was a guarantee of his or her respectability, even to those outside the sect. Once more, such confidence extended by the members of the sect obligated them to come to the aid of any of their number suffering from hard times. Bringing in a new member obligated them to the maintenance of their own confidence, and that of the world, through guaranteeing the reliability of the new member.[7]

For Weber, the consequences of such reinforcing demands for confidence led beyond capitalism to pure confidence itself. He decried the "iron cage" of the spirit of capitalism, in which all religious foundations had dwindled away and the attempt even to justify the pursuit of wealth (or the confidence that stands behind the wealth) was no longer required. "In the field of its highest development, in the United States," he wrote, "the pursuit of wealth stripped of its religious and ethical meaning, tends to become associated with purely mundane passions, which actually give it the character of sport."[8] Similarly, in his essay "Science as a Vocation," published just before his death, Weber grieved that German life was being Americanized, much as he had earlier grieved that Lutheranism had been absorbed by Calvinism. The German university, he said, still writing from his sense of displacement in the world, was being subverted by American bureaucratic values much as capitalism had undercut the competency of artisans in earlier generations.[9]

Weber's peculiar struggle between his desire for confidence and his horror of it was explored within the context of international Calvinism and the United States of the Open Door. This made him sensitive to the fact that confidence was a cultural approach to the problem of power and value, which, while not invented in the United States, had been universalized into a national ideology by Americans. For this reason, the German sociologist provided a useful framework for those twentieth-century American critics such as Perry Miller, who posited a unique Anglo-American Protestant culture that had lost its mission, and Reinhold Niebuhr, who denied such a unique culture existed but affirmed that a unique mission persisted. For Weber himself, however, the United States had actually become a manifestation of the spirit of capitalism, returning to swallow up the Europe that had spawned it, very much as capitalism swallowed up the Calvinist asceticism that had delivered it into the world.

Weber struggled to restore a personal balance between despair and hope through his identification with a disenchanted world in terms of a limited responsibility rooted in the Lutheran ideal of vocationalism. Science was, for Weber, an ascetic variation on the spirit of capitalism, as were Calvinism and bureaucratic administration. Like these other expressions of the spirit of capitalism, science was an expression of rationalization. As such, admitted Weber, "science contributes to the technology of controlling life by calculating external objects as well as man's activities." On this level, he said, science amounts to no more than "the greengrocer of the American boy." But, continued Weber, science may provide something the greengrocer cannot: the methods and tools of thinking, upon which clarity of choice becomes possible. At this point, for Weber, science may balance the world of trust and confidence even if it confirms the impossibility of knitting them together again. For the integrity of the scientist must be expressed in his renunciation of a messianic calling of ultimate ends and the acceptance of the limited ends of a humble vocationalism of service in a disenchanted world of unresolvably divided loyalties.[10]

Citing the transvaluation of values of Nietzsche and Baudelaire, Weber posited the paradoxical witness of truth in the scientist who renounces progress and in the true teacher who renounces leadership.[11] Value and power may be divided, according to Weber, but by inverting the claims of each, in relation to each, science may affirm a paradoxical human integrity. "To the person who cannot bear the fate of the times like a man," said Weber, "one must say: may he rather return silently, without the usual publicity . . ." Science offered a silent, inverted return to the sacredness of Luther's workaday vocation through the confidence of ascetic discipline, a religious return through the disenchantment of the world. But, for Weber, science was itself decaying in Germany, much as the ascetic sects of religion had decayed under the ever-expanding spirit of capitalism. The death of his own hardfought synthesis was on his horizon, he believed, because he considered himself the beleaguered "professor of the old style," without a place in the large, innovative capitalist system of the Americanized university that was absorbing all in its path.[12]

Rather than the ideal teacher as a scientist of hidden integrity, he complained, the American teacher was the teacher as football coach: one who sells the student knowledge that the student buys with the father's money, much as the student's mother buys cabbage from the greengrocer. If, like the football coach, the teacher is a leader in his field, the teacher has his prestige and is considered worth the price. If not a recognized leader, he or she is merely another teacher. No one would even consider buying a worldview or code of conduct from such teachers. Thus, in Weber's apocalypticism of the mediocre, the German professor's moral challenge to renounce the romantic and spontaneous demands of students, clamoring for a messianic ideal after which to pattern life, must decay into Americanization. That is, it must inevitably disintegrate into the last stages of the spirit of capitalism in which "specialists without spirit, sensualists without heart; this nullity imagines that it has attained a level of civilization never before achieved."[13]

But this is a prophesy of despair that the ineffectual scientist of integrity, who is Weber's ideal, cannot challenge directly. Instead, Weber presented a hidden heroism in the scientist-teacher whose vocation is expressed in drawing forth from the individual student a life decision of equally hidden integrity. That student must freely choose to consider the fruits of disinterested scientific research as a possible basis for the accounting of the ultimate meaning of his own conduct. In the paradoxical inversions of power and value that Weber has located in the scientific calling, "Who knows if entirely new prophets will arise, or if there will be a great rebirth of old ideas and ideals, or if neither, mechanized petrification, embellished with a sort of compulsive self-importance."[14] Claiming to be neither seer nor religious virtuoso but a hidden Lutheran or Dostoyevskian man of faith with no faith, Weber held tight to the inversion of Calvinist determinism for one last fading moment of the unity of an enchanted medieval world on the brink of a final modern catastrophe.

The triumph of the instrumental emphasis on confidence that Weber associated with American national culture found an ironic confirmation after his death in 1920. Two of the prime early interpreters of Weber's thesis for the American public were the theologian Reinhold Niebuhr and the historian Perry Miller. They were enormously influential in using Weber's thesis to redefine the character of American national culture during the Cold War, especially in the years between 1930 and 1960, when the country's Anglo-Puritan roots were still unquestioned but when its Anglo-Puritan future was being fundamentally challenged by ethnic minorities, consumerism, and technological progress. They were products of the opportunities afforded to new cultural voices who could manage both to identify with and rebel against America's Puritan heritage, a role they shared with the Agrarian New Critics and the New York intellectuals.[15]

Perry Miller was introduced to Weber through Reinhold Niebuhr, who was among the earliest of Weber's English-speaking readers. In his 1953 book, the second volume of *The New England Mind*, Miller self-consciously used Weber's thesis to explain the failure of the Puritan errand in New England. "The more diligently people applied themselves," he said, "the more they produced a decay of religion, and a corruption of morals, a society they did not want, one that seemed less and less attractive."[16] Miller chronicled America's decline through success, as Weber had traced the decline of Germany through routinization, insisting that he did so out of a self-imposed mission to expound "the innermost propulsion of the United States." Miller's scholarly life was dedicated to showing that the American Way, like the Puritan Errand, was "a time bomb packed with dynamite, the fuse burning close." He had undertaken the personal mission to expose the failure of the Puritan mission, he said, in order not only to "foretell explosions, but predict the manifold directions in which the fragments fly."[17]

Miller reported that he experienced an epiphany concerning his life's mission on the banks of the Congo River in 1926, while unloading the oil drums of capitalist expansion and living a dissolute life. Like Kurtz in Joseph Conrad's *The Heart of Darkness*, who may have been Miller's model for this jazz-age confession, it was a horror of emptiness behind the facade of Western civilization from which Miller recoiled, not the loss of spontaneity and the religious enchantment in the world.[18] From this perspective, Miller's project to show that "in a century of American experience the greatness of man's dependency had unaccountably become a euphemism for the greatness of man,"[19] appears to mirror Weber's description of the Protestant ethic, becoming, in the spirit of capitalism, pure confidence. But Miller's description of the decay of the New England errand was meant to subtly shift the terms of Weber's analysis. Miller sought to reveal a secret behind the facade of American confidence. He wished to disclose the unacknowledged emptiness of chaos and despair behind American optimism, while at the same time affirming the tragic grandeur of his own mission—a mission he doubted his capacity to live up to, and which he feared would reveal him to be an academic sham. His strategy for navigating this doubtful channel, which, like that of the Puritans he had freely chosen to risk his life's meaning upon, was to affirm that the failed Puritan errand, in which he was too sophisticated to believe, was indeed the promise that had actually made America exceptional before it lost its way.

Though Weber had denied that a unique American identity existed, or that Puritanism might be located outside of the spirit of capitalism, Miller's New England was predicated on the opposite assertion: that a truly unique spiritual identity had unaccountably been lost over time, and with it had died a unique promise of the New England Way. Miller, like Weber, attributed the rise of capitalism to the internal logic of the Protestant ethic from which it had been constructed. But Miller thought the Puritan mission had been abandoned by America. It had turned out to be merely a "clown's act," which may be funny in the circus but not in history. As a former actor, obsessed with the masks of illusion that the actor dons to illuminate hidden truths, Miller compared the agony of the Puritan saints to an actor's nightmare. The actor has prepared for the greatest role of his career; he strides onto the stage, only to find the theater dark and empty and himself entirely alone.[20]

For Miller, Puritanism was a system for providing confidence that "supernatural beauty could be carried across the gulf of separation" between human faith and divine grace. The "Augustinian strain of piety," which was as medieval for Miller as was Lutheranism for Weber, "flows from man's desire to transcend his imperfect self, to open channels for the influx of an energy which pervades the world, but with which he himself is inadequately supplied." It is rooted in the realization, Miller explained in the first volume of *The New England Mind* (1939), that natural humanity is "not only minute and insignificant, but completly out of touch with both justice and beauty." All the anguish in the world may be reduced to the problem of the relation of the individual to the One, said Miller, interpreting Augustine, and the irrepressible drive for knowledge of God is fueled by this need of piety. But the internal logic of piety, though an expression of grace, is the need of reason. And ultimately reason is the enemy of the piety that calls it forth.[21]

The Puritan mission was predicated on the possibility and the necessity of forging a balance between these forms of grace and piety, inspiration and reason, which were, in turn, manifestations of trust and confidence. Miller wrote, "The Puritans were confident that whenever they sallied forth onto the plain of reason, the fortress of revelation remained an impregnable refuge to which they could retreat in case they were worsted in the field." For this reason, he concluded, the Puritans "felt they had done God a particularly valorous service when they defended truth by their own with without being forced to take shelter behind His ramparts."

The Puritans, for Miller, lived in an Enlightenment universe of absolute freedom. They were literally "masters of their own destiny, their fate in their own hands to make or mar at will." They lived, on the one hand, in the midst of a web of necessities, the subjects of an immutable pattern of ideas. Yet, on the other, they were the recipients of grace, a salvation dispensed without merit, which alone could extricate men and women from the web of those necessities. Out of this perfect balance of freedom and determinism, the Puritans had undertaken a covenant with God, upon which depended their future as individuals and as a society. "Success and morality here were linked together as nowhere else in the world by a specific promise of the same God who elsewhere regulated success or failure without the slightest regard for civic virtue."[22]

Miller departed very significantly from Weber in suggesting that the Puritans were aware of their fall, and that they literally turned that consciousness of despair into an artistic convention, which he identified as a jeremiad. More important, Miller claimed that, abandoned by God and man, the Puritan saints were forced to turn their freedom into a psychological escape, a mask that turned their confidence into a confidence game. For how, asked Miller, "could a universal which turned out only to be nothing but a provincial particular be called anything but a blunder, an abortion?" If the Augustinian strain of piety was the common possession of Europeans and Americans, only the errand was specifically American. If the errand appeared to have failed, then it could be salvaged only through the rhetoric of the jeremiad as a ritualized sermon-form, which, Miller informed his readers, was a literary convention "for making an intelligible order out of the transition from European to American experience."[23]

Originally, as the name suggests, the jeremiad had been based upon the lamentations of the prophet Jeremiah, and it served a dual purpose. The jeremiad could be leveled against a community for having failed in its contractual responsibility of faith, but it could also be used to bring history before the bar of the individual conscience for failing to sustain the community. The jeremiad was more than rhetoric, Miller insisted, because as an art form its conventions expressed a medium for vision, though over time it became a stereotype wielded to avoid vision. According to Miller, therefore, the aesthetics of the jeremiad, like its religious message, was formally suspended between spiritual hope and despair, between optimism and pessimism in human affairs.[24]

In the 1950s and 1960s, until his death in 1963, Miller's essays closely imitated the pattern Weber had established in his criticism of the spirit of capitalism. For example, his 1956 essay "The Plight of the Lone Wolf" echoed Weber's complaint against bureaucracy. However, in Miller's hands, this complaint became an elegy for the great individualist scholar who was "a kingdom unto himself, sole ruler and only citizen." Weber's ideal professor was a craftsman of integrity who functioned within a guild; Miller's was the professor as battleship, imposing in his aloofness and beyond hostility or friendship in complete self-containment.

In essays such as "The Responsibility of Mind in an Age of Machines" and "Europe's Faith in American Fiction," Miller expressed his Weberian fears within the context of American exceptionalism. He compared the exhausted America, rooted in European culture, to the vital, unpretentious dynamism of the second America, the America of reckless contempt for a dying European culture. This was the America of the lone wolf intellectual, of the true individual. But it was, he also recognized, the America of the machine. Europeans could not understand the passionate abandon to which Americans "flung themselves into the technological torrent, how they shouted with glee in the midst of the cataract, cried to each other as they went headlong down the chute that here was their destiny . . ." Machines were supposed to be creatures of the mind, the servants of the intellect. Instead, they ushered in the era of the third America, the age of stultifying conformity, of mindless orthodoxy. The mind had produced its own antithesis, he wrote, creating in nuclear weapons the mortal enemy of its own existence.[25]

Faced with a deadly, brain-numbed American public on one side, and with an enervated, world-weary Europe on the other, Miller saw only one avenue of escape: the second America, the America that was irreverent toward both "nice culture" borrowed from Europe and the mindlessness of the popular culture of assembly lines and "communication skills." This was the America of mission that Miller shared with Sinclair Lewis, who cried out in European streets, "I love America . . . I love it, but I don't like it." Miller passionately believed that such an America could offer a way out of the modern predicament. But the measure of his disillusionment may be gauged by a recognition that this second America was only possible through the irreverent passion of the individual. The lone wolf professor saw himself as engaged in the same mission as the lone wolf novelists such as Hemingway and Sinclair Lewis. In his 1951 essay, significantly entitled "The Incorruptible Sinclair Lewis," Miller wrote that the story of Sinclair Lewis "was the story of the artist in America. . . . It may have been bad manners, but it was freedom, passionate and consuming. It was the elan that went into the writing of the great novels of the twenties which make them in the guise of ferocious attacks upon America, celebrations of it."

Miller wrote of the terror at being present at the death of a lion, to which he compared Lewis, who drank himself to death. The novelist might have been defeated, but he was uncorruptible in the dedication of his mission to America. "I wrote Babbit," Miller quoted Lewis as saying, "not out of hatred for him but out of love." Lewis's self-destruction was a final magnificent roar, "his last defiance from a cave in the rocks." Miller identified even more closely with Ernest Hemingway, whom he met during World War II, and whose suicide in 1961 seemed to propel Miller toward his own death of alcoholic despair in 1963, at the age of 59.[26]

Miller revealed his private identification with the American descent into the heart of darkness in *The Raven and the Whale* (1956), his study of Melville's eclipse in the nineteenth century. In that work, he repeated

Max Weber and the Spirit of Confidence   139

his claim that the Puritans had not failed in their errand, only found that it had been rendered absurd by the affects of time and a nation that would not listen. In this case, the mindless Young America movement and those who wished to ape English culture had divided literary sensibilities among themselves. Poor Herman Melville, foolishly accepting the shallow literary tastes of the Duyckinck circle of New York, blundered into the midst of their rivalries. But Melville had misread the literary establishment, who had welcomed his early sea adventures such as *Typee* and *Omoo*, and followed his misdirected muse to the conclusion of a monstrous abortion, which he called *Moby-Dick*. Melville lost his way, according to Miller, unaware that the foolish rivalries of the commercializers and Europeanizers had left the path of indigenous American literature. Melville sank into oblivion until the revival of 1920, which Miller suggests was rooted in the hatred of Puritanism, instead of an appreciation for its tragedy.[27]

The monstrously absurd failure of Melville, as Miller viewed it, repeated the monstrous failure of Puritanism. Both had been ensnared in an empty game behind the facade of the American Way. As Miller put it in 1954, Americans facing the monstrously great evil of death by hydrogen bomb or a monstrously mediocre death by smog have failed to see their similarities to the seventeenth-century Puritans. The fate of the New England Way and the fate of the American Way, he said, hinge together on the fate of the covenant, and that covenant "was progressively employed as a weapon to get public support for limited rather than communal ends."[28]

But how can such a society save itself? he asked. Miller's answer was revealing. It was not a positive answer but a negative one. After noting that H. Richard Niebuhr had pointed out that Miller's errand to remind Americans of their lost covenant was sterile because it was merely historical, Miller offered two ways that must fail. He attributed this advice to the Puritan theologian John Cotton, who offered his warning in a sermon he gave about 1633, leaving it behind when he escaped from England to America. The first response that must fail, Miller echoed Cotton, is when the righteous offer themselves as substitutes for others, when they try to take the afflictions upon themselves. The second response that must fail, he continued, is when they become "wrapt up in the same contagions of the sinners of the times and places they live in." The chosen people of God are left with an intolerable dilemma:

Unless they happen to be members of a society where holiness is virtually universal, they have the alternatives of recognizing that their virtue is too little to save the community, or else, by complying with the national ethos, of so acquiring the sins of the time and place as justly to be included in the national condemnation! In the one you must resign yourself to unpopularity and ineffectiveness, in the other to conformity and destruction.[29]

The terrible inner secret of the jeremiad, for Miller, was that since the nation had failed to follow the errand, the jeremiad could not be a vision. It could only be a dodge, a confidence game. Most horribly, in Miller's view this was not because the jeremiad was false, but precisely because it was true.

As an epiphany of emptiness, Miller's scholarly works on the jeremiad, ranging from the Puritan origins to the nineteenth-century writers like Poe and Melville to the twentieth-century writers like Hemingway and Lewis, followed a pattern of despair through history. The contemporary literary historian Sacvan Bercovitch, who is Canadian, and who has distanced himself from a personal identification with the jeremiad, has seen Miller's despair as an expression of Miller's naive victimization by a confidence game, which had never been anything else from the beginning.[30] As a Canadian looking at America through the lens of Vietnam, Bercovitch found it easier to follow Weber's original identification of America with pure confidence and to contrast it with the real thing, what he called a European jeremiad. In subverting Miller's anguish to reveal the scam at the heart of the idea of America, Bercovitch reaffirmed Weber's original analysis. But in doing so, he too found it necessary to appeal to confidence in his assault upon false confidence in the modern world.

In his influential study of the Puritan origins of the United States, *The American Jeremiad*, Bercovitch professed bewilderment that a diverse population created of numerous races and creeds could believe in an American mission, "and could invest that patent fiction with all the emotional, spiritual, and intellectual appeal of a religious quest." How was it possible, Bercovitch demanded rhetorically, that Americans were ever able to avoid the question "Who are we?" while repeating endlessly the millennial refrain, "How long, O Lord, how long."[31]

Bercovitch read the litany of lamentations and celebrations that constitute the jeremiad not as a simple cry of hope or of despair but as a clever confidence game. Rhetoric functions in culture to reflect and affect psychic, social and historical needs, he explained, denying Miller's contention that the jeremiad was more than rhetoric.³² For Bercovitch the rhetorical pattern of the jeremiad mediates the contradiction between appearance and expectation, but it does not function to divide vision from stereotype, as it did for Miller's Puritans. This means that for Bercovitch the role of the jeremiad is the same as the confidence artist's pitch. The jeremiad's rhetorical function, Bercovitch suggested, is to enfold the victim's desires into the reality of the experience, so that the victim's fears, doubts and resistances will confirm rather than shatter the illusion the artist seeks to sustain. Indeed, the confidence artistry of the jeremiad depends upon the desperate need to believe among the disillusioned. The jeremiad, as a rhetorical strategy, is fashioned to manipulate its litany of hope, and for Bercovitch, this demolishes the case for ambiguity that Miller made for it.

Clearly, both Miller and Bercovitch agree in their definition of the jeremiad as a confidence game. For Miller, the tragedy of this confidence game is that it is not a result of a dishonest errand. It is the result of history having failed to follow the path that allowed the jeremiad to be formally true. By making the Puritan errand an abortion, history, or the God the Puritans worshiped, mocked them with their own covenant. The emptiness of history, not the emptiness of the Puritans themselves, made the jeremiad a confidence game. For Bercovitch, in contrast, the errand was itself a fiction, and the mission was a ruse to sustain endless confidence by establishing a pattern of promise, decline, and prophesy of return that is impervious to events or to time. The worse the news, suggested Bercovitch, the more compelling the message of promise that the jeremiad affirms.³³

Either of these variations on the jeremiad as a confidence game might have been derived from Weber's ambiguous conclusion to *The Protestant Ethic*, in which he eschewed predictions as to whether the future would be one of some new order, a rebirth of the old ideals and values, or a state of "mechanized petrification." Weber's Kantian ambiguity about the future derived from his unwillingness to embrace the messianic ideals that Miller attacked in disappointed love and that Bercovitch restored in derision, as the legacy of America's Puritan origins. Miller's and Bercovitch's opposing emphases on despair and hope in interpreting the jeremiad, therefore, follow a deep symmetry within the American culture of confidence. That symmetry of hope in despair and despair in hope may be seen in many examples of American popular art and political rhetoric, not just among such scholarly interpreters as Miller and Bercovitch. It is expressed not only in the tension between Burke's beautiful and sublime, but in Burke's characterization of the jaded age of revolutionary emotion, which he described in the *Reflections* as the tension between the sublime and the ridiculous.[34]

The distinction between the sublime and the ridiculous exists at the margin of aesthetic distance that separates the immediate experience of the beautiful from the sublime. Too much distance turns tragedy into pathos and the sublime into foolish posturing. Perry Miller tried to preserve the sublimity of his scholarly mission to describe a vision of the holy, which became a sublime art form in the jeremiad, only to become merely silly in the judgment of history. Sacvan Bercovitch admitted the embarrassment but, as a Canadian, he had his own sublime sense of distance from the United States to transcend it, and, as Melville recognized, the transcendent, like all expressions of the sublime, provides a refuge of height for the detached observer.

However, a confidence game when uncovered requires more, not less, confidence to escape the resulting feeling of despair. The alchemical skill to turn the ridiculous into the sublime by containing laughter and channeling it into new forms of meaning is vital in preserving authority and in maintaining a sense of social legitimacy. Carnival may spontaneously erupt to mock established forms of authority, but Weber's sociology would argue that it must become routinized if it is to be sustained over time. Consequently, carnival may never remain subversive in only a single direction of challenging power or oppression. Indeed, it must alternatively function as a formula for preserving the sublime against the immediacy of the jocular.

This suggests that any form of carnival, over time, will institutionalize anarchic laughter into a form of organized theater. For this same reason, the persistent pattern American comedy shared through minstrelsy, vaudeville, and then the Hollywood movie industry was a formula for rescuing the sublime from laughter through laughter. Such Marx Brothers films as *Animal Crackers* (1930), *Duck Soup* (1933) and *At the Circus* (1939) mercilessly attacked elite society, government authority and social convention. Eddie Cantor's redface film, *Whoopee!* (1930), leveled the separation between "real Americans" and immigrant-newcomers by making a transparently urban Jewish character dress as a "real Native American." In Judy Garland's *Wizard of Oz* (1939), clowns and a frightened school girl from Kansas went on a journey to find confidence, and found the wisdom to look inside themselves rather than to confidence artists like the snake-oil salesman who became the Wizard of Oz. Such pretenders, the film warned, as Dorothy first exposed and then was left behind by the departing Wizard, could provide only false confidence.

The ridiculous, each of these very different films of the 1930s suggested, is a falsified confidence. Through exposing its falsity, each of these variations on vaudeville proclaimed that confidence might be restored and the sublime revitalized. Similarly, the Busby Berkeley films such as *Dames* (1934), *Gold Diggers of 1935* (1935), *I Live for Love* (1936), and *Babes in Arms* (1939) exploited the dramatic tension of backstage fantasy and real performance. The Berkeley musical formula often began with a staged rehearsal. The backstage challenges to the individual performer's confidence and to the company's ability to persevere were then resolved by the final extravagant and stylized production. The realism of backstage events contrasted with the artificiality of the construction of the show. The fanstastic elements of the final production contrasted with the reality of the immediate performance. The final return to the stage at the end of the film marked the triumphant moment of success for the cast before the staged audience. It reinforced the sublime sense of approval that the film audience shared with the staged audience. But the film viewer, unlike the apparently real audience in the film, shared the intimacy of the actors' private struggles and ridiculous moments of self-disclosure on the way to the final scenes of glory. The sublime was, therefore, made believable for Depression-era Americans, and performance was shown to be more real than reality. But this would be true only if the viewer preserved his or her confidence in the truth of a film that flaunted its artificiality both by its stage-setting and the mechanical fantasy of the film's musical productions.

Perhaps the most sophisticated and enduring of the films of the 1930s and 1940s to acknowledge the crisis of confidence in America and to use laughter to restore the credibility of the sublime upon which that confidence rests, however, were those of Frank Capra. Capra used the emotional realism of melodrama and romantic comedy to take his confrontation with the ridiculous beyond the minstrel and vaudeville formulas for exposing false confidence in order to rebuild confidence. Indeed, Capra, the Italian-American, made films of complaint about America that were as much confrontations with the absurd as were the scholarly confrontations with the public ritual of the jeremiad made by Perry Miller, the Anglo-American. Capra's reluctant heroes and holy clowns poignantly paralleled Miller's post-Menckian version of the Puritan's errand. His films paralleled the space between Miller's academic vision of the sublime and the ridiculous, but they are also interesting because they anticipated Bercovitch's post–1960s vision that the ridiculous lurks in the sublime itself. Capra's films, analogous to both Miller's and Bercovitch's versions of Weber's social analysis of charisma and the spirit of capitalism, illustrate the power within the ridiculous to restore the sublime and the power of doubt to restore confidence. Capra's films *Mr. Deeds Goes to Town* (1936), *Mr Smith Goes to Washington* (1939), and *Meet John Doe* (1941) all reflect this double vision of American confidence. Each is a morality tale of disillusionment and affirmation in an errand to redeem the "common man" and American political institutions, and each ends by promoting confidence as the only redemptive vision capable of restoring a sublime meaning for the individual and community.

Mr. Deeds Goes to Town tells the story of a typical Capra "idiot-hero" who inherits twenty million dollars during the Depression, and is immediately assailed by confidence artists of every stripe. He is an easy mark, and in his naivete is victimized by lawyers and by the woman he loves. Longfellow Deeds, who is as simple as the world is cynical, makes a moral decision to use his money to subsidize desperate farmers who embody the ideals of the American way of life. Deeds's voluntary charity is at once simple and simplistic. It is an appeal to personal piety and an attack upon the economic injustice and greed of Capra's contemporary urban America. *Mr. Deeds* is a Populist attack on the corruption of New Deal America and a celebration of New Deal generosity. It is an indictment of lawyers and the legal system that would destroy idealism and a defense of the system for preserving itself despite itself. Capra, therefore, manages to argue for both cynicism and idealism, and for neither, just as he uses Deeds the simpleton for laughs while also portraying him as a Christ-figure, lonely and suffering in the completion of his errand.[35]

Mr. Smith Goes to Washington is also a tale of errand. Its plot juxtaposes another "idiot-hero," a Boy Scout leader and citizen-senator named Jefferson Smith, with corrupt Senator Joseph Paine. Again, land speculation and government corruption figure strongly in the plot, which Capra turns into both a burlesque on Smith's credulous piety concerning American history and political institutions and into an affirmation of his idealism for fulfilling the promise of American institutions despite their corruption. In one segment of the film, Capra makes Smith an unwitting embodiment of Abraham Lincoln, America's patron holy fool. Finally, the venial senators, moved by Smith's simple Christ-like or Lincolnesque virtue (as is, presumably, the audience watching the film), are redeemed. This emotional response to the actor James Stewart and to the noble foolishness of his mission constitutes a basis for confidence in America that transcends the sentimental and the cynical aspects of the fictional hero's quest.[36]

Similarly, the Mr. Doe of *Meet Mr. Doe* is born as a publicity invention of a desperate newspaper columnist. The idea of a Mr. Everyman has become a fraud, and as such serves as the perfect confidence scam to be manipulated by a nihilist communications magnate named D. B. Norton. Long John Willoughby, a failed baseball player with a believable face, is hired to play the role of the fictional Mr. Doe, who is supposed to have threatened suicide because of his disillusionment with America. Willoughby is packaged and promoted to become the leader of a mass national movement of sinister design. Norton's nihilism and Willoughby's idealism are portrayed as the two symmetrical sides of Mr. Doe and his mass appeal. As a washed-up baseball player speaking in a baseball stadium to thousands of fans, John Doe becomes the embodiment of a jeremiad against the idea of American history and its corruption in mass society. Mr. Doe's selfless sacrifice to preserve an ideal behind Norton's confidence game and confidence in the faith that idealism may be organized among the members of the corrupt "John Doe" clubs is finally a promise of rebirth out of destruction. It is a vision deeply rooted in American millennialism and in the cycle of a regenerating frontier in which democracy is continually reborn out of corruption.[37]

Perhaps the best example of this theme in Capra's films, however, is *It's a Wonderful Life*. Although it has become his most popular film, it was not especially successful when it opened. The film shows that political and economic institutions had become indivisible for Capra in the Cold War America of 1946, and that anxiety over the American way of life remained central. *It's a Wonderful Life*, like Capra's other films, revolves around the ambiguous line between self-sacrifice and self-destruction. George Bailey, the hero of the film, is about to kill himself when an ineffectual angel, Clarence Oddbody, is sent to save him. We see George's previous life, one of quiet heroism and dignity but also of misunderstandings and missed opportunities. Bedford Falls, George's hometown, is small-town America; it offers a life that both frustrates and affirms the hero.

George Bailey's controversy with Bedford Falls turns on the competing conventions of vocation and calling that Weber and Miller also made central to their understandings of the triumph of the spirit of capitalism over a world no longer balanced between trust and confidence. George's vocation is found in continuing his father's commitment to a small-time savings and loan, which the greedy banker, Mr. Potter, has long wished to swallow up into his financial empire. However, for Capra's hero, the idea of vocation has become synonymous with narrowness and routine, while the idea of the calling has become romantic and liberating—just the reverse of Weber's dichotomy of romantic Lutheranism and realist Calvinism but not of his prophesy for the future of the United States. George wants to travel and to make his fortune, but events and, above all, his sense of duty conspire to force him to accept the limited world of Bedford Falls, and, with it, the lack of opportunities for advancement and the restless confinement of the burden of being a husband and father.

The film, as critics have observed, is neatly divided into two parts. The first half shows George's growing nihilism, his sense of having been betrayed by history and his loss of confidence. This leads him to ask why he was ever born, and he goes into a spiraling despondency, heading towards the moment of self-destruction. The second half of the film, under the influence of Clarence, who may or may not have been the result of too many drinks or a bad bump on the head, is an exploration of the question "What if I had never been born?" George Bailey is permitted to view the world as it would have been without him. This returns to him a feeling of self-worth and a sense of the meaningfulness of history. However, for this renewal of George's faith in himself and in Bedford Falls to be inspiring, Capra found it necessary to carefully avoid exposing the contradiction of individualism within the idea of American exceptionalism.

George Bailey's frustrated individual ambitions, Capra suggests, could not be resolved on the personal or family level, or on the community and national levels, except through a cosmic synthesis knitting these elements together. George's wife, Mary, has the vision to make an abandoned house into a home, but personal security is not sufficient for George. He must make homes for others through his self-sacrificing work at the building and loan. Potter, who tells him that he is wasting his talents on the "garlic eaters" and other undesirables, represents temptation that George will choose individual success over his errand to the community. But the community is flawed, and nearly abandons George and the building and loan during the Depression, when personal needs outweigh community responsibility. George, with Mary's understanding of his vocation, must sacrifice their pleasure and spend their honeymoon money to keep his customers from switching accounts to Potter's bank.

Besides being a scrooge who denies loans to the deserving poor, Potter is also portrayed as head of the draft board, who unfairly sends men without political or economic clout to fight in World War II. George's failure to serve the nation, due to an ear injury he got in service to others, denies him the heroism afforded his decorated brother, and leaves him inescapably trapped in the Bedford Falls Building and Loan he so desperately wishes to escape. All of these contradictions between selfless service and selfish ambition are brought into a cosmic resolution, however, when Capra makes it clear that the United States is on the side of the angels in World War II. Capra makes his film angels cheer enthusiastically for the American crusade. This cosmic justification of George, who could not fight because he saved the life of his brother who did, affirms George's value for the nation, the community and for himself. But in cosmically sanctifying George Bailey, Capra also neatly sidesteps the implication of the war and his own argument for despair. For the premature violent deaths of millions of other Georges in a world in which each individual's life is essential to all others bespeak a human tragedy beyond calculation or resolution. Only divine sanction could turn such unspeakable tragedy for individualism into a celebration of its endurance. The absurd is rendered meaningful by divine intervention, but, more important, Clarence's ridiculousness serves as a sublime defense of the foolish George Bailey and his dreams.

For this reason, too, the restoration of George's shattered life and vocation is a story of the renewal of a covenant. As such, as Perry Miller recognized in his discussion of the Puritan covenant, George Bailey's neighbors had to affirm his errand into the wilderness, and George had to deserve their confidence. In this case, it was the wilderness symbolized by Bailey Acres, the undeveloped meadowland which, without George's vision of building his neighbors' homes, would have become a desolate Potter's field. Capra, therefore, did not end the film with George's personal epiphany, or Potter's redemption, after the model of Dickens's *A Christmas Carol*. Instead, Potter's plan for sending George Bailey to jail and literally destroying the town is foiled by the people of Bedford Falls themselves, who discover the sublime selflessness that democracy may bring forth in moments of crisis.

Thus, Potter's mean-spirited greed is overcome, not by George Bailey's faith alone, nor even by the angels who are essential in mediating the sublime meaning of democracy to George. Rather the world is harmonized because at the last moment the people of Bedford Falls, whose prayers for George open the film, come bearing gifts to pay back the deficit at the building and loan, proving their confidence in George and justifying his confidence in them. The film ends with George's renewal having become a parable of Christmas, in which confidence is born in a manger, as it were, and Clarence receives his wings due to George's fortunate fall—all because of Clarence's confidence in George.

Clarence Oddbody, the holy clown, is hardly a theological principal. He does, however, represent Capra's recognition that any affirmation of confidence in America rests upon theological underpinnings and that a restoration of confidence in America in 1946 required a reevaluation of the relation between the national covenant and individual liberty. Capra used the horror of the war to challenge the mockery of the ordinary that threatened to destroy all George Bailey's self-worth, even as it threatened each member of the theater audience. Capra demonstrated that the absurd, engendered by the ordinary, could be tamed. The ridiculous evoked pathos, which, in turn, could be used ironically to reaffirm the aesthetic power of the sublime. It is, therefore, significant that a German-American clergyman, Reinhold Niebuhr, should have used the language of dramatic tragedy to attack the ridiculousness of pathos, and to gain unprecedented influence over Anglo-American efforts to solve the problem of political confidence, at the same moment that Capra, a Sicilian-American, was offering his tragicomic vision of democratic redemption in American theaters.

Niebuhr, like his contemporary, Capra, had experienced intense prejudice as an outsider in a still-insular Anglo-American society when he began his career. In each case Niebuhr and Capra made emotional breaks with their communities and embraced an ideal of American democracy that they recognized did not heal the divisions within themselves. Each, however, won acceptance and honor within the Anglo-American culture he affirmed through criticism. Though working in very different media, Capra and Niebuhr both used dualistic confrontations with despair and hope and motifs of light and dark to fashion their defenses of democracy and of personal meaning in a corrupt society. Each found Abraham Lincoln to be a heroic ideal for an antiheroic era, and, of course, each presented his message in theological form. Consequently, Niebuhr's books published in the 1930s and 1940s, such as *Moral Man and Immoral Society* and *The Children of Light and the Children of Darkness* expressed a blend of romantic realism remarkably similar to Capra's *Meet John Doe*, *Mr. Smith Goes to Washington*, and *It's a Wonderful Life*. Indeed, Capra's World War II propaganda film, *Why We Fight*, with images of a world of darkness and of light and an emphasis upon the demonic antireligious and antidemocratic character of the enemy, might almost have been scripted by Niebuhr.[38]

In the 1920s Niebuhr, the son of a pietistic German minister, had almost naturally assumed that Germany was a harbinger for the future of the United States. He did so, in part, because he was influenced by Max Weber's writing. Indeed, Reinhold Niebuhr and his brother H. Richard, were, in the 1920s, among the earliest interpreters of the still-untranslated Weber.[39] Once more, since German theology and social philosophy were so intertwined, Niebuhr was indirectly reading Weber's themes in his most important sources during the 1920s, such as the writings of the great liberal theologian Ernst Troeltsch. Troeltsch was a close friend and collaborator of Weber's. He was also, by Niebuhr's own account, among the most profound influences on the shaping of Niebuhr's theological principles. During the 1920s, Troeltsch explicitly developed Weber's linkage of Protestantism and capitalism in his own theological and ethical writings. Together, Troeltsch and Weber also influenced Paul Tillich, another of the most significant sources for Niebuhr's political and theological thought.[40]

Socialist critics like Tillich attacked capitalism and liberalism in the post–World War I period, appealing to the economic analysis supplied by Marx, on one side, and the antiprogressive individualism of Søren Kierkegaard, on the other. The desperation felt by Germans in the twenties had led to a recovery of Kierkegaard's anti-Hegelian writings, as well as new approaches to Marxism such as those later developed by the Frankfurt School, with which Tillich was associated after 1929.[41] Niebuhr absorbed these ideas and fashioned them into a prophetic warning to Americans, who he believed were artificially insulated from the realistic lessons of the German tragedy by virtue of their shallow lives of affluence. In a 1925 article in the *Atlantic Monthly*, Niebuhr sought to teach his American readers a moral lesson through the example of Germany's victimization by social evil. "Nowhere will they discover the forces which contend for mastery in a modern state more clearly defined, or the moral impotence of modern industrial civilization more obviously revealed" than in Germany, he wrote. Similarly, a year earlier, he had warned that the potential threat of the American Klu Klux Klan could be gauged by the rise of a virulent German version in the aftermath of the war. "If there is any comfort in finding your vices and weaknesses shared by others," he wrote, "it ought to be welcome news to Americans that our Klan is not as uniquely American as we believed."[42]

Weber and Troeltsch, however, gave Niebuhr more than a foundation for equating the tragedy of defeated Germany with the optimism of an expanding America. They also provided a basis for the shocking conclusion that in neither case would the Protestant conscience ever extirpate the evils of capitalism, since they, too, were merely extensions of each other. Weber had further complicated any revolutionary alternative by arguing that politics is a form of violence, which, paradoxically, is also the only means for keeping social peace. In Paul Tillich's theological language, this meant that politics, as an "ultimate concern," must necessarily participate in the demonic—a concept, he insisted, that he could not have developed "without the groundwork laid by Lutheran mysticism and philosophical irrationalism." For Tillich, the demonic expressed the recognition that the creative and destructive sides of human culture are inescapably bound together, as they were symbolically linked in Dionysus, Greek god of the theater.[43] For modern men and women, said Tillich, the demonic exists wherever the finite masquerades as a timeless universal, as it does, he said in 1927, in nationalism and capitalism.[44] In 1956 Tillich specifically related the concept of the the demonic to the Cold War when he wrote that "we are in continual social neurosis by the split consciousness and possession which is implied in this inescapable structure in which everything which is done is, either in reality or by suspicion of the other, that which strengthens the destruction of mankind."

Tillich described himself as living on the boundary between possibilities, rather than being committed to dogmatism, which as a partial human truth may always participate in the demonic if uncritically accepted. Consequently, he wrote, "at almost every point, I have had to stand between alternative possibilities of existence, to be completely at home in neither and to take no definitive stand against either."[45] The demonic, he explained, may be discerned at the junctions of the creative and destructive sides of all power, including religious and political institutions. All forms of human power outside of the holy are counterfeit, according to Tillich, because they lack the universal authority which, by definition, only the holy may embody. The demonic, as any partial authority which claims universality, is inherently self-destructive. It lacks the predictability of mere artifice, and it is too volatile, too unstable, to be dependably reproduced or to be used instrumentally for a predetermined end. Since it may not be contained if it is invoked, he warned further, ultimate sanction must not be given to any act of human creativity. This meant, for Tillich, the necessity of applying the "Protestant Principle" to all aspects of human culture, including Protestantism itself. For Protestants living within the heritage of the Lutheran Reformation, Tillich explained, this means that Protestant culture must be eternally critical of itself as a foundational, prophetic principle against its own false messianism. Otherwise, he said, it will not be possible to resist the political temptation of modern times to turn a finite national interest into a fraudulently universal civil religion of nationalism, as occurred during the First World War, or, as he later wrote, to sanction the use of nuclear weapons, which he considered to be a demonic manifestation of the meeting of creativity and destructiveness and therefore impossible to use rationally in a policy of mutually assured destruction.[46]

Reinhold Niebuhr, in his 1932 book, *Moral Man and Immoral Society*, attempted to apply Tillich's and Weber's jeremiads against the evil of modern politics but to escape the resulting crisis of confidence in the possibility of creating a just society at the same time. He proclaimed the failure of modern human pride and sentimentality, and unequivocally rejected any national claims for moral superiority. "The most significant moral characteristic of a nation is its hypocrisy," he wrote. But Niebuhr also insisted that such dishonesty of the nation is a necessary aspect of political policy. It is the only means by which the nation can "gain the full benefit of a double claim on the loyalty and devotion of the individual, as his own special and unique community and as a community which embodies universal values and ideals."[47] These two claims, one emotional and one rational, are incompatible, he wrote, and therefore hypocrisy is a necessary condition of political life. Departing from Weber and Tillich, Niebuhr attempted to resolve the internal contradiction of nationalism through casuistry. This new casuistry was what Niebuhr called Christian realism, after Tillich's phrase, "believing realism," but with very different connotations. "We live in an age in which personal moral idealism is easily accused of hypocrisy and frequently deserves it," Niebuhr explained. "It is an age in which honesty is possible only when it skirts the edge of cynicism."[48]

Niebuhr argued that Weber's paradox of politics and Tillich's demonic may be escaped in the Burkean terms of using deception, or illusion, to subvert reality in the name of preserving order and political confidence. Tillich's position had been closer to the classical aesthetic of Greek tragedy and Longinus's description of the sublime as emotional transport. He had argued that any form of identification with the demonic must result in self-destruction. Only the act of exposing the demonic through calling it by name, as in exorcism or drama, could achieve power over its destructive force.[49]

Tillich's distinction between the holy and the demonic, like Dewey's distinction between the holy and the lucky, was based upon Kant's solution to the fragmentation of human experience at the Enlightenment frontier of the natural and the artificial.[50] Kant had admitted that the sublime and the holy, art and religion, belong to different categories, but he suggested that each participates in the noumenal sphere, a reality that may not be directly experienced but nevertheless conceptually exists. On this basis, John Dewey had linked the holy and the lucky in his *Quest for Certainty*, which he published in 1929, just three years after Tillich's linking of the holy and the demonic in his writing in Germany.

Tillich had been influenced by the German theologian Rudolf Otto, whose classic study in comparative religion, *The Idea of the Holy*, had conflated the holy and the sublime.[51] Otto had criticized the idea of semantic transformation, arguing that association of ideas could not call into existence new ideas that were not already there. He also argued that the sublime and the beautiful are so categorically similar to the holy that distinctions between them are less relevant than the distinction between the holy and the profane. Tillich, who had been shaken by the catastrophic consequences of the First World War, came increasingly to fear the modern forms of false, or partial, powers that masquerade as universals, meaning that the demonic might masquerade as the holy. But, like Otto and most German idealists after Kant, and even empiricist psychologists such as Wundt, Tillich failed to recognize the efficacy of the sublime as an instrumental approach for manipulating power. Tillich followed Kantian idealism, rather than the practical power politics of Burke, and allowed himself to be drawn into aesthetic experience as a redemptive escape from life's divisions.[52]

Niebuhr, in contrast to Tillich, offered a Burkean escape from the classical problem of tragedy. He suggested the possibility of preserving a delicate balance between the destructive poles of brutal realism and romantic idealism, or, as Weber saw it, politics as violence and politics as order. This could be done, he wrote, within the dramatic realm of illusion. By applying Weber against Tillich, Niebuhr offered a way to use the demonic to bring about a limited good of ethical responsibility within the flawed realm of politics. The redemption of politics could be achieved, he wrote, by "men who have substituted some new illusions for the abandoned ones."

> The most important of these illusions is that the collective life of mankind can achieve perfect justice. It is a very valuable illusion for the moment; for justice cannot be approximated if the hope of its perfect realization does not generate a sublime madness in the soul. Nothing but such madness will do battle with malignant power and "spiritual wickedness in high places." The illusion is dangerous because it encourages terrible fanaticisms. It must therefore be brought under the control of reason. One can only hope that reason will not destroy it before its work is done.[53]

Niebuhr had subtly transformed the demonic into a form of support for his mission to establish confidence in the hope for human justice through a new casuistry. His project of imparting wisdom through deception, as he conceived it, could only be achieved through a version of a confidence game based on the neoclassical terms of the Burkean sublime.

Hitler's brutal rise to power by 1933 convinced Niebuhr that such illusions, and the sacred responsibility for constructing them, were more vital than ever. Niebuhr's Christian realism told him that the greater demonism of fascism justified the lesser evil of capitalism, which was at least compatible with democracy. This casuistic compromise with relative forms of evil was couched in the language of the theater in *Beyond Tragedy*.[54] This book of sermon-essays, published in 1937, reflected more than an allusion to Nietzsche's *Beyond Good and Evil* in order to turn Nietzsche's "transvaluation of values" to Niebuhr's own purposes of witnessing to the Christian transvaluation of despair into hope. It represented Niebuhr's successful subversion of Tillich's concept of the demonic into a redemptive, dramatic alternative to the pessimism he associated with Greek tragedy.

Tillich's association of the demonic with tragedy had originally grown out of his experience in the First World War. It was in part an expression of Tillich's anguished repudiation of his own confidence game as he came to consider his inspirational role as a chaplain in the German army, when he had urged men to sacrifice themselves to the horrors of trench warfare. Tillich, who had had a nervous breakdown after preaching endless funeral services at Verdun, believed he had witnessed the inevitable linkage of the creative and destructive sides of dramatic illusion as he watched German culture and religion merge to play the leading role in a world tragedy.[55]

In 1933 Tillich was among the first professors to be singled out for removal by the Nazis. Hitler's rise to absolute power in Germany reaffirmed Tillich's certainty of the role of the demonic in the modern condition. "It was our feeling," he later confessed, "that only in Germany was the problem of how to unite Christianity and the modern mind taken absolutely seriously.... And then it happened that at the end of the road of German philosophy and theology, the figure of Hitler appeared."[56] Reinhold Niebuhr, however, offered Tillich a refuge in America in 1933, confirming his belief that the United States represented a refuge for freedom for the world, as well. Niebuhr, who was increasingly frustrated by American isolationism, wished to inspire confidence in his American audience, not to depress them by emphasizing the universal tragedy of the human condition. At that time, however, Niebuhr was only dimly aware of the dramatic possibilities of irony for subverting Tillich's message that the effort to escape from tragedy must lead to self-destructive mediocrity. The universal truth of the Dionysian theater, Tillich had suggested, is that greatness and tragedy are inherent in the human condition because they are linked ambiguously together by hubris. Hubris, he pointed out, is not the same thing as arrogance. It is the condition of being responsible for what no individual has the power to see: the moment in space and time when the creative elevation of the self beyond finitude becomes the destructive failure to recognize the finitude of the self.[57]

As Tillich had made Germany the model of the tragedy of false self-confidence through the concept of the demonic, Niebuhr would redefine the demonic in order to offer an escape from tragedy. He would do so in the same terms in which the dramatist Machiavelli had approached Greek drama, and which Burke inherited—an approach promising that illusion could redemptively restore faith in necessary illusions. Through the terms supplied by Machiavelli's convention of the confidence-artist as hidden hero, which Burke translated into the sublime, Niebuhr conceived his mission for sustaining the Puritan identification of America as a refuge for confidence in a false and untrustworthy world. His personal mission was not, as it was for Perry Miller, to explain the tragedy of how the errand had turned into a deception; to the contrary, it was to deceptively deliver the truth that confidence was still possible because it was necessary.

Niebuhr initiated his assault on tragedy in *Beyond Tragedy* by quoting St. Paul's self-identification of ministers "as deceivers, yet true." Truth, he explained, is deeper than appearance. Christian symbolism contains "a certain degree of provisional and superficial deception."[58] Christian truth, like the artist's truth, is based on the use of symbols in one dimension to create the illusion of a reality in another dimension of space and time that does not really exist as it is presented. Similarly, Niebuhr said, since the truths of this world are derived from the eternal world and are not complete in themselves, no statement based on human judgment can ever be wholly true as it is presented; the seeming and the real never completely coincide in time. Therefore, ultimate trust is impossible to offer or sustain in this world. This misplaced faith, he continued, is the mistake of the Marxists who trust in the proletariat. "Trust no man," warned Niebuhr in a chapter entitled "Ultimate Trust." "Every man has his own capacities but also his weaknesses," just as every aspect of the temporal world has its capacities and weaknesses, neither entirely good nor entirely evil, neither entirely true nor entirely false. "Ultimate confidence in the goodness of life can, in other words," explained Niebuhr, "not rest upon confidence in the goodness of man." Such confidence must end in disillusionment. If the false optimism of trusting in human virtue leads to despair, however, so too does the opposite view that this world is a "vale of tears." The Christian recognizes that this world is good despite its corruption. "He has confidence, in other words, that evil cannot overwhelm the good."[59]

If the former of these statements was aimed at Marxist "trust in the poor man," the latter was aimed at the pessimism of Tillich and Freud, whom Niebuhr identified with the classical god Dionysus: "Greek tragedy declares that the vitality of life is in conflict with the laws of life," he wrote. The elitism of the classical hero makes him undemocratic, and his romanticism makes him self-absorbed. Needing lesser men and women to weep for his inevitable self-destruction, Niebuhr argued, the Greek tragic hero, whether Promethean or Dionysian, must end as the pathetic poseur. "Christianity," he insisted, "stands beyond tragedy." It reveals that "life is not only good but capable of destroying the evil which has been produced in it."

> It declares that what seems to be an inherent in life itself is really a contingent defect in the soul of each man, the defect of the sin which he commits in his

freedom. If he can realise that fact, if he can weep for himself, if he can repent, he can also be saved. He can be saved by hope and faith. His hope and faith will separate the character of life in its essential reality from life as it is revealed in sinful history.[60]

Though buttressed by sophisticated theological and political theory, Niebuhr's solution was not dissimilar to the Burkean plea for a revitalized confidence through tradition and the neo-Burkean belief in democratic capitalism that Frank Capra was then expressing in film.

In 1937, Niebuhr was still only dimly aware of the possibilities of irony for challenging Tillich's concept of the demonic, and he still had not developed an alternative to Weber's thesis in *The Protestant Ethic* for accommodating his new acceptance of capitalism. However, from the publication of *Beyond Tragedy* on, Niebuhr increasingly began to appeal to the Romantic conventions of the Schlegels, to use theatrical phrases like "the drama of human existence" and "the vastness of the historical drama," and to define the political environment as a stage, after the pattern of Edmund Burke. In *The Self and the Dramas of History*, which appeared in 1955, for example, Niebuhr appealed to Martin Buber's concept of life as dialogue to argue that history is a drama that integrates the individual and community.[61] But, Niebuhr insisted, Christianity is essentially Hebraic rather than Greek; therefore, the Judaic-Christian interpretation of history is neither Dionysian nor Promethean. It is, in other words, beyond tragedy and beyond the false optimism of science. This means, he said, that Freudianism, which he associated with Tillich's interpretation of the demonic, could never accurately describe the dramatic patterns of the self. For similar reasons, he argued, history may only reveal dramatic patterns of conflict but never the definitive answers promised by scientific progress.[62]

In *Beyond Tragedy*, he had anticipated these later themes by challenging both the Dionysian and Promethean attitudes of defeatism and arrogance in the name of a chastened but confident stance toward human potential. He had offered the idea of a divine comedy of redemption through suffering as a Christian alternative to the pessimistic lament of Dionysian tragedy. Though *Beyond Tragedy* has been considered one of Niebuhr's less successful efforts, the perspective he developed there eventually matured into his enormously influential concept of irony. In Niebuhr's moralistic interpretation, irony can be contained by humility. If irony could be depended upon to shatter the security of the arrogant, it could be equally depended upon to serve as a comfort to the meek.[63]

In Niebuhr's definition of an ironic situation, as distinguished from a pathetic one, the individual bears some measure of responsibility for his or her fate. It differs from the tragic in that the weakness is unconscious and not the result of a resolution. The implication of irony for Niebuhr is that, given a large dose of humility and some serious self-examination, the individual, the community and the nation may escape the wages of their folly and reaffirm the values from which they have strayed. Consequently, Niebuhr's irony, fully developed in *Irony of American History* in 1952, became his mature formulation of the Protestant jeremiad itself.

Though irony was an aesthetic category that Tillich, in his concept of the demonic, insisted could not be contained, Niebuhr was willfully blind to aesthetics in an effort to construct a purely Hebraic ideal of Christianity. For Niebuhr, therefore, irony did not appear to be an aesthetic category. It masqueraded, in his analysis, as a political law of the universe. It divinely resolved all the contradictions, through humility, which Tillich had associated with the demonic condition of human finitude. In turning Christian humility into a shield against hubris, Niebuhr was able to use it, instrumentally, to transcend tragedy and to ethically challenge the aesthetic categories used by Tillich to question all forms of political confidence.[64]

In the years following *Beyond Tragedy*, Niebuhr also began to celebrate the political cleverness of Roosevelt, which he had still decried in the 1936 election. In 1940, he published *Christianity and Power Politics*, cutting his ties to the "old illusions" of socialism and Christian passiveness. He changed the name of his quarterly from *Radical Religion* to *Christianity and Society*. He retreated from what had been the very sources of his prophetic formula for challenging America since the 1920s, legitimating capitalism, embracing Roosevelt's use of propaganda, and applauding the fiction of "lend-lease." Niebuhr was desperately rejecting a path that he, still a proponent of the Progressive social gospel at heart, believed instinctively must lead away from confidence and into political despair.[65]

"Loyalty to the truth requires confidence in the possibility of its attainment," Niebuhr wrote in his second volume of *The Nature and Destiny of Man*, which appeared in 1943. "Toleration requires broken confidence in the finality of our own truth. But if there is no answer for a problem to which we do not have the answer," he continued, "our shattered confidence generates either defeat (which in the field of culture would be scepticism); or an even greater measure of pretension, meant to hide our perplexities behind our certainties (which in the field of culture is fanaticism)."⁶⁶ Therefore, as we have seen, finding a basis for confidence became Niebuhr's obsessive mission. It was a mission that privately led him to seek psychiatric help for intense feelings of inadequacy by the mid-1950s, while permitting him to provide, through irony, the theoretical moral foundations for the American security state that emerged from World War II.⁶⁷

The integration of capitalism and democracy that Niebuhr achieved during this period helped link anticommunism with civil rights and American foreign policy with human liberation, without defending the discredited ideal of American national exceptionalism. Niebuhr's ability to offer such a powerful reformulation of an American mission was, in part, a result of his refashioning of the terms of the American jeremiad that Weber had supplied in *The Protestant Ethic*. By challenging the terms of Weber's jeremiad and its confidence-shattering implications for figures such as Perry Miller and the Americans Miller mourned in his scholarship, Niebuhr restored a foundation for confidence and for a reassertion of the Protestant Reformation as the foundation of a corporate American nationalism.

This challenge, though implied in *Moral Man and Immoral Society* and his subsequent works, was systematically presented for the first time in *The Nature and Destiny of Man*. Here, Niebuhr refashioned Weber's thesis in *The Protestant Ethic*, which had posited a tragic Reformation, into a thesis positing a tragic Renaissance. In doing so, Niebuhr substituted a "spirit of optimism" as the tragic flaw in Western culture for Weber's "spirit of capitalism."⁶⁸ Now Niebuhr simply needed to reintegrate the Lutheran and Calvinist reformations, and he had the basis for a new confidence in the mission and future of American democratic institutions. The aim of this synthesis is what he called "prophetic messianism."⁶⁹

Niebuhr specifically identified the Renaissance, as the spirit of optimism, with the problem of confidence. By transmuting Christian eschatology into an instrumental form of history called progress, "the classical confidence in rational man was dissociated from the historical pessimism of classical culture and made the instrument of historical optimism," he explained. Whereas Weber had written of the spirit of capitalism growing out of Calvinism, Niebuhr wrote of the spirit of optimism having grown out of science. Thus, for him, Renaissance meant not just the Italian Renaissance, but the spirit of optimism that also included Cartesian rationalism, the French Enlightenment, the liberal idea of progress, sectarian utopianism and Marxist catastrophism, as well.[70]

Niebuhr traced the tragic consequences of the spirit of optimism from two different sources: first, the confidence of classicism, and second, the Christian traditions of sanctification. Perfectionist sects, like science, he argued, had their origins in the spirit of optimism of the Renaissance. The messianic excesses of Calvinism, therefore, grew not out of the double vision of history as fulfillment and judgment that was characteristic of the Reformation, but out of the single, instrumentalist view of history as fulfillment that was a legacy of the Renaissance. The Renaissance had given the West valuable qualities, such as scientific progress and democracy, which the Reformation's sense of limits could not have provided. But the absolute triumph of the Renaissance in the modern era meant that the Reformation tradition was lost. As a leading spokesman for the Reformation tradition in America, Niebuhr had the responsibility to reclaim that lost tradition and replace the false Renaissance-inspired confidence of Marxism, liberal progressivism and even of Catholicism. To do so, he would turn Tillich's Protestant Principle on its head to negatively restore the authority of the Reformation out of its very weakness.

Niebuhr began by repeating Weber's analysis of the Lutheran and Calvinist sides of the Reformation. A measure of the complexity of the problem the Reformation balanced, Niebuhr explained, was the leading of Lutheranism into the trap of "supramoralism, not to say, antinomianism," while "the Calvinistic Reformation is imperilled by the opposite danger of a new moralism and legalism."[71] If such narrow legalism destroyed Puritanism, he said, its opposite tendency had fatally compromised the legacy of Luther. If Luther made too little of sanctification, Calvin made too much of it. Once more, Niebuhr charged, Calvin's ethical system is antidemocratic and arrogant, "for it gives the Christian an unjustified confidence in the transcendent perfection of the moral standards which he had derived from scripture and obscures not only the endless relativities of judgement involved in applying a scriptural standard to a particular situation, but also the historical relativities which are imbedded in these Scriptural standards themselves."[72]

These twin failures of perfectionism as narrow legalism, on the Calvinist side, and antinomianism on the Lutheran side, permitted the more unified instrumentalism of Renaissance optimism to triumph over both. But, said Niebuhr, a new synthesis was now both possible and necessary.

It was necessary, he said, because "we have lived through . . . centuries of hope and we are now in . . . a period of disillusionment. These centuries of hope have nearly destroyed the Christian faith as a potent force in modern life." A new synthesis, which rejects both the Catholic-Renaissance ideal of perfectionism of the Middle Ages and the scientific-Renaissance synthesis of the modern era, he said, could reestablish the legitimacy of the Protestant Reformation through the "creative despair which induces a new faith." A new synthesis of the Renaissance and Reformation, he suggested, could retain the optimism of the former, but reassert the spiritual and ethical demands of the latter. This new synthesis of the Renaissance and Reformation would reassert meaning for modern men and women "without placing an abortive confidence" in mere historical growth, as the triumph of the Renaissance spirit of optimism had done.[73]

The synthesis that Niebuhr offered carefully avoided mention of the problem of capitalism so central to Weber's analysis. It balanced Lutheran antinomianism against Calvinist legalism, and Lutheran defeatism against the Calvinist will, in order to construct a religious and ethical standard for Christian realism. Relying neither on false optimism nor perfectionist ideals, it would be based on the standard of "indeterminate possibilities"—an acquiescence to the inevitability of corruption in human affairs that must last until history comes to a divinely ordered end.[74] Niebuhr thought that a chastened Renaissance hope could bridge the gap between the two Reformation traditions to provide a ground between the two jeremiads that Weber had found to be incompatible.

On the Lutheran side, Niebuhr drew upon the antiprogressive and prophetic jeremiad of Søren Kierkegaard, who had attacked the idea of Christendom itself as a false abstraction in the nineteenth century. Niebuhr then linked Kierkegaard's jeremiad to the discredited jeremiad of Puritan messianism. Niebuhr did not view Kierkegaard as prophetic corrective to Lutheranism, as Kierkegaard had seen himself. Rather he used Kierkegaard's criticism of Lutheranism, in the context of American political exceptionalism, as a corrective to the same Calvinist messianism that had brought about the Civil War and World War I. From this unlikely pairing of Kierkegaardian individualism with Calvinist institutionalism, Niebuhr fashioned a prophetic messianism out of the negative balance of each side of the Reformation against the other. The result was that Niebuhr was able to preserve confidence in the mission of America through realism while disavowing national exceptionalism through idealism. Abraham Lincoln, as the messianic warrior of prophetic sorrow, served as the embodiment of Niebuhr's refashioned jeremiad.[75] As a man of political acumen and theological sophistication, Niebuhr had accurately recognized that confidence in an American mission could be restored only negatively in the second half of the twentieth century.

Niebuhr's synthesis remained powerful during the Cold War and the concomitant development of the civil rights movement. Only in the 1970s did the internal contradictions of the two jeremiads he had fused begin to unravel. However, even as Vietnam shattered the synthesis of anticommunism and civil rights, and as irony undermined the legitimacy of American power rather than affirming it, the quest for confidence that was behind Niebuhr's synthesis never abated. Already during the 1950s, science, which Weber associated with the "spirit of capitalism" and which Niebuhr associated with the "spirit of optimism," had entered into a crisis of confidence concerning the future of the environment and the continued existence of human life itself.

It was in the context of such doubts that Thomas Kuhn's highly regarded book, *The Structure of Scientific Revolutions*, appeared in 1962.[76] Kuhn used history to challenge the Whiggish interpretation of science as a universal form of progress. Kuhn's critique of Progressive conceptions of science grew directly out of the counter-Progressive historiography of Miller's and Niebuhr's generation. Indeed, as Gene Wise noted, Niebuhr provided the paradigm revolution which, in principle, synthesized similar challenges to either the privileged status of scientific or religious ways of knowing.[77] Kuhn himself recognized that his ideas were not new, only newly applied to the philosophy of science. Indeed, Kuhn offered little more than Carl Becker had already said in his classic 1931 essay, "Every Man His Own Historian," with the important exception that Kuhn located the power of coercion in professional communities themselves, while Becker located it in the public at large. Similarly, as suggested earlier, the philosopher Richard Rorty has noted the compatibility of Kuhn's science with Dewey's philosophical system.[78]

Like Becker or Dewey, Kuhn did not describe scientific truth as a set of universal principles beyond culture but as a social discourse on agreed-upon paradigms. He drew a parallel between politics and science, suggesting that revolutions occur in each area for approximately the same reasons and in the same ways. Individuals, he said, become more and more estranged from the establishment; they form themselves into competing parties, and eventually this minority of marginal figures takes power. Kuhn pointed out that no paradigm is fully legitimate, with those winning over rival paradigms to become "normal science" doing so through mass persuasion and even by force. The "abnormal science," or heresies, under the old regime, becomes the new orthodoxy. But in deposing the old order and installing a new one, a confidence game is inevitably played out. A messy and erratic change of paradigms, said Kuhn, is turned into an orderly march of progress, confirming the rationality of the scientific process and reaffirming the authority of the scientists to the public as well as to themselves. In short, Kuhn wrote, the textbooks "have to be rewritten in the aftermath of each scientific revolution, and, once rewritten, they inevitably disguise not only the role, but the very existence of the revolutions that produced them." Since no paradigm is ever completely satisfactory, the questions asked about it within the scientific community are circumscribed by the political influence of those who hold allegiance to the paradigm. Troublesome problems are dismissed as metaphysical, or irrelevant, until anomalies pile up beyond the ability to avoid them.[79]

Kuhn's description of paradigm revolution essentially follows Machiavelli's description of the Prince's fate. Like Machiavelli, he places the inevitable role of deception at the center of a process that revolves around the problem of confidence. For Kuhn, scientific knowledge, like politics, has become a structure of confidence rather than a foundation upon which to build confidence. For Kuhn, too, as for Niebuhr, Becker, Dewey, Miller and Bercovitch, paradigms, like jeremiads, have lost their privileged status as foundational truths. Science, like religion and politics, appears as particular strategies for interpreting purely formal systems of meaning.

Kuhn's description of scientific progress as a series of collapsing paradigms, however, did not make him lose confidence in scientific progress, as many of his readers assumed. To the contrary, for him as for Machiavelli, innovation was justified because it preserves the tradition it destroys. This Machiavellian faith in regeneration through destruction, in the context of Kuhn's theory, is the paradox that paradigmatic revolution preserves the assurance that the puzzle-solving identity of normal science will be retained when the order is restored. As a result, for Kuhn, the progress of science is cyclical rather than linear, making Einstein closer to Aristotle than Newton, but better than either. Under force and deception, which Kuhn identifies with the breakdown and rebirth of patterns of meaning, he sees the vindication of a community's highest ideals of progress—a position indistinguishable from Machiavelli's plea for a prince to liberate Italy, which, having suffered a fortunate fall, is now "ready and willing to follow any standard if only there be some one to raise it."[80]

Kuhn's defense of the democratic implication of this process, and his faith that it will reveal a true science rather than a false one, however, most closely parallels Reinhold Niebuhr's arguments concerning politics and religion and Niebuhr's faith in the casuistic process for creating a democratic future. Their common Machiavellian conventions for establishing confidence may be seen even more clearly through the writings of Stephen Jay Gould, a contemporary paleontologist and popular essayist, who has written extensively on the theme of evolutionary science, progress and individual freedom.

Gould has argued persuasively for a democratic paradigm for faith in science by attacking the same "spirit of optimism" that Niebuhr attacked in order to restore the primacy of the Reformation. Like Kuhn, Gould has seen normal science as a threat to democratic science, and has attacked the textbook process of erasing history to create a false confidence in the progress of science.[81] As a student of evolutionary science, however, Gould has been able to challenge the Weberian pessimism concerning the disenchantment of the world accepted by both Niebuhr and Kuhn. He has argued that biological catastrophism—extinction—is a proof of the contingency of all life, including human life, and, therefore, of its historicity. For Gould, Frank Capra's *It's a Wonderful Life* presents a paradigmatic statement of this new scientific appreciation for contingency. His book on the Burgess shale and the nature of history, published in 1989 and entitled *Wonderful Life* in honor of Capra's film, is a radical affirmation of the scientific vocation as a contingent cultural practice and is a redemptive vision of the insignificance of history that Capra had been unwilling fully to face.[82]

Gould's effort to establish confidence in science as a cultural activity, which is neither relativistic nor dogmatic, may be seen in an earlier essay on the history of geology, *Time's Arrow, Time's Cycle*. In that essay, he identified the discovery of deep time, a fundamental principle of modern science, as at once a vindication of the spirit of discovery and a profound crisis of confidence in Western institutions and values. Gould voiced this paradoxical position in the opening words of his reflection on history in *Time's Arrow, Time's Cycle*. "Sigmund Freud remarked," he wrote, "that each major science has made one signal contribution to the reconstruction of human thought—and that each step in this painful progress had shattered yet another facet of an original hope for our own transcendent importance in the universe."[83]

For Gould, the discovery of deep time was as shattering to confidence in a human-centered world and universe as Galileo's, Darwin's, and Freud's revolutions were before and after it. Yet Gould equally professed to see, within the discovery of deep time as presumably in these other revolutions, a confirmation of the positive cultural partnership between scientific innovation and Judaic-Christian religious tradition—a partnership that affirmed a basis for real confidence in the progress of science, as opposed to a sham confidence, formulated out of Whiggish "textbook cardboard" versions of the history of science, which, he said, ingenuously pit rational and empirical science against a superstitious, obscurantist church.

Gould's unlikely hero in revealing this partnership was the villain of textbook accounts of the history of science, the Reverend Thomas Burnet, the seventeenth-century author of a classic millennialist text, *The Sacred Theory of the Earth*. Rather than retarding the march of science, Gould argued, he codified the very terms by which deep time could become intelligible to Western science. He merged myth and metaphor with empirical observation to make the inconceivable an object of thought and to place the ages before the advent of human time into a pattern of history.

In doing so, the theologian provided an aesthetically pleasing theory for reconciling the contradictions of a natural history based on the linear conventions of time's arrow and the repetitious pattern contained within time's cycles. The endless repetition of creation and conflagration, based on the liturgical calendar and millennial clock, in which God's days correspond to human years, finally completing God's great year encompassing all of created time, would ultimately lead to "a new order of things." For, according to Burnet, "the earth must be reduced into fluid mass, in the nature of chaos, as it was at first; but this last will be a fiery chaos, as that was watery; and from this state it will emerge again into a paradisiacal world." Burnet's vision, as illustrated in the famous frontispiece to *The Sacred Theory*, is, said Gould, a detailed correspondence "between present and future, the two great cycles of our planet's course; but history moves inexorably forward as it cycles. Dark chaos lies under Christ's left foot, marking our beginnings; but the bright star of our ending closes the circle of the great year."[85]

Gould saluted Burnet's millennial vision of creation because it gave voice to the common cultural heritage out of which came the theories of James Hutton and Charles Lyell, who, in turn, formed the basis for modern scientific knowledge of the origins of the earth. But Gould's challenge to Whiggish history in the name of democratic science suggests another reason for his warm regard for Burnet. It is a reason echoed in his sincere identification with James Hampton's millennialist sculpture, *The Throne of the Third Heaven of the Nation's Millennium General Assembly*.

Hampton was a black janitor who created, out of bits of aluminium foil and found objects, a great throne room based on the Book of Revelation. Gould viewed Hampton's masterpiece at the Smithsonian Institution, where it has been on display since Hampton's death in 1967. It struck him that the symbolism used by the artist Hampton was identical to Burnet's, and that consequently science could be harmonized with the Judaic-Christian tradition in all its variations. For Gould, this was a profoundly moral conclusion, as well as an affirmation of the possibility of scientific progress in a contingent world. For a Jewish-American scientist of the late twentieth century to find a common democratic thread with which to bind the seventeenth-century Calvinist Burnet and the African-American Hampton together was also to share Burnet's and Hampton's dream. This was the dream, in Burnet's words, of "Happy days of peace and righteousness, of joy and triumph, of external prosperity and internal sanctity, when virtue and innocency shall be on the throne, vice and vicious men out of power and credit, as propheseied of in scripture, and promised to the church of God."[86] In Gould, as in the seventeenth-century millennialist Burnet and the twentieth-century millennialist Hampton, this is a call for confidence in a messianic future, not a prophetic challenge against dogmatism. As Ernest Lee Tuveson noted, Burnet was offering a political and social ideal of utopia, not merely a description of the course of natural history. So, too, in the final analysis, are the counter-Progressive scientist-historians Thomas Kuhn and Steven Jay Gould.

Reinhold Niebuhr and Frank Capra, each in his own very different way, used the conventions of classical theater and the masques of illusion to help establish a pattern for a new counter-Progressive historical understanding of the United States. This was a pattern that scientific theorists such as Thomas Kuhn and Stephen Jay Gould were able to apply to nuclear-age science, as well. Each used the aesthetics of the sublime to preserve a fading utopian promise for Enlightenment politics and science as agencies for preserving confidence both in social institutions and in human freedom. However, the sociologist and theologian Will Herberg, perhaps Niebuhr's most visible disciple in the 1950s and 1960s, had already consciously applied Niebuhr's thought to this end as early as the 1930s.

Though Herberg was an atheist and a leading theorist for the American Communist Party during the 1920s, he had experienced a crisis of faith in universal science by the time he discovered and appropriated Niebuhr's religious synthesis in the 1930s. But by the 1960s, Herberg had become convinced that confidence in universal natural law might only be preserved by sacrificing human freedom itself. Will Herberg's spiritual journey from the Left to the Right, from being a messianic Marxist to a messianic theist who subsequently moved from embracing existential religious philosophy to identifying tradition with the police, sounds a discordant note to Kuhn's and Gould's confidence that democratic science may balance freedom and order in a contingent universe. For the equally historicist Herberg, the metaphysical threat to confidence posed by the spiritual anarchy of freedom ultimately appeared to be too much to risk. Herberg explicitly argued that the utilitarian requirements of confidence necessarily demand the surrender of romantic trust if order is to be preserved. However, far from seeing this admission as a repudiation of Niebuhr's counter-Progressive legacy, Herberg, by the 1960s, was convinced that he was completing Niebuhr's own mission for restoring confidence in the United States during the Cold War.

7

Will Herberg's Crusade against Authenticity

If Cold War America were to have had an official prophet of confidence, in the Hebraic sense of a God-intoxicated individual whose message of redemption is focused through the struggles of his own life, that prophet would have been Will Herberg. Herberg's personal odyssey, from his birth in Russia in 1901 to his death in 1977, took him from the shtetel to the theological faculty of Drew University, from editing the communist newspaper *Revolutionary Age* to being religion editor of the conservative *National Review*, and from admiring Karl Marx to becoming an exponent of Edmund Burke.

In each phase of his life, Herberg identified with a movement or social philosophy that promised to achieve a marriage between universal laws of social redemption and his hunger for personal meaning. In each instance he ultimately failed to sustain his attempt to balance materialism and idealism, until he finally rejected the effort in the 1960s, repudiating the possibility of an authentic self. Herberg, therefore, began with a search for confidence and ended by concluding that doubt could only be contained at the price of trust. In his personal odyssey through "the American Way of Life," as he characterized the shared quest for meaning within a Judeo-Christian political community, he made use of a series of masks, invented identities, and rhetorical pyrotechnics. He was a showman, he himself admitted. Actually, he was something more. He was a twentieth-century intellectual Barnum. Like his nineteenth-century counterpart, he needed to appear sincere before the public and to expose confidence artists and their scams in order to redeem his own deceptive behavior through service to a transcendent cultural ideal.

His public role of playing impresario in regard to the ecumenical wisdom of Martin Buber, Paul Tillich, Jacques Maritain, and Nicolai Berdyaev was as integral to high Cold War American culture as was the promotion of abstract expressionism by art critic Clement Greenberg, the attack upon the culture industry by Dwight Macdonald and the Frankfurt school, or the period's films, music, and novels of youthful alienation. As a Cold War Barnum, Herberg had an eye for acts that the public would pay to see. That faculty made him successful despite, and even because of, the fact that he personally contributed little original insight and played only a minor role in interpreting the intellectual ferment of the time. For Herberg's influence was not the result of bold new ideas. It was rather that he promoted the ideas of others who had confronted the question of personal responsibility in an age of collective power, and that he did so with the authoritative assurance of an expert guide, through which he successfully appealed to an anxious and alienated American middle class. Herberg, in short, made his place in post–World War II America as an impresario of confidence, whose province was neither the arts, as was Greenberg's, nor entertainment, as was Macdonald's, but science, social theory and theology.

Herberg's penchant for exploiting rhetoric may be seen at its most characteristic in his scholastic skill at devastating a position that he might then turn around and uncompromisingly expound. Jay Lovestone's secretary, Edward Sagarin, for example, reported to Alan Wald that Herberg had thoroughly and permanently overwhelmed him in the 1930s with the logic against God's existence. Then, almost immediately, Herberg had embraced orthodox Jewish practice, and established himself as a major authority on American religion. By the late 1940s, he had achieved the self-appointed role of interpreter of the Judeo-Christian tradition for modern Americans. By the late 1960s, with equal assurance, he could repudiate from the pages of William F. Buckley's *National Review* both the Pauline theological tradition and the reforms of Pope John XXIII. In each instance, he did so in the name of preserving what he called the Judeo-Christian civilization from its own misguided traditions.[1]

To describe Herberg as an apologist for the "American Way of Life," a value system he placed in capital letters, and as an impresario of existentialist philosophy and theology is not to say that he was superficial or that he was inconsistent in his changing enthusiasms. To the contrary, Herberg's biographers agree that he remained committed to essentially the same principles at the end of his life, when he was writing in service to the New Political and Religious Right, that he had held at the beginning of his career, when he wrote in service to the Communist Party. Herberg disclosed an important reason for this continuity in his last years. In 1973, when his health began deteriorating from the brain tumor that would end his life, he wrote in the margin of Ruth Baven's book, *Marx and Burke: A Revisionist View*, that "Both [Marx and Burke] were socially and culturally conservative." Indeed, as early as 1953, Herberg praised Burke's realism and his posititive influence on British Whigs such as Lord Acton and on the American founding fathers. In 1959, Herberg accurately recognized that Reinhold Niebuhr's theology spoke so profoundly to Cold War Americans because it was a bridge between Burkean and Marxian versions of historicism.[2]

Perhaps because of his insight into the Burkean implications of his earlier Marxist approach to antisectarianism, Herberg anticipated by a decade or more Robert Bellah's identification of civil religion as the central Cold War convention shared by all Americans. In the late 1940s, Herberg was entirely critical of civil religion, viewing it as a manifestation of the demonic character of modern nationalism. By the early 1950s, however, he had become more ambivalent about the legitimacy of civil religion, though not about its efficacy as a force for social order and cohesion. By virtue of his Marxist training and his neo-Burkean analysis, Herberg presented a more complex picture of civil religion by the mid-1950s than would Bellah, whose famous 1962 article emphasized only the common elements of the sacred shared by Americans. Herberg, instead, stressed the paradoxical implication for viewing civil religion in the United States as simultaneously a fraudulent religion and a true source of unity, as both a source of false democracy and the ground of an authentic national identity.

The American Way of Life, Herberg wrote in *Protestant, Catholic, Jew* (1954), a work that delicately balanced Herberg's Marxism and neo-Burkean historicism, is based on "America's *faith in faith.*" It is not a faith in anything in particular, he insisted, so much as "just faith, 'the magic of believing.'" There were two sources for this cult of religiosity that supported the general popular belief in the American Way of Life, Herberg wrote: one was faith healing, which grew out of the nineteenth-century New Thought and Christian Science movements; the other was simply "positive thinking." Gradually, Herberg explained, these affirmative attitudes merged to become "an appeal to maintain a 'positive' attitude to life and not to lose confidence in oneself and one's activities."[3]

In *Protestant, Catholic, Jew* Herberg also associated civil religion with nationalism. He warned that the identification of religion with national purpose was almost inevitable when religion was so frequently associated with belonging, as it was among Americans. In its crudest form, this identification of religion with the national purpose generates a national messianism, he said, "which sees it as the vocation of America to bring the American Way of Life, compounded almost equally of democracy and free enterprise to every corner of the globe; in more mitigated versions, it sees God as the champion of America, endorsing American purposes, and sustaining American might." Yet, ultimately, Herberg affirmed civil religion because, in its "highest form" of the interfaith movement, it provided an overarching unity. Such unity, he said, is mandatory if democracy is to function. Herberg recognized the interfaith movement as a political expedient, but argued that it extends "far beyond such necessity; the very notion of tripartite arrangement is something that increasingly recommends itself to the American mind as intrinsically right and proper because it is so obviously American and so obviously all inclusive of the total American community."[4]

It was this shift to a utilitarian acceptance of civil religion, despite his acknowledgment of its inescapably pseudoreligious character from the perspective of orthodox Judaism and Christianity, which marked the beginning of Herberg's return to Leninism through Burke. Indeed, in 1971 the ex-Leninist Herberg essentially read the Augustinian tradition out of Judeo-Christianity as right-deviationists, who threatened universalism by their insistence on individualism.[5] It was a return that was, finally, not based upon ideological commitment or fear of anarchy but upon Herberg's continuing need to preserve the Enlightenment foundations of confidence. Herberg's changing positions as Lovestonite communist, Jewish theologian, and neo-Burkean social critic were rooted in his service to the logical necessities that such a quest required of him as a prophet of confidence in Cold War America.

Will Herberg's search for confidence in America began with his father, Hyman Louis, who lived his early life in a small Russian village near Minsk. Educated and progressive enough to work as an electrical contractor, Hyman Louis dreamed of American opportunity, and he brought his family to New York in 1904. He did not prosper, however; he neglected his business, quarreled with his wife, and by World War I had left his family and disappeared. One story says that he ran off with another woman and lived in South America; another, that he died a pauper in a New York apartment.⁶ Regardless of his eventual fate, Will's disillusionment with his father and his country may be indicated by his conflict with the officer in charge of his required military class at City College of New York (CCNY) in 1920. The cause of Herberg's rebelliousness is not known, although, at the time, Americans were disillusioned with the consequences of World War I. Many felt that the war had accomplished nothing tangible but an economic depression. Freud was in vogue, and Herberg was reading him avidly.⁷

The nineteen-year-old student of psychology, languages, literature, mathematics and science dropped out of school rather than participate in ROTC. He became active in the Young Workers League. He quickly rose to the directorship of the agitprop section of the politburo and to membership in the editorial committee of the *Young Worker*. But by 1926 he was writing in favor of military training for young communists in the league's summer schools. How could communists advocate summer military training when other communists were protesting required ROTC classes at state universities? Herberg asked rhetorically. The answer, he said, was simple. Military training on college campuses advanced the cause of imperialism, while such training at YWL camps advanced the cause of revolution. Young communists, Herberg said, must "purge themselves of pacifist illusions."⁸

Herberg's entire life to this point had been directed towards achieving universality. As a student of Hebrew and French, Freud and mathematics, the young communist organizer had avoided the problem of his particularity as a Jew and an American. He had also sidestepped the ethical responsibilities of being an individual of conscience. He had neutralized every particular contradiction through the larger movement of natural law that was dynamically creating an international human community in history. Indeed, history itself held little interest for Herberg at this stage of his life. He looked to the future as the promised land of personal and communal harmony.

Herberg was, therefore, unprepared for the ethical and intellectual earthquake that struck in 1929. The earthquake was not the Great Depression, which for Herberg only confirmed his confidence in Lenin's prophecy of the necessary collapse of capitalist societies. Rather, he was deeply shocked and angry to discover that just when world capitalism was on the brink of destruction before the natural laws of international revolution, Stalin had betrayed international communism. As it turned out, Stalin was not the leader of a universal movement of international liberation. Instead, he discovered, Stalin was merely another sectarian political leader who was willing to squander universal laws of social reconstruction for partisan political and personal ends. Herberg had found security in his identity within the party. Suddenly, through unexpected events of history, he found himself marginalized, both as a member of the Communist Party and as a Marxist.

Herberg shared with Jay Lovestone, the leader of the American Communist Party, full confidence in the Leninist vision of international communism. They were able to balance their Marxist perspective with their American identities, or their universalist doctrine of natural law with their personal sense of their own contexts, through the doctrine of American exceptionalism. That interpretation of the character of the revolution did not mean that Lovestone and Herberg questioned the inevitable collapse of capitalism in the United States and the rest of the world. Rather, they argued that the particular historical conditions of the United States should not be forced into a rigid and false universalism that would only artificially repeat the Russian pattern. To the contrary, Lovestone and Herberg argued, the natural law of revolutionary Leninism required revolutionaries to adapt to the particularities of the historical situations in which they found themselves until the completion of the universal revolution in the future. Though Jay Lovestone had the support of the majority of the American party in holding this interpretation of Leninist principles, he made a devastating tactical mistake, which plunged him and his party into chaos. He backed what he thought was party cohesion by supporting Nikolai Bukharin, Stalin's ally, against Trotsky in the struggle for leadership among Lenin's heirs in the Soviet Union. Lovestone could not have imagined that as soon as Stalin defeated Trotsky, in the name of party unity, he would turn on Bukharin. Thus, in November of 1929, Lovestone and the American communists he led were caught in the cross fire of Stalin's own sectarian ambitions for power.

The struggle among the founders of the revolution and the Americans who lined up in response indicated more than an internal battle for control of the party. It embodied a contradiction at the very heart of an international revolutionary faith. The party acted objectively in history for the proletariat, not subjectively for itself. The party, unlike bourgeois capitalism, could not contradict itself, so the party had to be followed regardless of personal or doctrinal disagreement. When Trotsky had become a dissident within the party, he had fostered sectarianism and, therefore, he had denied the basic values of Leninism as well as the meaning of the October Revolution. However, as Marxists, the Lovestonites could not accept the abuse of Lenin's internationalist values for the provincial and particular advancement of Stalinism any more than they could justify Trotsky's sectarianism. They therefore fought back when Stalin attempted to silence them. They took their case to Russia and to the executive committee of the Comintern.

Stalin attended the meeting and denounced the Lovestonites as "strikebreakers and anarchists," or, in other words, sectarians. The Lovestonites who had come to the Comintern with 90 percent of the party membership in the United States returned with their leader expelled and reduced to a remnant of a mere two hundred members. In response, they desperately held on to their claim of being the true universalists and defenders of Lenin's doctrine of "democratic centralism"; that is, they claimed to be a loyal, not a sectarian, opposition. The little remnant launched their own journal, *Revolutionary Age*, which they considered a resuscitation of the newspaper that John Reed and Lovestonites Ben Gitlow and Bertram Wolf had published after World War I. Herberg became managing editor.[9]

In February 1930, writing in *Revolutionary Age*, Herberg defended the Lovestonite claim to the revolution by writing a tribute to the German socialist martyr Rosa Luxemburg, whom Lenin had praised despite her criticism of the doctrine of democratic centralism. Rosa Luxemburg, Herberg intoned, "does not belong to the workers of any country." She represented the revolutionary consciousness and will of the class "whose historical mission it is to overturn the very basis of modern society in order to rebuild it on new foundations."[10] That March, Herberg directly attacked Stalin, calling for an internationalist perspective against a provincial Russian one. The party, he wrote, must return to the tactical flexibility advocated by Lenin. By January of 1931, Herberg had lost all patience. "Whatever Stalin the theoretician touches," he complained, "he vulgarizes beyond recognition." It was Stalin who appeared to be backing away from revolutionary confrontation with capitalism, Herberg charged. Stalin was suggesting that Russia should accommodate the capitalist West, he complained. The Lovestonites had championed Leninism without compromise, predicting the rebuilding of capitalism after the First World War, in their doctrine of American exceptionalism. Yet it was the fate of the Lovestonites to be expelled by the duplicitous Stalin as right deviationists![11]

At the same time that Herberg was defending the Lovestonites against

Stalin in the pages of the *Revolutionary Age*, he undertook a series of articles on the relation of science to communist doctrine. The theme of these articles was always the same: history and natural law must be harmonized through the dialectical achievement of science. Indeed, in the midst of his anguished political struggle within the party, Herberg falsely reported that a paper entitled "The Philosophy of Science and Scientific Philosophy" was his doctoral thesis at CCNY.[12] The complementary relationship between those subjects, as a crisis in the Enlightenment foundation of confidence, was also the foundation of his own confidence game as a respected academic. It was fundamental to Herberg's later turn to theology.

For Herberg, science was not a dry or abstract set of dogmatic principles. He characterized it as a "permanent and ever renewing bond" with life that was the source of its fertility. It was, therefore, essential for physical science, as well as for economic science, that history and natural law should exist in harmony. Practically, this meant that Marxian science dictated that the party must avoid sectarianism both internally and externally. In late 1931, he explained that this did not mean the false idealism of formal democracy. The hopelessly corrupt middle class could not be the source of renewal. The bourgeois partisanship of intellectuals lacked the social solidarity required for real change. Like the "greedy Jewish sweat shop exploiter" or the "corrupt Negro politician," bourgeois intellectuals failed to submerge themselves in the universality embodied in the proletariat. Because the proletariat was the lowest common denominator of all humanity, he reasoned, all humanity would find justice when the proletariat achieved it, and only then.[13]

Shortly after his warning against intellectual isolation from the perspective of the masses, he castigated the official Communist Party in the same terms. A planned march against hunger that was to be staged by the party had failed to include the poor themselves as equals in the planning. But, said Herberg, only protestors "in the closest organic contact" with the unemployed and the workers could have any lasting effect. Making the march a private affair of the party, the Lovestonite exile wrote, could only be self-defeating. The mobilization of the masses could never occur on the basis of "sterile sectarianism," he complained. "The breath of sectarianism is death."[14]

Science, for Herberg, was the very essence of the modern. It should have ushered in a resolution to the contradiction between the particulars of history and the universal natural law of Marxism. But Herberg's dilemma during the 1930s was that his faith in the eventual triumph of modern progress through Marxism had been complicated by his discovery that there was not a single modern. There were, instead, ideologically competing forms of the modern. The science that had first been produced during the the Enlightenment was the product of bourgeois idealists who were able to "look the world of nature confidently in the face and make a bold effort to dominate it." The bourgeois scientists of the eighteenth and nineteenth centuries had such confidence, he said, because the bourgeois class was itself simultaneously "making a gigantic and successful effort to dominate the world of society." The successful revolution in Russia, he argued, had inaugurated a new era of confidence. Revolutionary science would fulfil Enlightenment dreams through the rise of the proletariat. Precisely because of this modern material triumph, the bourgeoisie who had initiated the drive toward the modern now felt frightened and unconfident. When they had been in a period of cultural and economic ascendency, they had neither questioned the validity nor the desirability of scientific determinism. Now that they were in retreat, as victims of the dialectics of their own drive to power, the bourgeoisie were drawn to the scientific idealism of Eddington's and Jeans's physics and the relativism suggested by Einstein's special theory. The middle class now wished to hear that the very foundations of science, materialism and determinism, were "empty illusions." The modern turn to mysticism in science, as in the religion of Marx's day, Herberg suggested, was a sign of decadence and cultural defeatism. It was, he argued, an escape both from history as lived experience and from science as the practical formulation of natural law. Its final result was self-annihilation for a class whose day was nearly spent.[15]

But, behind his bravado, Herberg had been shaken by the same contradiction of history for the communist errand that led Perry Miller into despair as he contemplated the failure of the Puritan errand: the universal mission had turned out to be a mere particular. For Herberg, Einstein and the new physics confirmed that history and natural law had become divorced from each other. The new physics appeared to discredit scientific materialism, Herberg admitted, because the theory of relativity placed objective reality outside the powers of human apprehension. Einstein had shown that all knowledge of the physical universe is necessarily a function of the relativism of observation. Physicists such as Eddington and Jeans had interpreted the concept of indeterminacy as a confirmation that the universe could only be experienced as an idea. It appeared that, just as Bishop Berkeley had believed, the universe was an intellectual construction, a creation of the human mind.

Herberg's defense of orthodox Marxist materialism against this interpretation was essentially the same one Perry Miller would say had been mounted by Jonathan Edwards and the Puritans against the opposite problem that the Newtonian physics had presented for them. First principles could never be observed, Miller's Puritan apologist Edwards pointed out. "The natural world is, therefore, reasonable yet mysterious—and so infinitely susceptible to spiritualization," despite its apparent materialistic determinism. The natural world, for the Marxist apologist Herberg, was mysterious yet reasonable and, therefore, infinitely susceptible to materialization. Einstein, Herberg concluded, only appeared to confirm the idealism of the universe. It was true that Einstein had denied the existence of absolute space and time, Herberg admitted, but he had still confirmed the reality of the relation between objects and between events. The scientist had affirmed that what defines a thing is its measurement. Without real objects and actual events, there could be neither time nor space and, hence, no measurement. Therefore, Herberg reasoned, because men can only know what enters their experience, the relativistic measurement of matter and energy proves that the universe has objective material existence. In fact, Herberg argued, rather than threatening the Marxist view of the universe, Einstein had succeeded in confirming the fundamental tenet of Leninism: "the definition of a thing must be given through its relation to human practice." The implication for Herberg, in his attempt to preserve his Marxist faith, was that the Lovestonite position could be defended as ideologically pure Leninism and as compatible with the new physics. It is not surprising, therefore, that Herberg would later develop an affinity for Jonathan Edwards and that, like Miller, he would find Reinhold Niebuhr a valuable guide for the perplexed.[16]

Similarly, Herberg challenged the false modern of Darwinism, as he began to read American history more seriously, paying special attention to Vernon Parrington's *Main Currents in American Thought*. Preoccupied with the failure of the Russian Revolution, Herberg had been drawn to Parrington because of his interest in discovering the reasons for the failure of the American revolutions of 1776 and 1865. Herberg sympathized with Parrington's disillusionment with these failed revolutions, but was unmoved by Parrington's jeremiad calling for a return to nature to cure the corruption of the nation's history. The legacy shared by Einstein,

Darwin and Marx, Herberg insisted against Parrington, was that nature could not exist outside of history. Nineteenth-century science had been mistaken in its static metaphysical concept of the universe, he explained in an article comparing Darwinism and Marxism. Like Parrington, nineteenth-century science before Darwin had failed to regard nature as developing through time. Darwin had forever exploded the myth that nature was ahistorical, and, in doing so, had demolished Parrington's romantic naturalism. But Darwin had, at the same time, enshrined a false modernism, just as Einstein had done in his new physics. Evolutionism had made possible the false conclusions of social Darwinism as one way in which a supposed pattern disclosed in nature could be inappropriately and ahistorically applied to other situations. This, of course, is what Herberg had been accusing Stalinists and Trotskyists of doing to Leninism. Proponents of Darwinian evolutionism, therefore, were mistaken in forgetting the dialectical character of all progress. Revolutions, like science, he triumphantly concluded, move forward through contradiction.[17]

As an American independent communist, Herberg had been compelled to argue that the dialectical process must be pluralistic. He had defended the existence of differences in perspectives within the Marxist fold concerning the development of the modern, as well as the existence of alternatives within the modern itself. He recognized in the new physics a modern avant-garde that was dangerously defeatist. His resolution of progress through contradiction revealed a considerable strain on the idea of the modern as an eschatological culmination of time. Ironically, Herberg had to place the natural law of Marxism more firmly in history during the 1930s in order to retain his faith in progress. Thus, he argued, "the science of the future must be built on the science of the past," so that he could escape the mystical implications of the new physics, on one side, and Parrington's romantic naturalism, on the other. At this same time, Herberg wrote critically of Edmund Wilson's Trotskyist contention that the avant-garde of bourgeois literature would become the basis for a Marxist literature. Marxists, Herberg warned, could not simply appropriate the latest bourgeois style, as they could appropriate the latest bourgeois technology. Marxists would need to return to earlier forms of artistic expression that were more in tune with Marxist values.[18]

Politically, scientifically, and artistically, Herberg had come to the edge of a position of antimodernism by 1933, the year Hitler and Roosevelt came to power. His emphasis on history had made the integrity of the relation between means and ends and form and content vital to his ability to retain his faith in an exceptional communist future. His new emphasis on history had made the events appearing in the headlines of his newspaper determinative of the validity of his theory and his political faith.

Herberg struggled to retain his confidence in the revolution through the gloom of Hitler's rise to power and the accompanying destruction of the German Party, the rumbling of fascism in America, and his increasingly bitter opposition to Stalin's policies. In the November 1934 edition of *Workers Age*, the Lovestonite paper that had replaced the defunct *Revolutionary Age*, he celebrated seventeen years of "socialist construction" in the Soviet Union. In the article, he defended the Soviet system against the attack of Trotskyist sectarians, and explained away the failures of the regime.[19] But Herberg had not changed his mind or retracted his opposition to Stalin. Instead, he was expressing his support of Jacobinism, which was really a version of casuistry. It was a convenient equivocation of ethical standards that allowed him at once to support and to repudiate Stalin's leadership, in the interests of his transcending faith in the revolution. By 1936 and the Spanish Civil War, he was engaged in preserving an ever more precarious casuistic position. Like the French revolutionists, Herberg claimed, the Lovestone Communists would help fight the enemies of the revolution, even as they were locked in bitter contest with the official leadership of the party. The Lovestonites would defend Stalinists in Spain, as the force of liberation, knowing that as Jacobins they would remain enemies of Stalin. After the inevitable defeat of fascism, Herberg prophesied, the real battle for the revolution would be fought between the liberal bourgeoisie, supported by Stalin, and the peasants who were the proletariat of true Leninism.[20]

Herberg later wrote that his break with Marxism resulted from his inability to escape the implications of power that he confronted at this time. The democracies, despite official neutrality, cynically supported the fascists in Spain for their own economic interests, regardless of ideological distaste for both Franco and Stalin. Stalin, in his cynical support of the bourgeoisie, was as unconcerned with revolutionary principles as were the capitalists and fascists. It appeared to Herberg that all power, by its very nature, was sectarian. By the end of the decade, he was vociferously attacking both the democracies and the Stalinists for their indistinguishable pursuit of unprincipled power. His denunciations included the Catholic Church, which he described as the "mother of totalitarianism." Everywhere Herberg looked, in the ruthless rise of Nazism, the amoralism of Stalin in Spain, in the infamous Moscow Trials of 1937, and in the influence of Catholicism lurking behind fascism, the immorality of power seemed inescapable.[21] It was in this state of disillusionment that he discovered Reinhold Niebuhr through his book *Moral Man and Immoral Society*. Like Niebuhr, Herberg abandoned his confidence in Marxism and his belief in the Soviet Union as a redeemer nation. "Humanly speaking," Herberg confessed, Niebuhr's book had converted him, "for in some manner I cannot describe, I felt my whole being and not merely my thinking, shifted to a new center." Although he was pulled intellectually to Protestantism and now emotionally to Catholicism, he finally chose Judaism, again through Niebuhr's influence.[22]

In articles written during the 1940s in the Jewish Frontier, Herberg's deep disgust and sense of despair over "the demonic nature of all power" poured out. Power, he wrote in 1944, is dialectical, but it is dialectic without future hope. It is "a particularly detestable form of idolatry; it is devil worship in its modern form." The political machine survives, but the idealism behind it is killed, he wrote. Consequently, he charged, the self-serving character of power is misjudged by perfectionists and the cynically Machiavellian. Borrowing from Niebuhr's *The Nature and Destiny of Man*, Herberg complained that the former is "fatuously optimistic," only to become cynical. The absolutist, he said, refuses to participate in politics because he or she wishes to remain pure. Perfectionists, therefore, can offer no guidance to those caught in the contradictions of power. The Machiavellians, by which Herberg seems to have meant James Burnham's political realists as he described them in his 1943 book *The Machiavellians*, openly and unashamedly worship power. They duplicitously justify any evil in the name of an ultimate utopia. Both positions fail, Herberg insisted, because they do not understand that power stems from mixed motives and therefore must have tragic consequences. The relation between means and ends must become a central concern, he reasoned, once political power is recognized to be a form of evil, though a necessary and unavoidable evil, for human society.[23]

Herberg, through his reading of Niebuhr, Martin Buber, and Paul Tillich, had come to see political power as potentially dehumanizing, because he had concluded that the sublime experience of power no longer could be accepted as an expression of the universal. It now represented to him the usurpation of universal and transcendental values by mere particulars. Marxism, not just Stalin or Trotsky, had taken the jeremiad of innocence, fall, and redemption from its religious source and rigidly and inappropriately applied it to secular time. For Herberg, that artificial association explained the potent attraction of Marxism and why its sublime vision had collapsed into totalitarianism. The Marxist sublime had taken Judeo-Christian symbolism out of its religious context. It had rendered the natural artificial. Marxism, in the guise of the party or the proletariat, became the universal transcendent, absolutized by its followers, and, therefore, an ideology of self-aggrandizing power. Marxism, Herberg concluded, had proven to be destructive of the very values and ideals that it had borrowed from an older and more natural source. Clearly, Herberg argued, the historical source of Marxist values was Judaism, and this organic religious tradition was better able to sustain an ethic of means and ends in a world of power than could the ideological heresy of Marxism.[24]

Herberg's critique of Marxism was precisely the same critique that he had presented against the false modernism of Darwinism in 1932. By 1943, Judaism had replaced Marxism for Herberg as the sound historical basis for natural law. In that year, he defined Marxism as having ahistorically and inappropriately applied ideas and explanations out of context, as he had accused the Social Darwinists of doing a decade earlier. Similarly, when Herberg, as a young communist, was dreaming of an international revolution that would liberate a universal proletariat from bondage, he had viewed Judaism as a sect. His Jewishness had left him among the alienated in an Anglo-Protestant land. Suddenly, Judaism was revealed to him to be a universal religion and the Jew to be a universal man. "Israel is not simply the history of an ethnic or cultural religious group," he wrote, "it is a light unto the nations. . . . The message of Israel is universal." The Jewish God transcends nature, and yet works actively in history. As a universal, expressed entirely in time yet guaranteed by a God outside of history, Judaism would not be subject to the disillusioning failure of Marxism. Judaism could not fall prey to the sublime error of absolutizing itself into becoming its own god. Therefore, for Herberg, Judaism could defend the autonomy of the particular individual against the false universals of ideologies. Indeed, Herberg believed at the end of the 1940s that the turn to Judeo-Christianity anticipated the exhaustion of ideologies and the triumph of postmodernism.[25]

The revitalization of Judeo-Christianity, Herberg further claimed, constituted a defense of democracy. However, as he had done as a communist, Herberg made a distinction between false democracy and true democracy. Indeed, true democracy for Herberg remained indistinguishable from his Leninist ideal of "democratic centralism," even after he embraced Judaism. Genuine democracy, he explained, is based upon Judeo-Christian realism about human sinfulness, and, therefore, on the limitation of the power that one person should wield over another. By definition, he said, the true democracy that is embodied in the Federalist papers and the Constitution can not permit either the rulers or the masses to absolutize themselves. True democracy, therefore, recognizes itself to be derivative and dependent upon the universal of Judeo-Christianity, just as "democratic centralism" had once been derived from the universalism of the party. The significance of the institutional controls on power extends far beyond mere mechanical operation, Herberg explained. It organically balances motives and interests to preserve ideals in a world of power. "It promotes in rulers a wholesome humility which discourages inordinate pretensions to play the role of gods and saviors of their peoples. In short, . . . by limiting power it limits the corrupting effects of power."[26]

Herberg strongly supported a messianic role for Judaism, just as he had for communism. His reading of Protestant theology, especially Paul Tillich's pre–World War II writing that had so influenced Reinhold Niebuhr, filled Herberg with a sense of *kairos*, a moment when eternity intersects time to make the redemption of history possible. Like the neo-Orthodox Protestant theologians whom Herberg felt Judaism should emulate, he identified himself as a democratic socialist in the tradition of religious socialism. Herberg, however, had returned to the Judaism of his youth through Reinhold Niebuhr, who in turn, as we have seen, had been profoundly influenced by Martin Buber and Paul Tillich. As a result, Herberg never directly identified with either of these central influences upon twentieth-century religious thought. While Niebuhr warmly acknowledged his indebtedness to both theological thinkers, he also felt inadequate before their intellectual capacities. As he grew in stature in the public arena and his sense of inadequacy sharpened, he increasingly stressed political realism against their emphases on personalism. As late as 1955, however, Niebuhr still acknowledged his indebtedness to Buber, to whom he dedicated his book *The Self and the Dramas of History*.[27] It was quite natural, therefore, that Herberg would attempt to follow Niebuhr's lead and identify himself as closely as possible with Buber. Indeed, Herberg aspired to be an American Buber, the translator of ancient Judaic values for American Christian society, as he had once adapted Leninism for American Marxists.

Once more, as a religious socialist who opposed capitalist exploitation and Marxist collectivism, Buber offered an avenue of escape from the corruption of power for Herberg. Buber, who had studied social theory with Simmel and Dilthey, had also been an active Zionist and enemy of Nazism. He had dissociated what he called "Hebrew humanism" from the Western political tradition, which he felt was trapped in a false confidence on one side and despair on the other. Buber felt that such false confidence and disillusioned resignation both failed to acknowledge the practical responsibility to harmonize means and ends.[28]

Historian Friedrich Meinecke provided Buber with one side of the failure of Western political thought after World War I. He defended the Bismarckian ideal of realpolitik, because, he said, security and peace are possible only within the inevitable conditions of power politics. Meinecke, therefore, celebrated the potential for creative social change through war. The opposite position was suggested to Buber by Max Weber, with whom he developed a friendship between 1916 and 1918. Weber noted that one source of the disaster of World War I had been conservative leaders and the other source had been the socialist revolutionaries who challenged them at the war's end. Weber's ironic conclusion was that politics and ethics were divided by exigencies of power, on the one hand, and the requirements of the individual conscience, on the other. The irony of the corruption of power, the sobered Weber of 1918 argued, is that high purpose may lead to evil and that less-than-lofty notions sometimes may lead to reform. Buber countered both Meinecke and Weber by saying that a bifurcated person whose morality and politics are lived in separate spheres can only become an individual who lives as an accomplice to a cynical and violent future. He hoped that "Hebrew humanism" could provide a historical tradition of dialogue as an alternative to Meineckian nationalism and Weberian pessimism.[29]

Buber acknowledged that injustice could not be avoided in politics, no matter how virtuous the cause or the community. He also insisted that evil means could not eventuate in good ends. His alternative was a "prophetic politics." That phrase could easily be misread, as indeed Will Herberg did, to mean "messianic politics."[30] Buber, however, who had advocated a binational state in Palestine, insisted that prophetic politics required a sense of limits. It would be a politics without pretensions of universal solutions. "The Hebrew prophets," he explained, "invariably are only given a message for a particular situation . . . [the prophet] sets no universally valid image of perfection, no pantopia or utopia before men." Concrete events and specific choices constantly open the situation at hand to new possibilities, Buber said. Therefore, the individual in a political community must listen for new solutions and struggle towards making them possible. The Jews, Buber insisted, were not a light unto the nations; even in biblical times, he emphasized, they were by no means asked by the prophets to consider themselves as an example to other nations. Rather, they were to attempt to be the best among the gentiles, a category that necessarily included the Jewish nation along with all others.[31]

However, Buber said, this did not mean that Jews were strictly like everyone else. A biblical tradition had shaped their identity as a people. He cautioned that the identity he was referring to was not an identity of blood. Many years later, in an effort to show that the appeal to authenticity must lead to an ethical cul-de-sac, Herberg hinted that Buber had been infected by a somewhat Nazi-tainted Hegelianism.[32] However, Buber's actual position was that the particular historical choices and experiences of a given group of people form together as a certain kind of community. That community is not merely symbolic. Individuals are born into it over generations, and that history provides rootedness in the world. Such a community is not a nation. As early as 1909, Buber had contrasted the religious community with the polis. In 1928 he explained that his concept of prophetic, or limited, politics meant that attempts to make actual the values of the community require the practical recognition that the messianic world cannot be prepared, but only prepared for.[33] To this prophetic politics he contrasted the messianic faiths of Moscow and Rome. The first, he said, is a democracy without a demos — that is, a political entity without a responsibility to its own idea, which, therefore, ends by absolutizing itself. The second, fascist Rome, he said, has no idea, only a will to power: "Lenin fashioned because he had a vision; Mussolini undertook time and again to fashion what he had contrived. Lenin strove for power because he strove to promote his cause as no other could, and because he could provide it with this service only if he ruled. Mussolini wants to rule because he does not want to serve."[34]

In contrast, the idea of Jerusalem, as Martin Susser characterized Buber's third way, is to be located in a line of demarcation, rooted in Jewish history but redrawn and reconsidered at every moment of crisis. "I cannot see the God-willed reality of justice," Buber wrote to Reinhold Niebuhr, "anywhere other than in being just, and this means, of course, being just insofar as it is possible here and now, under the artful conditions of actual society."[35]

Buber defined the "line of demarcation" as an alternative to casuistry, which might preserve an ethics of dialogue when political interests and contradictions failed to practically sustain such relational values. Buber complained, however, that Herberg misunderstood this concept because Herberg viewed dialogue institutionally, while he viewed it personally. Herberg similarly insisted on interpreting Buber's *I and Thou*, which divided the world according to instrumental and relational speech, as triadic, just as he had identified the interfaith movement as an authentic civil religion in *Protestant, Catholic, Jew*. In this context, Herberg meant that a relation may exist separately between individual and individual and between the individual and God. This compartmentalization of social roles and personal values, reason and faith, and politics as instrument of expediency and ideal of community preserved the flexibility of identifying with contradictory institutional values. Buber countered that he rejected the dualism that was inherent in this interpretation of his philosophy. God, he said, was not an absolute other in the sense that an "I" and a "thou" are exclusive of each other. Individuals and God are I and thou to each other, said Buber, and he generalized this concept to include the relation between human beings and the environment, as well.[36]

In substance, this was an argument over the question of whether a break, separating modernism from past ages, had occurred in the contemporary world. Buber, in contrast to Walter Benjamin and other members of the Frankfurt school of sociologists, denied that a break was possible so long as a community remembered a responsibility and world beyond itself. Instead, he suggested that an eclipse might more accurately portray the crisis because it cannot be known beforehand that a break is definite. Will Herberg associated the personal with the particular, which was condemned to historical irrelevance. For Herberg, such personalism was evidence of a lingering mysticism, which he felt was a form of escape from the realities of a world of power and injustice.[37]

The Herberg of the 1950s, who had gained national recognition through *Protestant, Catholic, Jew*, was engaged in a desperate struggle to escape the implication of his Weberian resignation to the existence of an institutional gap between power and morality. To do so, quite to the contrary of Buber, he invested Judaism with a universal mission. Rather than viewing Judaism relationally, as having a historical responsibility to preserve dialogue as the ground for prophetic politics, he attributed to

Judaism an institutionalized mission to warn against the moral consequences of a reliance on the false security of limited human power. Such power, Herberg explained, echoing Tillich and Niebuhr, demonically tries to absolutize itself to disguise the reality of its own weakness.[38]

But, as early as 1949, in an article entitled "Has Judaism Still Power to Speak?", Herberg had already expressed his concern for the failure of Jewish tradition to effectively present its case to the modern world. Though full of praise for Buber, he otherwise saw only mediocrity in the intellectual life of Jewry and a tendency to degenerate into a culture-religion. In contrast, he pointed to the vigor of Protestant theological thought. The renunciation of theology among modern Jews, he said, was a break with tradition. It must be admitted, however, that aspects of the tradition had made this possible, he complained. The emancipation during the age of Enlightenment had left too many Jews confused and lost. "In the self-hatred that this period of demoralization bred, theology was rejected not only because it was theology but also because it was Jewish." As a result, he wrote, in an age in which ideologies were becoming exhausted, Judaism was unprepared for its mission of promoting a religious alternative. Rabbis and scholars did not speak from the depth of religious wisdom, the frustrated Herberg wrote, but "Ersatz Jewish faiths, especially Zionist nationalism . . . claim it is they who are exercising the prophetic function." Echoing his charges as a Lovestonite Leninist, Herberg concluded that they offer only a "pseudo-prophetism."[39]

Herberg's classic work, *Protestant, Catholic, Jew*, reflected this disillusionment with Judaism. He still identified with Judaism as a source of historic universalism, but not as a vehicle for supplying its wisdom to modern individuals. It therefore marked the beginning of his transference of universalism from Judaism to an American nationalism, or civil religion, which included Protestant and Catholic elements, as well as Jewish historicism. As in his Leninist distinction between true and false democracy, the sociologist Herberg made a distinction between true and false civil religion in what he called "the American Way of Life."[40] But for him, as a neo-Burkean as well as a former Leninist, that distinction was true because it was practically useful, not because it was a metaphysical truth.

Protestant, Catholic, Jew traced American Protestantism through its Turnerian frontier stage to the twentieth century, when it merged into the American Way of Life. Through the process of exhaustion of subsequent frontiers, the European churches were slowly transformed into

American churches. It was a process reproduced again and again from Jonathan Edwards and the Great Awakenings to the neoorthodox intellectual cross-fertilization of theology by the Niebuhrs and Paul Tillich. Protestantism, despite its numerical majority, he wrote, "no longer regards itself either as a religious movement sweeping the continent or as a national church representing the religious life of the people; Protestantism understands itself today primarily as one of the three religious communities in which twentieth-century America has come to be divided."[41] Similarly, Catholics became Americanized when they began to view themselves as members of one of the three religious communities instead of the one and only Universal Church. Jews, on the other hand, according to Herberg, first had to gain a sense of security and confidence as Americans in the second generation in order to regain their sense of religious identity in the third generation. As Jews approached the mid-twentieth century, their confusions began to subside. "The American Jewish community became integrally part of American society; the American Jew was now in the position where he could establish his Jewishness not apart from, nor in spite of, his Americaness, but precisely through and by virtue of it." Judaism, had attained the status of "one of the three religions of democracy." Judaism, however, because of its historical development in America, was the one of the holy trinity capable of sustaining loyal opposition. It was this third element of loyal opposition that made the Jewish claim for American universalism a genuine, rather than fraudulent, identity.[42]

Herberg needed to find confidence in a universal American identity through his Jewish identity. Despite his resolution of his Americanness with a bibical tradition that could not be equated with any civil religion, he remained threatened by the possibility that he was only trapped in a confidence game. The individual is always attempting to secure a center of meaning to life beyond life, he explained. "He is always searching for some god and some way of salvation from the fears, futilities and frustrations of life." The universal message of Jewish-Christian faith, however, is that so long as the individual seeks his own self security, relying on his own virtue, wisdom or piety, it will not be God that he finds but an idol—a mirror image of his or her self, or some aspect of that self which is writ large, projected, and worshiped.[43]

Sinfulness pervades the religious as well as every other aspect of human experience, he warned his readers. Religion, therefore, is "an ambiguous and doubtful thing, requiring careful scrutiny on the part of a man of faith." The unknown god of Americans, he warned, appears to be faith in faith. Rather than religious truth, Americans seek something called "peace of mind," which permeates and invades every aspect of contemporary American life, turning it into an endless search for adjustment and an exercise in therapy. Yet, in this ambiguity between false religion and the true religious quest, lay the promise of universalism in the American Way of Life that Herberg hoped to attain.[44]

In *The Christian Century*'s "How My Mind Has Changed" feature for 1959, Herberg reported that in the age of conformity and mass culture, the problem of social justice and economic concerns no longer moved him. Rather he had become concerned about the quality of life. It was a concern, he said, that had no villains. One could not blame the capitalist system; yet, demonstrably, modern life was in crisis and people faced a void in their personal lives. As a result, Herberg said, he had gained a new appreciation for the importance of historicism as a guide for stabilizing society. Besides discovering that history was all important, he professed to have found a new appreciation for natural law. Herberg called history a touchstone for modern man in search of meaning. He had retreated from his Marxist obsession with economics but also his Hebraic expectation of messianic redemption. He no longer lived in expectation of significant social change, he said, as he had a decade earlier. He lived, quoting Tillich in his post-World War I sense of despair, "in the situation of the void." It was, he said, "a period of crisis in which the preservation of historical stabilities and continuities against the incursion of the demonic becomes the primary concern and responsibility."[45] However, it was not Leninism that provided the historical anchor against sectarian deviation and the false policies of ultra-leftism and rightest opportunism. It was at this stage of his career that Herberg gained a special appreciation for Edmund Burke and a new view of himself as a conservative, "but not for what passes for conservatism in contemporary America."[46] The mindless vacuity of American democratic life distressed him as the mediocrity of contemporary Judaism disturbed him. Indeed, as Herberg looked around himself in the dawning 1960s, Protestantism and Catholicism, which he had once admired as bulwarks of tradition, also seemed to be foundering. Nothing in his understanding of social ethics, he complained, had prepared him to understand the most significant shift in moral development of his time: the turn inward, from the public to the private and domestic realm. Nevertheless, in the general chaos of the time, Herberg took comfort from a sense that the historical grain was running in accord with Anglo-American constitutional democracy, "which needs no ideology because it has a history." In 1960 the former editor of *Revolutionary Age* and *Workers Age* joined the staff of the *National Review* as religion editor.[47]

During the first half of the 1960s, Herberg struggled to construct a foundation of cultural values borrowing from both Athens and Jerusalem that would guarantee political stability but also religious individualism in a mass culture of hedonism and mindless conformism. "Religion is the spring of civic virtue," he wrote in 1961. "It binds the community together, it hallows custom and softens the harsh outlines of power." Yet, he still insisted, the stabilizing quality of religion must not be permitted to be used by the state or it becomes "an idolatrous cult sanctifying every social order simply because it is the social order that happens to prevail."[48]

Consistently over the years, Herberg had divided religion, as he had divided Marxism, modernism, and democracy itself, into the real and the fraudulent, mirroring Herberg's own doubt as well as confidence in the American Way of Life. On a political level, he felt that conservatism threatened religion by turning it into a stabilizing defense of the status quo, while liberalism undermined religion by reducing it to a purely personal and private concern. The liberal error was the more dangerous one, he had decided, because the liberal is really a Jacobin, "sans guillotin."[49]

Herberg's equation of liberalism with Jacobinism is significant, first, because he identified it with a subversive strategy, and second, because he had personally embraced Jacobinism in the 1930s. While he had promoted Jacobinism as a legitimate strategy for preserving traditional Leninism against sectarianism and liberalism in the 1930s, he had come to view Jacobinism in the Burkean terms of revolutionary antitraditionalism by the 1960s. He justified this rhetorical reversal by citing the fact that Lenin, like contemporary liberals, viewed religion as a private matter. On the one hand, draining religious symbolism from the national culture would undermine the real American Way of Life, yet, on the other, ascribing public religious symbolism to the national culture might lead to idolatry. So, despite his rhetorical attack on liberalism, Herberg had still not found a way to sustain both real religion and real Americanism. That unhappy tension was summarized in his May 1965 Spaulding Lecture, entitled "Athens and Jerusalem: Confrontation and Dialogue," which he presented at the University of New Hampshire.[50]

In that lecture, Herberg expressed concern that religion in America might become reduced to a defense of a cult of nationalism. Yet, convinced that only a historical foundation of natural law could protect the American democracy from itself and its enemies, he called for a rapprochement between the two communities of Athens and Jerusalem. Unfortunately, the immanence of Greek thought is in conflict with the transcendence characteristic of Hebraic thought, he acknowledged. The former is naturalistic and the later is supernaturalistic; the former encloses the individual in the totality of the polis, while the latter liberates the individual through a covenantal community. Perhaps, he suggested, these tensions, which have caught up every member of our culture, might find a basis for dialogue through existentialist philosophy. However, he concluded darkly, though existentialism might mediate the contradiction of Athens and Jerusalem, existentialism is unable to resolve it. For even in its religious forms, existentialism remains in the philosophical category of Athens, and, the dualistic Herberg explained, Athens must try to destroy Jerusalem.[51]

On June 14, 1965, Martin Buber died, and Herberg acknowledged his passing in the June 29 issue of the *National Review*. He took note of Buber's personal integrity, but emphasized the political disappointments that had accompanied the last thirty-five years of his life. Buber had been relegated from the mainstream of Zionism to a minority position without influence in Israeli affairs, he pointed out. Buber had not been able to make himself heard in the chauvinistic clamour in which the state had been founded, and the kibbutz, in which he had placed such hope for communitarian social change, had rejected him as well. Buber was dead and buried in an Israel on a collision course with its Arab neighbors.[52] More immediately, for Herberg, there was a rising tide of racial violence and anti-Vietnam confrontation at home. Herberg seems to have concluded that Athens and Jerusalem could not be held together through personal freedom. Instead, having surrendered trust in the free and authentic self, he placed his confidence in the faith that confidence could be preserved through the enforcement of order.[53]

Two weeks after his eulogy of Buber, on July 13, Herberg lashed out against the failure of the universities to preserve the authority of Athens against the forces of chaos. The article, entitled "The Professors and the Teach-ins," criticized the use of "teach-ins" by professors who opposed the Vietnam conflict. Herberg did not defend the war. He felt that the Vietnam conflict was a result of a muddled and dubious policy. Instead, he argued that even well-intentioned disruptions to the university, as the guardian of civilization, fostered chaos and violence. *"La traison des clercs"* was an ominous sign. The new professional class was handing over the universities to a self-indulgent and mediocre generation of youth.[54]

A few months later, in September, Herberg raised the alarm in the *National Review* that both Athens and Jerusalem were endangered by the destabilizing violence of racial unrest. Though a year earlier he had attacked Martin Luther King's civil disobedience on the basis of the tradition of Paul, Augustine, and Luther, in September of 1965 he hinted that that very tradition was to blame. Herberg now identified the Augustinian tradition of grace with antinomianism, and antinomianism with frontier violence.[55] American civil religion had laboriously transformed antinomian Protestantism into an organic unity of Protestant, Catholic and Jew. King's faulty theology, though well intentioned, had brought "corruption and demoralization," which were destroying black children and their futures. The handiwork of King and his followers had lured the children "away from the steady path of decency and self-government to the more exhilarating road of 'demonstrating'—and rioting." Civilization was a thin veneer for "covering up and holding down a veritable hell of aggression, anarchy and chaos," he wrote. Custom and respect for constituted authority, tradition and the police, were the institutionalized forces for saving civilization from itself.[56]

Herberg did not defend racism in September any more than he had defended the Vietnam War in July. Both issues, however, were personally threatening to him because they were closely associated with Reinhold Niebuhr's Cold War balance between order and justice, community and conscience, and messianic and prophetic politics. Herberg had built his reputation as one of America's foremost interpreters of religion by pretending to be a close friend and confidant of Niebuhr's.[57] His carefully crafted public image of himself as an insider, created through his fictional association with Niebuhr, gave him the license to criticize American civic and spiritual values in his own right, not just to serve as an impresario who promoted the voices of briefly fashionable existential writers such as Buber, Tillich and Berdayev. Herberg had used his insider status as a former Communist and Niebhurian realist to lift himself beyond the crank image of conservatives such as Richard Weaver and Russell Kirk. Therefore, Herberg's own credibility depended upon his ability to promote Niebuhr's Burkean credentials against civil rights leaders such as Martin Luther King and antiwar writers such as Robert

McAfee Brown, who claimed Niebuhr's inspiration. This was rendered necessary and made possible because Niebuhr was sick and mostly vacant from direct engagement in the turmoil of the times, and because, as we have seen, Herberg shared Niebuhr's contempt for Buber's and Tillich's mysticism, which both ex-Marxists identified with Romanticism. Despite the profound influence that each had on Niebuhr's own development, therefore, it became necessary to remove the existential side of Niebuhr's theological and political synthesis, and to emphasize the political associations of Lincoln's Christian realism over the Augustinian roots of Niebuhr's neoorthodox Protestant theology. Herberg attempted to establish the real Niebuhr against the fraudulent Niebuhr, a dichotomy that itself reflected the fact that Vietnam had shattered the two sides of Niebuhr's Calvinist and Lutheran jeremiad.[58]

Consequently, Herberg, aside from using Niebuhr for personal self-aggrandizement, also needed the legitimizing authority of Niebuhr to confront in Protestantism the same flaw of false modernism that he had earlier attributed to Stalinism, Darwinism, and scientific idealism. Protestantism, he concluded, was fatally compromised in its ability to fight the evils of the modern world because it lacked a natural law tradition. Without the foundation of natural law, it was paralyzed before the storm of rioting in contemporary American cities as it had been paralyzed before the scourge of Nazi ideology. The second of the three American religions identified in *Protestant, Catholic, Jew* did have such a natural law tradition, he said, but it too was losing its way through the *aggiornamento*, or revision of tradition, which Pope John XXIII was making the basis of Vatican Council II. For Herberg, a false Catholic modernism threatened to transform the movement toward ecumenical unity into a pathetic form of social conformity, at the same time that primitive frontier impulses were defeating Protestantism.[59]

As rioting and political assassination rocked the nation, Herberg compared primitive but authentically American frontier violence, which was direct and nonideological, with European violence, which was artificial and ideological. Frontier violence, which he associated with Jack Ruby's murder of Lee Oswald, as a personal act of retribution, was disappearing. Such violence, he said, echoing Turner, had never been significant in the established eastern states, and could not long persist in the West under the conditions of urbanization and nationalism. While this Turnerian view of the necessary historical evolution of American institution had seemed optimistic when applied to religion in 1955, it appeared apocalyptic a decade later when he applied it to social violence. American vigilantism, he now argued, was the national institution that was in the process of becoming replaced by European-style political murder. That process was behind the ominous 1968 political assassination of Robert Kennedy by Sirhan Sirhan in Los Angeles, California.[60]

Herberg described this transformation from frontier violence to ideological violence as an inevitable product of historical development. It was, he argued, the result of the vast immigrant influence on late nineteenth-century America and the turn of the United States to economic imperialism in the twentieth century. Under these twin influences, the nation began a process of Europeanization that ethnically and politically would turn the United States into a staging ground for exiles from foreign lands to carry on their ideological battles. This European type of violence had always been present, he said, as illustrated by John Wilkes Booth's assassination of Lincoln to vindicate the South. On that occasion, for the first and only time, the bonds of the Constitution were nearly broken, and America nearly fell victim to European passion and ideological violence. Now, in the late twentieth century, the United States faced the historical summation of the passing of frontier violence and the consequences of imperialism. Instead of achieving the American Way of Life, in which sectarianism gave way to unity through a genuine civil religion, as he had prophesied in *Protestant, Catholic, Jew*, a different historical pattern could now be discerned on the horizon: the end of American exceptionalism. "There are no foreign quarrels," he wrote, saying that "every foreign quarrel is, at least potentially, an American quarrel."[61]

The end of American exceptionalism meant that what had been European was now American and what was politically European or Asian was now global. In that sense, he admitted, it was inaccurate to call the growing ideological form of violence he decried "European." It had truly become American, and it would only become more pervasive in the immediate future. "I have been told that this conclusion reflects a bleak and pessimistic outlook on the world," he concluded. "So it does. But if you want a happy optimistic outlook, you should have made arrangements to have been born in some other place and some other century."[62] Ironically, by 1968 Herberg was retracing William Appleman Williams's revisionist history of American foreign policy in the pages of the *National Review*. The inevitable end of American ideological innocence and the fading of the frontier ethos of American exceptionalism meant a new political era of Wilsonian internationalism for Herberg, just as it had for

Williams a decade earlier. But Herberg's sense of dialectics was too keen for him to have escaped recognizing that his communist faith in internationalism in the 1920s had paradoxically already anticipated the failure of the American exceptionalism he saw approaching in 1968.

Herberg had long since lived through one failed internationalist frontier before Williams described the failure of America's in *The Tragedy of American Diplomacy*. In 1964, Williams provocatively offered Karl Marx as a prophet to Americans, but Herberg had long ago abandoned Marx as a legitimate prophet. Williams argued in *The Great Evasion* that American economic and political leaders had confused supernationalism with true internationalism, a confusion that Williams said Frederick Jackson Turner had already recognized in the 1890s. Turner had seen that Americans had used the abundance of nature to evade the demands of living closely and responsibly and creatively in community with others. As Americans entered into a new era of internationalism and cybernetic production, Williams saw a new opportunity to reject empire, which, in 1964, threatened to go beyond continents and into the infinity of space itself. Herberg also believed that the frontier could no longer sustain the needs of community in an increasingly internationalist social context. Williams found promise for the end of the great American evasion in "the confrontation between the reality of Marx and the reality of America." But for Herberg, disappointment with the frontier experience of America and with Charles Beard's revision of it in the promise of democratic industrialism could not become the basis for confidence in internationalism twice.

After 1970, Williams, too, came to consider Marx a false prophet. Marx and his supporters embraced the same instrumentalist ethic and corporate view of economics that characterized the American Open Door empire, Williams said. In his disillusionment with the Left and the Right, he denied the legitimacy of corporate economic values for a life of limits in which community, rather than production and consumption, was paramount. Williams's conservative jeremiad called for the end of confidence in the modern search for universals, while embracing a utopian ideal of community based upon a recovery of the primacy of persons, rather than systems.[63]

Herberg, in contrast, identified with a conservativism that could provide a new foundation in reason to salvage a shipwrecked political and religious tradition and make it "solid, safe and impregnable to the challenge of the Thrasymachuses and even the conservative Protagorases of the time," and of prophets who were "a 'stabilizing element,' striving to reduce the ground gained in revelation to order and coherence. In contrast to a true conservatism of tradition and institutions," Herberg wrote in 1971, there is a false conservatism "that is radically different." This pseudotradition, he said, is mired in the antinomianism of the frontier. "We might begin with Augustine," Herberg wrote, but instead he spelled out his position using Kierkegaard: "The decision [Kierkegaard tells us] lies in the subject. The thing is determined not by the *what* but by the *how*." This advice, Herberg pointed out in his article "The 'What' and the 'How' of Ethics," was derived from Augustine, who said, "Love, and do what you will." This sentence, Herberg claimed, formed the nucleus of a nearly antinomian system of ethics—a pseudotradition, leading from Paul and Augustine to Luther, Kierkegaard, and Buber and to Jean-Paul Sartre and Simone de Beauvoir. "Parodying, but hardly parodying, Augustine, we might set up the formula for existentialist ethics as, 'Be authentic, and do what you will.' " In dispensing with standards, the *what*, "authenticity itself, becomes something dark, and demonic."

The end of such ethics is inescapable, Herberg said. Nothing in Buber, Kierkegaard or Luther can counter the logic of Sartre's philosophy or the words of Mme. de Beauvoir: "Owing to his headstrong sincerity, he [the Marquis de Sade] deserves to be hailed as a great moralist." Herberg wrote: "Here we have it. This sick and sickening Marquis de Sade, who stands self-condemned as a gross and brutal hedonist by any moral code known to man, is hailed by Mme. de Beauvoir as a 'great moralist' because of his 'headstrong sincerity'! Of course! since the 'what' is nothing, the 'how' ('sincerity') is everything. Buber would say, 'Be authentic! Do what you do with the whole of your being!' " He would undoubtedly argue that the Marquis de Sade could not have been "sincere," Herberg continued, "that is, whole-hearted in his wickedness." But obviously Simone de Beauvoir thinks otherwise.[64]

Herberg had lost his ability to preserve his confidence in the American Way of Life and the frontier conventions upon which it must be sustained, as had William Appleman Williams. But as an American prophet of confidence, Herberg had also unconsciously participated in pointing towards new sources, from which a new confidence in the American Way of Life could be resurrected, even as he, and his own, died. Herberg fulfilled his office of prophet to the American Way of Life by anticipating the rise of the Religious and Political Right through his own estrangement from existentialism and rapprochement with the editorial views of

William Buckley and the *National Review*. Second, and simultaneously, he surrendered his faith in the possibility of an authentic self, which he equated with the frontier, as a place of individual performance. He replaced it with an unquestioning allegiance to tradition because of its efficacy as a standard in preserving social order. Third, by the 1970s, the disillusioned Herberg had unconsciously come to equate "authenticity" with "sincerity." In doing so he restored the promise of the frontier as a place to gain confidence through performance, and replaced personalism with a cult of personality. Herberg failed to recognize the usefulness of his own variation on Burke's classic formula of "the beautiful and the sublime" in "the authentic and the sincere." He saw sincerity not as sublime but as terror in which the chaos of pure political theater had triumphed over established order. However, it was a formula that proved politically useful for a countermovement against antiestablishment politics during the Nixon presidency, because it supported a neo-Burkean emphasis upon manners and the rhetoric of law and order and against the political voices of conscience against war, class division, and race and gender discrimination.

However, at the same time that Herberg and Williams were losing their confidence in the frontier, a former cowboy-actor named Ronald Reagan, who had turned politician, was exploiting his image of sincerity and perfecting his performance of "The Speech," through which he was becoming the standard-bearer for a new conservative coalition following Goldwater's defeat in the 1964 election. He became the governor of America's most populous state two years later. Ronald Reagan was only a decade younger than Herberg, and he was proving that the American Way of Life included a second chance at life for a washed-up actor, at an age when most men and women were forced to accept the end of their dreams. As Herberg was dying of cancer in 1976, he told a reporter that "if I expected to have an effect, I would end in despair all the time. Never do I expect to have an effect. Never!"[65] In 1976, however, Reagan expected to have an effect. He set his sights on the Republican nomination for president of the United States. Although he lost to Gerald Ford, he became the leader of the right wing of the party, and, despite concern that at sixty-nine he would be too old to run in 1980, Reagan's handlers began preparing the groundwork for the next presidential contest. "I often wondered whether Reagan could really taste defeat, the way Nixon did," said his admiring campaign manager, John Sears. "Nixon had no inner confidence. But this guy did." Reagan remained confident, even in defeat, of his eventual success and the success of his anti-New Deal vision of "the American spirit unleashed once again; to make this land a shining, golden hope God intended it to be."[66]

8

Performance, Politics and Personality
RONALD REAGAN, JAMES BALDWIN AND NORMAN MAILER

Ronald Reagan needed confidence when Hollywood returned to business at the end of the war. He clung to a fading career by hosting television's "General Electric Theatre" between 1954 and 1962, while he invested what was left of his celebrity status to position himself to run for political office. His campaign biography, *Where's the Rest of Me?* (1965), suggests that the new conditions in Hollywood left him profoundly disillusioned. The old Hollywood, he said, had been created out of "thin blue sky and ideas." The taste in drama of men like Louis B. Mayer might have been questionable, he said, but they were true individualists who "built an empire out of faith and hope and a good deal of charity." The old Hollywood was from its beginnings a pure American enterprise, built upon private thought and execution, with its own voluntary morality codes and control of the distribution of its product to the consumers who desired it. "More than any other industry, its founders worked with raw materials that had no other markets but people's emotions," he said. That Hollywood died in 1948, Reagan complained, when the federal government invoked antitrust laws against the major studios.[1] It was also the point at which Reagan used his position as president of the Screen Actors' Guild to sell packaging rights to the Music Corporation of America. Reagan's deal helped cement the marriage of Hollywood to television by permitting corporate producers to double as actors' agents, thus destroying the very studio system that Reagan had eulogized in *Where's the Rest of Me?*. Everyone in show business has two businesses, Reagan explained, show business and their own.[2]

The MCA deal, which led to a Justice Department probe of Reagan, also led directly to a contract to host "G. E. Theatre." Reagan, who was technically hired by the advertising firm of Batten, Barton, Durstine and Osborn through his agent, MCA, remembered that, with his career fading, it was like having the cavalry come riding to his rescue.[3] In *Where's the Rest of Me?*, Reagan emphasized that "G.E. Theatre" began as a mixture of film and live broadcasting, and that this was reflected in the fact that the shows were produced from both New York and Hollywood. Reagan expressed pride in having participated in the transformation of television drama from live to filmed production. In eight years, he said, "G.E. Theatre" had cast over one hundred Academy Award winners, many for the first and only time on television. Some of those finding work on shows such as "G.E. Theatre" were new talents nurtured by the opportunities afforded by commercial television. Others were old stars like himself, who no longer were wanted at the Hollywood studios but were "much beloved by the people."[4]

Reagan wrote, with a hint of bitterness, that Hollywood was making five hundred pictures per year, and over ninety million paying customers went to the theater each week when the government and television arrived together in 1948. Reagan's pride in negotiating the MCA deal and in his association with "G.E. Theatre" reflected his ability to survive and to turn the destruction of the Old Hollywood, which had given him wealth and fame, to his own ends. "The Hollywood I knew is gone," he said, "to some fond nostalgic nook bathed in a golden haze." Reagan, however, claimed to have no nostalgia for the old live television of his early "G.E. Theatre" days. Actors may have gotten an emotional kick from making a live broadcast successful, he said, "but we aren't supposed to be in this business for our own kicks, and the audience doesn't really care how we manage the backstage tricks: they want to see the play without the seams showing." The basis of all dramatic entertainment is the emotional catharsis obtained by the audience, Reagan explained. Our modern lives, he said, have lost a certain amount of excitement and "we've kept a little stardust in our lives by identifying with make-believe characters in make-believe adventures in the house of illusion—the theatre."[5]

But, as the old Hollywood died, and with it his acting career, Reagan found a way to use his celebrity status to keep stardust in the popular eye and to serve new corporate interests. Reagan described the beginning of his political career as a new part he was hired to play. As host of "G.E.

Theatre," MCA arranged for him to give personal appearance tours for G.E.'s Employee-Community Relations Program. He was used by General Electric as a celebrity-morale builder because of his name and face recognition, but he used G.E. to make new opportunities for himself as a spokesperson for corporate American values. "No barnstorming politician ever met the people on quite such a common footing," he remembered. "I had the awesome, shivering feeling that America was making a personal appearance for me, and it made me the biggest fan in the world."[6]

The Ronald Reagan of 1949 had surrendered the personal freedom and fulfilment he had once associated with acting to survive in a new economic and aesthetic order. "So much of our profession is taken up with pretending, with the interpretation of never-never roles," Reagan explained, "that an actor must spend at least half his waking hours in fantasy, in rehearsal or shooting." With all that acting had given him, the disillusioned Reagan said, something was missing. He had become like the figure in his most famous role, Drake McHugh, in *King's Row*. He felt "like a shut-in invalid, nursed by publicity." Reagan insisted that this was not because acting, per se, was confining, but that it had become so since the end of World War II. He suggested that acting had served as a personal frontier of expression and opportunity, but that frontier had failed him. He had "always liked space, the feeling of freedom," Reagan wrote. But he had come to view himself as victimized by Hollywood, despite all he had gained from it in the past. "I had become a semi-automaton, Reagan confessed, " 'creating' a character another had written, doing what still another person told me to do on the set."[7]

Reagan successfully navigated the new economic order of Cold War Hollywood by repudiating his former liberal political ties—1948 was the last time he voted Democratic—and by embracing, in 1949, a new role as a public relations figure for the Motion Picture Industry Council. He attempted, as cochair of the public relations campaign, to counter the image of Hollywood as a den of moral iniquity and a hotbed of communism. Then, in 1954, Reagan used his charisma as a celebrity in film and television to create effective live performances for political change. Reagan "opened" at G.E. plants across the country, and went on to public forums that quickly brought him to elective office in the mid-1960s.[8]

Ronald Reagan was, therefore, an artist of public relations, an actor and an advertiser, who used his skills and personal assets to turn his entrapment in defending the Hollywood that had abandoned him by 1945 into new opportunity through television and political revival meetings across the country. He used Hollywood as a cultural space of performance, attacking its false theatricality, building upon the same impulses of disillusionment and optimism felt by the public regarding the American Dream, or what Will Herberg called "the American Way of Life," which brought religious revivalism into the mainstream of American national culture at that same time. Indeed, Ronald Reagan had grown up with revivalism, and was influenced by its emotional rhythms and appeals from an early age. His mother, Nelle, was a convert to the evangelistic Disciples of Christ. Young Ronald was spiritually nurtured in Disciples churches before enrolling in Eureka, a Disciples college.[9]

Nelle Reagan, however, was both a pious member of the church and an avid performer in mostly religious plays and skits. Ronald Reagan referred to his mother as "dean of dramatic recitals for the countryside," and as a "frustrated actress."[10] Her blend of theatrical performance and Christian witness, therefore, was the most direct and obvious influence on Ronald Reagan's own blend of acting and witnessing, which Hollywood only rarely permitted him to use as an actor, expecting him then to perform in service to the Motion Picture Industry Council, even as his own opportunities for significant roles evaporated before his eyes.

Reagan later proudly remembered his roles as George Gipp in *Knute Rockne, All American* (1940) and Drake McHugh in *King's Row* (1942), because they permitted him to play inspirational roles that confirmed the higher purpose of acting. His playing the part of Gipp, which he won because his college football photographs confirmed his believability for the role, also turned out to provide a moment of redemption for his alcoholic father, the Irish-Catholic Jack Reagan. Jack lived up to Nelle's pious faith in him when he avoided embarrassing his son in his moment of glory by remaining dry during the premier of the film at Notre Dame. Reagan suggested his theatrical view of morality in viewing his father's successful completion of that confidence as a final victory over his personal weakness. Jack charmed the Mother Superior, and, when he died soon after, Reagan was sure that his father knew that the actors were there, in the little church off Sunset Boulevard, to say good-by to their new friend. In Ronald Reagan's other inspirational role, Drake McHugh overcame adversity to realize that his life was not in his lost legs, and that disaster and disillusionment might be turned into opportunities for individual success and a return to social harmony.[11]

Drake McHugh also represented, for the Reagan of *Where's the Rest of Me?*, an allegory of his own slow growth in awareness and his own pilgrim's progress towards becoming politically born again. Initially, he wrote, that awareness expressed itself in 1945, when he spoke out against neofascism. The Russians were still America's allies, Reagan said, and Communists were still influential in Hollywood because of their deceptive behavior. They masqueraded as liberals, he explained, so liberals like himself "bedded down with them," without thought about the Communist's true motives. "Thus," Reagan remembered, "my first evangelism came in the form of being hell-bent on saving the world from neofascism." Only when "a rather diffident local minister" challenged the liberal Reagan to prove his principles by opposing the tyranny of communism as vigorously as he assaulted fascism did Reagan find himself becoming an evangelical witness.[12]

Reagan had returned to postwar life in Hollywood, he remembered, with a commitment to work with the tools of his trade—his thoughts, speaking abilities, and reputation as an actor—to try to bring about the regeneration of the world he believed should have automatically appeared. Instead, he said, he was introduced to the real world, as opposed to one of make-believe. "To this day," he wrote in 1965, "I am trying to assess what the slow awakening of my faculties cost me." When that awakening did come, however, "it was hard-hitting enough to rid me of all illusion." Hollywood had revealed itself to be an island from which he would have to venture into the real world, once he had found the rest of himself and become whole.[13]

The message of Reagan's campaign biography was that, by 1949, the Reagan who was lost now was found, and the Reagan who had been blind now could see. In that same year, the Luce publishing empire, the backbone of the Old Political and Religious Right, launched the national career of a young evangelist named Billy Graham. Henry Luce, the son of Presbyterian missionaries, with his wife, Congresswoman Clare Booth Luce, was not only an enthusiastic supporter of Graham's ministry, but had embraced the antiliberal Reinhold Niebuhr of the 1940s and was a close confidant of Cardinal Spellman and his protégé, Monsignor Fulton Sheen.[14] Luce's print-media linkage of religious morality and militant anticommunism helped forge the religious ecumenicalism that Will Herberg identified with American civil religion in *Protestant, Catholic, Jew* in 1954, but which still did not exist during World War II when anti-Semitism and anti-Catholicism remained strong influences on American life. Luce's postwar commitment to promoting a national revival through Billy Graham helped spark similarly popular national television crusades by the neo-Pentecostal Oral Roberts, and thus promoted the careers of legions of regional evangelists such as Rex Humbard of Akron, Ohio, who found in television a new and useful approach to spreading their messages. The favorable Luce press also gave Bishop Fulton J. Sheen, who had recently baptized Clare into the Catholic Church, the positive exposure that helped him make the transition from being on radio to being a television personality. Indeed, Bishop Sheen considered the nature of commercial television to be so naturally ecumenical that he viewed himself as an evangelist with a nondenominational message, as well.[15]

The New Evangelicals and Bishop Sheen shared a moderate Eisenhower Republicanism and a militant anticommunism with Luce. Reagan similarly described himself through the 1950s as a Democrat for Eisenhower.[16] As Reagan, a self-styled political evangelist, recognized in the new medium of television a valuable new form of theater, which he later used in service to the New Political and Religious Right, the New Evangelicals, Sheen, Graham, and Roberts, opened up new techniques of communication and performance that the New Political and Religious Right would appropriate and build upon in the 1970s.

Bishop Sheen's "A Life Worth Living" first aired in 1952, opposite "Amos 'n' Andy." By 1954 Sheen was attracting twenty-five million viewers, despite competing against Milton Berle and Frank Sinatra for prime-time ratings. Sheen spoke without notes or props for a half hour each week on topics ranging from Stalin to God's sense of humor. He used dramatic lighting to add a glow of inspiration to his eyes and wore the impressive robes of his office and his zucchetto to add a theatrical gravity to his presence. Sheen had a powerful instinct for the dramatic, and felt strongly the potential of television as a medium for indirect persuasion, which was different from the direct communication characteristic of an effective radio address. However, Sheen's influence was cut short because of increasing tension with his superior and patron, the ultraconservative and ambitious Cardinal Spellman. Their mutual hostility led Spellman to remove Sheen from television in 1957, and, though he briefly returned two years later, routinely visiting the talk shows, Sheen's star waned.[17]

Other New Evangelists, particularly Billy Graham and Oral Roberts, borrowed from Sheen. But they also responded to the potential of television in their own right. Indeed, they innovatively translated the sawdust trail of Protestant revivalism into the mainstream American popular culture of television, film, and finally Hollywood entertainment, as well as of radio and comic books. Sheen cultivated an image of urbanity and cultural sophistication in order to appeal to a general audience including Jews, Protestants and unbelievers. Graham and Roberts, in contrast, became international celebrities while they cultivated their rural southern images as simple and sincere men of plainspoken truth from America's forgotten frontier. Sheen noticed that while letters of bigotry declined, neurotic letters increased. He responded by offering the way to inner peace to an audience in search of a vague sense of spirituality. Graham concentrated on releasing individual consciences from the cost of anxiety obtained through living in a false and materialist society. The faith healer Oral Roberts, the least conventionally legitimate of the three national evangelists, emphasized the redemptive possibilities of faith, which may begin in honest doubt, but ends in being "supernaturally emptied of doubt."[18]

Ronald Reagan, like Bishop Sheen, was the son of an Irish-Catholic father from rural Illinois who had been unlucky in business. As a result, Reagan said of himself, he knew how to appeal to the warm sentimentality of the "shillelagh psyche" — to be lusty but not vulgar and a rigid moralist but with a twinkle in the eye. Yet, unlike Sheen's mother, Reagan's was a pious Scots-English Protestant, who had weaned him from his father's faith and had him rebaptized into the Protestant evangelical community. In 1965, candidate Reagan suggested that he had learned from his father's weaknesses that there was danger in that "blarney green in the blood of most Sons of the Old Sod" — a condition proved by recent political history, he said, no doubt thinking of the Kennedy brothers, John and Robert, whom Sheen warmly admired. In Reagan's view, his father was in rebellion against the universe, while his mother was a practical do-gooder. His father, outstretched on the front porch "as if he were crucified," was a victim of alcohol, while his quietly forgiving mother was a surviver and a reformer. It was, therefore, with his mother's sincerity and belief in the power of human initiative, as preached by Disciples revivalists, that Reagan identified, rather than with his father's fatalism and "democratic sentimentality."[19]

But if the political evangelist Reagan sold sincerity as the road to recovering individual initiative in postwar America, so too did Graham and Roberts, who became the soul-doctors of America's national culture and of many of the political and entertainment celebrities who led it. In 1949 the struggling young evangelist Graham took Los Angeles by storm. After the "Sixth Great Sin-Smashing Week," celebrities such as Gene Autry and Jane Russell began to attend his crusade. Cecil B. De Mille offered him a screen test, and Louella Parsons, Ronald Reagan's angel from Dixon, who held court over Hollywood careers, declared Graham a "really naive, humble man." Graham immediately began to consider film as a vehicle for spreading his message and advertising his crusades. In 1951 he began broadcasting the "Hour of Decision" on television, and the next year warned Americans that God was watching them on his T.V. He grew out his blond hair for a better television appearance, taking on the aura of a prophetic movie star when he frequented talk shows such as that of Bishop Sheen's personal friend, Jack Parr.[20] Oral Roberts was constantly compared to Graham by the news media, and was warmly accepted by Graham himself. As Roberts's national image spread, he too embraced filmmaking, and by the mid-1950s was regularly seen on television. Roberts put show business swing into his choir, the World Action Singers. By 1968, after shedding his Pentecostalism for a more mainstream Methodism, he was producing prime-time specials with Hollywood stars such as Jimmy Durante, Lou Rawls, the Lennon Sisters and Johnny Mathis.[21]

The electronic church helped translate religion to a new standard of performance, which, in turn, helped reconfigure the American national culture of confidence between 1949 and 1968. It found its way to the center of the American political, economic, and entertainment systems from its roots in revival tents and radio. It did so through an aggressive use of television; through public association with mainstream Hollywood films with an evangelical message such as *Quo Vadis* (1951), *The Robe* (1953), *The Ten Commandments* (1956), *Ben Hur* (1959), and *The Greatest Story Ever Told* (1965); and through attachment to the personalities at the highest levels of national government. The New Evangelicals emphasized religious confidence in an age of anxiety. Their corporate campaigns successfully absorbed the older prophets of individual confidence, such as Dale Carnegie and Norman Vincent Peale, connecting them to the worlds of mass entertainment and media politics, much as the New Evangelists' programming linked such dramatic religious productions as "Frontiers of Faith," "Lamp unto My Feet, and "Directions" with a cult of the hero of faith as celebrity.[22]

The New Evangelical celebrities witnessed to divine power and judgment, and exhibited sublime attributes in their own personalities, as larger-than-life performers in God's theater. Perhaps more important for explaining the continuing public appeal of the New Evangelists, they served as living instruments through which the public, as a gallery of spectators, could expropriate the masculine associations of power from the sublime. This secondary, instrumental quality of the charismatic personality, through which ordinary men and women could vicariously participate in sublime emotion, was classically Burkean. Although Burke's impassioned defense of the monarchy in the *Reflections* was presented long before there was a sociological concept of charisma and before the mass communication made possible by the electronic media, his appeal to a cult of celebrity is instructive concerning gender and the modern preoccupation with personality.

Burke, as we have seen, associated the sublime with masculine power and the beautiful with the feminine. This artificially gendered association of power necessarily required him to challenge the masculine associations of revolutionary violence, which he described as "a new conquering empire of light and reason," and for this he found an emphasis upon the queen strategically useful. The value of the monarchy, however, including male and female members, the British politician insisted, was that through it, the public could participate in sublime emotion. Burke identified the monarchy with a tamed animal, though he carefully avoided drawing attention to that simile. Through the agency of the monarchy, spectator-citizens could appropriate the fierceness of raw nature without risking their lives. For Burke, sentiment and tradition — social mores — had been the agency for taming the power of the monarchy, with kings being "mitigated into companions and raised private men," like Burke himself, "to be fellows with kings." Burke went on to explain that "Without force or opposition, it subdued the fierceness of pride and power, it obliged sovereigns to submit to the soft collar of social esteem, compelled stern authority to submit to elegance, and gave a dominating vanquisher of laws to be subdued by manners."[23]

For Burke, it was the political utility of this tamed monarchy that was compelling, not the moral or religious authority of the monarchy, or even the tradition it represented. Indeed, Burke recognized that the queen as easily functioned to sustain the public's sublime emotion as did the king, since the sublime is not actually patriarchal, despite its conventional associations with masculine power. However, by stripping the king and queen of their "charisma" — by reducing a king to a mere man, the queen to a mere woman—it must follow, Burke said, that "a woman is but an animal, and not of the highest order." Mixing metaphors for the sublime, he warned that the "pleasing illusions which made power gentle and obedient" would be "dissolved," and that "all the decent drapery of life is to be rudely torn off." The masculine associations of power will be unleashed and the "defects of our naked, shivering nature" will be exposed to ridicule.[24]

Max Weber, who sociologically identified the character of charisma before World War I, along with his myriad post-World War II interpreters, similarly recognized that charisma is not an expression of a cult of persons, either masculine or feminine, but of *personality*, which is a gender-neutral instrument of self-projection. Charisma may be manifested in either "priestly"—that is, institutionalized, form—or in a "magical," or antinomian form. According to Weberian sociology it may be "wild" or "tamed," "raw" or "cooked," individualistic or routinized, and applied to either revolutionary or conservative ends.

The "charisma" Burke associated with the church, monarchy, and state, and echoed by Cold War religious leaders such as Billy Graham and Oral Roberts, political leaders such as John Kennedy and Richard Nixon, and even actors as different as the romantic James Dean and the stolid John Wayne, therefore, did not rest in the patriarchal character of the sublime. Rather, in each case, their masculine charisma was dependent upon some greater routinized center of corporate power. As the very practice of performance by evangelists, politicians, and actors on the television, movie screen and stage assumes, the sublime may be evoked and directed by appropriating the *conventional* masculine through imitation. Indeed, those gay Hollywood actors who, like Rock Hudson, became the ideal of heterosexual manhood, perfectly illustrate the Burkean sublime, as does the transvestism in Andy Warhol's films and iconographic art. Similarly, the long public fascination with Madonna resulted from her provocative extension of the logic of the sublime to a female performance that appropriated masculine power. This apparent iconoclasm by a musical performer, however, repeated the very pattern that Susan McClary has suggested conventional classical music has privileged through its "masculine endings," and Wayne Koestenbaum has attributed to the Enlightenment origins of opera. It is this same convention behind the minstrel show that Eric Lott has appropriately characterized as a musical performance of racial expropriation, based upon *Love and Theft*.[25]

American social scientists after World War II were professionally organized around the problems and needs of a growing corporate economy. They characteristically used their discipline to identify and explore new forms of personal performance. Social scientists attempted to map the character of an exceptional American national culture (behind which stood a security state of awesome technological and bureaucratic scope), as well as to provide legitimacy to its corporate and bureaucratic systems. Max Weber's sociology became widely influential among intellectuals, both as the basis for an individualist challenge to a mass society of bureaucracy and consumerism, and, paradoxically, as an apology for it. Talcott Parsons, the leading Cold War functionalist sociologist, popularized Weber, as did C. Wright Mills, Parsons's leading critic. So too, did David Riesman, the author, with Nathan Glazer and Reuel Denney, of *The Lonely Crowd* (1950) and *Individualism Reconsidered* (1954).[26]

Riesman wrote in celebration of contemporary explorers of new frontiers of consumption in popular and professional journals such as *Commentary*, *Psychiatry*, and *American Scholar*. He called for personality engineers and a new Taylorism, not to eliminate false and unnecessary labor for a more efficient industrialism, but to eliminate false and unnecessary personalism in the coming culture of consumption.

Riesman identified three character types that he said were available among post–World War II Americans: the anomic, the adjusted, and the autonomous. It was the last of these, neither underconforming nor overconforming, that became Riesman's ideal. The ideal autonomous self promised to preserve individualism in an organic nationalism, while eliminating the problems associated with personalism for maintaining the class and bureaucratic interests in what Riesman called an "other-directed" society.

In an other-directed society, the office secretary, for example, imaginatively experiences her boss's hopes and fears, and expects to be treated reciprocally as a person by her boss. Riesman pointed out that such personalism is enormously problematic, both emotionally for the boss and secretary and bureaucratically for the system in which they work. This holds true in any bureaucratic setting, according to Riesman's Taylorist logic, because system needs and personal emotional needs may not coincide or may even be inimical. Similarly, he said, service attendants at the gas pumps create an uncomfortable and time-consuming dilemma for the other-directed. Such consumer-personalism creates the opportunity for many false, or inappropriate, claims upon the consumer's emotions.

In this case, he said, a new generation of engineers must eliminate service attendants and permit autonomous consumers to fill their own automobile gas tanks.[27]

Riesman's solution of substituting autonomous individualism for the reciprocity of personalism fostered celebrity personalities for much the same reason that Burke wished to preserve the monarchies. Celebrity personalities at once replaced personal relationships and responsibility for them, exhibiting the superior freedom and liberty that autonomous individualism makes possible. On the negative side, Riesman recognized that autonomous individualism, as an alternative to personalism, tends to replace social bonds with manipulative behavior. The very essence of the successful confidence game is an imaginative identification by the confidence artist with his or her mark. However problematic the appropriation of patriarchal power by secretaries and service station attendants — and, by extension, every manifestation of gender, race and class challenge to patriarchal privilege in an "other-directed society" — it can not be completely eliminated by personality engineers. It is vital for manufacturing public confidence in a consumer democracy that makes possible "the American Way of Life."

Therefore, professional sociologists such as David Riesman shared with sociologist Will Herberg a responsibility for eliminating personalism as a social model, while preserving the ideal of the celebrity personality. For, without the heroic personality, the autonomous individual would fall victim to anomic maladjustment or conformism — the twin dangers of a consumer-oriented society to the preservation of confidence. Consequently, throughout the Cold War era and after, jobs were eliminated, gender-based poverty and violence accelerated, and inner cities deteriorated, while the emphasis upon celebrity personalities in sports, entertainment, politics and business continued to expand through advertisement, public relations, and news programming.

It was this Cold War defense of autonomous individualism against personalism and conformism that led the literary critic Lionel Trilling to favorably review Riesman and to integrate his views into his own work. Trilling was the most respected critic of the late 1950s and early 1960s. Intellectually and politically, he embraced Richard Hofstadter, Seymour Martin Lipset, Edward Shils, and Daniel Bell, as well as Riesman, to promote neoconservatism, which may more accurately be termed neo-Burkeanism, since it appealed to both liberals and conservatives. The sociology of Erving Goffman, Nelson Foote, Peter Berger, and Ernest

Becker, among other dramaturgically oriented social psychologists, offered another formula of neo-Burkeanism, which complemented B. F. Skinner's psychology of performance. Skinner owed as much to Stanislavsky as to Pavlov in calling for a behavioristic model for assessing motivation. Skinner challenged the efficacy of the revolutionary ideals of "freedom and dignity," declaring that they were invitations to social chaos. Although he criticized the Enlightenment ideal of the autonomous individual, he defended the autonomy of the Taylorist engineers who would eliminate the baleful effects of both personalism and conformity on society in the classical Enlightenment convention of the formal garden. That is, Skinner preserved the Enlightenment ideal of the frontier as the sublime space between the natural and the contrived that is the province of the gardener, of the monarch, and of the celebrity.[28]

Not every social and psychological approach to the problem of performance in the post–World War II period was Burkean. But the very emphasis upon performance, and therefore on confidence, made Burkean solutions to aesthetic, social and political dilemmas increasingly popular and successful. Perhaps the best illustration of this may be seen in the similarities and contrasts between two of the most famous Cold War novelists and social critics, James Baldwin and Norman Mailer. Baldwin participated in the cult of personality that both advanced and fatally co-opted the civil rights movement. He brought an existential approach to the issues of race, gender and power. Preoccupied with personalism rather than autonomous individualism, Baldwin attempted to wear the charismatic mantle of artist-celebrity as a witness to the emptiness of the ideal of the autonomous individual. He remained alienated from political authority in both the civil rights and government establishments, very visibly separating himself, in the 1950s, from those New York intellectuals who identified with Burke.[29]

Among these was Norman Mailer. Mailer brought together the post–World War II vogue of existentialism and performance to create a celebrity personality, as did Baldwin. But Mailer's whole literary and public career was identified with the search for confidence rather than for the trust associated with personalism. Mailer embraced establishment politics, twice running for mayor of New York, as Baldwin chastised him for abandoning his responsibility as an artist. Mailer moralized over the quality of power, whether political, technological or individual, not over the quality of personal relationships, as did Baldwin. By the 1960s Mailer self-consciously abandoned a rather superficial Marxism, declaring himself a Burkean left-conservative. By 1968, Mailer would express political empathy for Richard Nixon, though he ultimately withheld his political support.[30]

As two of the best-known literary artists and social critics of the high Cold War, Baldwin and Mailer led their generation of writers in transferring the problem of how to escape conformism on one side and alienation on the other into the literary mainstream and the public controversies of their time. In fact, in a 1954 review, Mailer criticized Riesman because the sociologist's scientific style failed to achieve an artist's standard of emotional realism. Mailer's sympathy for abstract expressionist art was evident in his stylistic assault on Riesman's conventional academic writing style: "Far more important than the data are the attitudes and preconceptions with which the artist or *equally* the sociologist begins his work," Mailer chided Riesman, and, more obliquely, Lionel Trilling, "not to mention the energy and ambition."[31]

If Mailer used Riesman to challenge the patriarchal authority of Lionel Trilling and the New York literary establishment, Baldwin similarly leveled his aesthetic criticism at Richard Wright and the protest novel. Baldwin criticized Wright's sociological style for its lack of emotional realism. "We find ourselves bound, first without, then within, by the nature of our categorization," Baldwin wrote of the African-American experience in 1949. "We take our shape . . . within and against that cage of reality bequeathed us at our birth; and yet it is precisely through our dependence on that reality that we are most betrayed." The tragedy of *Native Son*'s Bigger Thomas, he wrote, was not his poverty but his theology, which denied him life. The failure of the protest novel, he concluded, is in its rejection of life. It is only the category of the personal acceptance of self "which is real and cannot be transcended." In a 1951 article in *Partisan Review*, Baldwin returned to the same theme. He warned against the Negro's acquiescence to the "obliteration of his own personality," through "surrendering to those forces which reduce the person to anonymity and which make themselves manifest daily all over the darkening world."[32]

The two young and ambitious artist-social critics, who wrote these essays near the beginning of their literary careers, were closely associated with *Commentary* and the New York intellectual community. Both had been drawn to the anti-Stalinist Left in the 1940s but in the 1950s embraced existentialism. They made existentialism central to their writing and to their social philosophies by linking it to the burgeoning opportunities for performance that came with the new age of American stage, film and television. Both celebrity-writers were products of the same pressures of advertisement and publicity that created the Actors Studio after World War II, and, not surprisingly, both Baldwin and Mailer were active in the studio, though ultimately held opposing assessments of its value.[33] Both men were unabashedly theological. Mailer presented his Manichean message of a cosmic struggle between the forces of good and evil through Jewish mysticism. Baldwin presented his message of personal salvation through an evangelical voice and the rhythms of the gospel blues. They both shared an apocalyptic language with the New Evangelists, who spoke and performed to the "Judeo-Christian" America of the 1950s and 1960s, all warning of a national moral crisis of cancerous conformity and spiritual alienation.

Baldwin was a child-evangelist, and, in significant ways, remained an evangelist all his life. The adolescent Baldwin precociously garnered praise and prestige, as well as a measure of protection from an abusive stepfather, through his role as God's messenger of judgment and redemption to Harlem churches. He remained in the pulpit through high school, even as he gravitated to writing plays and short stories, was introduced to the pleasures of theater and film, and recoiled from the terrors of sexuality and poverty. "Being in the pulpit was like being in the theatre," he wrote in *The Fire Next Time*. "I was behind the scenes and I knew how the illusion was worked." So intertwined were Baldwin's experiences with evangelism and theater that, like Melville's protagonist in his short story "The Two Temples," Baldwin remained unsure all his life whether the sincerity he found in art was recognizable because of the insincerity of the church, or whether the artifice of theater seemed sincere because it imitated religious truth.[34] Significantly, like Melville and Henry James, Baldwin distrusted sincerity, because he viewed it as a cultivated performance belonging to the surface of human interaction rather than to its substance. Americans have tremendous sincerity, he explained in an interview given a year before his death in 1987, about everything from Disneyland to football games. They are sincere about the Russians, he supposed, and "they are certainly sincere about what they call the 'Negro problem,' and about the Indians; they're sincere, in fact, about everything. And they understand nothing." It was for this insight into the American character, he said, that he appreciated Henry James, and he believed that this explained James's unwillingness to celebrate the American rise to dominance, which made him a lonely figure among American writers.[35]

The price for public adulation and the support of a beloved community was that the substance of the young evangelist's life was inseparable from his image. The adolescent preacher, like the adolescent choirboy, must appear to retain a pure innocence, and his words must dispense the gift of confidence to uplift his desperate and doubting listeners. Baldwin suggests in *Go Tell It on the Mountain* and *The Fire Next Time* that, as the choirboy's image must crack with his adolescent voice, the young evangelist was overwhelmed by the hypocrisy of his position, both in his sexuality and his morality. The first left him feeling degenerate and undeserving, and the second filled him with righteous indignation. The bisexual young black man felt guilt that outsiders were excluded from the grace of fellowship, and that fallen brothers and sisters, acting on the same impulses he secretly felt, were driven away while he was feted.[36]

Baldwin sought out the support of Beauford Delaney, a minister's son who had become a successful artist in Greenwich Village. Delaney, who, as David Leeming has written, eventually succumbed to his own inner sense of desolation, served as the most important in a series of surrogate fathers for Baldwin, including director Elia Kazan, psychologist Kenneth Clark, and poet Sterling Brown. Delaney offered Baldwin friendship and taught the aspiring writer to use words to reveal the rhythms of light and music in the pain and joy of African-American life. Unquestionably, Beauford Delaney comforted Baldwin in his loneliness and doubts about his inner life. His friendship may well have saved Baldwin's physical life at a critical time, and certainly it made Baldwin's artistic life possible. Delaney, however, could not resolve for the young Baldwin, or ultimately for himself, whether an artist's personal identity could be sustained through the sublime mission of dedicating his or her artistic creativity to the salvation of others. Nor could Delaney guarantee that celebrity-fathers would make such dedication any more personally fulfilling than had evangelists such as Baldwin's stepfather or the preacher who first called him out, Mother Horn of Mount Calvary of the Pentacostal Faith.[37]

In 1943, after years of personal doubt and conflict, Baldwin left home and moved to Greenwich Village. He was befriended, through Delaney, by Connie Williams, a Trinidadian who owned a bar called the Calypso, across the street from the Provincetown Playhouse on McDougal Street. There Baldwin found a gathering of artists, actors, writers, musicians and political writers who sustained him at a "welcome table" of fellowship, which replaced the church. The regulars at the Calypso included blacks and whites, laborers, sailors, and such celebrities as C.L.R. James, Burt Lancaster, Eartha Kitt, Paul Robeson, Claude McKay, Malcolm X, and Marlon Brando. Baldwin at this time was so drawn to theater that he briefly attended classes at the New School, with the intention of becoming an actor and playwright. In fact, Baldwin met Brando during the time when Brando was playing in Kazan's and Clurman's *Truckline Cafe*, and as the Actors Studio was forming out of the nucleus of that play. Subsequently, Baldwin became closely involved with Kazan, an association that led to the Actors Studio's staging of *Blues for Mister Charlie* (1964) on Broadway.[38]

Baldwin's early and critically acclaimed work reflected his mission to redeem Americans from their alienation from themselves and each other through love and to locate hope through merging religious rhythms and sensibilities with the sublime instrument of art. *Go Tell It on the Mountain* (1953), *Amen Corner* (1954), *The Fire Next Time* (1963), and *Tell Me How Long the Train's Been Gone* (1968) also expressed Baldwin's sense of responsibility to use his celebrity personality to save lost young people, as he was saved by the love of Delaney. The counterthemes of otherness and brotherhood in all Baldwin's writing, especially *Giovanni's Room* (1956), *Another Country* (1962), *Just Above My Head* (1979), and *Tell Me How Long*, suggest that racism was only the occasion for a more basic truth of American life: the fear of "seeing through to the reality of others." This fear results in a loss of self for the victim and oppressor. Whiteness, he insisted, is merely a metaphor for power. It is the name of the curse that results when one defines one's brothers and sisters out of one's community. The consequence of this God-like expulsion from Eden is that love, the act of recognizing oneself by recognizing the humanity of the other, becomes a crime. Where brotherhood and sisterhood is legally or viscerally made criminal, sexuality becomes incest, a crime against nature, or it becomes violent.[39]

Baldwin had looked to theater to find a place of community since the 1940s, but as early as 1961 he perceived that that community was as problematic as the one provided by the church he had left. The method acting he observed at the Actors Studio productions and on the movie screen reinforced, rather than challenged, the emotional unreality characteristic of both American theater and American life. "The characters played by the white actors," he wrote, "however untruthful they may essentially be, do depend—indeed, must depend—on the accumulation of small, very carefully observed detail." So an unreal character may be mimicked and the audience may easily be misled into believing that they recognize the character's realism. "But the characters played by Negro actors do not have even this advantage." White audiences do not know enough about the lives of black Americans to know which details to look for or how to interpret the ones with which they are presented.[40]

The black actor must act more in the casting office than he or she is likely to have an opportunity to do on stage. Whatever the black actor's training "he is not there to get a role he really wants to play; he is there to get a role which will allow him to be seen." The aspiring black actor, therefore, "dissembles his experience in the office, and he knows that he will probably be lying about it onstage. He also knows why; because nobody wants to know the story."

And, as the years went on, I was to be more and more struck by this numb passivity on the part of characters, who, after all, were part of the most active and optimistic nation in the world. They were helpless, they were stricken, from the moment the curtain rose. They seemed unable utterly to suspect any connection between their personal fortunes and the fortunes of the state of which they were a part, and rarely indeed was their heroism anything more than physical.

Most roles played by white actors "could only be played by means of tricks, tricks which would never help one to come closer to life, and all of which one would have to discard in order to play even one scene from Ibsen."[41]

Theater in America, Baldwin concluded, was "perishing for lack of vitality." The source of all theater is life, but the life being led in America is not what Americans pretend it to be. Blacks are very different from what they are permitted to show. This false image must be cracked, he wrote, because "the Negro in America is increasingly the central problem in American life, and not merely in social terms, in personal terms as well."[42]

Blues for Mister Charlie was Baldwin's great hope for cracking that image and delivering theater from commercialism and moral dishonesty. His play, made possible by his achievement of celebrity status through his success as a novelist, would inaugurate a new kind of Broadway theater production. He would use art to force confrontation instead of to facilitate avoidance of facing the self. *Blues for Mister Charlie* promised to make possible a theatrical-religious moment for breaking through the isolation of the silenced personal in America, the root of America's rage against blacks and against the world. Baldwin, therefore, refused to follow Kazan into his new home, Lincoln Center, because he wanted his play to be accessible to ordinary blacks who were excluded from Broadway by its sterile culture and its costs. But Baldwin could not make his communal vision of theater felt by Lee Strasberg, Cheryl Crawford, or by the actors from the studio.[43]

The artistic failure of *Blues* also coincided with a number of real or perceived personal betrayals, which increased Baldwin's growing pessimism about the possibility of providing meaning for others through his personality as a celebrity. He published a pessimistic book entitled *Nothing Personal* with fashion photographer Richard Avedon in 1964, which portrayed a devastating falseness at the core of American consumer culture. In 1964, too, he began work on the novel *Tell Me How Long the Train's Been Gone*, which failed critically when it appeared in 1968 but was perhaps the strongest apology Baldwin produced for his personal, artistic and political values.[45]

The protagonist of *Tell Me* is a celebrity actor, Leo Proudhammer, whose devastating heart attack both shatters his old life and forces him to recognize that the failure of theater means a crisis in the redemptive power of the celebrity's personality. The young Leo had been baptized as a new Adam through his success in the theater. "There is no baptism like the baptism of the theater, when you stand up there and bow your head and the roar of the people rolls over you," says Leo. He felt that if only he could keep the faith of the theater, he could transform his sorrow into life and joy, for while his life might be filled with pain, he would not be useless. "If I kept the faith, I could do for others what I felt had not been done for me, and if I could do that, if I could give, I could live." But even on this first mountaintop experience as celebrity-savior, he felt isolated and empty. It is this unbearable aloneness that brings on the middle-aged Leo's heart attack. "I don't think I'd have minded," Leo says, "if I could have found a role with some relation to the life I lived, the life I knew, some role which did not traduce entirely my own sense of life, my own life." He played the available roles for a black actor — waiters, butlers, porters, and clowns — but since they did not exist, he had no conceivable way to play them. Consequently, Leo was forced to rely upon tricks, which led to contempt for the audience, and with contempt came an actor's death. "One was imitating an artifact," he explained. "One might as well have been an icon, and one's performance depended not at all on what one saw — still less, God forbid, on what one felt—but on what the audience had come to see, had been trained to see." Acting had to "change the beat," and not serve as a sinister and fearful confidence game in which the actor must make the audience know he or she is happy, so that they may be sure they are happy.[46]

Baldwin, in *Tell Me*, berates the falseness of acting that fails to remember that the actor wears disguises to approach the truth rather than to flee from it. "If it is true, as I suspect, that people turn to each other in the hope of being created by each other then it is absolutely true that the uncreated young turn, to be created, toward their elders," Leo Proudhammer says. "Thus, whoever has been blessed with the power of enchantment is guilty of something more base than treachery whenever he fails to exercise the power on which the yet-to-be created, as helplessly as newborn birds, depends." Leo remembers one instance of that treachery from his early adolescence. He and his brother, he says, entered a sort of "cathedral," with photographs of movie stars on the walls, to attend the movie *King's Row*. Though he suspected that these cheerful white faces mounted prominently on the wall lacked acting ability, "lights and makeup and an innocence as brutal as it was despairing did marvelous things for these sons and daughters of the one and only God, and very nearly reconciled me to Ronald Reagan's teeth." In the dark theater, which he describes as a cave, Leo watched the young people scattered around him, despising them in his arrogance. But as a middle-aged and heartbroken celebrity, Leo acknowledges that his masks are not so different from those of the young people who sat around him in that platonic cave of his youth.[47]

Perhaps in parody of Reagan's 1965 autobiography, *Where's the Rest of Me?* and thinking of the former actor's election to the governorship of California, Baldwin portrays these young people as unaware of the preposterous falsehoods that were being presented to them on the screen. His memory of the film, he says, will be forever distorted by the uncontrolled laughter that the dishonest acting and story of a father's incest elicited from his brother, Caleb, the same brother who later awoke from a terrified dream about his degrading sexual experience in prison. The unreality of Reagan's performance in the dark cave of the theater is inseparable from the pain in the dungeon, for both resulted from the twisted psyches of those who deny the humanity of others and turn the act of love into a transgression.[48]

The second instance of treachery appears in the character of a thinly disguised Lee Strasberg of the Actors Studio, with a version of Stanislavsky's method. Saul San-Marquand, the white-haired and thin-lipped director of The Actors' Means Workshop, impresses Leo Proudhammer as a Jeremiah who never had any convictions. San-Marquand is manipulative and impersonal. He hides behind a facade of dedication to theater, while using the method to dominate actors rather than to bring out their personal sense of truth. Indeed, Baldwin suggests that Strasberg's method is a kind of rape. Leo attends an acting class at Saul's house, "where students performed, or exposed themselves, ordinarily, and where celebrities, at parties did likewise." Leo's role in this improvisation class is Kazan's role of the hack driver from *Waiting for Lefty*. Saul first subtly discredits the personal motivation of the actors and then insists that an artist's execution must be impersonal, because the body is an instrument. Saul reminds Leo that he was a revolutionary in the 1930s, and directed this revolutionary play before he was born. But Leo recognizes that the control of The Actors' Means Workshop over the bodies of actors is destructive to theater, as is the control of a man of power over another's sexuality. The new theater is no more real than the old commercial films of Leo's youth.[49]

Leo's heart attack forces him to realize that "there is a truth in the theater and there is a truth in life—they meet, but they are not the same, for life, God help us, is the truth." He discovers that he lives a life of frontiers, and that "the most dramatic, the most appalling remains that invisible frontier which divides American towns, white from black." He finds that frontier stretching out beneath the sublime mountain of his celebrity, where he makes living contact only with another celebrity, Barbara King. The love of two celebrities, safe in their equal achievement, is sublime but necessarily incestuous. The love of celebrities who do not belong to themselves must be for the young and uncreated. The love of the pure young revolutionary and child of the future, Black Christopher, alone, can confirm the authenticity of the celebrity's creative life. But Black Christopher must go his own way and make his own life after climbing to safety through the celebrity's gift of himself. Thus, Baldwin's celebrity must learn to ride his pain as a horse, while acknowledging that his pain is no horse and he is no rider. But does the responsibility of the celebrity to use sublime power to save Black Christopher from self-destruction include supplying money to buy guns to save him from falling under the feet of horses?[50]

In response to this frontier conundrum, Baldwin's existential performer accepts the fleeting transience of personal meeting. Neither Leo

Proudhammer nor his creator is prepared to abandon his mystical faith in the redemptive power of the heroic personality of the celebrity, but the strain on Baldwin's faith is evident as he moves towards a rapprochement with the evangelism of his youth and an apocalyptic vision of a coming day of revolutionary judgment at the conclusion of the novel. Though still clinging to his sublime celebrity, the new Leo is under surveillance by the people as well as the police. He has become a witness, and a witness does not share with others, but only reports, without answers. Leo acknowledges that he is divided between himself as a celebrity and as a person and also between the church and his art as expressions of dedicated performances that only gain meaning as a gift to others. As a celebrity personality, he has conquered the city, but the city, he ruefully acknowledges, has the plague. The essayist Baldwin says much the same thing in his own voice four turbulent years later, in *No Name in the Street* (1972).[51]

As Baldwin faced the deaths of Medgar Evers, Malcolm X and finally, in 1968, Martin Luther King, he found the destruction of the personal and the isolation of the mountaintop experience of his celebrity-personality to be overwhelming. Baldwin could no longer fulfil the role of purveyor of confidence for Americans, a confidence game that he had long since given up as an evangelist only to preserve as an artist. However, he wrote, "Since Martin's death in Memphis, and that tremendous day in Atlanta, something has altered in me, something has gone away."[52]

No Name in the Street took its title from the Book of Job. Baldwin's identification with Job marked his rejection of his role as Jeremiah and his charge that the jeremiad had become a rhetorical form for exploiting the suffering of blacks, rather than a litany of hope in despair. It also pointed to his personal loss of a vital connection with the Harlem community of his youth, which he had vowed to serve, and of his inability to bridge the gap between Beverly Hills and the valley where Watts lay in the wake of King's death. Indeed, this elegy to the three great celebrity-martyrs of the civil rights movement was equally a confession of Baldwin's growing distance from those he wished to save. When Dr. King was assassinated in Memphis, Baldwin was still bearing witness to his enduring faith in the American Dream: the uncreated potential for humanity among his countrymen, which he sought to redeem through the resources of Hollywood. Baldwin's attempt to negotiate a screenplay on the life of Malcolm X failed, however, and King, like Malcolm a creation of the people's need and taken away in violent death, became hot commercial property. Baldwin was forced to admit to himself that he was, in reality, powerless to use his celebrity status artistically to fulfil the people's need. Nor could he use his fame to shield young revolutionary Black Panthers from government violence, or to deliver his young friend, Tony Maynard, from the worldwide arm of the police. In other words, Baldwin had begun to suspect that his achievement of celebrity status, as a sacred trust and charismatic office, might have made him an accomplice in a national confidence game. Baldwin felt implicated in the worldwide racism which was destroying his friends at home and abroad, since at home he was a star who was a protected commodity, and, as an American abroad, his passport insulated him from the danger that stalked the poor and despised.[53]

In Baldwin's last years, he continued to dream of a "welcome table," voicing his faith in the possibility of a "New Jerusalem," but those dreams were cruelly mocked in the murder of black children in Atlanta by an individual who must have been an elder of the community, and whom the usually wary street children fatally trusted. Baldwin's anguished report of this apocalyptic irony and his biting portrait of the accused murderer, Wayne Williams, whom Baldwin described as a scapegoat and a failed celebrity, constituted the subject matter of his last book, *The Evidence of Things Not Seen* (1985). It was a despairing witness to a black imitation of the murder of young Emmett Till, the event that had been the source for *Blues for Mister Charlie*. These murders of unrecognized black children of poverty, however, did not occur because of white police or governmental indifference, but under Andrew Young's mayoral administration. It confirmed the end of Baldwin's hope that his celebrity personality could convince America to affirm community, which, as he understood it, "simply means our endless connection with, and responsibility for, each other." Yet not even a despairing Baldwin could surrender his confidence in America as "the only nation under heaven that contains the universe," the last hope for a nation which might liberate mankind from "the strangling idea of national identity."[54]

It was precisely the success of his effort to attach himself to the national identity of confidence that separates Norman Mailer from Baldwin and links him to Ronald Reagan and the frontier tradition. Mailer was able to project his celebrity-personality and engage the public in the most challenging dilemmas of the Cold War by provocatively defining race, sex, and politics in terms of psychic war. The ideal of the celebrity-artist, as described by Mailer, is a modern equivalent of the frontier scout, the patrol leader on jungle reconnaissance. The patrol leader works "the structure of an art in his sleep" on the uncertain conclusions of what he has seen the day before. The "small facts, experience, and touch of instinct would have their unconscious war, and leave him in the morning with a new sense of form which was the record of that psychic war." It is a process, Mailer said, that makes no military sense, but if the patrol leader is a good one, and the good ones always have something of the artist in them, "he will gamble on his perceptions because it was the only way for him to grow," and this is, paradoxically, the best chance that the men he leads will escape death by ambush. For, if he does not follow his instincts and try to take the hill, he will not know if his suspicions of the hidden presence of the enemy, waiting in ambush, are right or wrong. The next time he must call on "a collaboration between his paranoia and courage his instincts will be slack with untested questions."[55]

Mailer characterized postwar Americans as living in a new era of totalitarian conformity and depression in which "a stench of fear has come out of every pore of American life, and we suffer from a collective failure of nerve." His solution for restoring confidence might have been as old as Buffalo Bill Cody's, but he would have been unable to achieve Cody's fame without a new international expression of that solution for the conditions of the twentieth-century cultural Cold War. A New Yorker, Mailer found that style by touring Paris, much as Buffalo Bill had found his by touring New York. Buffalo Bill turned himself into a celebrity-scout; the new urban frontiersman, Mailer, turned himself into an existentialist celebrity.

An "existentialist celebrity," a category created by Jean-Paul Sartre at the end of World War II, was identified by William Barrett as a contradiction in terms. Mailer discovered Sartrean existentialism in the Paris of 1947, where the young author of *The Naked and the Dead* traveled in imitation of ex-patriots such as Hemingway and Fitzgerald. Sartre then dominated the Paris literary scene. Though Sartre later confessed that he had never personally experienced dread but only exploited it because it seemed fashionable, his calculated effort to create a reputation for himself eclipsed the reputations of Albert Camus and Gabriel Marcel, who were his contemporaries. He took in innocents such as Mailer, who had probably never read a word of existentialism, but also the American philosopher Walter Kaufmann, who made existentialism his life study.[56]

Mailer shared with Sartre the dream of turning the anguish of the human condition in the twentieth century into personal fame. While he was in France, Mailer learned that he had succeeded in his ambition through his first novel, *The Naked and the Dead*, which had become a best-seller back in New York. *The Naked and the Dead* was a Freudian novel about war and self-mastery, but it was most depressingly about power and how modern militarism reduces individuals to the "insignificance of insects traversing an endless beach."[57] Sartrean existentialism, with its mixture of Freudianism, Marxism and individualism, offered Mailer a formula for transcending the contradictions of power and for turning the meaninglessness of existence into a glamourous act of conservative rebellion. He could move beyond writing the great novel of World War II, fusing political theater, the new journalism, and metaphysics to affirm his own ambition and America's capacity to lead the world.

In the 1960s, as Mailer began to identify himself as a Burkean, he also became impressed with Andy Warhol, who masterfully produced ominously inane images of consumer goods, consumed celebrities, and consumed consumers—from Brillo pads to Marilyn Monroe to graphic scenes of automobile accidents. Warhol built his successful career as a fine artist—or confidence artist—by cogently recognizing and shamelessly exploiting the sublime tensions between terror and triviality in the ordinary processes and images of the working commercial artist's world (in mass-produced silk screens and paintings), in his films, and in his capacity to turn inarticulation into self-promotion.

Warhol straddled the line between simulation and dissimulation and between optimism and despair. He was the only other man in America who could sense the shifts and trends in the culture six months to a year ahead of everyone else, Mailer said. Warhol's underground films particularly interested Mailer, because they permitted an artist to project his or her vision of reality more immediately than either the novel or theater. In this sense, Mailer's forays into films and into electoral politics were part of the same artistic process. Mailer's personality, like Warhol's, was his true artistic medium, and he would use it to heal the slack, featureless, and symptomless disease that was wasting the national soul. Mailer had looked around and seen no political leader, with the partial exception of John Kennedy, to accept the messianic responsibility of saving the nation through a revolution in consciousness. He therefore made that mission his own during the 1960s.[58]

In a 1971 review of Mailer's film, *Maidstone*, Richard Schickel noted that it takes a supple and intelligent view of the self, such as Mailer has, to successfully manage the contradictions of the modern celebrity game. The model of the Hollywood star, who properly belongs to exotic locations and studio backstage lots, he said, no longer suffices. For the star, Schickel explained, has become the extension of the director's vision.[59] When the star—as evangelist, artist or politician—appears, it is increasingly in terms defined by someone else, as James Baldwin discovered in one way and Ronald Reagan in another. Mailer, like Warhol, assured his stardom by making himself the director of the events that surrounded him. By defining himself as an existential hero, and by recognizing that in twentieth-century America, as Schickel saw, all celebrity is political, Mailer successfully promoted himself into fame and wealth on the currents of Cold War paranoia.[60]

Mailer essentially laid down this life project in his 1957 essay, "The White Negro," following the critical failures of *Barbary Shore*, an existential attack on liberalism, and *The Deer Park*, a critique of the false celebrity values of Hollywood that was strongly reminiscent of Dos Passos. In "The White Negro," Mailer wrote that collective death was the overwhelming reality of the twentieth century, whether experienced through concentration camps, nuclear weapons, totalitarian politics, or conformism. The individual in twentieth-century America may only live by heroically risking death at every moment and "encourag[ing] the psychopath in oneself, to explore that domain of experience where security is boredom and therefore, sickness, and one exists in the present, in that enormous present which is without past or future, memory or planned intention, the life where man must go until he is beat, where he must gamble with his energies through all those small or large crises of courage and unforseen situations which beset his day, where he must be with it or doomed not to swing." The unstated essence of Hip, he wrote, as a cultural expression of "psychopathic brilliance," is the mystical imparting of new levels of knowledge through one's entire being with every victory over boredom or desperation. "One is Hip, or one is Square (the alternative that each new generation coming into American life is beginning to feel), one is a rebel or one conforms, one is a frontiersman in the Wild West of the American night life, or else a square cell, trapped in the totalitarian tissues of American society, doomed willy-nilly to conform if one is to succeed."

Baldwin criticized Mailer for creating an artificial black man who lived a life of posturing no African-American could afford. But Mailer's hipster was meant to be an entirely artificial creation of the natural Adam—

that is, a symbolic manifestation of sublime power. Mailer's evangelism for the psychopathic hip fit the apocalyptic mood of the 1950s. In the 1960s Mailer was becoming conscious of his Jewishness, and brought his Cold War version of cabalism, as an American Walter Benjamin or Georg Lukács, to the pages of *Commentary*. Norman Podhoretz encouraged him by introducing him to Jewish tradition at about the same time Podhoretz was also encouraging Baldwin to write about the black Muslims. That was the genesis of Baldwin's apocalyptic essay, *The Fire Next Time*.[61]

Perhaps because Sartre was increasingly criticized in the 1950s as a mere *litterateur*, or because French rationalist atheism was alien to Mailer's personality and background, he was strongly attracted to the same messianic blend of politics and mysticism that characterized the postwar phase of the Frankfurt school of sociologists and the writings of Walter Benjamin and Georg Lukács.[62] In addition, perhaps because of the apocalyptic implications of the Cold War tensions, theology resonated with the American political culture, as it had with the culture of early modernism in Europe. For whatever reasons, the nominally Jewish Mailer found himself attracted to the mystical thesis that God and the devil were engaged in a cosmic struggle for the forces of freedom and personality against the forces of totalitarianism and conformity. Perhaps, too, the then-languishing author needed to be taken seriously again, and to do that he needed to demonstrate his intellectual acumen to the New York intellectual establishment, many of whom were Jewish ex-Marxists. In 1962, therefore, as Lukács had done in 1911, Mailer explored the mystical themes of Buber's *Tales of the Hasidim*, and in remarkably similar terms.[63]

Lukács was, like Mailer after him, an exponent of revolutionary conservatism. Though drawn to mysticism and religious transcendence, Lukács, again like Mailer, was an assimilated Jew who was not conventionally religious. Lukács was shaped by the political and cultural crises of war, as was Mailer, and both found in existentialist philosophers such as Kierkegaard and Dostoyevsky confirmation of their feeling of alienation from bourgeois society and of a psychological split between metaphysics and politics. As abstract expressionism was for Mailer, postimpressionist art, for Lukács, was a cultural harbinger of a crisis in Western culture that required the individual to face an age of insecurity and anxiety with emotional realism. The artist, they agreed, must take the aesthetic moment and expand it to fill the entire world by an act of creative will.[64]

As was so for Lukács, Mailer's existentialism was an aesthetic gesture, through which he transformed the "authentic" of personalism into an individualist act of pure performance. Mailer's Hipster embodied the same combination of primitive purity, violence and transcendence that Lukács celebrated in primitiveness and Bolshevism. Mailer, of course, lived on the other side of twentieth-century totalitarianism and was not tempted to become a communist, as Lukács had been in the Hungary of 1918. Instead, Mailer was deeply influenced by John Dos Passos, as well as by Dwight Macdonald and the Marxist writer Jean Malaquais. He identified himself as a Marxist-anarchist, and then, as he wrote in 1967, "he tried to think in the style of Marx in order to attain certain values suggested by Edmund Burke."[65] Both ideologically and physically, Mailer embraced violence as an act of self-regeneration, brawling in bars and at parties. In 1960, he stabbed his second wife, Adele Morales. In another instance, Mailer defended the prison writer Jack Abbott, after Abbott murdered a man following his release in 1981. Mailer argued that, since saving the nation's honor had justified a gamble with nuclear weapons during the Cold War, "I'm willing to gamble with a portion of society to save this man's talent."[66]

Though Mailer never discussed Lukács, their similar fascination with violence and their double consciousness towards modernism as terror and promise led them to the same preoccupation with confidence. Though both Mailer and Lukács were drawn to the drama and mystical struggle between good and evil in Martin Buber's Hasidic tales, neither was interested in the central concepts of dialogue and trust, the I and thou, that Buber emphasized in his interpretations of the tales. It was instead the metaphysics of confidence that defined their political visions, and, ultimately, their acceptance of the logic of violence and even murder in the name of a higher courage. For Lukács, that celebration of confidence, as a manifestation of the sublime, may be seen in his decision to embrace the ethically unspeakable crimes of Bolshevism as an act of logical and rational necessity for creating a new world—an act made all the more heroic because it required a courageous renunciation of his own ethical standards. For the Mailer of *Advertisements*, the hipster-hero must creatively encourage the psychopath in himself, because "one murders not only a weak fifty-year-old man, but an institution as well.... The hoodlum is therefore daring the unknown, and so no matter how brutal the act, it is not altogether cowardly."[67]

For Mailer, the social gamble involved in allowing a prison writer to develop his creative potential, or in going to the moon, is the same as the individual artist's gamble with his talent and nerve in making an experimental film or in writing a fictional biography of Marilyn Monroe or a factual novel about the execution of Gary Gilmore, while courting financial disaster. Mailer sees these acts as a placing of the self organically within a sublime flow of cosmic energy, which both threatens to crush the isolated individual and lifts him or her into a transcendent universalism. Mailer's "nuclear sublime" defines his artistic oeuvre, from "White Negro," to *Ancient Evenings*. It links the mystical power of ego and karma to the technological ambition of astronauts and the political power of presidents. It offers intimations of the spiritual power of reincarnation to restore the vitality of rebirth after rebirth, into infinity, through the act of sexual performance and through artistic performance, in which a new self is created and expressed again and again.[68]

But the metaphysics of confidence is, inescapably, also a metaphysics of doubt. The Cold War might have come because of the communist threat to freedom, or because capitalism could not survive without it, he wrote in 1964, or both. "Who could know? Who could really know? The center of our motive was the riddle wrapped in the enigma—was the country extraordinary or accursed?" Similarly, in 1971, the "prisoner of sex" reflected that "he had by now lost the essential belief in himself which was critical to the idea that one could improve the world (and he knew he might not regain that belief until he had succeeded in passing judgement on himself—if indeed, one could) no, now there were days when he wondered if that continuing revolution of reason which the Renaissance had begun was not a war to liberate man but to pollute him by the wastes of his vanity, huge scientific vanity now destroying every natural act of nature." Women's liberation had forced him to ask the same question Goldwater had made him ask about what Lyndon Johnson meant for the country's future: Was the revolution, whether political or sexual, a beautiful or diabolical idea? No thought was so painful as the idea that sex had meaning, he wrote, "for give meaning to sex and one was a prisoner of sex—the more meaning one gave it the more it assumed, until every failure and misery, every evil of your life, spoke their lines in its light, and every fear of mediocre death. Worse. It was not an age to look for meaning in one's acts—a dread of the future oozed from every leak in the social machine. . . ." Mailer concluded with the ominous possibility that an artificial karma and reincarnation would invade not just nature but metaphysical reality as well. The genetic engineer might in the future create a new breed of human being, one capable of changing sex repeatedly after birth, to create an artificial reincarnation that mocks the artist's self-invention, much as in *The Executioner's Song* (1979), the doubt concerning Gilmore's executioner was as central as the indeterminate meaning of the song.

Gilmore's prison was not just metaphorical, nor was his death only symbolic, as he worked out his karma and gave witness to his deadly faith in reincarnation. But Mailer remained unsure as to whether Gilmore was an artist of confidence, who found metaphysical confirmation of his courage in facing a firing squad, or a confidence artist who manipulated others to fill his emptiness, or both. Gilmore was a product of the open spaces of the western frontier, but his life had become fatally defined by the confined space of the prison he carried around inside himself, and which he read in the psyches around him. Mailer suggested this reading of his novel in "the old prison rhyme," with which he began and ended *The Executioner's Song*. Actually, however, it was not an old prison rhyme, he admitted, but one written by himself a decade before: "Deep in my dungeon/I welcome you here/Deep in my dungeon I worship your fear/Deep in my dungeon I dwell/I do not know if I wish you well . . . A bloody kiss from the wishing well."[69]

Perhaps Mailer's most concise statement of the metaphysics of confidence as a Burkean approach to power, however, may be found in his celebration of boxing, as violence and as theater. The boxer became Mailer's primary metaphor for the existentialist hero as political leader, replacing the hipster, during the national election of 1964. The American people, Mailer said, faced a political choice between an insane liberal totalitarianism and a conservative apocalypse. Lyndon Johnson had led the country into the quicksand of Vietnam, while Barry Goldwater might lead America over the precipice into nuclear war. Since "there was nothing in our growth which was organic," the neo-Burkean Mailer surmised, the country had become confused. It had lost its bearings, and was adrift between madness and inauthenticity.[70] For Mailer, the lesson of the boxer in the arena—sport or political—was a lesson for a people who had to learn to live with pain and blurred vision from too many blows. Mailer was no professional boxer, but the reporter had gone his share of rounds in the ring and on the street. He wrote from personal experience, therefore, when he reflected in 1971 that

> there was only one way in which boxing was still like a street fight, and that was in the need to be confident you would win. A man walking out of a bar to fight

with another man is seeking to compose his head into the confidence that he will certainly triumph—it is the most mysterious faculty of the ego. For the confidence is a sedative against the pain of punches and yet is the sanction to punch your own best. The logic of the spirit would suggest that you win only if you deserve to win; the logic of the ego lies down the axiom that if you don't think you will win, you don't deserve to. And, in fact, usually don't; it is as if not believing you will win opens you to the guilt that perhaps you have not the right, you are too guilty.

So training camps are small factories for the production of one rare psychological item—an ego able to bear huge pain and administer drastic punishment.[71]

In 1968, Mailer's political sympathy went out to a fighter he hoped had learned the lessons of defeat, but whom the reporter had previously dismissed as an arrogant lightweight. Richard Nixon's heroic appeal for Mailer, and he suspected for American voters, was in his comeback after his career seemed over. The new Nixon, he said, had finally acquired "some of the dignity of the old athlete and the old con—he had taken punishment, that was on his face now, he knew the detailed schedule of pain in a real loss, there was an attentiveness in his eyes which gave offer of some knowledge of the abyss, even the kind of gentleness which ex-drunkards attain after years in AA."[72]

Mailer's new sympathy for Nixon was not a reaction of fear because of the violent excesses of the Left. He had defended the need to pay the price of violence too often to have been so easily frightened into a turn to the political Right. Rather, Mailer needed to believe in Richard Nixon because that would permit him to preserve his confidence in America itself. Only Nixon's comeback could restore Mailer's faith in the national destiny, he knew, because winning would prove that Nixon had learned something that permitted him to deserve to win. The successful return of Nixon meant, Mailer said, that some previously overlooked virtue in the man had come to maturity; it "might even be a measure of the not entirely dead promise of America, if a man as opportunistic as the early Nixon could grow in reach and comprehension and stature to become a leader." More ominously, if Nixon could not perform with a newfound authority and grace, "to weed the garden of tradition," then Ronald Reagan might win the nomination for the New Religious and Political Right.[73]

Ronald Reagan, Mailer suggested, was either a confidence artist, or, even more dangerous, a man with greater confidence than the establishment politician fighting against the tides of his squandered past. First, the insurgent Reagan was a serious opponent because he had the psychological edge of an electoral victory in a big state that Nixon lacked. Second, "he had incorporated the confidence of an actor who knows he is popular with interviewers." Indeed, his manner, in contrast to Nixon's, was so natural that his faults seemed inconsequential. Mailer stood before Nixon in the convention hall considering all this, and reported that he could think of only one question: "What, sir, is the state of your familiarity with the works of Edmund Burke?"[74]

As Mailer sized up the new Nixon, who had to contend with the Hollywood actor Reagan, he saw a man with good voice and plenty of acting potential but felt the despair of a drama coach. Perhaps, Mailer thought, Nixon was not a bad actor, only the product of bad training. Indeed, his artificiality and reputation for being boring made him seem all the more sincere. Perhaps he was, after all, the great educator, the man to bring the warring halves of the nation together, "and bring back the faith of other nations to a great nation in adventurous harmony with itself. . . ." If that were possible, Mailer concluded, then all things were, indeed, possible. The country might survive the bad years of its history and not be stripped of its blessings. If the old Nixon was a devil, then the new Nixon might be a devil who had been improved by the suffering of God's striving. That, it seemed to Mailer, would be the ultimate theological assurance of the national hope for salvation.[75]

Mailer had not surrendered to the sublime appeal of Nixon's political personality, which, in a street crowd, he said, "is *radiant* with emotion to reach across the prison pen of his own artificial moves and deadly reputation and show that he is sincere." But he was emotionally moved by it, and felt the strength of Nixon's appeal to the Protestant center of the national culture, especially to Billy Graham, who had long since surrendered to "Tricky Dick's" sincerity. For Graham had so identified his message and ministry with Nixon's leadership that he considered an open endorsement of Nixon in 1968, and he offered the closing prayer following Nixon's acceptance speech at the convention in Miami, before participating in a meeting to discuss possible running mates. Graham was not alone among the New Evangelists in feeling a special kinship with Nixon, which dated back to his days as vice president. Nixon had relationships, though less intimate ones, with Oral Roberts and Fulton Sheen, as well.[76]

In gaining empathy for Richard Nixon, Mailer was gaining empathy for the nation under siege that had given him fame and wealth. He was beginning to find more and more common ground with the neo-Burkeans to his political right, even as he remained opposed to the Goldwater-Reagan forces gathering on the far right. This Luce-Eisenhower base, which included the neo-Burkeans and which Nixon inherited in 1968, was an informal coalition of evangelicals and intellectuals, alienated middle-class Americans, and corporate leaders. But the Religious and Political Right, which briefly came to power with Reagan, was built from that same Cold War coalition. It included other factions and networks of influence, some of which Nixon added through his southern strategy, but it was not originally a paranoid fringe of eccentric Taft Republicans, as the neo-Burkean sociologist Daniel Bell characterized them in his *The New American Right* (1955) and *The Radical Right* (1963).[77]

Rather, the origins of the New Religious and Political Right, whom Reagan endorsed, and who joined in awarding Reagan his electoral victory, grew out of the very Luce-backed forces for whom Bell worked at *Fortune* Magazine from 1948 to 1958. For, contrary to Bell and his associates at *The New American Right* and *The Radical Right*, Luce and Eisenhower silently supported McCarthy and virulent anticommunism and used McCarthyism for their own political ends as long as it remained useful to do so. The Luce-Eisenhower forces differed from the Religious and Political Right in their ability to control the Burkean images of moderation and naturalness. They were, therefore, able to simultaneously co-opt and absorb former leftist radicals such as Bell himself, Stevenson Democrats such as Reinhold Niebuhr and Lionel Trilling, and the New Evangelicals who wished to distance themselves from strict fundamentalism.[78] The tactics used to mold the public's perception of the world in terms of the "American Century" helped move the nation further to the corporate right, and, perhaps more important, legitimized casuistry in the battle against communism and reinforced the primacy of performance over principle in the national culture.

The result was that a celebrity personality on the right, appearing sincere and championing a return to traditional values and a natural economy purged of artificial governmental influences, could eventually capture the Burkean conventions of political theater. This was a distressing surprise to Daniel Bell. Despite his own attraction to a postmodern "return of the sacred," he was shocked to discover that such "neoconservative" friends as Norman Podhoretz and Irving Kristol had become ardent supporters of Ronald Reagan and allies of the Christian Religious

Right.[79] However, Mailer's attention to the politics of personality permitted him to see that potential already inherent in the 1960 election of John Kennedy, even as he supported his nomination. "I was forcing reality," Mailer admitted, in his positive description of Kennedy in *Superman Comes to the Supermarket*. "I was not writing with the hope that perchance I could find reality by being sufficiently honest to perceive it, but on the contrary," Mailer wrote in *The Presidential Papers*, "was distorting reality in the hope that thereby I could affect it."[80]

Mailer said that he supported Kennedy for his potential as a personality and not for his politics, which he expected to be conventional at best. The night Kennedy was elected he felt uneasy. "It was a spooky emotion," he said, but he felt that in writing with the casuistic purpose of affecting the election and Kennedy's image, he had entered into a Faustian bargain. He felt a sense of woe, as if he had betrayed the Left, and himself. "In the wake of the election one note was clear—the strength the Left had been gaining in the last years of Eisenhower's administration would now be diluted, preempted, adulterated, converted and dissolved by the compromises and hypocrisies of a New Democratic administration." In 1968, Mailer was further drawn to the Right in the politics of sincerity over authenticity, as he found the new Richard Nixon to be the most interesting figure at the Republican convention.[81]

But it was Ronald Reagan who particularly excelled at the Burkean virtue of appearing sincere, and Lionel Trilling, in his 1972 book *Sincerity and Authenticity*, unconsciously touched upon Reagan's appeal before Reagan discovered it himself. Trilling insisted that manners and cultured behavior were better defenses of social health than romantic authenticity. Sincerity was more serviceable for preserving social order than was the demonic volatility of the authentic.[82] Trilling's direct Burkean appeal to sublime sincerity over the unmediated beauty of the religious conscience was rooted in the same doubts about the "adversary culture" that Daniel Bell embraced and that led Mailer to reappraise Nixon in 1968. For Will Herberg and for Daniel Bell, it meant the complete rejection of existentialism, with its emphasis upon the authentic, as a dangerous form of individualism.[83]

The reissue of Trilling's 1947 novel, *The Middle of the Journey*, in 1975, therefore, is significant for its anticipation of the attraction of ex-communists to the sincerity of the New Religious and Political Right, through the sympathetic portrayal of the character Gifford Maxim's conversion from communism to Christianity. Maxim was based directly upon Whittaker Chambers. The *Time* editor's 1948 testimony before HUAC, in which he charged former state department official Alger Hiss with spying for the Soviet Union, electrified the nation. Chambers's testimony provided Richard Nixon with a national reputation, and turned Chambers into a media symbol of the anticommunist as penitent sinner.

Trilling, who was not an observing Jew, felt uneasy about the religious message Chambers and Maxim represented but also an attraction for its commitment and authority. Communism had "presented the world as in movement and drama, had offered the possibility of heroism or martyrdom, made available the gift of commitment and virtue to those who chose to grasp it," Trilling's liberal protagonist, John Laskell, acknowledged. But Laskell saw that "the intellectual power had gone from the system of idealism, and much of its power of drama had gone." Times were changing, and a competing system must come with the swing of the pendulum. Maxim—and Chambers—were riding that pendulum of religious idealism in 1947.[84]

By 1980, Ronald Reagan could successfully ride that pendulum beyond his 1976 defeat to capture the presidency for the right wing of the Republican Party. He did so by first assuring the 1976 election of another evangelical, Democrat Jimmy Carter, by mounting a divisive primary challenge to incumbent Gerald Ford. Reagan won in 1980 with the support of the still anxious and disaffected Democrats and white southerners whom Nixon had brought together through his "southern strategy." Reagan's victorious campaign staff relied both on their candidate's charisma and on continuing doubts and disillusionments felt by the majority of American voters toward the political process. They successfully exploited the failure of the Carter administration to heal the national "malaise" and "crisis of confidence" and to restore the economy and national honor.

Then, in 1984, Reagan preserved his political coalition to turn those unresolved doubts about the economy and military preparedness into a referendum on confidence in America. Ronald Reagan and the Political and Religious Right did not long hold the national culture in their sway. Televangelist Pat Robertson and columnist Pat Buchanan failed to win the Republican nomination from George Bush in 1988. Though lacking Reagan's charisma, Robertson could nevertheless manufacture and direct the media and the networks of power, which Reagan served but never controlled. Indeed, Robertson, following his electoral defeat, continued to construct a powerful global television conglomerate and to wield considerable influence through the Christian Coalition, which claimed over one million members in the 1990s.

In the future, the web of connections among the rising stars of the Political and Religious Right may again dominate the national culture through new styles of performance promoted through national and international media. Certainly, the wedding of religion, politics and the media has grown far beyond what the New Evangelists of the Cold War era dreamed possible. For the moment, however, the close of the Reagan era and the end of the Cold War have resulted in a fragmented competition among those who identify themselves with the values and agendas of the Political and Religious Right. As in the 1950s, the Burkean patterns of American national culture have returned to the hands of a more moderate political and economic leadership; what is different is that no identifiable alternative to a corporate culture of celebrity and performance can be discerned on the post–Cold War horizon.

Afterword

> At the theatre, the crowd would applaud and acclaim him, surge homeward with the heroic artist in their midst, to honor him with a magnificent banquet. For intelligence has got the upper hand to such an extent that it transforms the real task into an unreal trick and reality into a play.
> —Kierkegaard

In an article in which Paul Tillich sought to introduce existentialism to an American audience in 1944, he noted that England was the only European country in which that philosophical movement had failed to take hold in the years between 1830 and 1930. Tillich explained this anomaly to his Anglo-American readers by pointing out that in England religious faith remained stronger than anywhere else in Europe. He said that the English had largely been spared the anguish of struggling towards a new personal meaning to life, because in that country religious faith and positivism lived side by side, united through social conformism. This situation illustrated the dependence of existentialism on the breakdown of religious tradition through the impact of Enlightenment rationalism and instrumentalism, he said.[1]

In its nineteenth-century manifestation, Tillich explained, existentialism provided a focus for challenging such Enlightenment conventions as the Cartesian division between object and subject, in a conservative effort to restore medieval symmetry to social experience. As community was sapped of its internal vitality by mechanistic forms of social and technological power, Tillich suggested, existentialists sought to conserve it through flight from the calculation and control of objectivity into subjectivity.

The existential philosophers, supported by poets and artists throughout Europe, were aware of the estrangement that had invaded the fabric of life under the impact of modern instrumentalist strategies. They tried to resist the slow sapping of vitality in the community and its institutions with a desperation that sometimes led to excessive, paradoxical, fragmentary and ecstatic language, Tillich wrote. But, he concluded, their provocative forms of speech and artistic expression did not prevent them from achieving sociological insight into the dynamics of modern instrumentalist power and the psychology that motivated the drive to objective control and away from personal responsibility for a life of choice in concert with other selves.[2]

Tillich's accuracy in characterizing existentialism as both a desperate conservative struggle against Enlightenment instrumentalism and an ethical responsibility to community may be illustrated in the person of Søren Kierkegaard. Perhaps the most pivotal of the existentialist philosophers for defining the character of the movement, Kierkegaard has been stereotyped in the public imagination as an individualist who radically rejected community as a force of social conformism. Daniel Bell, for example, insisted that Kierkegaard's radical commitment to authenticity made "the gesture" everything, leading him to repudiate marriage with Regine Olson and spurring at least one of Kierkegaard's readers, Georg Lukács, to make a leap of faith into revolutionary terrorism. However, Lukács actually criticized, rather than applauded, Kierkegaard's gesture. Paul Breines concluded, contrary to Bell's assertion, that "it should be clear without being inevitable, the 'leap' from this singular cosmic realm to the camp of communist revolution may well be short and rational." Nor does Bell's equation of the two leaps explain why Lukács remained within the bureaucratic fold of the Hungarian Communist Party, repudiating his bourgeois individualist ideas of ethical purity in the name of political casuistry, while Kierkegaard repudiated his own gesture, writing in his diary "had I faith, I should have remained with Regine."[3]

The very terms of the existentialists' response to Enlightenment instrumentalism and the loss of religious immediacy resulted in their opposition to attempts to bring together the objective and the subjective, the sublime and the holy, and civil and religious traditions, as Hegel advocated in his absolutist philosophy. As a result, Kierkegaard consciously rejected Hegel's system, but also, coincidentally and quite unintentionally, repudiated the principles and strategies of expedient conformism advocated by Burke. Indeed, Kierkegaard's 1846 *The Present Age* may legitimately be read as an oppositional statement to Burke's 1756 *A Vindication of Natural Society* and his *Philosophical Enquiry into the Origin of Our Ideas of the Sublime and Beautiful*, published the following year.[4] For Kierkegaard deceptively subverted the aesthetic distance of the sublime for the ends of communicating personal responsibility for, and relational trust in, religious choice. Those ends, which he believed could be served only by an indirect appeal to the subjectivity of the individual conscience, flatly contradicted Burke's equally deceptive ends of social conformism through performance and his instrumental advocacy of the sublime over the beautiful to preserve political order.

The nineteenth-century existentialism of Kierkegaard, Nietzsche, and Dostoyevsky, mediated for Americans by Martin Buber, Albert Camus, and Paul Tillich, among many other literary, philosophical, theological and artistic voices, was undeniably dominated by the Enlightenment conventions of scientific rationalism and aesthetic romanticism. Existentialists were locked within the assumptions of the Kantian philosophical tradition, with its strengths and weaknesses for creating alternatives to the modernity they wished to escape, and the postmodernism they helped spawn. Indeed the preoccupation of the existentialists with doubleness and deception confirms the Enlightenment conventions out of which that sensiblity was formed and against which they were in rebellion.

But the importance of existentialism for twentieth-century Americans was not in its unassailability as a philosophical approach. Its importance was that it provided the last manifestation of a common Western language and moral focus for challenging the instrumental conventions of the Enlightenment and the cultural imperatives of the American commitment to confidence. Existentialism provided a broad conservative cultural framework for recognizing and speaking to the need for personal responsibility, anticonformity, and the values of dialogue, in opposition to an instrumentalist framework of performance and commercial manipulation. It gave coherence to a conception of a life of limits, lived on boundaries between dogmatisms rather than on frontiers with messianic possibilities without limit.

The existenialist moment in the United States was, however, a brief one. It quickly ended under the impact of Cold War politics and burgeoning consumerism. Existentialist personalism was absorbed into the cult of the celebrity personality, a co-option that was encouraged, at least in part, by the existentialists themselves. For the existentialist strategy of using aesthetic deception and imitation to awaken others to authenticity necessarily ushered it into postmodern space, where simulation meets dissimulation—the ambiguous space of the Actor, Advertiser and Artist. Postmodernism undermined existential choice, raising suspicions about the very possibility of an authentic self or experience, as existentialism had earlier undermined modern objectivity and the authority of bureaucratic systems and institutions. Ironically, while the Cold War passed into history, so too did the last Western cultural expression of opposition to a corporate American market ethos. But in its wake was left an ever greater need for confidence, precisely because social reality had become so visibly determined by confidence games in every aspect of social experience.

When militant fundamentalists identify with the tactics of the promoters of ruthless expediency, when the legal system becomes at once a form of popular entertainment and a coercive system of punishment, and when constitutional amendments to protect the flag are couched in antigovernment rhetoric, we must recognize that the post–Cold War era of American national confidence has already begun to embody the consequences of the doubts that must invariably accompany it.

In such a time of transcendent confidence and insidious doubt, remembering that trust remains vital for preserving and reweaving the fabric of community life has become a radical political and moral stance. It is an affirmation that, even within the disenchantment that has permeated Western institutions and values, one can choose to practice a politics, an aesthetics, or a religion that refuses to be normative yet preserves a ground of principled integrity. That choice, however, promises neither a revitalization of national unity nor a return to "family values." What it does promise is the preserving of a place for critical intelligence and genuine dialogue in opposition to an ethos that has confidence only in power.

Notes

Preface

1. Henry Miller, "Money and How It Gets That Way," in *Stand Still Like a Hummingbird* (New York: New Directions, 1962), 119–56.
2. Max Weber, *The Protestant Ethic and the Spirit of Capitalism*, trans. Talcott Parsons (New York: Charles Scribner's Sons, 1958), 13–27, 47–78. See Anthony Quinton, *Francis Bacon* (New York: Hill and Wang, 1980), 1, 9–10; Francis Bacon, *The Great Instauration and New Atlantis*, ed. J. Weinberger (Arlington Heights, Ill.: Harlan Davidson, 1980), 1–9.
3. See Morris Berman, *The Reenchantment of the World* (New York: Bantam, 1984), 13–37, for an exploration of this Enlightenment perspective through a consideration of Bacon, Descartes and Weber.

Introduction

1. Will Herberg, *Protestant, Catholic, Jew: An Essay in American Religious Sociology* (New York: Doubleday, 1955), 270, 289. Herberg appropriated this term from Paul Tillich. See also Mark Silk, "Notes on the Judeo-Christian Tradition in America," *American Quarterly* 36.1 (spring 1984): 65–86.
2. Herberg, *Protestant*, 271–81.
3. Robert Bellah et al., *Habits of the Heart: Individualism and Commitment in American Life* (New York: Harper and Row, 1985), 28–41.
4. Herberg, *Protestant*, 69–77; and Bellah, *Habits*, 41–48, 22–26. Riesman used the categories of the anomic, the adjusted, and the autonomous. See David Riesman et al., *The Lonely Crowd: A Study of Changing American Character* (New York: Doubleday, 1950), 276. Alisdair MacIntyre used the aesthete, the bureaucrat and the therapist in *After Virtue* (South Bend: Notre Dame University Press, 1981). For MacIntyre, the seventeenth-century problem of distinguishing the "seems" and the "is" constitutes the essential break between the modern and the medieval (76–77).
5. Bellah, *Habits*, 296.
6. John P. Diggins, *The Lost Soul of American Politics: Virtue, Self-Interest, and the Foundations of Liberalism* (Chicago: University of Chicago Press, 1984), 296.
7. See, for example, M. M. Bakhtin, *The Dialogic Imagination*, ed. Michael

Holquist, trans. Caryl Emerson and Michael Holquist (Austin: University of Texas Press, 1981); Steven Kepnes, *The Text as Thou: Martin Buber's Dialogical Hermeneutics and Narrative Theology* (Bloomington: Indiana University Press, 1992), 62–72, especially p. 171, n. 14.

Chapter 1

1. William Appleman Williams, *The Tragedy of American Diplomacy* (New York: World, 1959), 15–17, 46–48, 210–12.

2. Norman Mailer, *Advertisements for Myself* (New York: Signet, 1959), 20–21. *Imitation of Life* (Universal-National Studios, 1959), directed by Douglas Sirk, screenplay by Eleanore Griffin and Allan Scott from the novel by Fannie Hurst. See Lucy Fischer, ed., *Imitation of Life: Douglas Sirk, Director* (New Brunswick, N.J.: Rutgers University Press, 1991). This collection includes the continuity script (43–156), interpretive essays, and interviews with the director. See especially pp. 221–31.

3. Mailer, *Advertisements*, 18–20, 424–26; Fischer, *Imitation of Life*, 53.

4. Williams added this appeal to conservatism to the revised edition, *The Tragedy of American Diplomacy* (New York: Delta, 1962), 308–9.

5. "Crazy Like a Fox," *Newsweek*, 31 August 1959, 57; Maria Reidelbach, *Completely Mad* (New York: Little, Brown, 1991). In 1959 *Mad* was rated as the favorite magazine of 58 percent of college students and 43 percent of high school students in the United States.

6. Williams, *Tragedy*, 55–56; Mailer, *Advertisements*, 305; commentaries by Michael Stern, Marina Heung and Sandy Flitterman-Lewis in Fischer, *Imitation*, 279–88, 302–38.

7. See, for example, *Time* 47.5 (3 August 1959): 13; and *Newsweek*, 17 August 1959, 19. Nixon used the account of the Moscow trip for its public relations value in 1962. Richard Nixon, *Six Crises* (New York: Doubleday, 1962), 253–314. See also Milton Rokeach, *The Three Christs of Ypsilanti: A Psychological Study* (New York: Random House, 1964).

8. *Time*, 3 August 1959, 11–16; *Newsweek*, 3 August 1959, 16; *Life* 47.14 (5 October 1959): 35; Ernest Lee Tuveson, *Redeemer Nation: The Idea of America's Millennial Role* (Chicago: University of Chicago Press, 1968).

9. *Time*, 3 August 1959, 12–13; *Life*, 5 October 1959, 35; and *Look*, 21 July 1959, 52–54.

10. Rokeach, *Three Christs*, 1.

11. Ibid., 1–15; Rob Wilson, *The American Sublime: The Geneology of a Poetic Genre* (Madison: University of Wisconsin Press, 1991). 1–15.

12. The classical definition of the sublime first captured the Enlightenment imagination through the recovery and translation of Cassius Longinus, *On the Sublime*. See *On Great Writing (On the Sublime)*, trans. G. M. A. Grube (New

Notes to pages 17–26   239

York: Liberal Arts Press, 1957). See also John Baille, *An Essay on the Sublime* (Los Angeles: University of California Press, 1953); and, for an interpretive overview, Peter de Bolla, *The Discourse of the Sublime: Readings in History, Aesthetics and the Subject* (Oxford: Blackwell, 1989). De Bolla notes that there were three translations of Longinus's treatise, in 1712, 1724 and 1739, reflecting its central importance to eighteenth-century Enlightenment culture (31–44).
  13. Rokeach, *Three Christs*, 324–32; Wilson, *American Sublime*, 228–36.
  14. Rokeach, *Three Christs*, 324.
  15. Ibid., 22–36.
  16. Ibid., 23.
  17. Ibid., 75–92, 122–72.
  18. Ibid., 19–23.
  19. Ibid., 314.
  20. Ibid., 190.
  21. Ibid., 332.
  22. Ibid., 334.
  23. Richard Nixon, quoted in *Time*, 3 August 1959, 12–13.
  24. Editorial, *Wall Street Journal*, 13 May 1960, 8.
  25. *Paris Is Burning* (Off-White Productions, 1990), directed by Jennie Livingston, produced by Livingston and Barry Swimar.

Chapter 2

  1. Richard Morin and Maralee Schwartz, "Trust and Parry Politics: The GOP Focuses on Winning Voter Confidence," *Washington Post National Weekly Edition* 9.40 (31 August-6 September 1992): 13; Ann McDaniel and Howard Fineman, "Whatever It Takes to Win," *Newsweek*, 21 September 1992, 38–39; George Bush interview with Kenneth T. Walsh, "Bush on the Attack," *U.S. News and World Report* 113.7 (17 August 1992): 20–24; Paul Gigot, *Wall Street Journal* editorial, 28 August 1992, A 10.
  2. Michael Kramer and Henry Mullen, "Bush on the Record," *Time* 148.8 (24 August 1992): 24. See also Robert J. Samuelson, "The New Nixon," *The Washington Post: National Weekly Edition* 9.40 (10–16 August 1992). "Watergate wouldn't have happened if Nixon had been more confident. . . . Bush has undermined his own popularity by his preoccupation with staying popular. . . . Bush's experience has gone awry, because it has made him unpresidential. . . . The best politics is not to look political" (29). See also Fred Barnes, "Cool Hand Bill Clinton's Amazing Confidence Trick," *New Republic* 207.21 (16 November 1992): 12–13.
  3. Garry Wills, *Reagan's America* (New York: Penguin, 1988), 1–5.
  4. Hugh Sidey, "You Shouldn't Win 'Em All," *Time* 138.17 (28 October 1991): 27.

5. Oliver L. North and William Novak, *Under Fire* (New York: Harper-Collins, 1991).

6. Ibid., 114–19.

7. Quoted by Barrett Seaman, "The Unsinkable Ollie North," *Time*, 28 October 1991, 69.

8. Cornel West, "Black Leadership and the Pitfalls of Racial Reasoning," in *Racing, Justice, En-gendering Power: Essays on Anita Hill, Clarence Thomas, and the Construction of Social Reality*, ed. Toni Morrison (New York: Pantheon, 1992), 392–96. See also John C. Danforth, *Resurrection: The Confirmation of Clarence Thomas* (New York: Viking, 1994), and Jane Mayer and Jill Abramson, *Strange Justice: The Selling of Clarence Thomas* (New York: Houghton Mifflin, 1994).

9. Nancy Gibbs, "An Ugly Circus," *Time* 138.15 (21 October 1991): 35.

10. See Neal Gabler, "Persona Goeth Before a Fall," *The New York Times*, 12 December 1993, 1, 34.

11. Ibid. "The essential dilemma," writes Gabler, "is that celebrities cannot defy their image lest we punish them, but neither can they remain static lest they become irrelevant" (34). On Madonna and the image of authenticity redefined as a performance, see Andrew Goodwin, *Dancing in the Distraction Factory: Music, Television and Popular Culture* (Minneapolis: University of Minnesota Press, 1992), 34–35.

12. See Eric Lax, *Woody Allen: A Biography* (New York: Knopf, 1991), 9, 285. Allen's real name is Allen Stewart Konigsberg. He renamed himself in 1952 and became a cartoon character in 1976; his persona has continued to evolve. See also Roger Rosenblatt, "Bananas: Has Woody Lost It?", *New Republic* 207.13 (21 September 1992): 10–12. A similar association of cartoon character and performance with minstrelsy as a manifestation of the sublime may be found in Bell Hooks's discussion of Madonna in *Black Looks: Race and Representation* (Boston: South End Press, 1992), 151–55.

13. Gary Hart attempted and failed to refashion American political theology by merging Jeffersonian populism with Kierkegaardian existentialism and Wesleyan evangelism. See Gary Hart, *The Good Fight: The Education of an American Reformer* (New York: Random House, 1993), 16–52. To compare Niebuhr's successful Cold War synthesis of the Puritan jeremiad and Kierkegaardian existentialism during the 1930s to the 1950s, see chapter 6.

Jim Bakker was the subject of a sex and blackmail scandal in 1987, and Swaggart was caught in sexually compromising activities in 1988 and 1991.

14. The relation of law to performance in American popular culture is discussed by Anne Norton, *The Republic of Signs: Liberal Theory and American Popular Culture* (Chicago: University of Chicago Press, 1993), 139–54. *Cool World* (Paramount Studios, 1992) was directed by Ralph Bakshi; *Lawnmower Man* (New Line, 1992) was directed by Brett Leonard; *Aladdin* (1992) was produced and released by Walt Disney Studios. See also Warren Susman, *Culture as His-*

tory: The Transformation of American Society in the Twentieth Century (New York: Pantheon, 1984), 196–97.

15. Richard Rorty, *Philosophy and the Mirror of Nature* (Princeton: Princeton University Press, 1979), 3–13, 42–45.

16. Thomas Kuhn, *The Structure of Scientific Revolutions*, 2d ed. (Chicago: University of Chicago Press, 1962), v-xii; Daniel Bell, "The End of Ideology in the West: An Epilogue," in *The End of Ideology: On the Exhaustion of Political Ideas in the Fifties*, rev. ed. (New York: Free Press, 1960), 393–407. See also Job L. Dittberner, *The End of Ideology and American Social Thought, 1930–1960* (Ann Arbor: UMI Research Press, 1979).

Rorty discusses the Cold War origins of his disillusionment with objective truth in "Trotsky and the Wild Orchids," in *Wild Orchids and Trotsky: Messages from American Universities*, ed. Mark Edmundson (New York: Penguin, 1993), 29–50.

17. Rorty, *Philosophy*, 7–8; Bell, "The End of Ideology," 393–95. Bell, like Rorty, quotes Bacon's *Novum Organum*, in which he sought to release Reason from "the imperfections of the mind" through a description of different forms of distortion. Besides *The Idols of the Tribe* and *The Idols of the Cave*, Bell recounted, Bacon included ". . . *The Idols of the Market-Place*; and *The Idols of the Theatre* ('because in my judgment all the received systems [of philosophy] are but so many stage-plays representing worlds of their own creation after an unreal and scenic fashion')," n. 395.

18. Edmund Burke, "A Letter to a Member of the National Assembly," in *Reflections on the Revolution in France and Other Essays*, ed. A. J. Grieve (London: J. M. Dent, 1951), 249–50.

19. Rorty, *Philosophy*, 389–94; and Richard Rorty, "Science as Solidarity," in *The Rhetoric of the Social Sciences: Language and Argument in Scholarship and Public Affairs*, ed. John Nelson, Alan Megill and Donald McCloskey (Madison: University of Wisconsin Press, 1987), 38–52. See also Richard Rorty, *Contingency, Irony, and Solidarity* (Cambridge: Cambridge University Press, 1989), 189–98.

20. Rorty, *Philosophy*, 42 n. 10, 156–57, 296–97; Josiah Royce, "The Rediscovery of the Inner Life," in vol. 1, 275–81, and "The Philosophy of Loyalty," in vol. 2, 855–1013, in *The Basic Writings of Josiah Royce*, ed. John J. McDermott (Chicago: University of Chicago, 1969). Although Rorty expresses some reservations concerning both Royce and Charles Sanders Peirce, it is Peirce's emphasis upon semiotics and truth as convention that provides the philosophical link between Rorty's neopragmatism and Royce's metaphysical faith in fidelity. A similar link may be found between Rorty and Wilfred Sellars. See Rorty, *Contingency, Irony and Solidarity*, 1, 190–92. See also David L. Hall, *Richard Rorty: Prophet of the New Pragmatism* (Albany: State University of New York Press, 1994), 70–71, 117–20.

21. Josiah Royce, *The Feud of Oakfield Creek: A Novel of California Life* (Boston:

Houghton Mifflin, 1887). See also Rorty, "The Contingency of Selfhood," 23–43, and "The Contingency of a Liberal Community," 44–72, in *Contingency*; and Richard Rorty, "On Ethnocentrism: A Reply to Clifford Geertz," 203–10 in vol. 1, *Objectivity, relativism, and truth: Philosophical papers* (Cambridge: Cambridge University Press, 1991).

22. Arthur Vidich and Stanford Lyman, *American Sociology: Worldly Rejections of Religion and Their Directions* (New Haven: Yale University Press, 1985), 270–75; William James, "The Will to Believe," in *The Will to Believe and Other Essays in Popular Philosophy and Human Mortality* (New York: Dover Publications, 1956), 1–31. See also Joseph Brent, *Charles Sanders Peirce: A Life* (Bloomington: University of Indiana Press, 1993), 258.

23. Burke, *Reflections*, 135; Royce, "Philosophy of Loyalty," 864–74, and "The Hope of the Great Community," 1145–63 in vol. 2, *Basic Writings*; Rorty, *Philosophy*, 373–75, 391 n. 29; George Herbert Mead, "The Problem of Society," in *George Herbert Mead: On Social Psychology*, ed. Anselm Strauss (Chicago: University of Chicago Press, 1965), 34–42.

24. See Vidich and Lyman, *American Sociology*, 267, 271–76.

25. Charles Horton Cooley, *Human Nature and the Social Order* (1902; reprint, New York: Schocken, 1967), 330.

26. Ibid., 332.

27. Edward A. Ross, *Sin and Society: An Analysis of Latter-Day Iniquity* (New York: Harper, 1907), 4–7, 58–63.

28. Letter from Henry James to William James in 1907, quoted in Van Wyck Brooks, *New England Indian Summer* (New York: Dutton, 1940), 228; Henry James, *The Art of the Novel* (New York: Charles Scribner's Sons, 1934), 15–16, 277–78, 346.

29. Henry James, "The New Novel," in *The Art of Fiction and Other Essays* (New York: Oxford University Press, 1948), 207–8.

30. Brooks, *New England Indian Summer*, 398–403, n. 403.

31. James, *Art of Fiction*, 173–76, 182–83.

32. Henry James, "The American Scene," in *Collected Travel Writings: Great Britain and America* (New York: Library of America, 1993), 426–28. James's essentially theatrical orientation may be recognized by comparing this well-known section to his discussion of the New Theater on pp. 518–19.

33. Walt Whitman, "Democratic Vistas," in *Prose Works 1892: Collect and Other Prose*, vol. 2, ed. Floyd Stovall (New York: New York University Press, 1964), 369–70.

34. Cooley, *Human Nature*, 223; Miles Orvell, *The Real Thing: Imitation and Authenticity in American Culture, 1880–1940* (Chapel Hill: University of North Carolina Press, 1989), 28, 302 n. 10.

35. Walt Whitman, *Notebooks and Unpublished Prose Manuscripts*, vol. 4, ed. Edward Grier (New York: New York University Press, 1984), 1569.

"We see London, Paris, Italy—not original, superb, as where they belong," Whitman wrote. "We see the shreds of Hebrews, Romans, Greeks; but where on our own soil, do we see in any faithful highest, proud expression, America herself?" Whitman, *Prose Works*, 2: 411. See also Tim Sweet, *Traces of War: Poetry, Photography and the Crisis of the Union* (Baltimore: The Johns Hopkins University Press, 1990).

36. Liah Greenfield, *Nationalism: Five Roads to Modernity* (Cambridge, Mass.: Harvard University Press, 1992), 1-6; Vidich and Lyman, *American Sociology*, 281-82.

37. See Dorothy Ross, *The Origins of American Social Science* (Cambridge, Mass.: Harvard University Press, 1991), for a comprehensive discussion of the history of the American social sciences. Ross sees the development of American social science as a response to a crisis in the republican political tradition. See also Robert M. Crunden, *Ministers of Reform: The Progressives' Achievement in American Civilization, 1889-1920* (New York: Basic Books, 1982). Crunden emphasizes the Protestant religious origins of the American social sciences.

38. David Potter, *People of Plenty: Economic Abundance and the American Character* (Chicago: University of Chicago Press, 1954), 23-31, 84-90, 93-100.

39. Frederick Jackson Turner, *The Frontier in American History* (Malabar, Fla.: Krieger, 1920), 33-34. Woodrow Wilson was committed to a Burkean view of politics as a sublime rhetorical formula of power. See, for example, young Wilson's commonplace book in *The Papers of Woodrow Wilson*, ed. Arthur Link et al. (Princeton: Princeton University Press, 1966), 94-98, 110; and presidential candidate Wilson's appeal to Burke against socialism in *Papers*, vol. 24 (Princeton: Princeton University Press, 1977), 365; Woodrow Wilson, *Congressional Government: A Study in American Politics* (New York: Houghton Mifflin, 1925), 209; and Woodrow Wilson, *Mere Literature and Other Essays* (Boston: Houghton Mifflin, 1896), especially pp. 68-160.

40. Frederick Jackson Turner, "The Significance of Section," in *Frontier and Section*, ed. Ray Allen Billington (Englewood Cliffs, N. J.: Prentice Hall, 1961), 115-35. Turner wrote that by "section" he meant what "Professor Josiah Royce defined as a 'province' "—that is, "any part of a national domain which is geographically and socially sufficiently unified to have a true consciousness of its own ideals and customs and to possess a sense of its distinction from other parts of the country" (131).

41. Turner, "The West and American Ideals," in *Frontier and Section*, 90-114.

42. Turner, "Frontier and Section," in *Frontier and Section*, 153.

43. Turner, "The West and American Ideals," 106.

44. John Dewey, *Democracy and Education* (New York: Macmillan, 1916), 174.

45. John Dewey, "Impressions of Soviet Russia: A New World in the Making," in *John Dewey: The Later Works, 1925-1953*, ed. Jo Ann Boydston (Carbondale: Southern Illinois University Press, 1984), 3: 215-16.

46. Ibid., 215, 222–23.

47. Dewey, "Impressions of Soviet Russia: A Country in a State of Flux," 213–14; and "The Great Experiment and the Future," in ibid., 250. See also "Impressions of Soviet Russia: New Schools for a New Era," 233–41. "Those whom I met," Dewey wrote of his sojourn to Russia in 1928, "had a vitality and a kind of confidence in life—not to be confused with mere self-confidence—that afforded one of the most stimulating experiences of my life" (236).

48. John Dewey, *The Quest for Certainty: A Study of the Relation of Knowledge to Action* in *Dewey: Later Works*, 4: 1–10.

49. Ibid., 28–39, 178–83, 195.

50. See John Dewey et al., *The Case of Leon Trotsky: Report of Hearings on the Charges Made Against Him in the Moscow Trials* (New York: Merit Publishers, 1937), 584–85. "Esteemed Commissioners! The experience of my life, in which there has been no lack either of success or failures, has not only not destroyed my faith in the clear, bright future of mankind, but, on the contrary, has given it an indestructible temper," Trotsky stated at the closing of the proceedings. "In the very fact of your Commission's formation—in the fact that, at its head, is a man of unshakable moral authority, a man who by virtue of his age should have the right to stay outside of the skirmishes in the political arena—in this fact I see a new and truly magnificent reinforcement of the revolutionary optimism which constitutes the fundamental element of my life.... And allow me, in conclusion, to express my profound respect to the educator, philosopher *and personification of genuine American idealism* [emphasis added], the scholar who heads the work of your Commission."

51. Alan Wald, *The New York Intellectuals: The Rise and Fall of the Anti-Stalinist Left from the 1930s to the 1980s* (Chapel Hill: University of North Carolina Press, 1987), 128–39.

52. Edmund Wilson, *To the Finland Station: A Study in the Writing and Acting of History* (Garden City, N.J.: Doubleday, 1940), 444.

53. See Josiah Royce, *Race Questions, Provincialism and Other Problems* (New York: Macmillan, 1901); and Vidich and Lyman, *American Sociology*, 274–77. On Park, see also Fred H. Matthews, *Quest for an American Sociology: Robert E. Park and the Chicago School* (Montreal: McGill University Press, 1977) and Winifred Raushebush, *Robert E. Park: Biography of a Sociologist* (Durham, N.C.: Duke University Press, 1979).

54. Robert Ezra Park, *Race and Culture: Essays in the Sociology of Contemporary Man* (New York: Free Press, 1950), v-ix. Relevant essays include "Education in its Relation to the Conflict and Fusion of Cultures," 261–283, "The Mentality of Racial Hybrids," 377–92, and "Personality and Cultural Conflict," 357–76.

55. Park, "Behind Our Masks," in ibid., 244–55.

56. Ibid., "Personality and Cultural Conflict," 360, and "Our Racial Frontier in the Pacific," 149–51.

57. Henry Nash Smith, *Virgin Land: The American West as Symbol and Myth* (New York: Vintage, 1950).
58. Theodore Roosevelt, *The Autobiography of Theodore Roosevelt* (Elm Grove, Wis.: Grove Press), 1: 32–33, 59.
59. Ibid., 60.
60. Ibid., 38.
61. Ibid., 103–4. See also Chris Bruce et al., *Myth of the West* (Seattle: University of Washington Press, 1990), especially Brian W. Dipple, "Frederic Remington's West: Where History Meets Myth," 79–89, and Paul Fees, "In Defense of Buffalo Bill: A Look at Cody in and of His Time," 141–52.
62. Smith, *Virgin Land*, 113–25; Richard Slotkin, *Gunfighter Nation: The Myth of the Frontier in Twentieth-Century America* (New York: Atheneum, 1992), 70–79; and Arthur Kopit, *Indians* (New York: Hill and Wang, 1969).
63. Smith, *Virgin Land*, 120.
64. See William F. Cody and Frank Bliss, *The Life of the Honorable William F. Cody, Known as Buffalo Bill, The Famous Hunter, Scout and Guide: An Autobiography* (Hartford, Conn.: Frank E. Bliss, 1879), 310–11; and Don Russell, *The Lives and Legends of Buffalo Bill* (Norman: University of Oklahoma Press, 1960), 9, 182.
65. Cody and Bliss, *Life*, 330–36.
66. Ibid., vi–vii, 281, 295–305.
67. Ibid., 340–50; Russell, *Lives and Legends*, 209–13, 221–35, 287–92.
68. Russell, *Lives and Legends*, 360–61.
69. Ibid., 294–95, 321–22; Slotkin, *Gunfighter Nation*, 67, 169–71. See also Ben Yagoda, W*ill Rogers: A Biography* (New York: Knopf, 1993), 68–75, 171–74. Charles Russell was among the cowboys who made southern California a regular stop in their work cycle between fall and spring roundups, once the making of movies became concentrated there. This second generation of cowboy performers is illustrated by Russell's friend Will Rogers. Rogers began his performing career under the tutelage of the adopted son and protégé of Buffalo Bill's friend and fellow performer, Texas Jack Omohundro.
Rogers later rode with Zack Mulhall's Congress of the Rough Riders, featuring Geronimo, at the same St. Louis Purchase Exposition in which Max Weber and Ernst Troeltsch read academic papers.
70. Lloyd Goodrich, *Thomas Eakins: His Life and Work* (New York: Whitney Museum, 1933), 102–3.
71. See Elizabeth Johns, *Thomas Eakins: The Heroism of Modern Life* (Princeton: Princeton University Press, 1983), 158–59. Johns notes that Eakins identified his mission as a painter with that of anthropologists such as Cushing. In an article published in 1882, Cushing described himself as a "black sheep" among the Zuni because of his sketching and notetaking. See Frank Hamilton Cushing, "My Adventures Among the Zuni," *Century Magazine* 25 (1882): 203.

72. See Frank Hamilton Cushing, "The Zuni Social, Mythic and Religious Systems," *Popular Science Monthly* 21 (June 1882): 186–92. After introducing his Zuni "friends" to the gentlemen of the National Academy of Sciences, Cushing explained that to comprehend the mythology of a people "we must learn their language, acquire their confidence, assimilating ourselves to them by joining in their everyday life, their religious life, even as far as possible in their intellectual life, by remembering with intense earnestness our own childhood, by constantly striking every possible chord of human sympathy in our intercourse with those whose inner life we would study" (186). See also Theodora Kroeber, *Ishi in Two Worlds: A Biography of the Last Wild Indian in North America* (Berkeley: University of California Press, 1961), 134–37.

Hamilton Cravens describes the professional success of this anthropological approach in *The Triumph of Evolution: The Heredity-Environment Controversy, 1900–1941* (Baltimore: The Johns Hopkins University Press, 1988), 92–93, 105–10.

73. William James, *The Will to Believe*, 31.

74. See, for example, Jean Baudrillard, "Simulacra and Simulations," in *Jean Baudrillard: Selected Writings*, ed. Mark Poster (Stanford: Stanford University Press, 1988); Jean-François Lyotard, *The Post Modern Condition: A Report on Knowledge* (Minneapolis: University of Minnesota Press, 1984); Neville Wakefield, *Post Modernism: The Twilight of the Real* (London: Pluto, 1990).

75. The Simpson trial was far more pervasive as a media event than any previous trial in American popular culture. See "Blood, race, celebrity, lust, love, sex, brutality: this case had it all ... Rev up your TV sets," quoted in Larry Reibstein et al., "And Now the Trial," *Newsweek*, 23 January 1995, 44–51; and Howard Fineman, "Revenge of the Right," *Newsweek*, 21 November 1994, 36–57.

76. Garry Wills, "The Visionary," *New York Review of Books*, 23 March 1995, 4–8; Michael Kelly, "Rip It Up," *The New Yorker*, 23 January 1995, 32–39.

Chapter 3

1. Alexis de Tocqueville, *Democracy in America*, trans. Henry Reeve, rev. Phillips Bradley (New York: Knopf, 1945).

2. Ibid., 2: 8–12.

3. See Richard S. Moore, *That Cunning Alphabet: Melville's Aesthetics of Nature* (Amsterdam: Rodopi, 1983), 17–19. Melville's literary contemplation of such social violence as slavery, coupled with his own crisis of mental instability and domestic violence, made the connection between the sublime, terror, and confidence central to his work. Consider Melville's "Benito Cereno" in *The Piazza Tales and Other Pieces* (Chicago: Northwestern University and Newberry Library, 1987), especially pp. 115–17 in comparison to Elizabeth Renker's criticism of Melville's own patriarchal violence in "Herman Melville, Wife Beating,

and the Written Page," *American Literature* 66.1 (March 1994): 123–50. See also Robert K. Wallace, *Melville and Turner: Spheres of Love and Fright* (Athens: University of Georgia Press, 1992). Part of the sublime authority of authors, for literary critics and readers alike, appears to be their belief that artistry should signal a personal transcendence over the concerns described in the artistic work.

4. Moore, *That Cunning Alphabet*, 1–4.

5. Herman Melville, "The Two Temples," in *Great Short Works of Herman Melville*, ed. Warner Berthoff (New York: Harper and Row, 1969), 151–58.

6. Ibid., 158–64.

7. Ibid., 164.

8. Ibid. See also Michael Paul Rogin, *Subversive Genealogy: The Politics and Art of Herman Melville* (New York: Knopf, 1983), 197–207, 232–35.

9. Melville, "Benito Cereno." See note 3 above and note 25 below.

10. Ibid., 115.

11. Ibid., 116–17.

12. Herman Melville, *The Confidence-Man: His Masquerade* (Chicago: Northwestern University and Newberry Library, 1984). See also John Bryant, *Melville and Repose: The Rhetoric of Humor in the American Renaissance* (New York: Oxford University Press, 1993), 70–87.

13. P. T. Barnum, *The Life of P. T. Barnum* (New York: Redfield, 1855), 46–47, 214–25, 387–99. Barnum's experience as a blackface performer is also the subject of a revealing story. Barnum says that he very narrowly escaped death when he once confronted a violent white man after a performance. Thinking Barnum was a Negro, the man threatened to shoot him. Barnum saved himself by impetuously rolling up his sleeves and declaring "I am as white as you are, sir" (189–90).

14. Ibid., 225–27, 374–77.

15. See John Bryant, "*The Confidence-Man*: Melville's Problem Novel," in *A Companion to Melville Studies*, ed. John Bryant (New York: Greenwood, 1986), 315–50.

16. Melville, *The Confidence-Man*, 10–17.

17. Ibid., 144–51.

18. Immanuel Kant, *The Critique of Judgment*, trans. James Creed Meredith (Oxford: Clarendon, 1911), 128–29.

19. Ibid., 111.

20. Ibid., 125–27.

21. Ibid., 114–15, 130–33. Quotation is from Immanuel Kant, "The Metaphysics of Morals," second section, The Great Books edition of *Kant*, trans. Thomas K. Abbott (Chicago: Encyclopedia Britannica, 1952), 262. See also Shirley M. Dettlaff, "Melville's Aesthetics," in *A Companion to Melville Studies*, ed. Bryant, 640–42; and Moore, *That Cunning Alphabet*, 17–21.

22. Kant, *Critique of Judgment*, 110–13, 120.

23. Ibid., 129.
24. Melville, *Confidence-Man*, 144.
25. The source was chapter 6 of James Hall, *Sketches of History, Life and Manners in the West*, vol. 2 (Philadelphia, 1835), reproduced in Melville, *Confidence-Man*, 501–10. Melville uses this same conflation of the fictional and factual and the real and artificial in "Benito Cereno." See Delano, *A Narrative of Voyages and Travels*, chapter 18, reproduced in Melville, *The Piazza Tales*, 809–47.
26. Barnum, *Life*, 225.
27. Benedict Anderson, *Imagined Communities: Reflections on the Origins and Spread of Nationalism* (London: Verso, 1983), 13–16.
28. Riesman, *The Lonely Crowd*; Potter, *People of Plenty*; Seymour Martin Lipset, *The First New Nation: The United States in Historical and Comparative Perspective* (Garden City, N. J.: Doubleday, 1967), 17–18.
29. R. W. B. Lewis, *The American Adam: Innocence, Tragedy and Tradition in the Nineteenth Century* (Chicago: Phoenix, 1955), 1–10.
30. Ibid., 195–98.
31. Ibid., 66–73; Michael Kramer, "The Truth About Bush's Hypocrisy," *Time* 140.14 (5 October 1992): 44; "How Bush Could Win It All," *U. S. News and World Report* 113.12 (28 September 1992): 40–44; Michael Duffy, "The Race in Key Places," *Time* 140.11 (14 September 1992): 34–45; Michael Kramer, "It's Clinton's to Lose," *Time* 140. 16 (19 October 1992): 26–30.
32. Lewis, *American Adam*, 77–79, 90.
33. Morton Kondracke, "Slick Willy," *New Republic* 205 (21 October 1991): 18; Joe Klein, "A Memo to Candidate Bush," *Newsweek*, 29 June 1992, 23; and Klein, "Clinton: The Survivor," *Newsweek*, 20 July 1992, 23–25. See also Norman Mailer, "By Heaven Inspired: The Republican Convention Revisited," *New Republic* 207.16 12 October 1992): 22–27, 30–35.
34. The New Covenant theme was incorporated into the Democratic platform for the 1992 election and into Clinton's acceptance speech, *The New York Times*, 15 July 1992, A 10, and 17 July 1992, A 14–15. In Clinton's November 1992 speech, he promised to empower individuals instead of establishment bureaucracies, to promote economic growth and the free market while supporting the middle class, and to require corporations to act responsibly.

See Charles F. Allen and Jonathan Portis, *The Life and Career of Bill Clinton, Comeback Kid* (New York: Birch Lane, 1992), 7–9. Clinton was actually raised in Hot Springs, a gambling town with a public image very different from Hope's, the latter being featured in Clinton's convention video, produced by Linda Bloodworth Thomason. See also Fred Barnes, "The New Covenant: Clinton Speech at Notre Dame," *New Republic* 207.20 (9 November 1992): 32–33. See P. Magnusson, "A Trust Fund That Will Have No Funds and Inspire No Trust," *Business Week*, 31 May 1993, 31.

Gingrich amassed more than seventeen million dollars in funds between 1986 and 1995 from a variety of sources. See "For Gingrich, '94 Vote Was a Plan Realized," 1, 18, David Shribman, "No More Business as Usual," and Michael Rezendes, ". . . And Death and Taxes, Too," *The Boston Globe*, 20 November 1994, 85, 86; Dale Russakoff, "The Search for Newt Gingrich," and Dale Russakoff and Dan Balz, "Play Rough and Never Say Die," in *The Washington Post National Weekly Edition*, 2–8 January 1995, 6–8, 9–10; Thomas Ferguson, "What the Voters Really Said," *The Nation*, 26 December 1994, 792–98.

35. Ed Gillespie and Bob Schellhas, *Contract With America: The Bold New Plan by Representative Newt Gingrich, Representative Dick Armey and the House Republicans to Change the Nation* (New York: Random House, 1994), 5.

36. Michael Rezendes, "Doing the Minimum," *The Boston Globe*, 29 January 1995, A29–32.

37. Howard Fineman, "A Round of 'Idiotic Game Playing,' " *Newsweek*, 29 November 1993, 42.

38. Ibid., A32.

39. Lewis, *American Adam*, 128–52, 198.

40. Ibid., 132–34, 152.

41. Ibid., 129, 197.

42. Ibid., 197–98. See also Russell Riesing, *The Unusable Past: Theory and Study of American Literature* (New York: Methuen, 1986), 113–29.

43. Anderson, *Imagined Communities*, 50–52.

44. Laural Thatcher Ulrich, *Good Wives: Image and Reality in the Lives of Women in Northern New England, 1650–1750* (New York: Vintage, 1991), 36–50; Linda K. Kerber, *Women of the Republic: Intellect and Ideology in Revolutionary America* (New York: Norton, 1986), 120–21, 128–29, 252–53.

45. Mary Wollstonecraft, *A Vindication of the Rights of Woman: With Strictures on Political and Moral Subjects*, ed. Charles Hagelman, Jr. (New York: Norton, 1967).

46. Wollstonecraft, *Vindication*, 50–54, 285–86; Kerber, *Women of the Republic*, 222–25.

47. Wollstonecraft, *Vindication* 287. Wollstonecraft suggests that female folly and cunning reflect a universal response to oppression. Her analysis of gender parallels later descriptions of race and the appeal of minstrelsy to white audiences; see, for example, Eric Lott, *Love and Theft: Blackface Minstrelsy and the American Working Class* (New York: Oxford University Press, 1993). See also Kerber, *Women of the Republic*, 278–83, and Hugh Henry Brackenridge, *Modern Chivalry* (New York: American Book Co., 1937). A contemporary burlesque of Wollstonecraft's earlier *Vindication of the Rights of Men: In a Letter to the Right Honourable Edmund Burke* (New York: Scholars' Facsimilies and Reprints, 1975) reinforces this association with minstrelsy. See Thomas Taylor, *A Vindication of the Rights of Brutes*, ed. Louise Schutz Boas (Gainesville, Fla.: Scholars' Facsimilies and Reprints, 1966).

48. Lott, *Love and Theft*, 112–22, 136–53.
49. Greenfield, *Five Roads*, 1–8, 487–88.

Chapter 4

1. Thomas Paine, *The Rights of Man, Part I* in *Political Writings*, ed. Bruce Kuklick (Cambridge: Cambridge University Press, 1989), 51–118.
2. See Russel B. Nye, *This Almost Chosen People: Essays in The History of American Ideas* (Toronto: Macmillan, 1966), 264–65.
3. Wollstonecraft, *Vindication of the Rights of Men*, 115. Burke, Wollstonecraft perceptively noted, succeeded in defining respect and love as antagonistic principles instead of mutual ones.
4. For discussions of Burke's equation of power with the aesthetic sublime, see de Bolla, *Discourse of the Sublime*, 59–75, and J. T. Boulton's introduction to Edmund Burke, *A Philosophical Enquiry into the Origin of Our Ideas of the Sublime and Beautiful* (New York: London, Routledge and Paul, 1958), xv-cxxx. Burke's early political writings reveal a similar use of imitation to defend artificiality over the natural. See Edmund Burke, "A Vindication of Natural Society," in *Pre-Revolutionary Writings*, ed. Ian Harris (Cambridge: Cambridge University Press, 1993), 4–57.
5. Burke, *Enquiry*, 47.
6. See Peter H. Melvin, "Burke on Theatricality and Revolution," *Journal of the History of Ideas* 36 (1975): 447–68. Peter de Bolla, in *Discourse of the Sublime* (63 n. 5), comments on the similarity of Burke's approach in the *Enquiry* to certain descriptions of history writing, especially Hayden White's *Metahistory* (Baltimore: The Johns Hopkins University Press, 1973). This appeal is evident and self-conscious in Gertrude Himmelfarb's *The New History and the Old* (Cambridge, Mass: Belknap, 1987), 108–13.
7. Paine, *Rights of Man, Part I*, 53.
8. Paine, *Rights of Man, Part II*, 164.
9. Burke, *Reflections*, 1–12, 23–24.
10. Ibid., 24, 67, 77.
11. Ibid., 87–90.
12. Ibid., 7–8, 62–65, 14–23, 29–41; Burke, *Enquiry*, 47, 76; Paine, *Rights of Man, Part I*, 53.
13. Burke, *Reflections*, 77–78, 189–90; "Letter from Mr. Burke to a Member of the National Assembly," in Burke, *Reflections*, 254–55, 262–63.
14. Burke, "Letter," 264.
15. Richard Weaver, *The Ethics of Rhetoric* (Chicago: Regenery, 1953), 55–84. See also Friedrich A. Hayek, "Why I Am Not a Conservative," postscript to *The Constitution of Liberty* (Chicago: University of Chicago Press, 1960), 400–11; and Irving Kristol, *Reflections of a Neoconservative: Looking Back, Looking Ahead* (New

York: Basic, 1993), 105, 152. Hayek and Kristol similarly view Burke as a casuist rather than a cultural conservator.

16. Perez Zagorin, *Ways of Lying* (Cambridge, Mass.: Harvard University Press, 1990), 153–62; and George Mosse, *The Holy Pretense: A Study of Christianity and Reason of State from William Perkins to John Winthrop* (Oxford: Basil Blackwell, 1968).

17. See Richard Nelson, "Liberalism, Republicanism and the Politics of Therapy: John Locke's Legacy of Medicine and Reform," *The Review of Politics* (winter 1989): 29–54. See also Bruce Kuklick, *Churchmen and Philosophers: From Jonathan Edwards to John Dewey* (New Haven: Yale University Press, 1985), 15–65; and Jonathan Edwards, "Narrative of Surprising Conversions" (revised account), "A Divine and Supernatural Light," and "Religious Affections," in *Jonathan Edwards*, ed. Clarence H. Faust and Thomas H. Johnson, (New York: Hill and Wang, 1962), 85–154, 206–54.

18. Burke, *Enquiry*, lxxix-lxxxi, 16–17, 165–66; Edwards, "Sinners in the Hands of an Angry God" and " A Funeral Sermon," in *Edwards*, 155–205.

19. Burke's fascination with the emotional power of the Romantic painters' tricks of illusion is evident in the *Enquiry*, 44, 49–50. Burke, however, considered rhetoric to be superior to painting for the application of these techniques, 174–75.

20. Burke, *Reflections*, 10, 88–100.

21. See Burke, *Enquiry*, 110–12, 124–25; and Edwards, "Religious Affections," in *Edwards*, 245–48.

22. Weaver, *Ethics*, 57–58, 61, 83; Russell Kirk, *The Conservative Mind* (Chicago: Gateway, 1953), 5–10.

23. See Steven Blakemore, ed., *Burke and the French Revolution* (Athens: University of Georgia Press, 1992). Particularly relevant essays are Frans De Bruyn, "Theatre and Countertheatre in *Burke's Reflections on the Revolution in France*," 28–68; Peter J. Stanlis, "Burke, Rousseau and the French Revolution," 97–119; and Daniel E. Ritchie, "Desire and Sympathy, Passion and Providence: The Moral Imaginations of Burke and Rousseau," 120–43. See also Steven Blakemore, *Burke and the Fall of Language: The French Revolution as a Linguistic Event* (Hanover, N. H.: University Press of New England, 1988). A useful insight into the theatrical sublime that the French Revolution helped codify for all nationalistic ideologies may be gained from George Mosse, *Fallen Soldiers: Reshaping the Memory of the World Wars* (New York: Oxford University Press, 1990), especially pp. 9–23.

24. J. G. A. Pocock, *The Machiavellian Moment: Florentine Political Thought and the Atlantic Political Tradition* (Princeton: Princeton University Press, 1975), 509; Peter Viereck, *The Shame and Glory of Intellectuals: Babbit Jr. vs. the Rediscovery of Values* (New York: Capricorn, 1965), 10–11.

25. Viereck, *Shame and Glory*, 5–7, 302.

26. Ibid., 9–10, 201.
27. Ibid., 10–12, 200, 289–90.
28. Ibid., 203–4, 290–93.
29. Ibid., 330.
30. See Daniel Bell, ed., *The Radical Right: The New American Right Expanded and Updated* (Garden City, N.J.: Doubleday, 1962).
31. Louis Hartz, *The Liberal Tradition in America: An Interpretation of American Political Thought Since the Revolution* (New York: Harcourt, Brace, 1955), 142, 145–55, 172.
32. Ibid., 22, 59–66, 197–200; Viereck, "The Revolt Against the Elite," in *The Radical Right*, 164–65.
33. Kirk, *Conservative Mind*, 521–28.
34. Diggins, *Lost Soul*, 347–52.
35. Bell, *End of Ideology*, 395.

Chapter 5

1. Karl Marx, *The Eighteenth Brumaire of Louis Napoleon* (New York: International Publishers, 1969), 15; Burke, "Letter to a Member," 249–51. Marshall Berman, *All That Is Solid Melts into Air* (New York: Simon and Schuster, 1982), 109–10, 157, suggests that Marx and Burke began with similar insights, but that Marx sought to tear away social masks "with a violent *grand geste*," while Burke tried to use them dramatically. The social criticism of both, Berman argues, hints at vaudeville, slapstick and the metaphysical clowning of Chaplin and Keaton. "It points forward to a century whose heroes will come dressed as antiheroes, and whose most solemn moments of truth will be not only described but actually experienced as clown shows, music-hall or nightclub routines—Shticks" (157).
2. See Mary C. Henderson, "Against Broadway: The Rise of the Art Theatre in America, 1900–1920," in *1915: The Cultural Moment*, ed. Adele Heller and Lois Rudnick (New Brunswick: Rutgers University Press, 1991); and the Report of the New Society of American Artists in Paris, in *The New York Times*, 12 March 1908. Manifesto quoted in "The First American Secessionists," 4, by D. Scott Atkinson, is in the catalogue for the exhibition at the Queens Museum, February 1-April 6, 1986, 1–15.
3. See Martin Jay, *The Dialectical Imagination: A History of the Frankfurt School and the Institute of Social Research* (Boston: Little, Brown, 1973).
4. Tillich's views on expressionist art are discussed in Wilhelm and Marion Pauck, *Paul Tillich: His Life and Thought* (New York: Harper and Row, 1976), 1: 75–79; Paul Tillich, "Protestantism and Artistic Style," *Theology of Culture* (New York: Oxford University Press, 1959), 68–75; and Paul Tillich, *On Art and Ar-*

chitecture, ed. John Dillenberger in collaboration with Jane Dillenberger (New York: Cross Roads, 1987), 67–69, 131–38.

See also Richard Crossman, ed., *The God That Failed* (New York: Harper, 1949); William Barrett, *The Truants: Adventures Among the Intellectuals* (Garden City, N.J.: Anchor, 1982); and Norman Podhoretz, *Breaking Ranks: A Political Memoir* (New York: Harper and Row, 1979).

5. Alan Wald, *New York Intellectuals*, 3–24; Mary McCarthy, "Naming Names," *On the Contrary* (New York: Octagon, 1962), 151–53; Bell, *End of Ideology*, 393–407.

6. Bell, *End of Ideology*, 405.

7. Clement Greenberg, "*Avant-Garde* and *kitsch*," in *Clement Greenberg: Collected Essays and Criticism*, ed. John O'Brian (Chicago: University of Chicago Press, 1993), 1: 5–22.

8. See Greenberg, "The Case for Modern Art," in *Greenberg*, 4: 75–84; and "Modernist Painting," in *Greenberg*, 4: 75–106. Art critic T. J. Clark has described Greenberg's position in the 1940s as "Eliotic Trotskyism." But the combined influences of Eliot and Babbitt and Kant suggest closer affinities to Burke than to Trotsky. See Robert Hughes's review of *Clement Greenberg: Collected Essays and Criticism*, in *The New York Review of Books* XL. 17 (21 October 1993): 44. See also similar Burkean perspectives in Dwight Macdonald, who brought Greenberg to *Partisan Review* in 1940 (Michael Wreszin, *A Rebel in Defense of Tradition: The Life and Politics of Dwight Macdonald* [New York: Basic Books, 1994]), 92–93, 321.

9. See Townsend Ludington, *John Dos Passos: A Twentieth Century Odyssey* (New York: Dutton, 1980), 2–13, 95–110.

10. Alfred Kazin, introduction to *1919: U.S.A.* by John R. Dos Passos (New York: New American Library, 1969), xvii-xviii; Miles Orvell, *The Real Thing*, 258–72.

11. For an overview of *The Masses*, see Eugene E. Leach, "The Radicals of *The Masses*," in Heller and Rudnick, *1915: The Cultural Moment*, 27–47.

12. Melvin Landsberg, *Dos Passos' Path to U. S. A.: A Political Biography* (Boulder: Colorado Associated University Press, 1972), 107, 145–52; Ludington, *John Dos Passos*, 123.

13. Ludington, *John Dos Passos*, 237. The most complete discussion of Dos Passos as a New Playwright is George Albert Knox, *Dos Passos and the "Revolting Playwrights"* (Upsala: Lundequistska, 1964). See also John Dos Passos, "Is the 'Realistic' Theatre Obselete?", *Vanity Fair*, 24 May 1925, 64, 114.

14. Landsberg, *Dos Passos' Path*, 154–60; Ludington, *John Dos Passos*, 269–70. See Dos Passos, "The New Theatre in Russia," *The New Republic* LXII. 802 (16 April 1930): 236–40. Dos Passos acknowledged the problems of government control, but felt these drawbacks were offset by a life and variation of experience in the Russian theater, as compared to American and European the-

ater. It was this variety that appealed to him in American jazz, vaudeville, burlesque and some musical comedy, he suggested.

15. Dos Passos reveals that ambivalence in "Wanted: An Ivy Lee for Liberals," *The New Republic*, 13 August 1930, 371–72: "The thought of what Eddie Bernays or Ivy Lee would do in the inconceivable possibility that enough money could be collected to hire one of those super-public-relations counsels and put him on the job is not entirely futile. After all, if by propaganda you can make women wear corsets and everybody believe cigarettes are good for the voice, it's conceivable that by propaganda you can make them hate cruelty or tolerate the idea of change."

16. Ludington, *John Dos Passos*, 331–32.

17. Ibid., 255–56, 273–77, 490–97; and John R. Dos Passos, *The Anglo-Saxon Century and the Unification of the English-Speaking People* (New York: Putnam, 1903), 88.

18. Elia Kazan, *A Life* (New York: Knopf, 1988), 22–45, 98; Ludington, *John Dos Passos*, 22–34, 50–85, 530.

19. See Victor Navasky, *Naming Names* (New York: Viking, 1980), 199–222; Ludington, *John Dos Passos*, 455, 464; John P. Diggins, *Up from Communism: Conservative Odysseys in American Intellectual History* (New York: Harper and Row, 1975), 138–55, 245; John Dos Passos, *Most Likely to Succeed* (New York: Prentice Hall, 1954).

20. Kazan, *Life*, 71–73.

21. See Paul Gray, "From Russia to America," in *Stanislavsky and America*, ed. Erika Munk (New York: Hill and Wang, 1966), 140; see also Cheryl Crawford, *One Naked Individual* (New York: Bobbs-Merrill, 1977).

22. Harold Clurman, *The Fervent Years* (New York: Knopf, 1945), 37–38; Kazan, *Life*, 64–67.

23. Clurman, *Fervent Years*, 43. See also Wendy Smith, *Real Life Drama: The Group Theatre and America, 1931–1940* (New York: Knopf, 1990) for a comprehensive discussion of the history of the Group Theatre.

24. Clurman, *Fervent Years*, 43–44.

25. Ibid., 8–9; Kazan, *Life*, 142–52; Smith, *Real Life Drama*, 3–33.

26. See Lee Strasberg, *A Dream and a Passion: The Development of The Method*, ed. Evangeline Morphos (Boston: Little, Brown, 1987). The central problem of the actor that "the Method" resolved, he wrote, is "How can the actor both really feel and also be in control of what he needs to do on stage?", 6. See also Kazan, *Life*, 55, 64–67, 719.

27. Smith, *Real Life*, 37–54, 179–84; Kazan, *Life*, 51, 101–3, 115–17.

28. Kazan, *Life*, 606–7.

29. Kazan was assistant director. His Group Theatre experience helped him to offer expert advice on what made a scene convincing. See Frank T. Adams, *James Dombrowski: An American Heretic, 1897–1983* (Knoxville: University of

Tennessee Press, 1992), 104–5, 126; Kazan, *Life*, 105; Thomas Pauly, *An American Odyssey* (Philadelphia: Temple University Press, 1983), 41.

30. Kazan, *Life*, 106–17.
31. Ibid., 115.
32. Ibid., 275–77, 290–92.
33. Ibid., 300–1; Pauly, *American Odyssey*, 4.
34. Arthur Hill, "The Actors Studio the First Year: The Directors' Attempt to Unify American Acting Practice" (master's thesis, University of Maine, 1991). On the first meeting of the Actors Studio, see John Garfield, *A Player's Place* (New York: MacMillan, 1980), 52–54.
35. Kazan, *Life*, 302; Richard Pells, *The Liberal Mind in a Conservative Age: American Intellectuals in the 1940s and 1950s*, 2d ed. (Middletown, Conn.: Wesleyan University Press, 1989), 371–74. Pells's association of the inarticulate hero with all method acting is inaccurate, but it suggests that an inarticulate Andy Warhol was self-consciously parodying that stereotype to create his own media image as an artist and filmmaker in the 1960s.
36. Garfield, *Player's Place*, 72–73.
37. Erving Goffman, *The Presentation of Self in Everyday Life* (Garden City, N.J.: Doubleday, 1959), 254–55.
38. Erving Goffman, *Stigma: Notes on the Management of Spoiled Identity* (Englewood Cliffs, N.J.: Prentice-Hall, 1963), 122.
39. Ibid., 1–19; Richard Wright, *Pagan Spain* (New York: Harper and Row, 1957).
40. "Baffling U.S. Art: What Is It About?", *Life*, 47.19 (December 1959): 68–77.
41. The existentialist criticism of society as theater should not be confused with antitheater; it was quite the opposite. See Christopher Norris, "Fiction of Authority: Narrative and Viewpoint in Kierkegaard's Writing," in *The Deconstructive Turn: Essays in the Rhetoric of Philosophy* (London: Metheun, 1983), 84–106; Søren Kierkegaard, *Crisis in the Life of an Actress and Other Essays on Drama*, trans. Stephen D. Crites (New York: Harper, 1967), 67–91; and Kierkegaard's *Diary of a Seducer* (New York: F. Ungar, 1966). See also Friedrich Nietzsche, "The Case of Wagner," in *The Basic Writings of Nietzsche*, trans. Walter Kaufmann (New York: Modern Library, 1968), 611–56. In declining culture, Nietzsche wrote, "authority becomes superfluous, disadvantageous, a liability. Only the actor still arouses great enthusiasm" (635).
42. Tillich, *Theology of Culture*, 113–15; Martin Buber, "The Crisis and Its Expression," in *Between Man and Man*, trans. Ronald Gregor Smith (New York: Macmillan, 1965), 157–208 and afterword, 209–24.
43. Christopher Lasch, "The Cultural Cold War: A Short History of the Congress for Cultural Freedom," in *The Agony of the American Left* (New York: Vintage, 1969), 61–114.

44. Kirk, *Conservative Mind*, 214.
45. Marvin Meyers, *The Jacksonian Persuasion: Politics and Belief* (Stanford: Stanford University Press, 1957).
46. Meyers also quoted Burke in the preface, ibid., xi-xii; Goffman, *Presentation of Self*, ix, 102. See also Dennis Brissett and Charles Edgley, eds., *Life as Theatre: A Dramaturgical Source Book* (Chicago: Aldine, 1975) for examples of the popularity of symbolic interactionism and other forms of dramaturgical social psychology in the United States in the 1950s and 1960s.
47. Meyers, *Jacksonian Persuasion*, xi, 3–15.
48. Ibid., 234–75.
49. Ibid., vi.
50. Ibid., 34–35, 39–46.

Chapter 6

1. Susman, *Culture as History*, xxviii.
2. Weber, *Protestant Ethic*, 71–81, 126–27.
3. Ibid., 85–92, 95–128, 159–62.
4. Ibid., 82.
5. See H. H. Gerth and C. Wright Mills, eds., introduction to *From Max Weber: Essays in Sociology* (New York: Oxford University Press, 1946), 15–23.
6. Max Weber, "The Protestant Sects and the Spirit of Capitalism," in Gerth and Mills, *From Max Weber*, 312, 319.
7. Ibid., 302–5, 320–22.
8. Weber, *Protestant Ethic*, 180–83.
9. Weber, "Science as a Vocation," in Gerth and Mills, *From Max Weber*, 129–33.
10. Ibid., 148–50.
11. Ibid.
12. Ibid., 149–56.
13. Ibid.; Weber, *Protestant Ethic*, 181–83.
14. Weber, "Science as a Vocation," in Gerth and Mills, *From Max Weber*, 129–31, 154–56; and Weber, *Protestant Ethic*, 182.
15. See Richard Nelson, *Aesthetic Frontiers:The Machiavellian Tradition and the Southern Imagination* (Jackson: University Press of Mississippi, 1990).
16. Perry Miller, *The New England Mind: From Colony to Province* (Boston: Beacon, 1953), 51. Weber's influence on Miller's scholarship is underscored by the fact that Miller entitled the chapter in which the quotation appears "The Protestant Ethic" (40–52).
17. Perry Miller, *Errand into the Wilderness* (Cambridge, Mass.: Harvard University Press, 1956), viii.
18. Ibid., vii.

19. Miller, *New England Mind: From Colony to Province*, 485.
20. Miller, *Errand*, 11–12.
21. Perry Miller, *The New England Mind: The Seventeenth Century* (New York: Macmillan, 1939), 8.
22. Ibid., 197, 484.
23. Miller, *Errand*, 12; Miller, *New England Mind: From Colony to Province*, 31.
24. Miller, *New England Mind: From Colony to Province*, 31–38.
25. Perry Miller, "Plight of the Lone Wolf," 8–14; "The Responsibility of Mind in an Age of Machines," 195–213; and "Europe's Faith in American Fiction," 122–33, in *The Responsibility of Mind in a Civilization of Machines*, ed. John Crowell and Stanford J. Searl (Amherst: University of Massachusetts Press, 1979). See also Gene Wise, *American Historical Explanation: A Strategy for Grounded Inquiry* (Minneapolis: University of Minnesota Press, 1980), 272–75; and Reising, *Unusable Past*, 56–57.
26. Perry Miller, "The Incorruptible Sinclair Lewis," in *Responsibility of Mind*, 114–15; and Kenneth S. Lynn, "Perry Miller," *American Scholar* 52 (1983): 221–27.
27. Perry Miller, *The Raven and the Whale: The War of Words and Wits in the Era of Poe and Melville* (New York: Harcourt, Brace, 1956), 3–7.
28. Miller, "The Social Context of the Covenant," in Crowell and Searl, *The Responsibility of Mind*, 137.
29. Ibid., 139–40.
30. Miller, in *Errand into the Wilderness*, used the metaphor of a modern soldier parachuted behind enemy lines to perform a meaningless act of valor. He described the Puritans as "sent, as the devestating phrase has it, upon a fool's errand, than which there can be a no more shattering blow to self-esteem," 11; Miller, *New England Mind: From Colony to Province*, 197, 198; Sacvan Bercovitch, *The American Jeremiad* (Madison: University of Wisconsin Press, 1978), 10, 17–18.
31. Bercovitch, *Jeremiad*, 10–11.
32. Ibid., xi.
33. Ibid., 9–10, 17–26. Note the ambiguity in the meaning of confidence in Miller's descriptions of the jeremiad in *The New England Mind: From Colony to Province*: "So, by an exceedingly oblique device, the more these people accused themselves of having shirked their covenant, the more they asserted that they had not lost confidence"(26); but "The Jeremiads came from something deeper than pious fraud, more profound than cant: they were the voice of the community bespeaking its apprehensions about itself" (47). David W. Noble called attention to Bercovitch's failure to acknowledge the implications of this ambiguity in *The End of American History: Democracy, Capitalism, and the Metaphor of Two Worlds in Anglo-American Historical Writing, 1880–1980* (Minneapolis: University of Minnesota Press, 1985), 4–8.

34. Burke, *Reflections*, 75–78. See, for example, Dominick LaCapra, *Rethinking Intellectual History: Texts, Contexts, Language* (Ithaca: Cornell University Press, 1983).

35. Michael Rogin, "Making America Home: Racial Masquerade and Ethnic Assimilation in the Transition to Talking Pictures," *Journal of American History* 79, no. 3 (December 1992): 1050–77. On Busby Berkeley's films, see Ronald Davis, *The Glamour Factory: Inside Hollywood's Big Studio System* (Dallas: Southern Methodist University Press, 1993), 182–85. See Joseph McBride, *Frank Capra: The Catastrophe of Success* (New York: Simon and Schuster, 1992), 329–50; *Mr. Deeds Goes to Town* (1936), screenplay by Robert Riskin, is from the story "Opera Hat" by Clarence Buddington Kelland. Ronald Reagan, who was ideologically to the left of Capra until the 1950s, quoted Deeds in an October 5, 1981, speech before the National Alliance of Business.

36. *Mr. Smith Goes to Washington* (1939), screenplay by Sidney Buchmann and (uncredited) Myles Connolly, from the novel *The Gentleman from Montana*, by Lewis Foster, is discussed in McBride, *Frank Capra*, 408–24.

37. *Meet John Doe* (1941), screenplay by Robert Riskin and (uncredited) Myles Connolly and based on the story "A Reputation" by Richard Connell, is discussed in McBride, *Frank Capra*, 429–41.

38. *It's a Wonderful Life* (1946), screenplay by Frances Goodrich, Albert Hackett, Frank Capra, and (uncredited) Michael Wilson, Dulton Trumbo, Clifford Odets, Marc Connelly, and Dorothy Parker from the story "The Greatest Gift" by Philip Van Doren Stern, is discussed in McBride, *Frank Capra*, 503–34, and in Robert B. Ray, *A Certain Tendency of the Hollywood Cinema, 1930–1980* (Princeton: Princeton University Press, 1985), 179–215. Ronald Reagan's corporate populism, like Niebuhr's, was similar to Capra's. Like Burke, Niebuhr and Capra could appear to be liberals or conservatives, depending upon the context of the interpretation. The *Why We Fight* series was conceived in 1942 and is discussed in McBride, *Frank Capra*, 467–80. The similarly casuistic use of illusion for a higher end provides one basis for a comparison between Reagan, Capra and Niebuhr. Their Manichaean view of good and evil provides another. See Reinhold Niebuhr, *The Children of Light and the Children of Darkness* (New York: Charles Scribner's Sons, 1944) and Capra's *Why We Fight: Prelude to War* (1942), released May 13, 1943.

39. Richard Fox, *Reinhold Niebuhr: A Biography* (New York: Harper and Row, 1985), 102.

40. On Ernst Troeltsch and his influence on Weber, Tillich and the Niebuhrs, see Wilhelm Pauck, "Ernst Troeltsch," in *From Luther to Tillich: The Reformers and Their Heirs*, ed. Marion Pauck (New York: Harper and Row, 1984), 106–38.

41. Tillich was at Frankfurt University from 1929 to 1933. Theodor Adorno had been one of his students, and wrote a dissertation on Kierkegaard under

Tillich's direction. In 1931, Tillich helped his friend Max Horkheimer assume the directorship of the Institute for Social Research. Tillich was also a close friend of Karl Mannheim's, with whom he cotaught seminars. Those ties were preserved in America. See Pauck and Pauck, *Paul Tillich*, 116; and Jay, *Dialectical Imagination*, 24–25.

42. Reinhold Niebuhr, "Germany and Modern Civilization," *Atlantic Monthly* 135 (June 1925): 843. On Tillich's influence on Niebuhr, see C. W. Kegley and R. W. Bretall, *Reinhold Niebuhr: His Religious, Social and Political Thought* (New York: Macmillan, 1956); Niebuhr's articles: "The Contribution of Paul Tillich," *Religion in Life* 6 (autumn 1937): 574–81; and "Biblical Faith and Socialism: A Critical Appraisal," in *Religion and Culture: Essays in Honor of Paul Tillich*, ed. W. Leibrecht (New York: Harper and Row, 1959), 78–80. Richard Fox, *Reinhold Niebuhr*, 160–61, 257–59, emphasizes their differences as they grew older.

43. Weber, "Politics as a Vocation," in Gerth and Mills, *From Max Weber*, 121–28. See Paul Tillich, *On the Boundary* (New York: Charles Scribner's Sons, 1966), 40, 76–79.

44. Paul Tillich, "The Demonic," in *The Interpretation of History*, trans. N. A. Rasetzki and Elsa Talmoy (New York: Charles Scribner's Sons, 1936), 77–122. At the time he named nationalism and capitalism as two demonic systems in the world. He added Bolshevism in 1937. See Paul Tillich, "The Kingdom of God in History," a paper delivered at the Oxford Conference on Life and Work (1937) and published in H. G. Wood et al., *The Kingdom of God and History* (London: Allen and Unwin, 1938); and Tillich, "Religion and Marxism," *Modern Monthly* 8 (February 1938): 712–14. See also Wolfgang Zucher, "The Demonic from Aeschylus to Tillich," *Theology Today* 26 (1969): 48–50.

45. Tillich, *On the Boundary*, 13.

46. Pauck and Pauck, *Paul Tillich*, 316 n. 23, 257. Reinhold Niebuhr, in *Irony in American History* (New York: Charles Scribner's Sons, 1952) placed the dilemma within the conventions of confidence and doubt: "Though confident of virtue, it [the free world] must yet hold atomic bombs ready to use so as to prevent a possible world conflagration. It may actually make the conflict the more inevitable by this threat; and yet it cannot abandon the threat" (1). See also Paul Tillich, "The Protestant Principle," in *The Protestant Era*, trans. James Luther Adams (Chicago:University of Chicago Press, 1948), 161–81.

47. Reinhold Niebuhr, *Moral Man and Immoral Society: A Study in Ethics and Politics* (New York: Charles Scribner's Sons, 1932), pp. 95–97, 221–35.

48. Ibid., 276.

49. Ibid. Niebuhr pointed out that such sublime madness must be directed rationally to avoid smashing the illusion before its work is completed. For a contemporary challenge to the Niebuhrian sublime, see Noam Chomsky, *Necessary Illusions: Thought Control in Democratic Societies* (Boston: South End Press, 1989).

50. Pauck and Pauck, *Paul Tillich*, 15, 113; Crunden, *Minister of Reform*, 52.

51. Rudolf Otto, *The Idea of the Holy: An Inquiry into the non-rational factor in the idea of the divine and its relation to the rational*, trans. John W. Harvey (London: Oxford University Press, 1958), 12–24, 41–42, 62–71.

52. Ibid., 1–11, 42. See, for example, Tillich, *On the Boundary*, 24–30; and Tillich, "Art and Society" (1952) in Dillenberger and Dillenberger, *On Art and Architecture*, 11–41.

53. Niebuhr, *Moral Man*, 277.

54. Reinhold Niebuhr, *Beyond Tragedy: Essays on the Christian Interpretation of History* (London: Nisbet, 1930).

55. Pauck and Pauck, *Paul Tillich*, 40–53.

56. Tillich, *Theology of Culture*, 163–64.

57. Paul Tillich, *Systematic Theology* (Chicago: University of Chicago Press, 1957), 2: 50–51.

58. Niebuhr, *Beyond Tragedy*, 3–24.

59. Ibid., 127–32.

60. Ibid., 155–69.

61. Reinhold Niebuhr, *The Self and the Dramas of History* (New York: Charles Scribner's Sons, 1955). Niebuhr dedicated the book to Buber, but Niebuhr's Burkean interpretation is clearly present, and serves as the basis for his anti-Rousseauvian stance (149, 174). Niebuhr described the self as an actor in a play (7–8).

62. Ibid., 49. Niebuhr was an enthusiastic amateur actor; see Fox, *Reinhold Niebuhr*, 246.

63. Niebuhr, *Irony of American History*, 154–55.

64. Ibid., 368–69.

65. See Fox, *Reinhold Niebuhr*, 196–97.

66. Reinhold Niebuhr, *The Nature and Destiny of Man*, vol. 2, *Human Destiny* (New York: Charles Scribner's Sons, 1943), 243.

67. Fox, *Reinhold Niebuhr*, 259–60.

68. Niebuhr, *Nature and Destiny*, 2: 181.

69. Ibid., 181–83.

70. Ibid., 164.

71. Ibid., 198.

72. Ibid., 203.

73. Ibid., 204–12.

74. Ibid., 244–56.

75. See Niebuhr, *Irony of American History*, 171–74, and Niebuhr's response to Hans Morgenthau in *Reinhold Niebuhr: A Prophetic Voice in Our Time*, ed. Harold R. Landon (Greenwich, Conn.: 1962), 102, 121–22.

76. Kuhn, *Structure*. Kuhn revised and enlarged his original essay of 1959.

77. Wise, *American Historical Explanations*, 247–48, 296–314.

78. See Peter Novick, *That Noble Dream: The "Objectivity Question" and the American Historical Profession* (New York: Cambridge University Press, 1988), 526–35; and Richard Nelson, "Carl Becker Revisited: Irony and Progress in History," *Journal of the History of Ideas* 48.2 (April-June 1987): 307–23.

79. Kuhn, *Structure*, 137–52.

80. Ibid., 3–5, 93–94, 150–53; Niccolo Machiavelli, *The Prince and Other Works*, trans. Allan Gilbert (New York: Hendricks House, 1964), 87, 99–100, 122. The Prince was essentially a manual for fostering practical political confidence through which Niccolo attempted to gain the confidence of Lorenzo de' Medici (93–94, 168–69, 172–73). See also Wayne Rebhorn, *Foxes and Lions: Machiavelli's Confidence Men* (Ithaca: Cornell University Press, 1988), 40.

81. Kuhn, *Structure*, 100–10; Stephen Jay Gould, *Time's Arrow, Time's Cycle: Myth and Metaphor in the Discovery of Geological Time* (Cambridge, Mass: Harvard University Press, 1987), 4–7.

82. Stephen Jay Gould, *Wonderful Life: The Burgess Shale and the Nature of History* (New York: Norton, 1989), 287–90.

83. Gould, *Time's Arrow*, 1–2.

84. Ibid., 21–22, 181–208.

85. Ibid., 181–92. Burnet is quoted by the nonconformist minister Moses Lowman in *Paraphrase and Notes Upon the Revelation* in Tuveson, *Redeemer Nation*, 42. See also Miller, *The New England Mind: From Colony to Province*, 186–87.

86. Tuveson, *Redeemer Nation*, 42–43.

Chapter 7

1. The most comprehensive biographical information on Herberg may be found in Harry J. Ausmus, *Will Herberg: From Right to Right* (Chapel Hill: University of North Carolina Press, 1987).

2. Ibid., 216. See also Herberg, "The Dissection of Babbitt Junior" (a review of Peter Viereck's *The Shame and Glory of Intellectuals*), *Commonweal*, 3 April 1953, 653–55; "The History of a Great Historian" (a review of Gertrude Himmelfarb's *Lord Acton: A Study in Conscience and Politics*), *New Leader*, 13 April 1953, 23–24; and "Acton's Meaning for Today" (a review of Lord Acton's *Essays on Church and State* and G. E. Fasnacht's *Acton's Political Philosophy*), *New Leader*, 29 June 1953, 17–18. See Herberg, "Reinhold Niebuhr, Burkean Conservative," *National Review*, 2 December 1961, 379, 394.

3. Herberg, *Protestant, Catholic, Jew*, 85–97, 101–4, 275–76.

4. Ibid., 278–85.

5. Will Herberg, "The What and How of Ethics," *Modern Age*, fall 1971, 350–57.

6. Ausmus, *Will Herberg*, 1–2.

7. Ibid., 3.

8. Ibid., 5; Herberg, "Lenin and the Youth," *Workers Monthly*, February 1926, 166–71.

9. Ausmus, *Will Herberg*, 8–14; and Herberg, "The Tenth Plenum ECCI: A Political Analysis," *Revolutionary Age*, 15 November 1929, 17.

10. Herberg, "Rosa Luxemburg," *Revolutionary Age*, 15 February 1930, 12–13. Compare to Hannah Arendt's appreciation of Rosa Luxemburg in *Men in Dark Times* (New York: Harcourt, Brace and World, 1968), 33–56. Both view Stalin's rejection of Luxemburg's memory as proving a break in the tradition of socialist values, and both also view her as confirming a transcendent orthodoxy.

11. Herberg, "The New Turn and the Crisis in the CI," *Revolutionary Age*, 15 March 1930, 7; Herberg, "Stalin Speaks on World Politics," *Revolutionary Age*, 10 January 1931.

12. See the exchange between Lewis Feuer and Douglas G. Webb in *Canadian Review of American Studies*, fall 1978, 233–40, and fall 1980, 262–68. Herberg not only falsified his academic credentials but also his date and place of birth. Webb speculates that the falsification of credentials was a result of Herberg's sense of inferiority and that the changing of birth data stemmed from his desire to appear to be a "real American" (he dated his birth from his arrival in the United States).Certainly, these instances confirm the centrality of confidence to Herberg's life.

See, for example, Herberg, "Einstein and Marx," *Revolutionary Age*, 4 April 1931, 3–4; Herberg, "Communism and Science," *Revolutionary Age*, 13 June 1931, 4; and Herberg, "What the Theory of Relativity is All About," *Revolutionary Age*, 13 December 1930, 3.

13. Herberg, "Communism and Intellectuals," *Revolutionary Age*, 10 October 1931, 4.

14. Herberg, "Lessons of the Hunger March," *Revolutionary Age*, 10 December 1931, 3.

15. Herberg, "How Einstein 'Made' the First Page," *Revolutionary Age*, 13 December 1930, 3; Herberg, "Einstein and Marx," *Revolutionary Age*, 4 April 1931, 3–4; Herberg, "Communism and Science," *Revolutionary Age*, 13 June 1931, 4.

16. See Miller, *New England Mind*, 1: 443; Herberg, "Marxism and the History of Science," *Revolutionary Age*, 21 November 1931, 3.

17. Diggins, *Up From Communism*, 133; Herberg, "Darwinism and Marxism," *Workers Age*, 17 May 1932, 3–4.

18. Herberg, "About the Literary Class War," *Workers Age*, 14 May 1932, 3.

19. Herberg, "Seventeen Years of Socialist Construction," *Workers Age*, 19 November 1934, 1–2.

20. Herberg, "Jacobin Defense in the Spanish War," *Workers Age*, 15 September 1937, 2, and 29 September 1937, 4. See also similar positions in "Com-

munists and Abolitionists," *Workers Age*, 4 April 1932, 3; "Civil War in Spain," *Workers Age*, 15 August 1936, 3–4; and "The P. O. U. M. and the Spanish Revolution," *Workers Age*, 17 April 1937, 5.

21. Herberg, "Spain and the Great Democracies," *Workers Age*, 16 January 1937, 4; "The Problem of Defense," *Workers Age*, 6 July 1940, 4; "On the Political Nature of the Stalinist Party," *Workers Age*, 15 July 1939, 3; "The Inquisition Lifts its Head in America," *Workers Age*, 27 April 1940, 3.

22. See Ausmus, *Will Herberg*, 65–66 and 230–31 n. 12. See also Herberg, "From Marxism to Judaism," *Commentary* 3.1 (January 1947): 25–32.

23. Herberg, "Crisis of Socialism," *Jewish Frontier* 11.9 (September 1944): 28; Herberg, "The Christian Mythology of Socialism," in *Faith Enacted as History*, ed. Bernard Anderson (Philadelphia: Westminster Press, 1976), 182–86; and Herberg, "The Ethics of Power," *Jewish Frontier* 11.9 (September 1944): 19–22.

24. See Herberg, *Judaism and Modern Man: An Interpretation of Jewish Religion* (New York: Farrar, Straus and Young, 1951), 29–30, 231.

25. Herberg, "From Marxism to Judaism," *Commentary* 3.1 (January 1947): 25–32; Herberg, "Biblical Faith as 'Heilsgeschichte,' " in Anderson, *Faith Enacted as History*, 39–40.

26. Herberg, "From Marxism to Judaism," 29; "The Ethics of Power," 23; "Society, Democracy and the State," in Anderson, *Faith Enacted as History*, 222–40. See also "Do Communists Have the Right to Think?", *Revolutionary Age* 1 (February 1930): 10–11; "Workers Democracy or Dictatorship," *Workers Age*, 15 December 1934, 3; and "Professor Hook Loses His Temper," *Workers Age*, 6 July 1935, 3.

27. Fox, *Reinhold Niebuhr*, 256–60.

28. The most complete biographical study of Buber and his relation to the theological thought and political events of the twentieth century is Maurice Friedman's three-volume work, *Martin Buber's Life and Work* (New York: E. P. Dutton, 1981, 1983, and 1983).

29. See Paul R. Mendes-Flohr, ed., *A Land of Two Peoples* (New York: Oxford University Press, 1983), especially "A State of Cannons, Flags and Military Decorations," 35–38 and 35 n. 48. See also Friedrich Meinecke, *Machiavellism*, trans. Douglas Scott (London: 1947); and Weber, "Politics as Vocation," 77–156.

30. See Martin Buber, "Hebrew Humanism," in *Israel and the World: Essays in a Time of Crisis* (New York: Schocken, 1968), 240–52.

31. Quoted in Mendes-Flohr, *Land of Two Peoples*, 21.

32. Herberg, review of Martin Buber's *Eclipse of God*, in *Theology Today* 10.2 (July 1953): 289–90.

33. See Martin Buber, "Judaism and the Jews," in Nahum Glatzer, ed., *On Judaism* (New York: Schocken, 1967), 13–15; Buber, "The Faith of Judaism," in *Israel and the World*, 24.

34. Quoted in Bernard Susser, *Existence and Utopia: The Social and Political Thought of Martin Buber* (Toronto: Associated University Press, 1981), 115.
35. Quoted in Mendes-Flohr, *Land of Two Peoples*, 16–17, 20–21.
36. See Friedman, *Buber's Life and Work*, 3: 200–1.
37. See Martin Buber, *The Eclipse of God: Studies in the Relation between Religion and Philosophy* (New York: Harper, 1952). See also Martin Buber, *Paths of Utopia*, trans. R. F. C. Hull (Boston: Beacon, 1949), 136. On the differences between Buber, Walter Benjamin, and the Frankfurt sociologists, see Martin Jay, "The Politics of Translation," in *The Leo Baeck Institute Yearbook* (1976), 3–26; Gershom Scholem, *On Jews and Judaism in Crisis* (New York: Schocken, 1976); Gershom Scholem, *Walter Benjamin: The Story of a Friendship*, trans. Harry Zohn (Philadelphia: Jewish Publication Society, 1981); and Friedman, *Martin Buber's Life and Work*, 1: 178–258.
38. Herberg, *Judaism and Modern Man*, 171–75; and "Christian Faith and Totalitarian Rule," in Anderson, *Faith Enacted in History*, 243–57.
39. Herberg, "Has Judaism Power to Speak?", *Commentary* 7. 5 (May 1949): 455–57.
40. Herberg, *Protestant, Catholic, Jew*, 254–56, 285–89.
41. Ibid., 139–40.
42. Ibid., 213.
43. Ibid., 270.
44. Ibid., 272, 283–85.
45. Herberg, "Historicism as a Touchstone," *Christian Century*, 16 March 1960, 311–13.
46. Ibid.
47. Ibid.
48. Herberg, "Conservatives and Religion: A Dilemma," *National Review*, 30 September 1961, 230–32; and "Conservatism, Liberalism and Religion," *National Review*, 30 November 1965, 1087–88.
49. Herberg, "Conservatives and Religion: A Dilemma," 230.
50. Herberg's, "Athens and Jerusalem: Confrontation and Dialogue" actually appeared first in the spring 1958 issue of *Drew Gateway*. It was published in 1965 under the same title for the University of New Hampshire's Distinguished Lecture Series Number 3 by the university's press, Durham.
51. Herberg, "Athens and Jerusalem," 5–21.
52. Herberg, "Martin Buber, R. I. P.," *National Review*, 29 June 1965, 539–40.
53. Herberg, "Civil Rights and Violence: Who Are the Guilty Ones?", *National Review*, 7 September 1965, 769–70.
54. Herberg, "The New Estate: The Professors and the Teach-Ins," *National Review*, 13 July 1965, 590.
55. Herberg, "Civil Rights and Violence: Who Are the Guilty Ones?", 769.

56. Ibid., 770.
57. See Ausmus, *Will Herberg*, 230 n. 12.
58. Herberg, "Reinhold Niebuhr: Burkean Conservative," 379, 94; Herberg, "America's Civil Religion: What Is It and Whence It Comes," *Modern Age*, summer 1975, 227, 233; Herberg, "Anarchy on Campus," *Modern Age*, winter 1969–70; Herberg, "Civil Rights and Violence: Who Are the Guilty Ones?", 769–70.
59. Herberg, "Aggiornamento: The Plight of American Catholicism," *National Review*, 27 August 1968, 852–53; "The Plight of American Protestantism," *National Review*, 5 November 1968, 1109, 1126–27.
60. Herberg, *Protestant, Catholic, Jew*, 119–24. As Billy Graham, Oral Roberts and Ronald Reagan were beginning their climb to power and influence, Herberg wrote: "Baptists, Methodists, and later Disciples, frequently found themselves on the same frontier, in rivalry yet co-operating in revival enterprises" (119). See chapter 8 below. See also Herberg, "Two Historical Types," *National Review*, 2 July 1968, 668–69; and "Civil Rights and Violence: Who Are the Guilty Ones?", 769.
61. Herberg, "Two Historical Types," 669.
62. Ibid.
63. William Appleman Williams, *The Great Evasion* (Chicago: Quadrangle, 1964), 12–20, 25. The complementarity between Herberg's analysis of the American crisis of the 1960s and Williams's is interesting. Williams positively associated Marx with the prophetic tradition, while Herberg did so negatively. "If you have to have a religion," Herberg quoted Marx, "let it be that of the Old Testament prophets" (quoted in Ausmus, *Will Herberg*, 242 n. 13.

Both Williams and Herberg associated the assassination attempts against American political leaders with the antinomianism of frontier violence, and both promoted community as an alternative to the false standards of capitalist individualism. See William Appleman Williams, *America in a Changing World* (New York: Harper and Row, 1978), and William Appleman Williams, *Some Presidents from Wilson to Nixon* (New York: Vintage, 1972). For a discussion of Williams's changing views of Marx and Beard, see Noble, *The End of American History*, 133–40. Herberg reprinted Beard's articles in *Workers Age* during the 1930s.

64. Herberg, "The 'What' and the 'How' of Ethics," 350–57.
65. Interview with Herberg in *Jewish Post and Opinion* (Indianapolis: 18 January, 1976), quoted in Ausmus, *Will Herberg*, 211.
66. Reagan campaign manager John Sears, quoted in Jules Witcover, *Marathon: The Pursuit of the Presidency, 1972–76* (New York: Viking, 1977), 398.

Chapter 8

1. Ronald Reagan, with R. G. Hubler, *Where's the Rest of Me?* (New York: Duell Sloan and Pierce, 1965), 291–92.

2. Ibid., 292–93, 255. See also David F. Prindle, *The Politics of Glamour: Ideology and Democracy in the Screen Actors Guild* (Madison: University of Wisconsin Press, 1988), 80–91.
3. Reagan and Hubler, *Rest of Me*, 247.
4. Ibid., 253–55.
5. Ibid., 254–55, 293.
6. Ibid., 255–61.
7. Ibid., 6.
8. Ibid., 258–61.
9. See Wills, *Reagan's America*, 20–32.
10. Reagan and Hubler, *Rest of Me*, 15.
11. Ibid., 97–99.
12. Ibid., 141.
13. Ibid., 140.
14. See William Martin, *Prophet with Honor: The Billy Graham Story* (New York: William Morrow, 1991), 129–30; W. A. Swanberg, *Luce and His Empire* (New York: Charles Scribner's Sons, 1972), 290–91, 341.
15. D. P. Noonan, *The Passion of Fulton J. Sheen* (New York: Dodd, Mead, 1972), 95–98, 54–55; David Edwin Harrell, Jr., *Oral Roberts: An American Life* (New York: Harper and Row, 1985), 126–30.
16. Reagan and Hubler, *Rest of Me*, 139.
17. Ibid., 141; Noonan, *Fulton J. Sheen*, 55–60. A contemporary analysis of Sheen's message and appeal was provided in a 1955 study by Yale Divinity School. See Everett C. Parker et al., "Personality Traits in the Sheen Audience," in *The Television-Radio Audience and Religion* (New York: Harper and Row, 1955), 274–315.
18. Noonan, *Fulton J. Sheen*, 110–11; Marshall Frady, *Billy Graham: A Parable of Righteousness* (New York: Little, Brown, 1979), 213–16; Harrell, *Oral Roberts*, 451.
19. Fulton J. Sheen, *Treasure in Clay: The Autobiography of Fulton J. Sheen* (New York: Doubleday, 1980), 7; Reagan and Hubler, *Rest of Me*, 7–10.
20. Martin, *Prophet with Honor*, 112–20; "Sincerity—that key word stuck in this reporter's mind as the basic impression made by evangelist Oral Roberts during a personal interview." Jim Pharr, "The Word Is Sincerity," *The Fayetteville* (N. C.) *Observer*, 16 May 1959, quoted in Harrell, *Oral Roberts*, 177.
21. Harrell, *Oral Roberts*, 178–80. Harrell points out that by 1958, Oral Roberts's public relations account had reached $1,500,000. "You were quite an actor," Roberts's wife pointed out after watching a film of an early crusade. Roberts agreed: "You have to have enough results to inspire people in the audience, let them see that God is actually healing someone" and also establish "a credibility that the television audience will grasp" (101).
22. For a contemporary analysis of religious television programming in the

1950s among Protestants as well as Catholics and Jews, see Parker et al., *The Television-Radio Audience and Religion*. A brief description is provided by Kimberly A. Neuendorf, "The Public Trust and the Almighty Dollar," in Robert Ableman and Stewart M. Hoover, *Religious Television: Controversies and Conclusions* (Norwood, N. J.: Ablex, 1990), 71–83.

23. Burke, *Reflections*, 73–74.

24. Ibid. Anne Norton, in *A Republic of Signs*, suggests a similar Burkean interpretation of presidential candidates by their "handlers," and "spin doctors." The candidate is like "an unruly animal, less intelligent than the handler," requiring discipline and restraint. For the spin doctor, she says, the candidate is "the source of ungoverned, undirected energy." As a result, the "acts, speeches, appearances and offhand statements of contending candidates are merely raw material, a force to be controlled and directed by experts" (114–15).

25. See Weber, "The Sociology of Charismatic Authority," in Gerth and Mills, *From Max Weber*, 245–52; Wayne Koestenbaum, *The Queen's Throat: Opera, Homosexuality, and the Mystery of Desire* (New York: Poseidon Press, 1993), 154–56, 170; Susan McClary, *Feminine Endings: Music, Gender and Sexuality* (Minneapolis: University of Minnesota Press, 1991); Richard Meyer, "Rock Hudson's Body," in *Inside/Out: Lesbian Theories, Gay Theories*, ed. Diana Fuss (New York: Routledge, 1991), 259–90; Lott, *Love and Theft*, 19–37.

26. Terrance Ball, "The Politics of Social Science in Post-War America," in *Recasting America: Culture and Politics in the Age of the Cold War*, ed. Lary May (Chicago: University of Chicago Press, 1989), 76–92. Frederick Winslow Taylor (1856–1915) was a mechanical engineer who became famous for his advocacy of scientific management in industry. After his death, the Taylor society continued his efforts to make the American economy more efficient.

27. Riesman, *The Lonely Crowd*, 276–79, 303–12; and David Riesman, *Individualism Reconsidered* (New York: Doubleday, 1954).

28. B. F. Skinner, *Beyond Freedom and Dignity* (New York: Bantam, 1971), 22–40; B. F. Skinner, *Particulars of My Life* (New York: Knopf, 1976). The title was taken from *Henry IV, Part I*. Skinner wrote plays—after the style of Ibsen and Shaw—and poetry during college. He became convinced, however, that literature was dead, and that science was the art of the twentieth century (225–26, 239–43).

29. James Campbell, *A Life of James Baldwin* (New York: Viking, 1991), 38–45. See also Clayton Holloway, "When a Pariah Becomes a Celebrity: An Interview with James Baldwin," *Xavier Review* 7 (1987): 1–10; Alan Levensohn, "The Artist Must Outwit the Celebrity," a review of *Going to Meet the Man* in *The Christian Science Monitor*, 18 November 1965, 15; James Baldwin, "The Artist's Struggle for Integrity," *Liberation* 8 (March, 1963): 9–11; John Cawelti, "The Writer as Celebrity: Some Aspects of American Literature as Popular Culture," *Studies In American Fiction* 5 (1977): 161–74.

30. Norman Mailer, *Miami and the Siege of Chicago: An Informal History of the Republican and Democratic Conventions of 1968* (New York: Signet, 1968), 11–15, 16–18.

31. Mailer, "David Riesman Reconsidered," in *Advertisements*, 173–84.

32. James Baldwin, "Everybody's Protest Novel," 9–17, and James Baldwin, "Many Thousands Gone," 18–36; both reprinted from *Partisan Review* in *Notes of a Native Son* (New York: Bantam, 1955).

33. David Leeming, *James Baldwin* (New York: Knopf, 1994), 49–57, 150–51, 232–35; W. J. Weatherby, *Squaring Off* (New York: Mason/Charter, 1977), 138–48.

34. James Baldwin, *The Fire Next Time* (New York: Dell, 1962), 55; Melville, "The Two Temples," in Berthoff, ed., *Great Short Works of Herman Melville*, 164.

35. See David Leeming, "An Interview with James Baldwin on Henry James," *Henry James Review* 8 (fall 1985), 47–56. See also David Riesman on "the cult of sincerity," in *Lonely Crowd*, 224–26.

36. James Baldwin, "To Crush the Serpent," *Playboy* 34 (January 1987): 66–70.

37. Leeming, *James Baldwin*, 24–25, 32–43. See also Baldwin's introduction to his *Price of the Ticket: Collected Nonfiction 1948–1985* (New York: St. Martin's/Marek, 1985), ix-xx; and Baldwin, "On the Painter, Beauford Delaney," *Transition*, 18 April 1965, 45. Henry Miller shared Baldwin's admiration for Delaney's capacity to make others see the world in new ways. Henry Miller, "The Amazing and Invariable Beauford DeLaney" [sic], *Remember to Remember* (New York: New Directions, 1947).

38. Leeming, *James Baldwin*, 46–48.

39. See, for example, James Baldwin, *Go Tell It on the Mountain* (New York: Dell, 1953), 29–41, 92–115, 193–205 and *Tell Me How Long the Train's Been Gone* (New York: Dial, 1968), 160–63. See also James Campbell, *Talking at the Gates: A Life of James Baldwin* (New York: Viking, 1991), 265; Bruce Bawer, "Race and Art: The Career of James Baldwin," *The New Criterion*, November 1991, 16–26.

40. Bawer, "Race and Art," 24. Baldwin's self-identification with acting and the theater remained central throughout the 1960s. His writing on theater in *The Urbanite* in 1961, for example, already expressed the themes that he later explored in *Tell Me How Long the Train's Been Gone*. See James Baldwin, "Theatre: On the Negro Actor," *The Urbanite*, April 1961, 6, 29. See especially Richard Courage, "James Baldwin's *Go Tell It on the Mountain*: Voices of a People," *CLA Journal* 32 (June 1989): 410–23.

Courage says that critics of Baldwin have failed to notice the classical dramatic formula that informs his work. As a result they have often missed the fact that in Baldwin the persona of the narrator and the author's voice are not the same.

Instead, for Baldwin, "The narrator functions as a *persona*, of classical drama — the actor's mask through which sounded a voice appropriate to the character being represented. Trained in declamation, the classical actor possessed different voices for the different masks he donned" (411–12).

Courage suggests that Baldwin used this formula, as he used the blues, to express a polyphonic voice (411–12). The voice in *Go Tell It on the Mountain* is "neither infinite nor arbitrary. It embraces young and old, male and female, rough and refined, secular and religious, but finds a common matrix in the black experience, particularly the signposts of the Afro-American journey, the blues and Gospel shout" (424). This insight applies even more fully to Baldwin's plays, *The Amen Corner* (New York: Dial, 1968). Act I was first published in *Zero*, 2 July 1954, 4–11, 8–13, and *Blues for Mister Charlie* (New York: Dial, 1964).

41. Baldwin, "Theatre," 29; Baldwin, *Tell Me*, 266.
42. Baldwin, "Theatre," 29.
43. Leeming, *James Baldwin*, 231–42.
44. Ibid., 225–26, 233–34; James Baldwin and Richard Avedon, *Nothing Personal* (New York: Atheneum, 1964).
45. Leeming, *James Baldwin*, 277–83; Campbell, *Talking at the Gates*, 226–28.
46. Baldwin, *Tell Me*, 3–7, 264–66, 332.
47. Ibid., 62–63, 82–83, 175.
48. Ibid., 176–89.
49. Ibid., 214–33.
50. Ibid., 336, 368–70.
51. Ibid. Theater, Leo Proudhammer reminds his readers, began in the church; Ibid., 323, 361; James Baldwin, *No Name in the Street* (New York: Dial, 1972).
52. Baldwin, *No Name*, 9. See also "I Can't Blow This Gig," interview with G. Nagsta, *Cinema*, summer 1968, 2–3. Commenting on his screenplay about the life of Malcolm X, "One Day When I Was Lost," Baldwin said: "In terms of technique, I have more tricks than most writers ever learned, however, if I rely on my tricks or my technical skill, that would be the end. It's very easy to be a virtuoso. I'm a kind of virtuoso. I know that. I have to fight against it. Where it's at is the amount of truth I can dig out of my belly, my heart, the center of me. The terrifying thing about writing a screenplay, however, is that the camera can do nothing but lie. In fact, though people say exactly the opposite, you must force the camera to tell the truth" (3).
53. Baldwin, *No Name*, 53–59, 116–26, 144–46.
54. James Baldwin, *The Evidence of Things Not Seen* (New York: Holt, 1985), 23–31, 36–41, 123–24. "It is a very grave matter to be forced to imitate a people for whom you know—which is the price of your performance and survival—you do not exist. It is hard to imitate a people whose existence appears, mainly, to be made tolerable by their bottomless gratitude that they are not, thank heaven, *you*"(44).

55. Mailer, "Advertisement for Games and Ends," in *Advertisements*, 348–50.

56. Mailer, "The White Negro," in *Advertisements*, 304. A few paragraphs earlier, Mailer wrote, "... and so if in the midst of civilization founded upon the Faustian urge to dominate nature by mastering time, mastering the links of social cause and effect—in the middle of an economic civilization founded upon the confidence that time could indeed be subjected to our will, our psyche was subjected itself to the intolerable anxiety that death being causeless, life was causeless as well, and time deprived of cause and effect had come to a stop" (303). See also Barrett, *The Truants*, 128–29; Walter Kaufmann, *Existentialism from Dostoyevsky to Sartre* (New York: Meridian, 1957), 40–48.

Georg Lukács visited Paris in 1949 to lead the Marxist critique of Sartrean existentialism as a bourgeois expression of celebrity performance. See Arpad Kadarkay, *Georg Lukács: Life, Thought, and Politics* (Cambridge, Mass.: Basil Blackwell, 1991), 309–401.

57. Mailer, *The Naked and the Dead* (New York: Rinehart, 1948), 494. Mailer claimed in a 1951 interview with Harvey Breit that the authors who most influenced *Naked and the Dead* were James T. Farrell, John Dos Passos, and most especially Melville. See Michael Lennon, ed., *Conversations with Norman Mailer* (Jackson: University Press of Mississippi, 1988), 15.

58. Hilary Mills, *Mailer: A Biography* (New York: Empire Books, 1982), 308; Norman Mailer, *The Presidential Papers* (New York: Bantam, 1964).

59. Richard Schickel, "Stars and Celebrities," *Commentary*, August 1971, 63.

60. Ibid. "It has become almost impossible for young actors to work in three or four films a year as was the case when studios would put young people under contracts and build them into valuable properties by the simple process of repeatedly exposing them to the public gaze.

"But even if none of these factors had come into play, and even if the movies had not been economically reduced by television, I think it likely that the institution of stardom would have undergone the radical alteration we have been witnessing. To begin with, it must be remembered that stars were created and existed in a highly stylized world, that of the soundstage and backlot, and although Hollywood prided itself on its ability to reproduce reality in those confines, the fact is it never really did." Schickel's comments are exactly parallel to Ronald Reagan's in *Where's the Rest of Me?*, 292–95.

61. Mills, *Mailer*, 48; Mailer, "The White Negro," in *Advertisements*, 304–8; James Baldwin, "The Black Boy Looks at the White Boy," in *Nobody Knows My Name* (New York: Dell, 1963), 169–90.

"I want to know how power works," Baldwin quoted Mailer, "how it really works in detail." Baldwin wrote in response, "Well, I know how power works, it has worked on me, and if I didn't know how power worked, I would be dead. And it goes without saying, perhaps, that I have simply never been able to afford myself any illusions concerning the manipulation of that power. My revenge, I decided very early, would be to achieve a power which outlasts kingdoms" (183).

62. Mills, *Mailer*, 96; Kaufmann, *Existentialism*, 40.
63. See, for example, Mailer, *Presidential Papers*, 187–98.
64. On Lukács, see Mary Gluck, *Georg Lukács and His Generation: 1900–1918* (Cambridge: Harvard University Press, 1985), 69–75, 106–42, 145–54. See also Kadarkay, *Georg Lukács*, 29–42, 339–41. After repudiating existentialism as an empty gesture, Lukács remained devoted to realist theater. Lukács had immersed himself, as a critic and director, in anticommercial, experimental theater between 1902 and 1908. His biographer refers to him as a lifelong "theatromaniac." Ibsen, and later Shaw, particularly shaped his vision of aesthetic and political morality during his whole life.

In *Soul and Form*, trans. Anna Bostock (Cambridge, Mass.: MIT Press, 1974) Lukács makes clear his association of the illusions of theater with power. "The mystical experience is to suffer the All, the tragic one is to create the All," wrote Lukács. Mysticism leads to a cancellation of the self, he explained, but in tragedy "the self stresses its selfhood with an all-exclusive, all-destroying force, but this extreme affirmation imparts a steely hardness and autonomous life to everything it encounters and—arriving at the ultimate peak of pure selfhood—finally cancels itself out. The final tension of selfhood overleaps everything that is merely individual" (160). Like Burke and Mailer, Lukács practiced theater as countertheater to achieve political ends.

65. Norman Mailer, *Armies of the Night: History as a Novel, The Novel as History* (New York: New American Library, 1968), 206; Mills, *Mailer*, 97–99. Mailer was also influenced by Dwight Macdonald, who identified himself in the 1950s as a "conservative anarchist" with Burkean sympathies. See Dwight Macdonald, *Memoirs of a Revolutionary: Essays in Political Criticism* (New York: Farrar, Straus and Cudahy), 3–6; and Wreszin, *A Rebel in Defense of Tradition*, 237–39, 432.
66. Mills, *Mailer*, 13–19.
67. Mailer, "The White Negro," in *Advertisements*, 312. See Michael Löwy, *Georg Lukács: From Romanticism to Bolshevism*, trans. Patrick Camiller (London: NLB, 1979), 100–8. See also Lukács, *Soul and Form*, 160–61. Like Mailer, Lukács identified tragedy with the frontier. "The tragic life is, of all possible lives, the one most exclusively of this world. That is why its frontier always merges into death. Real, ordinary life never reaches the frontier; it knows death only as something frightening, threatening, meaningless, something that suddenly arrests the flow of life." Mystics overleap the frontier, said Lukács, and thereby rob death of its value. "But for tragedy, death—the frontier as such—is an always immanent reality connected with every tragic event." Lukács concluded that "the experiencing of the frontier between life and death is the awakening of the soul to consciousness, or self-consciousness."

"To be cool," Mailer wrote in "The White Negro," means that "it is more difficult for the next cat who comes along to pull you down. And of course one can hardly afford to be put down too often, or one is beat, one has lost one's confidence, one has lost one's will, one is impotent in the world of action and so closer to the demeaning flip of becoming a queer, or indeed closer to dying, and therefore it is even more difficult to recover enough energy to try to make it again, because once a cat is beat he has nothing to give and no one is interested any longer in making it with him" (317).

Mailer's homophobic assumption about "white negritude" presents a diametrically opposed view to Baldwin's view of sex, race and power in works such as *Giovanni's Room*, "The Male Prison," in *Nobody Knows My Name*, 125–30, *Another Country* (New York: Dell, 1962) and "Freaks and the American Ideal of Manhood," *Playboy*, January, 1985. Yet, surprisingly, much of the new queer studies fits the hipster-style of challenging heterosexual square, a perspective very similar to Mailer's.

68. See, for example, Norman Mailer, *Of a Fire on the Moon* (New York: New American Library, 1970), 273–74, 467–72; Melvyn Bragg, "Norman Mailer Talks to Melvyn Bragg about the Bizarre Business of Writing a Hypothetical Life of Marilyn Monroe," in Lennon, *Conversations*, 193–206; Mailer, "Before the Literary Bar," in Lennon, *Conversations*, 271–90; Norman Mailer, *Ancient Evenings* (London: Picador, 1983); and Robert Begiebing, "Twelfth Round: An Interview with Norman Mailer," in Lennon, *Conversations*, 306–29.

69. Norman Mailer, "In the Red Light," in *Some Honorable Men: Political Conventions 1960–1972* (Boston: Little, Brown, 1976), 90; Norman Mailer, *Prisoner of Sex* (Boston: Little, Brown, 1971), 56–57, 213, 214–18; Norman Mailer, *The Executioner's Song* (New York: Warner, 1979), 1019.

70. Mailer, "In the Red Light," in *Some Honorable Men*, 91. Mailer, an enthusiastic amateur boxer, had used the boxing metaphor earlier. See, for example, Mailer, "Ten Thousand Words a Minute," in *Presidential Papers*," 213–68.

71. See Norman Mailer, *King of the Hill* (New York: Signet, 1971), 62–64. Compare to Mailer's description of the Hipster in n. 67.

72. Mailer, *Miami and the Siege of Chicago*, 44.

73. Ibid., 50, 62.

74. Ibid., 70–71, 49.

75. Ibid., 62, 41–42, 44–50. See also n. 81 below.

76. Ibid., 41. This company included Norman Vincent Peale, who was a staunch supporter of both Graham and Nixon. See Carol V. R. George, *God's Salesman: Norman Vincent Peale and the Power of Positive Thinking* (New York: Oxford University Press, 1993), 147–49, 198–200, 202, 209–11, 214–15.

77. George, *God's Salesman*, 214–15. Peale also illustrates this continuity between Eisenhower, Nixon and Reagan. Having supported Reagan in 1970, he was awarded a Presidential Medal of Freedom in 1984.

78. In 1964 *Time* had a circulation of 2,900,000, *Life*, 7,000,000, *Sports Illustrated*, 1,005,000, and *Fortune*, 400,000. Including *House and Home*, *Architectural*

Forum and international editions of *Time* and *Life*, Luce's publishing corporation circulated 13,000,000 publications. The stories in *Time, Life* and *Fortune* were very much shaped by Luce policy decisions, leading Edmund Wilson to view *Time*, in particular, as dangerously propagandistic. See John Kobler, *Luce: His Life, Times and Fortune* (Garden City, N.J.: Doubleday, 1968), 2–3, 6–8, 112–13.

Henry Luce's call for a "new imperialism" in a February 17, 1941, *Life* editorial launched a broad agenda for a populist corporate consumerism at home and intervention abroad within American popular culture. "We stand in the great liberal tradition — with what some theologians might call Christian presuppositions," Luce wrote to Episcopal Bishop James Pike, who was confused by Luce's politics. "My own political hero was Theodore Roosevelt who, fallible though he was, did not hesitate to assert that 'righteousness' is relevant to politics and all the public affairs of men and actions" (quoted in Kobler, *Luce*, 276).

Daniel Bell's absorption into the Luce orbit is recounted in Howard Brick, *Daniel Bell and the Decline of Intellectual Radicalism: Social Theory and Political Reconciliation in the 1940s* (Madison: University of Wisconsin Press, 1986). As the title suggests, Brick sees Bell's odyssey as paradigmatic for his generation.

79. Daniel Bell, "The Revolt Against Modernity," *The Public Interest* 81 (fall 1985): 44–60; Irving Kristol, *Reflections of a Neoconservative: Looking Back, Looking Ahead* (New York: Basic Books, 1983), ix, 152. Kristol cited Burke's similar affection for Adam Smith as a justification for his own support of Reaganism. Norman Podhoretz, *Breaking Ranks*, identified the cultural left as a political and sexual threat to tradition and natural virtue (295–305, 362–64). See Peter Steinfels, *The Neoconservatives: The Men Who Are Changing American Politics* (New York: Simon and Schuster, 1979).

80. Mailer, *Presidential Papers*, 60.

81. Ibid., 61; Mailer, *Miami and the Siege of Chicago*, 50. In Mailer's essay "Of a Small and Modest Malignancy," in *Pieces and Pontifications* (Boston: Little, Brown, 1982), he expressed his disillusionment with Nixon following Watergate in theatrical terms. "He had always believed Richard Nixon was the most untalented actor he had ever witnessed, and Mailer had often brooded on the first meeting decades ago of Richard and Pat Nixon in an amateur theatrical company," Mailer wrote, "and wondered whether Nixon, if he had been somewhat better in those early years as an actor, would have become in later life, a politician more like Ronald Reagan." Instead, Mailer complained, Nixon's insincerity as an actor led to depression. Therefore, "Nixon's inability to act had always, by reflection, intimated that something in the American public must be atrocious if millions were ready to accept his transparent lack of sincerity, his push-button smile, and his simple lack of ability to offer even that resonance of the throat which is a ham actor's emotion."

Yet, marvelled Mailer, commenting on Nixon's interview with David Frost, the untalented Nixon had miraculously gained the talent of a Bogart, a Fonda, a

Tracy, or a Robinson: "... watching Nixon, it did not matter what the truth might be, any more than one would find fault with a great stage actor for bringing life and splendor and passion and the monumental echoes of tragic woe to lines that were not his own and that he could say in his sleep or while shaving, he had practiced them so well, yes, Nixon struck America with a miracle—a talentless actor had become a splendid actor—yes, Nixon now went to the root of good acting, where before he had lived in the center of bad acting" (79–80).

82. Lionel Trilling, *Sincerity and Authenticity* (Cambridge, Mass.: Harvard University Press, 1972), 1–12. Trilling noted that the word "sincerity" had entered the English language in the sixteenth century. Originally meaning pure or unadulterated, it soon gained the metaphorical connotation of lacking in dissimulation. "The sixteenth century," wrote Trilling, "was preoccupied to an extreme degree with dissimulation, feigning, and pretence. Dante had assigned those whose 'deeds were not of the lion but of the fox' to the penultimate circle of the Inferno, but Machiavelli reversed the judgement, at least in public life" (13).

83. Ibid., 94–99, 15–25. See Herberg, "The 'What' and 'How' of Ethics," discussed in chapter 7. See also Daniel Bell, "Beyond Modernism, Beyond Self," in *The Winding Passage: Essays and Sociological Journeys, 1960–1980* (New York: Basic Books, 1980), 275–302.

84. Lionel Trilling, *The Middle of the Journey* (New York: Harper, 1947), pp. 300–1.

Afterword

1. The epigraph is from Søren Kierkegaard, *The Present Age*, trans. Walter Kaufmann (New York: Harper and Row, 1962), 38; Paul Tillich, *Theology of Culture*, 108.

2. Tillich, *Theology of Culture*, 106.

3. See Michael Löwy, *Georg Lukács*, 100–8; Lukács, *Soul and Form*, 41: "And then," Lukács concluded, "his [Kierkegaard's] purest and most unambiguous gesture of his life—vain effort!—was not a gesture after all." See also Alexander Dru, ed., *The Journals of Kierkegaard* (New York: Harper and Row, 1964), 86; Daniel Bell, "The Return of the Sacred," 340–43; George Urban, "A Conversation with Daniel Bell," *Encounter* 60 (February 1983), 22.

Martin Buber overemphasized this difference to separate himself and his philosophy of dialogue from Kierkegaard in "The Question to the Single One," in *Between Man and Man*, 40–79. See also Robert Perkins, "Buber and Kierkegaard—A Philosophic Encounter," 275–96, and discussion, 297–300; and Walter Kaufmann, "Buber's Failure and Triumph," in Haim Gordon and Jochannan Bloch, eds., *Martin Buber: A Centenary Volume* (Negev: Ben-Gurion Univ., 1985), 3–24. Daniel Bell ignored his own similarities to Buber's position in developing his critique of existential authenticity, despite his reliance on the Hasidic tales that Buber had popularized.

4. In *A Vindication of Natural Society*, a young Burke satirically imitated the style of the deceased Lord Bolingbroke: "You are, my Lord, but just entering into the World; I am going out of it. I have played long enough to be heartily tired of the Drama. Whether I have acted my part well or ill, Posterity will judge with more Candor than I, or than the present Age, with our present Passions, can possibly Pretend to" (56–57).

Index

Abstract Expressionism, 105–06, 121–22, 210, 223
Action painting, 121. *See also* Pollock, Jackson
Action Theatre, 115
Actor, 7–8, 78, 213–14, 235
Actors' Means Workshop, 216–17. *See also* Actors Studio; Baldwin, James
Actors Studio, 116–18, 211, 213–17. *See also* Baldwin, James; Brando, Marlon; Clurman, Norman; Crawford, Cheryl; Garfield, John; Kazan, Elia; Mailer, Norman; Strasberg, Lee
Adam, American, 49, 68–79, 125–26. *See also* Clinton, President Bill; Eve, American; Lewis, R. W. B.
Advertiser, 7–8, 235
Advertising, 68, 115, 116, 124
Adler, Stella, 103, 113
Aladdin (animated Disney film), 30. *See also* Disney, Walt
Alexi, Russian Grand Duke, 53. *See also* Cody, William F. (Buffalo Bill)
Allen, Woody (Koningsberg, Allen Stewart), 28–29, 240n12
American national culture, 4–13, 22, 64, 78–79, 124, 127, 158. *See also* American Way of Life; Nationalism; National culture
American Sublime, 17. *See also* Sublime
American Trade Exhibit (Moscow), 14–16. *See also* Khruschev, Nikita; Kitchen Debate; Nixon, Richard
American Way of Life, 14, 127, 139, 168, 185, 208. *See also* Herberg, Will

Anderson, Benedict, 68
Anderson, Maxwell, 117
Artist, 7–8, 37, 91, 121, 235
Augustine, 135–36, 170, 190–91, 194

Backwoodsman, Melville's portrait of, 67–68, 78. *See also* Melville, Herman, *The Confidence-Man*
Bacon, Francis, 31, 89
Bailey, George. *See* Capra, Frank, *It's a Wonderful Life*
Bakhtin, Mikhail, 8
Baldwin, James: as evangelist, 211–13, 222; as celebrity, 215, 219; as frontier writer, 219; performance and, 8, 77, 209, 269n52; Kazan, Elia and, 212–15; Strasberg, Leo and, 215–17; King, Martin Luther, Jr., and, 218; Mailer, Norman and, 77, 209–11, 219, 222, 270n61; Malcolm X and, 213, 218–19, 269n52; Reagan, Ronald and, 216; Wright, Richard and, 210; *Blues for Mister Charlie*, 214–15, 219; *Evidence of Things Not Seen*, 219, 269n54; *Fire Next Time*, 211–13, 223; *Giovanni's Room*, 213; *Go Tell It on the Mountain*, 212, 268–69n48; *Just Above My Head*, 213; *Tell Me How Long the Train's Been Gone*, 215–18; *No Name in the Street*, 218–19
Baptists, 131
Barnum, P. T., 54, 64, 67, 77–78, 167, 168, 247n13
Barrett, William, 103, 220
Buffalo Bill. *See* Cody, William F.

Index

Baum, L. Frank, 68, 77
Becker, Carl, 161, 162
Bell, Daniel, 31, 100, 104, 123, 208, 229–30. *See also* End of Ideology; NeoBurkeans
Bellah, Robert, 4–7, 94, 169
Benjamin, Walter, 184, 223
Benson, Clyde, 18. *See also* Rokeach, Milton
Benton, Thomas Hart, 121
Bercovitch, Sacvan (*American Jeremiad*), 140–42, 162
Berdyaev, Nicolai, 168, 190
Berkeley, Busby, 143
Black Christopher, 217. *See also* Baldwin, James
Black-face, 64, 76. *See also* Minstrelsy
Blumer, Herbert, 35. *See also* Goffman, Erving; Mead, George Herbert
Boas, Franz, 55
Boleslavsky, Richard, 113
Boone and Crockett Club, 54
Boorstin, Daniel, 103
Brackenridge, Hugh Henry (*Modern Chivalry*), 76
Brooks, Van Wyck, 37–38
Brando, Marlon, 117, 213
Buber, Martin, 8, 123, 156, 168, 179, 181–85, 189–91, 194, 223–24
Buckley, William F., 165, 168. *See also National Review*
Bukharin, Nikolai, 172
Buntline, Ned, *King of the Border Men*, 52. *See also* Cody, William F.
Burke, Edmund: American national culture and, 43, 59, 78–79, 111, 232; Cold War interest in, 32–34, 78–81, 98–100; new casuistry of, 88–92; on confidence, 32–34, 83; organic community and, 35, 96, 124; performance and, 84–88, 92, 118, 205–06, 209; religion and, 83–84, 90–92; use of sublime by, 80–81, 90, 92, 154, 205–06; *A Philosophical Enquiry into the Origins of our Ideas of the Sublime and Beautiful*, 80–82; *Reflections on the Revolution in France*, 68, 82–85, 92; *A Vindication of Society*, 234–35, 250n4; Dos Passos, John R. (senior) and, 109; Edwards, Jonathan contrasted, 90–92; Greenberg, Clement and, 105; Hartz, Louis and, 97–98; Herberg, Will and, 170; James, William and, 59; Kant, Immanuel and, 65–67; Kierkegaard, Soren contrasted, 234, 275n4; Kirk, Russell and conservative ideal of, 92; Mailer, Norman and, 224, 228; Marx, Karl and, 102–03, 122, 252n1; Melville, Herman and, 60, 65–66, 81; Niebuhr, Reinhold and, 152–53; Paine, Tom and, 76, 82, 96; Price, Dr. Richard and, 82–85; Rousseau, Jean contrasted, 78, 93–94; Tocqueville and, 59–60, 81, 124; Turner, Frederick Jackson and, 42–43; Weaver, Richard critique of, 88, 92–93; Wilson, Woodrow and, 43, 93, 100, 243n39; Wollstonecraft, Mary and, 76, 80. *See also* Conservatism; NeoBurkeans; Performance
Burnet, Thomas, 164–65
Burnham, James (*The Machiavellians*), 103, 179
Bush, President George Walker, 24–28, 69–72, 231

Cable, George Washington, 36
Calvin, John, 91, 159
Calvinism, 89, 92, 128–32, 146, 158–60, 191
Cantor, Eddie (*Whoopee!*), 142
Capitalism, 15, 57, 120, 131–33, 135, 149–50, 156, 160–61, 173–74, 259n44
Capra, Frank, 26, 143–44, 156; Bercovitch, Sacvan and, 144; Niebuhr, Reinhold and, 148–49; Miller, Perry and, 143–44; *Mr. Deeds Goes to Town*,

Mr. Smith Goes to Washington, and Meet John Doe, 144–45; It's a Wonderful Life, 145–49, 163; Why We Fight, 149
Carnegie, Dale, 204
Carter, President Jimmy, 231
Carville, Jim, 72
Cassel, Joseph, 18. See also Rokeach, Milton
Casuistry, new, 58, 88–89, 151, 178, 229. See also Burke, Edmund; Niebuhr, Reinhold
Catholicism, 90, 178–79, 185, 187, 191, 202
Celebrity, 72, 120–21, 204–05, 209, 212, 217–19, 229, 240n11
Chopin, Kate, 36
Christian Coalition, 232
Christs of Ypsilanti (Three Christs of Ypsilanti), 16–22. See also Rokeach, Milton
Civil Religion, 3–4, 84, 87, 93–94, 169–70, 185
Civil Rights movement, 158, 161, 218
Clinton, President Bill, 25–29, 57, 59, 70–73
Clurman, Harold, 112, 113. See also Actors Studio; Group Theatre
Cody, William F. (Buffalo Bill), 52–54, 68, 77, 121, 220. See also Frontier; Performance
Cold War, 6, 8, 11–12, 16, 21–22, 92, 94, 103, 127, 208
Commentary. See Podhoretz, Norman
Communism, 9, 15, 95–96, 109, 111, 117, 123, 166, 172, 177–78. See also Lovestonites; Stalin, Joseph; Trotskyists
Confidence: defined, 32–33, 56; as foundation of Enlightenment, 35, 40, 44–46, 77, 89, 165–66, 226; contrasted with trust, 18–20, 63, 90–91, 129; and American national culture, 8, 23, 24, 41, 49, 59–65, 69, 131–32, 141, 195, 236; mentioned, 26, 38, 133, 146, 167, 194, 196–97. See also Doubt; Trust
Congress for Cultural Freedom, 23–24
Conservatism, 96, 97, 122, 123, 126, 187, 188, 193–94, 223
Contract with America, 71–72
Cooley, Charles H., 35–36, 39–40
Cotton, John, 139–40
Counter-Progressives (historians), 124, 165, 166
Coverture, laws of, 75
Crane, Stephen, 36
Crawford, Cheryl, 117
Cuba, 9, 10
Cushing, Frank Hamilton, 55, 246n72

Darwin, Charles, 164, 177
Darwinism, 176, 177, 180, 191
Deconstruction, 33, 57
Decter, Midge, 103
Delaney, Beauford, 212–13, 268n37
Demonic, 150, 152–54, 156–57, 179, 187, 194. See also Tillich, Paul
Denney, Reginald, 29
Descartes, René, 89, 233
Dewey, John, 33–35; industrial frontier of, 41–42, 44–48; Russia and, 44–45, 244n47; Park, Robert E. and, 47, 50, 56; Trotsky, Leon and, 46–47, 244n50; Democracy in America, 44; Quest for Certainty, 45–46
Diggins, John Patrick, 5–7, 99
Disciples of Christ, 200, 265n60
Disney, Walt, 21, 211; films of, 14, 30
Dole, Senator Robert, 72
Dos Passos, John R., 10, 77, 104, 106, 110; and New Playwrights, 103; and U. S. A., 106–07; Manhattan Transfer, 107; Most Likely to Succeed, 110–11; plays of, 107–08; and New Masses, 109
Dos Passos, John R. (Sr.), 109. See also Burke, Edmund

Index

Dostoyevsky, Feodor, 12, 122, 134, 223, 235
Doubt, 35, 50, 56–57, 76–78, 100, 106. *See also* Confidence
Duyckinck circle, 139. *See also* Melville, Herman

Eakins, Thomas, 54–55
Eastman, Max, 47, 103, 107
Edwards, Jonathan, 90–91, 122, 176
Einstein, Albert, 175–76
Eisenstein, Sergei, 108
Eisenhower, President Dwight D., 21, 22, 229–30
End of Ideology, 31, 104, 123. *See also* Bell, Daniel
Enlightenment, 30, 31, 33–35, 56, 79, 89, 93, 97, 166, 170, 185, 209, 233–35. *See also* Frontier
Evangelicals, New, 202–06, 211, 228, 229, 232. *See also* Graham, Billy; Roberts, Oral; Sheen, Fulton J.
Eve, American Adam and, 75; Whitman, Governor Christine Todd as, 72–73
Existentialism, 118–19, 122, 123, 189, 209, 220, 233–36

Falwell, Reverend Jerry, 5
Family values, 236
Farrow, Mia, 28–29
Fitzgerald, F. Scott, 11
Florio, Governor Jim, 72
Ford, President Gerald, 195, 231
Ford, John, 54
Frankfurt School of Sociologists, 102, 149, 168, 184, 223
Freud, Sigmund, 155–56, 163, 171
Freudianism, 102, 221
Frontier: Cold War and, 13; as Enlightenment convention, 33–34, 209; as stage, 35–36, 52, 89, 152, 271*n*67; and American National Culture, 41, 50–51, 55, 185–86, 190, 194–95, 220, 265*n*63; Dewey, John and industrial, 41–42, 44, 49–50, 56; Kennedy, President John F. and, 25, 71; Park, Robert E. and racial, 42, 44–47, 49–50, 56; Roosevelt, Theodore and, 51–52; Potter, David and artificial, 42; Turner, Frederick Jackson and agrarian, 42–43, 49–50, 56, 98, 191–93. *See also* Cody, William F.; Royce, Josiah

Gabor, Leon, 18. *See also* Rokeach, Milton
Garfield, John, 117–18
Garland, Judy, 142–43
Gibbs, Nancy, 27
Gilmore, Gary, 225–26. *See also* Mailer, Norman
Gingrich, Newt, 57–59, 71–72
Gipp, George (*Knute Rockne, All American*), 200. *See also* Reagan, Ronald
Goffman, Erving, 35, 119–20, 125
Goldenweiser, Alexander, 55
Goodman, Paul, 97
Gould, Stephen Jay, 163–66
Graham, Reverend Billy, 5, 201–04, 206, 228. *See also* Evangelicals, New
Gramm, Senator Phil, 72
Greenberg, Clement, 99, 102, 123, 164, 168. *See also* Abstract Expressionism
Greenfield, Liah, 40–41, 77
Group Theatre, 112–13, 116, 117. *See also* Adler, Stella; Clurman, Harold; Crawford, Cheryl; Kazan, Elia; Strasberg, Lee

Hampton, James, 165
Hart, Gary, 28, 29
Hartz, Louis (*Liberal Tradition in America*), 97–99, 124–25
Hegel, Georg, 48, 183, 234
Hemingway, Ernest, 10–11, 121, 220
Henri, Robert, 102, 107
Herberg, Will, 3–7, 166–80, 184–96, 201, 262*n*12

Hickock, Wild Bill, 53
Hicks, Granville, 103
Hill, Anita, 27
Himmelfarb, Gertrude, 103
Hipster, 222, 224–25. *See also* Mailer, Norman
Hitler, Adolph, 153, 177, 178
Hofstadter, Richard, 125, 208
Hollywood, 35, 106, 111, 115, 116, 142, 197–99, 201, 203–04, 206
Hook, Sidney, 103, 122
House Un-American Activities Committee (HUAC), 103, 110, 114, 115, 231
Horton, Willy, 27
Hudson, Rock, 206
Humbard, Reverend Rex, 202
Hurst, Fannie. *See* Sirk, Douglass

Ibsen, Henrik, 115, 271*n*4
Ideology: Marxist, 100, 103–05, 180, 185; Nazi, 191; republican, 11; of violence, 192
Imitation of Life. See Sirk, Douglass
Imitation, 39, 43, 52, 60, 77, 81, 87, 121. *See also* Looking-glass self; Mead, George Herbert; Simulacra; Simulation
Instauration, great. *See* Bacon, Francis
Iran-contra scandal. *See* North, Oliver; Reagan, Ronald
Irony, 157
Ishi, 55
It's a Wonderful Life. See Capra, Frank; Gould, Stephen Jay

Jacobinism, 178, 188
Jacksonian Persuasion. See Meyers, Marvin
James, Henry, 36–40, 211–12
James, William, 34, 37, 56, 59–60
Jefferson, Thomas, 71, 81, 94, 109
Jeremiad, 12, 140–42, 191, 193; defined, 157–58, 179. *See also* Bercovitch, Sacvan; Miller, Perry
Johnson, President Lyndon B., 226
Judaism, 179, 181, 183, 185–87, 223
Judeo-Christianity, 3–6, 164, 165, 168, 180

Kant, Immanuel, 31, 46, 65–66, 78, 105, 152. *See also* Sublime
Kaufmann, Walter, 220
Kazan, Elia, 104, 106, 110–11, 113–19, 212–13, 215, 217
Kazin, Alfred, 106–07
Kennedy, President John F., 22, 24–25, 26, 28, 203, 230
Kennedy, Robert F., 192, 203
Khrushchev, Nikita, 13–15, 21
Kierkegaard, Soren, 119, 122, 149, 160, 194, 223, 234–35
King, Reverend Martin Luther, Jr., 5, 190, 218
King, Rodney, 29
Kingsley, Sidney (*Men in White*), 138
Kirk, Russell, 92, 95, 99, 124
Kitchen Debate, 14–16. *See also* Khrushchev, Nikita; Nixon, Richard
Kopit, Arthur (*Indians*), 52
Kristol, Irving, 103, 229, 273*n*79
Kroeber, Alfred, 55
Kuhn, Thomas, 31, 33, 77, 161–63

Lawnmower Man (film), 30
Lawson, John Howard, 107, 110
Left, 104, 108–09, 188, 227
Lenin, V. I., 171, 173, 183
Leninism, 171–73, 176, 178, 181, 185, 187
Lewis, R. W. B., 69–70, 73–74, 78
Lewis, Robert, 117
Lewis, Sinclair, 138
Liberalism, 11, 93, 95–98, 100, 126, 188, 201
Liberache, 121
Lincoln, Abraham, 6, 141, 161, 191, 192

282 Index

Lipset, Seymour Martin, 68, 208
Livingston, Jennie (*Paris Is Burning*), 22
Locke, John, 89–90, 97–98, 124
Looking-glass self, 35, 36
Longinus, 77–78, 80, 152. *See also* Sublime
Lovestone, Jay, 168, 172
Lovestonites, 108, 176, 178
Luce, Clare Booth, 202
Luce, Henry R., 201–02, 229, 272*n*78
Lukács, Georg, 223–24, 271*nn*64, 67
Luther, Martin, 91, 129–30, 133, 159, 190
Lutheranism, 128–32, 134–35, 146, 150–60, 191
Lyell, Charles, 165
Lyman, Stanford, 41
Lynd, Helen (*On Shame and the Search for Identity*), 18–19

McCarthy, Senator Joseph, 95, 229
McCarthy, Mary, 103–04
McClary, Susan, 206
Macdonald, Dwight, 99, 168, 224
Machiavelli, Niccolo, 154, 163, 179
McHugh, Drake (*King's Row*), 200. *See also* Reagan, Ronald
MacIntyre, Alisdair (*After Virtue*), 5
Mad Magazine, 12
Madonna, 28, 29, 77, 206
Mailer, Norman, 40, 93, 209, 219–22, 224; *Advertisements for Myself*, 10–11, 224; boxing and, 225–26; *Executioner's Song*, 225–26; *Naked and the Dead*, 221; *Prisoner of Sex*, 225; *White Negro*, 222; and Hipster, 224–25, 271*n*67; and Goldwater, Barry, 225; and Lukács, Georg, 223–24; and Nixon, Richard, 210, 226–27, 228–29, 273*n*81; and Reagan, Ronald, 227–28. *See also* Baldwin, James; Burke, Edmund
Marx Brothers (films), 142

Marx, Karl, 100, 193, 224, 229. *See also* Burke, Edmund; Marxism
Marxism, 48, 102–03, 109, 118–19, 149, 155, 159, 166, 169, 174, 176, 177, 178, 179, 180–81, 187–88
Masses, 107
Mead, George Herbert, 8, 33, 134
Meinecke, Friedrich, 182
Melville, Herman, 60, 68, 78; *Billy Budd*, 73–74; *The Confidence-Man*, 63–65, 67–68, 75; *Piazza Tales*, 60–62; "Benito Cereno," 62–64, 246*n*3. *See also* Burke, Edmund; Kant, Immanuel; Sublime
Methodism, 204
Meyerhold, V. E., 108
Meyers, Marvin, and *Jacksonian Persuasion*, 125–26
Miller, Perry, 134–42, 154, 176
Minstrelsy, 76, 142, 206, 249*n*46
Modernism, 6, 32, 36, 40, 94, 102–03, 105–06, 174, 180, 184, 188
Moscow Art Theatre, 107, 113, 117, 225
Most Likely to Succeed (Dos Passos), 110–11
Moynihan, Daniel Patrick, 25
Mussolini, Benito, 183

National Review, 109, 189–90, 192
Nationalism, 15, 93–94, 127–28, 150, 185, 191
National culture, 12, 22–23, 88, 124. *See also* American National Culture
Native Son. *See* Wright, Richard
Natural Law, 103, 172, 191
Naturalism, 7–8, 86–87, 105
Nazis, 94, 95, 183, 191
NeoBurkeans, 97, 101, 170, 185, 209, 226, 229
Neoconservatives, 208–09, 229. *See also* NeoBurkeans
NeoPragmatism, 33–35. *See also* Rorty, Richard

New Agrarian Critics, 74, 78
New Deal, 144, 196. *See also* Roosevelt, Franklin Delano
New Masses, 107, 109
New Playwrights Theatre, 107, 108, 110
New Religious and Political Right, 25, 194, 229–30. *See also* Political and Religious Right
New Society of Artists, 120. *See also* Secessionists
New Theater, 108–12
Niebuhr, H. Richard, 139, 149
Niebuhr, Reinhold, 74, 130, 134, 148–51, 163, 179, 190; Herberg, Will and, 166, 179, 181, 190, 262n12; Capra, Frank and, 148, 258n38; *Beyond Tragedy*, 153, 155–57; *Children of Light and Children of Darkness*, 74, 148; *Christianity and Power Politics*, 157; *Irony of American History*, 74, 157, 259n46; *Moral Man and Immoral Society*, 158; *Nature and Destiny of Man*, 157–61; *Self and the Dramas of History*, 156. *See also* Confidence; Tillich, Paul; Weber, Max
Nietzsche, Friedrich, 119, 122, 153
Ninja, Willie, 22
Nixon, Richard M., 13–15, 20, 26, 116, 195, 206, 227–29, 231, 273–74n81
Norris, Frank, 36
North, Oliver, 26–27
Nuclear sublime, 17–19, 225

Oddbody, Clarence, 145, 147–48. *See also* Capra, Frank; Gould, Stephen Jay; *It's a Wonderful Life*; Niebuhr, Reinhold
Odets, Clifford, 115. See also *Waiting for Lefty*
O'Neill, Eugene, 108
Open Door, 9, 132, 193
Optimism, spirit of, 158
Orvell, Miles, and *The Real Thing*, 39, 107

Otto, Rudolph, *The Idea of the Holy*, 152. *See also* Sublime; Tillich, Paul

Paine, Thomas, 76, 80, 82, 96
Paris Is Burning (film), 22
Park, Robert Ezra, 42, 47–50. *See also* Frontier
Parr, Jack, 204
Parrington, Vernon, 176
Peale, Charles Wilson, 81
Peale, Norman Vincent, 204
Peirce, Charles Sanders, 33–34
Pells, Richard, 118
Performance, 15, 22, 50, 53–56, 94, 114, 118–20, 122, 195, 209, 216, 224, 232, 235
Performativity, 56, 77–78, 97, 116
Perot, H. Ross, 25–26
Personalism, 122, 207–09
Photography, 31, 39, 40
Podhoretz, Norman, 103, 129, 223
Political and Religious Right, 25, 123, 194–95, 201–02, 227, 229–32. *See also* Luce, Henry R.; Reagan, President Ronald
Pollock, Jackson, 121
Popular Front, 124
Populism, 22, 42
Postimpressionism, 223, 229
Postmodernism, 6–7, 33, 48, 57, 59, 180, 229
Potter, David (*People of Plenty*), 42, 78
Pragmatism, 37, 47, 55–56
Price, Dr. Richard. *See* Burke, Edmund
Progressives, 40–41
Puritanism, 135, 139–40, 145, 175–76. *See also* Calvinism

Ransom, John Crowe, 78
Reagan, Jack, 200, 203
Reagan, Nelle, 200, 203
Reagan, Ronald, 8, 24–28, 116, 195–96, 197–202, 216, 219, 229–32. *See also* North, Oliver

284 *Index*

Reformation, 91, 131, 158–60
Religious and Political Right. *See* Political and Religious Right
Remington, Frederic, 51, 54
Renaissance, 106, 160, 225
Ressentiment, 75, 76
Revolution, 24, 162, 164, 172, 223; American, 75, 127, 176; French, 82, 87, 127; Glorious, 84–85, 89, 101; Russian, 44–45, 103, 173, 176, 178
Revolutionary Age. *See* Herberg, Will
Rhetoric, confidence and, 25, 34, 99, 100, 104, 140–41, 157, 168, 188. *See also* Semantic transformation
Riesman, David, 68, 97, 125, 207–08, 210
Roberts, Reverend Oral, 202–04, 206, 228, 266n21
Robertson, Reverend Pat, 231–32
Rokeach, Milton (*The Three Christs of Ypsilanti*), 16–21
Rollins, Ed, 72
Roosevelt, Franklin Delano, 157, 177
Roosevelt, Theodore, 51–54, 57
Ross, Edward A., 36, 38, 40
Rorty, James, 33
Rorty, Richard, 30, 31, 33, 44, 161
Rousseau, Jean-Jaques, 33, 67, 78, 93–94. *See also* Burke, Edmund
Rousseauvians, 94–95
Royce, Josiah, 23–34, 35, 47, 241n20
Russell, Charles, 51, 54, 245n69

Saphir, Edward, 55
Sartre, Jean Paul, 119, 194, 220, 223
Schickel, Richard, 221–22, 270n60
Scholasticism, 91, 130
Schreyvogel, Charles, 51
Science, 20–21, 41, 50, 88, 131–33, 161–66, 173–77
Secessionist movement, 107
Sectionalism, 43–44. *See also* Frontier
Semantic transformation, 40–41, 152
Sheen, Bishop Fulton J., 202–04, 228

Shils, Edward, 125, 208
Sidey, Hugh, 25, 27
Simmel, Georg, 148, 182
Simpson, O. J., trial as media event, 57
Simulation, 40, 64, 77–78, 88–89
Simulacra, 31, 56
Sincerity, 62, 87, 92, 194–95, 203, 211–12, 228–30, 273n81, 274n82
Sirk, Douglass, 10, 11, 13
Skinner, B. F., 209
Slotkin, Richard, 52
Smith, Henry Nash, 52
Sociodicy, 41
Stalin, Joseph, 46, 108, 116, 171, 172, 173, 174, 178, 179, 191
Stanislavsky, Constantin, 115, 116, 216–17
Stanislavsky method, 12, 113, 115–17, 119, 124
Stieglitz, Alfred, 40
Strindberg, August, 115
Stoddard, Solomon, 91
Strasberg, Leo, 113, 115, 116, 118. *See also* Actors' Means Workshop; Actors Studio; Group Theatre; Stanislavsky method
Sublime, 17–19, 21, 27, 42, 45, 50, 58, 61–64, 76, 80, 126, 142–43, 147, 165, 179, 195, 217, 223, 225, 230; Burkean, 81–82, 85–87, 89–92, 118, 153–54, 205–06; Culture of confidence and, 77–78; Kantian, 65–67, 152; defined by Longinius, 77–78; Warhol, Andy and, 221. *See also* Burke, Edmund; Christs of Ypsilanti; Cody, William F.; Confidence; Melville, Herman
Susman, Warren, 128
Swaggart, Reverend Jimmy, 29
Sydenham, Dr. Thomas, 90
Symbol-myth School of American Studies, 50

Taft, Senator Robert, 29, 95
Taylor, Winslow, and Taylorism, 207, 209

Tragedy, 99, 141, 155–56, 158, 271n67
Teatro Nacional, 107
Theater, 29, 52, 61, 77, 84–85, 88, 103, 107–08, 110, 115, 117, 122, 153–54, 156, 195, 198, 200, 205, 211, 214–15, 255n41, 269n52. See also Action Theater; Baldwin, James; Group Theatre; Moscow Art Theatre; New Theater; New Playwrights Theatre; Performance; Performativity; Teatro Nacional
Terry, Randall, 5
Thomas, Clarence, 27–28
Tillich, Paul, 102, 123, 149–59, 168, 179, 181, 186–87, 190, 233–35
Tocqueville, Alexis, 4, 57, 59–60, 68, 78, 81, 124–27
Transvestism, 76, 206
Trilling, Lionel, 123, 208, 210, 230–31, 274n82. See also Sincerity
Troeltsch, Ernst, 149–50
Trotsky, Leon, 47, 172–73, 179, 244n50
Trotskyists, 100–01, 107–09, 172, 177
Truckline Cafe, 117, 213
Trust, 17, 30, 44, 60, 63, 70, 224, 235; contrasted with confidence, 18–19, 24–26, 32–33, 63–64, 67–68, 91, 130–31, 136, 155, 166, 209, 236. See also Burke, Edmund; Confidence; Melville, Herman; Weber, Max
Turner, Frederick Jackson, 41–44, 50, 55, 98, 185, 191, 193. See also Frontier
Twain, Mark (Clemens, Samuel), 54

Utilitarianism, 103, 130

Veblen, Thorstein, 109
Viereck, Peter, 94–99
Vietnam, 11, 25, 109, 161, 190, 191
Virtual politics, 50
Virtual reality, 30, 122

Waiting for Lefty, 115, 120, 217. See also Odets, Clifford
Warhol, Andy, 40, 221
Washington, Booker T., 48
Wayne, John, 52
Weaver, Richard, 88, 95
Weber, Max, 7, 128–36, 141, 146, 149–50, 152–53, 163, 182, 206. See also Confidence
West, Cornel, 27
Western films, 121
Whitman, Walt, 22, 36–40, 77
Wild West Shows, 52, 54, 115. See also Cody, William F.
Williams, Wayne, 219
Williams, William Appleton, 9, 11, 192–95, 265n63
Wilson, Edmund, 47, 177
Wilson, Rob, 17–18, 20
Wilson, Woodrow, 9, 43, 81, 94, 100, 102, 192, 243n39. See also Burke, Edmund
Wirth, Louis, 120
Wister, Owen, 54
Wollstonecraft, Mary, 75–76, 82, 93, 249n47
Workers Age. See Herberg, Will
Wright, Richard, 119, 120, 123, 210
Wundt, Wilhelm, 152

Yellow Hand, Cody, William F. and, 53–54
Young Worker, 171. See also Herberg, Will
Ypsilanti. See Rokeach, Milton; Three Christs of Ypsilanti

Zagorin, Perez, 89
Zionism, 182, 185, 189. See also Nationalism

www.ingramcontent.com/pod-product-compliance
Lightning Source LLC
Chambersburg PA
CBHW030336240426
43661CB00052B/1648